Bill Hefley and Wendy Murphy (Eds.)

Service Science: Research and Innovations
in the Service Economy

For other titles published in this series, go to
www.springer.com/series/8080

Haluk Demirkan • James C. Spohrer
Vikas Krishna
Editors

Service Systems Implementation

Foreword by Richard C. Larson

Springer

Editors
Haluk Demirkan
W. P. Carey School of Business
Department of Information Systems
Main Campus PO BOX 874606
85287 Tempe AZ, USA
Haluk.Demirkan@asu.edu

James C. Spohrer
IBM Research - Almaden
Harry Road 650
95120-6099 San Jose CA, USA
spohrer@us.ibm.com

Vikas Krishna
San Jose CA, USA
vikasconnect@gmail.com

Series Editors:
Bill Hefley
Katz Graduate School of Business &
College of Business Administration
University of Pittsburgh
PA 15260
USA
wehefley@katz.pitt.edu

Wendy Murphy
IBM c/o
1954 Rocky Cove Lane
Denton, NC 27239
USA
wendym@us.ibm.com

ISSN 1865-4924   e-ISSN 1865-4932
ISBN 978-1-4419-7903-2   e-ISBN 978-1-4419-7904-9
DOI 10.1007/978-1-4419-7904-9
Springer New York Dordrecht Heidelberg London

Library of Congress Control Number: 2011921337

Springer is part of Springer Science+Business Media (www.springer.com)

Foreword

Richard C. Larson

Engineering Systems Division, MIT

Number please. These words were once heard when picking up the telephone to make a call. Yes, a human telephone operator was involved in making each connection.

Floor please? Only a few decades ago, a human operator spoke these words as he maneuvered a long lever to get you to your desired floor. *Fill it up?* You heard this question when stopping to get gasoline in what is now called a 'full service' service station. *Do you want any large bills?* You might have heard this question from a bank teller upon cashing a check or withdrawing funds, prior to the wide-scale implementation of ATM's (Automated Teller Machines). These are but a few examples of how services have changed over the past 60 or so years. In many services, as with telephones, humans have been replaced by technology. In others, such as self-serve gasoline 'service stations,' the consumer has become the server! And in many cases, both changes have happened at once: technology removed the human server *and* the customer performs the service, as with ATMs and elevators.

The number of human elevator operators has dropped about 90% since 1950 (Hedberg 2010). Traditional telephone operators no longer exist for routine calls. These and many other older service jobs have dried up, replaced with technology and with new human-provided service jobs. Our lifestyles have changed forever. The result on the U.S. economy has been profound. After decades of stagnation, service productivity has increased dramatically, due in large part to technology and – in particular – information technology that has accelerated the two trends introduced above. With the majority of the U.S. economy in services, our standard of living, our very way of life, depends on continual improvements in the delivery of services, improvements in quality, choice, resiliency and cost.

Yet, 'services' has not been a focus of study, for students or their professors. Who graduates with a degree in Services Engineering, or Services Science, or Services Technology, or Services Management? With the importance so huge, the need for such programs is clear. And, as with any respected academic endeavor, the curriculum needs to be buttressed with active, productive research. Thus, the need to fill the gaps. Thus the need for books like this, to initiate the process.

Service Science is the focus of this book. To understand this, let's examine definitions of 'Science' and 'Service'. A typical dictionary definition of *Science* is, "… systematized knowledge derived from observation, study, and experimentation carried on in order to determine the nature or principles of what is being studied." Or, "… any specific branch of scientific knowledge, esp. one concerned with establishing and systematizing facts, principles, and methods, as by experiments and hypotheses,[1]" such as the science of physics. The word science comes from the Latin "scientia," meaning knowledge. So, science is a logical process for acquiring knowledge (definition 1) and can apply to any field that is being studied by the scientific method (definition 2). The well-known sciences are of the physical world, such as biology, physics, chemistry, and astronomy. Less well known as sciences are those focused on the human world of individuals and organizations, including psychology, political science, management science, economics and other social sciences.

To understand if it makes sense to create a science of services, let's now define *Services*. The service industry, as it comprises so much of the economies of the developed world, is defined more by what it isn't than by what it is. It is defined by subtraction! For our purposes, we will define services to include any and all economic activities that do not involve the production of a physical object. This means that every job that is not directly related to agriculture, manufacturing, or resource extraction and harvesting is a service job. In the United States, services represent 75–80% of the GDP. At the top of the service industry's wage distribution, we have occupations such as lawyers, doctors and university professors. At the bottom, we have security guards, cashiers, cleaners and waiters. In the middle, we have vibrant craft service-oriented professions such as those relating to maintenance and repair (e.g., plumbers, electricians, auto mechanics), and we also have a large number of shrinking occupations, many clerical. Services associated with health care comprise about 17% of the GDP, with education coming in second at about 10%. But services also include financial services, transportation and logistics, retailing, communication, government and much more.

The question is: "*With services so diffuse, so heterogeneous, so all-encompassing, does it make sense to say we can develop a science of services?*" I say, *No* in the small, and *Yes* in the large. The *No* refers to the focused definition of science such as that associated with physics or biology. Services are simply too all encompassing and diffuse to be mapped into one new focused science, admittedly a science of humans such as management science or economics. In my mind, to do so would be like merging all of the natural sciences and calling them "physical science." Such a field is simply too broad to be useful. We need to retain the individual parts. The *Yes* relates to a meta-science of services that constitutes the logical union and expansion of constituent parts of the science of services.

An illustrative 'constituent part' is queueing theory, from my own focused science of operations research. Queueing theory began in 1909 when the Danish engineer/mathematician A. K. Erlang invented a mathematical theory of queues to assist the then-new service – telephony, for the Copenhagen Telephone Company.[2]

---

[1] http://www.yourdictionary.com/science June 25, 2010.
[2] Erlang's primary works in queues were published between 1909 and 1917.

The problem was: "What should be the capacity of the new invention, the central telephone switch that allows all callers to connect with all others having telephones?" The capacity question traded off the likelihood of a busy signal – associated with a system having too little capacity – with cost of a system having too much capacity. This is engineering applied to the design of a new service system. Since Erlang's landmark papers, scores of books and thousands of papers have been written about queueing theory, extending now to the psychology of queueing as well as the physics and mathematics of queueing. While some of the queueing literature pertains to queues in manufacturing or other industries that create things, most has been motivated by problems in services. So, 'service science' 'in the small' in the form of queueing theory has existed for 100 years. It is doubtful if the substantial progress in queueing theory would have been made if this highly focused field had been folded into a mega-field called 'Service Science.' Queueing theory, like scores of other constituent parts of the study of services, needs its own domain, its own journals, its own professional societies. It makes no sense to swallow it in something we call "Service Science."

Another example is graph theory, invented by Leonard Euler in 1736, solving the "Seven Bridges of Konigsberg" problem. Now graph theory is used by almost every service industry. The field is robust, deep and dynamic. Recently, in 1962, we saw the "Chinese Postman Problem (Mei-Ko 1962)" the formulation and solution via graph theory of the routing of a postman – modeled as traveling on a graph representing his delivery route – so as to deliver mail to each address while walking or driving the minimum possible total distance. This is another example of service system engineering design. Graph theory, like queueing theory, needs its own experts, journals and professional societies.

What about non-engineering, more human-centered, sub-specialties in services? There are many. One robust new field is called Marketing Science. Born in the 1970s, this field applies major aspects of the scientific method to marketing products and services. Marketing is a service, with annual expenditures exceeding $10 billion/year. The field now has a world-class journal (*Marketing Science* http://mktsci.journal.informs.org/) and many tenured professors whose reputations are based on expertise in Marketing Science. It makes no sense to fuse marketing science into a mega-field called Service Science.

So, what do I mean by Yes in the large? The sub-sciences of what we might call Service Science are analogous to the constituent sciences of the physical sciences or of the social sciences. The good news is that each is accomplished, usually with great reputation. The bad news is that these fields are often over specialized, sometimes becoming deep narrow canyons of knowledge whose arcane vocabularies are so obscure that only a few hundred people in the world would understand them. For instance, I have seen mathematically rigorous research papers on queues that fewer than 100 people could fully understand. Impact levels can be astonishingly small, given the inability of the more general public to know about them and understand their relevance to everyday problems. Service Science can emerge from this set of deep canyons as a strong inter-disciplinary macro-science, building bridges across canyons, providing synergistic new knowledge and insights. The analysis across sub-disciplines in services will reveal holes or gaps in our integrated theories, holes that need to be filled with new research. So, in my view, Service Science is a bridging, integrative science that embraces all the service-relevant sub-fields that have gone before – several calling themselves *sciences* – and uses interdisciplinary approaches to develop new knowledge and new insights.

Consider urban traffic congestion as an example. A mathematical queue theorist sees this as a network of queues. But one familiar with the psychology of queues might see this as an environment that risks increased anxiety levels among drivers, perhaps even leading to 'queue rage', which sometimes leads to violence. An economist might focus on lost productivity due to time wasted in traffic. An environmentalist would be concerned with air pollution and the increased carbon footprint associated with gasoline used by vehicles delayed in traffic. A traffic engineer might focus on better timing of the traffic lights. And so on …. A Service Science specialist would be able to combine the best of all of these perspectives into an integrated, interdisciplinary analysis of urban traffic congestion. And she would frame the problem not in a canyon but on a wide prairie. She would include analysis of options not usually considered by canyon dwellers, options like negotiated staggered work times for key employers, bike lanes to encourage commuting by bicycle, congestion pricing such as is done in Singapore and London (Larson and Sasanuma 2010), incentives to use public transportation, incentives to car pool, local use of borrowed 'zip cars,[3]' tax subsidies for new infrastructure supporting electric vehicles, property tax relief for developers of high-density housing near public transport stations, and more. And her analysis would be just as rigorous as those of the canyon dwellers, so she must have considerably more expertise than that of a single-discipline professional. When she does not have the deep knowledge required for some aspect of her work, she knows how to assemble strong interdisciplinary teams, to get the best from each team member. The results of her work could be new fundamental research findings and/or a set of feasible and imaginative policy alternatives that are implementable and that satisfy the often-conflicting goals of multiple stakeholders.

I see several keys to success in developing this new field of Service Science. First, let us acknowledge the centuries-long tradition of studying services from more traditional disciplines. This is the legacy we start with. We should not be saying that Service Science is a brand new field, but rather one that builds on decades and even centuries of excellent work by those before us. Like its predecessor sub-fields, Service Science must follow the scientific method, must be rigorous and scholarly. To be less than that could quickly reduce people's perception of the field to images of consulting reports piled high. We need to acknowledge the earlier work of others in what we are now calling Service Science, in the large. Two illustrative books were published in 1988 by the National Academies, focusing on services innovation and employment (Guiles and Quinn 1988a, b). We need to develop graduate

---

[3]Zipcar is the world's largest urban car-sharing company.
http://www.zipcar.com/about/.

level curricula in Service Science. The straightforward part of that is to build a foundation on the decades-long sub-fields, all well established. A student majoring in Service Science must be competent in some critical subset of these sub-fields. The hard part is to develop courses and projects in the uniquely "in-the-large" part of Service Science, relating scientifically rigorous interdisciplinary programs that create what many are calling T people – skilled in traditional disciplines (the vertical part of the T) and in applications-oriented interdisciplinary analyses (the horizontal part).

This book and its companion contain some of the best attempts to date to create this new "in-the-large" Service Science. You will see that many authors acknowledge and build on the work of others, while creating new results corresponding to useful bridges across traditional deep canyons. Others are attempting to do original integrative research, using the scientific method, straightaway in Service Science. We hope you enjoy each of the chapters. And we hope that many of you will contribute yourselves to this exciting new – in-the-large – applied science.

References

Guiles, B. R. and Quinn, J. B. (1988a). *Managing Innovation: Cases from the Services Industries,* National Academy Press, Washington, D.C.

Guiles, B. R. and Quinn, J. B. (1988b). *Technology in Services: Policies for Growth, Trade and Employment,* National Academy Press, Washington, D.C.

Hedberg, K. (2010). Change in the Service Industry, post-WWII – present, June 10 (Unpublished, available from the author).

Larson, R. C. and Sasanuma, K. (2010). Urban Vehicle Congestion Pricing. *A Review. Journal of Industrial and Systems Engineering,* 3(4):227–242, Winter.

Mei-Ko, K. (1962). *Graphic Programming Using Odd or Even Points, Chinese Mathematics,* 1:273–277.

Prof. Richard Larson

Dr. Larson received his Ph.D. from MIT where he is Mitsui Professor in the Engineering Systems Division (ESD) where he is founding director of the Center for Engineering System Fundamentals. The majority of his career has focused on operations research as applied to services industries. He is author, co-author or editor of six books and author of numerous scientific articles, primarily in the fields of urban service systems, queueing, logistics, disaster management, disease dynamics, dynamic pricing of critical infrastructures and workforce planning. In 1993–1994, he served as President of ORSA (Operations Research Society of America), and in 2005 he served as President of INFORMS, INstitute for Operations Research and the Management Sciences. For more than 15 years, Dr. Larson was Co-Director of the MIT Operations Research Center. He is a member of the National Academy of Engineering and is an INFORMS Founding Fellow. He has been honored with the INFORMS President's Award and the Kimball Medal. Recognizing his research on pandemic influenza and disaster preparedness, he is a member of two Boards of the Institute of Medicine.

He is founding Director of LINC, Learning International Networks Consortium, an MIT-based international project that has held five international symposia and sponsored a number of initiatives in Africa, China and the Middle East.

Table of Contents

Preface

Service and service systems are not new things. They are as old as division of labor and family activities, and have been around a long, long time. Today, we live in and interact with many modern service systems that we depend on in our daily life. Many organizations have variety of service offerings, internally to employees and externally to customers. And these service systems have variety of configurations. While these configurations can take many, potentially infinite, forms, they can be optimized for the subject service to eliminate unnecessary costs in the forms of redundancies, over allocation, etc. So what is an ideal configuration that a provider and a customer might strive to achieve? As much as it would be nice to have a formula to compare all configurations, experience teaches us that innovation and subtle changes can make all the difference.

The concept of a service system is resonating well with academics from diverse disciplines and practitioners from diverse economic sectors. And yet, because this is such a new area, few compilations of the works of academics and practitioners exist. Therefore to fill the gap, these two inter-related peer reviewed volumes of the Service Science: Research and Innovations in the Service Economy Series on Advancement of Services Systems ("Service Systems Implementation" and "The Science of Service Systems") and are very specific in nature. They present multi-disciplinary and multisectoral perspectives on the nature of service systems, on research and practice in service, and on the future directions to advance service science. Service Systems Implementation intends to stimulate discussion and understanding by presenting application-oriented, design science-oriented (artifacts building: constructs, models, methods and instantiations) and case study-oriented research with actionable results. The Science of Service Systems intends to stimulate discussion and understanding by presenting theory based research with actionable results.

We know the importance of having to start "somewhere" to get the new ideas moving, and finding the appropriate collaborators to make some initial steps and advances in new knowledge possible. The editors would like to thank the Series Editors of the Service Science: Research and Innovations in the Service Economy Series, Bill Hefley and Wendy Murphy, and the Springer co-editors, Melissa Fearon and Jennifer Maurer, for their encouragement and guidance for development of these volumes; and leading thinkers in this field, Richard B. Chase and Richard C. Larson, who wrote forewords, and Mary Jo Bitner, Stephen W. Brown, Andrew Dingjan, Jay Kandampully, Suk Joon KIM, Jeong Hyop Lee, Michael Lyons, Kunihiko Niwa, Miguel-Angel Sicilia and J.B. Wood who wrote testimonials.

To edit these books, in addition to public call for chapter proposals, we also invited many professional and academic leaders, and successful organizations to share their knowledge and experiences. We had 80 articles and extended abstracts submitted for these two inter-related volumes. With so many submissions reflecting the interest of these topics among scholars and practitioners in our community, it was necessary for us to make some tough decisions as to papers to accept for further development, and those to pass back to submitting authors with indications of the work that they needed to do to put themselves in a better position to contribute to the service science literature. The articles in these volumes issue went through a three-cycle "review and revise" process. From original inception to completion this book project with two interrelated volumes took almost 3 years. We include total 34 chapters (17 chapters in each book) that represent research and practices from almost 20 countries including Amsterdam, Australia, Canada, China, Cypress, Germany, India, Ireland, Italy, Mexico, Netherlands, Singapore, Spain, Taiwan, Turkey, United Arab Emirates, United Kingdom, United States of America, and many others. These researches represent studies and practices from many universities, companies, government offices and public and private institutions.

We would especially like to acknowledge the anonymous reviewers, who so generously offered their time, effort and helpful insights for us to make the hard choice and for helping us with development and constructive reviewing that led to the final products that you see in the present edited volume. Finally, we thank the authors, including those whose works we accepted, and those whose efforts did not permit their research and practices to go the final distance to publication. They all were diligent and careful, and gave us private lessons along the way about what vibrant and creative research on service systems is. We look forward to the "next generation" of service science and systems research and practices.

HD, JCS, VK
San Jose, California
December 24, 2010

Contributors

Atreyi Kankanhalli is an associate professor in the Department of Information Systems at the National University of Singapore (NUS). She obtained her B. Tech. from the Indian Institute of Technology Delhi, M.S. from the Rensselaer Polytechnic Institute, and Ph.D. from NUS. Her research interests include knowledge management, IT-enabled organizational forms, and IT in public sector. Her work has appeared in top-tier journals such as the MIS Quarterly, JMIS, and IEEE Transactions on Engineering Management, and proceedings such as the ICIS. She serves on the editorial boards of the MIS Quarterly and IEEE Transactions on Engineering Management among others.

Balaji Sankaranarayanan is an assistant professor in the IPM department at Bentley University, Waltham, Massachusetts. He holds a Ph.D. in Information Systems from Indiana University, Bloomington. His dissertation focused on the various relationship, governance and learning factors that predict IS outsourcing effectiveness. His research interests include IS outsourcing and offshoring, and IS management in healthcare. Dr. Balaji's research publications include articles on IS offshoring capabilities in MIS Quarterly Executive, an outsourcing teaching case in Managing Information Technology (6th edition, Prentice Hall/Pearson, 2008), and other articles in the proceedings of ICIS, ECIS and HICSS conferences.

Carmel Laragy is a lecturer in social work at RMIT University, Melbourne, Australia. Before moving to academia, Carmel's background as a social worker in children, adult and elder services provided her with a well grounded understanding of service system requirements. Her current research focuses on flexible service delivery that meets the needs of service users and the challenges of successfully implementing change management strategies. She has published internationally in this field.

Carol V. Brown is a distinguished professor of Information Systems at Stevens Institute of Technology where she also serves as the Program Director for Healthcare IT. She has been developing curricula and teaching graduate students at Stevens, as well as at Purdue University and Indiana University, for over 20 years. Her research findings on IS strategy and management issues have been widely disseminated in research articles, and she co-authors a leading IT management textbook (Managing Information Technology, 6th edition, Prentice Hall/Pearson, 2008). She is currently serving as the editor-in-chief of MIS Quarterly Executive, and was previously the editor-in-chief of Information Systems Management. Dr. Brown's current research focuses on sourcing issues, including realigning IT resources in the context of mergers and acquisitions, and enterprise system implementation issues within healthcare delivery organizations.

Chee Wei Phang is an assistant professor in the Department of Information Management and Information Systems at Fudan University, China. He obtained his B.Comp and Ph.D. from the National University of Singapore (NUS). His work has appeared in journals including the IEEE Transactions on Engineering Management, Journal of the Association for Information Systems, Communications of the ACM, and Journal of Strategic Information Systems; and the proceedings of the International Conference on Information Systems (ICIS) and HICSS among others. His research interests include virtual communities, IT in public sector, and e-commerce.

Danny Zijlstra, B.Sc. is manager in Data Center Technologies & Operations (DCTO) at Accenture. He has over 10 years of experience in this field of practice in Consulting, Outsourcing and Infrastructure Management. His everyday work involves the optimization of ICT infrastructures at a wide range of clients and he is currently specialized in green IT initiatives, among others.

Erik den Hartigh is assistant professor of strategy and innovation at Özyeğin University in Istanbul and at the Delft University of Technology. He received his Ph.D. from the school of economics of the Erasmus University Rotterdam. His research is in corporate strategy, innovation and business networks, specifically about the strategic positioning of firms in business networks, and about the productivity of innovation systems. He has published on these topics through academic journals and conferences as well as through books and for-company reports. He is a part time consultant at TVA developments, a strategy consultancy firm in The Netherlands.

Gary Warnaby is a senior lecturer in marketing at the University of Liverpool Management School. His research interests include the marketing of places (in particular the marketing of towns and cities as retail destinations), town centre management and retailing more generally. Results of this research has been published in academic journals including Environment and Planning A, Marketing Theory, Journal of Marketing Management, European Journal of Marketing, Cities, Area, Local Economy and the International Review of Retail, Distribution and Consumer Research, as well as a variety of professional and trade publications.

Haluk Demirkan is a Professor of Information Systems and a Research Faculty of Center for Services Leadership. His doctorate is in Information Systems and Operations Management from University of Florida, and his research in service science, and service-oriented management and technology solutions have included recent industry-sponsored research projects with American Express, Intel, IBM, MicroStrategy and Teradata. His research appears in a number of journals, including Journal of Information Management Systems, Journal of the Association for Information Systems, Journal of Service Research, European Journal of Operational Research, IEEE Transactions on Systems, Man and Cybernetics, Electronic Commerce Research and Applications, Communications of ACM, and many other leading journals. He has authored or co-authored almost fifty articles in refereed journals or conference proceedings. He has fifteen years of consulting experience in the areas of service-oriented information systems and technology solutions, information supply chain, business intelligence and strategic business engineering with Fortune 100 companies. He is the recent recipient of the IBM Faculty Award for a research project titled "Design Science for Self-Service Systems."

Hossein S. Zadeh is the program director of Master of Business Services Science at RMIT University in Melbourne, Australia. Hossein has an extensive portfolio of research and consultancy in multicriteria optimization and outside of academia has held positions such as research scientist, senior system administrator, project manager, network manager, and senior computer system administrator. Hossein has taught undergraduate and postgraduate courses in Australia, Hong Kong, Vietnam, Singapore, and Sweden. He is currently on sabbatical at Almaden Services Research group of IBM Almaden Research Labs, Silicon Valley (San Jose), California, USA.

Howard W. Lightfoot works in the School of Applied Sciences and Innovative Manufacturing Research Centre at Cranfield University in the UK, where his research is focused on Product-Service Systems, the configuration of Servitized Manufacturing companies and Manufacturing Supply Chain Positioning. He has held senior operations and management positions within international UK manufacturing companies in the Automotive, Defence and Aerospace sectors and International business development experience gained in Western Europe, USA and the Far East.

Jaap Gordijn is professor of service science and innovation at the Faculty of Sciences of the Vrije Universiteit, Amsterdam. He obtained his Ph.D. degree from the Vrije Universiteit Amsterdam on e-business modeling. His research interest concentrates on innovative e-business applications. He is a key developer of the e3value e-business modeling methodology, addressing the integration of strategic e-business decision making with ICT requirements and systems engineering. He has been working on projects in the field of e-business such as Obelix, BusMod, Interop and FENIX. Before joining the Vrije Universiteit, he was a member of Cisco's Internet Business Solution Group and senior manager of the e-business group at Deloitte & Touche. As such, he was involved in rolling out e-business applications in the banking, insurance, and digital content industries.

James C. Spohrer is a Director of IBM Global University Programs since 2009, Jim founded IBM's first Service Research group in 2003 at the Almaden Research Center with a focus on STEM (Science Technology Engineering and Math) for Service Sector innovations. He led this group to attain ten times return on investment with four IBM outstanding and eleven accomplishment awards. Working with service research pioneers from many academic disciplines, Jim advocates for Service Science, Management, Engineering, and Design (SSMED) as an integrative extended-STEM framework for global competency development, economic growth, and advancement of science. In 2000, Jim became the founding CTO of IBM's first Venture Capital Relations group in Silicon Valley. In the mid 1990's, he lead Apple Computer's Learning Technologies group, where he received the DEST (Distinguished Engineer Scientist and Technologist) award. Jim received a Ph.D. in Computer Science/Artificial Intelligence from Yale University and a B.S. in Physics from MIT.

Jerry Luftman is the founder and Executive Director of Graduate Information Systems Programs, and Distinguished Professor at Stevens Institute of Technology, Hoboken, New Jersey. His career includes strategic positions in management (information technology, including being a CIO, and consultant), management consulting, information systems, and executive education. After a notable 23 year career with IBM, and over 15 years at Stevens, Dr. Luftman's experience combines the strengths of practitioner, consultant, and academic. His SAM model for assessing IT-business alignment maturity is considered key in helping companies around the world understand, define, and scope an appropriate strategic planning direction that leverages Information Technology. Dr. Luftman has authored/co-authored over a dozen books and dozens of articles.

John A. Ricketts is an IBM distinguished engineer. Formerly a consulting partner in IBM Global Services, John is currently a technical executive in IBM headquarters. Prior to joining IBM, Dr. Ricketts was a professor, manager of applied research, and director of software engineering. His doctorate combines information systems, computer science, and behavioral science. John's research and teaching have won awards from the Decision Sciences Institute and the Association to Advance Collegiate Schools of Business, as well as IBM. His recent book, Reaching the Goal: How Managers Improve a Services Business Using Goldratt's Theory of Constraints, was published by IBM Press.

Joris Hulstijn is assistant professor IT Audit at the Vrije Universiteit Amsterdam. His current research interests are: normative reasoning, auditing, information integrity, and the impact of regulatory compliance on information systems. Previously, he worked on multi-agent systems at Utrecht University and the AI department of the Vrije Universiteit. In 2000 Joris defended his Ph.D. on natural language dialogue systems at University of Twente.

Justin Nieuwerth, M.Sc. recently graduated on the Master's program of Business Informatics at Utrecht University, the Netherlands. This chapter describes his thesis research, which involved creating an assessment framework measuring the capability of companies to adopt an Infrastructure-as-a-Service architecture. This research is conducted on behalf of, and supported by Accenture Netherlands BV, situated in Amsterdam, as well as Utrecht University itself.

Linda Wilkins is an educational designer who has contributed to a number of cross-disciplinary national and international IS research projects. Many of these collaborations have been in association with industry partners. She has published widely in leading IS academic journals and co-authored several Australian state and federal government reports on the future of e-business. Her practice revolves around business service issues impacting on user uptake of innovative online technologies.

Marc Zegveld is partner in Strategy & Change IBM Netherlands. Marc focuses on strategy development and value creation. Marc has an engineering degree, received a business education at INSEAD and received his Ph.D. on a study on dual innovation strategies. Before joining IBM in 2008 Marc was director of TVA developments by, a strategy consultancy firm in The Netherlands. As an associate professor he led the Technology Strategy & Entrepreneurship section at Delft University of Technology. Marc published a dozen books, over 30 articles and almost 100 columns in the leading Dutch financial newspaper "Het Financieele Dagblad."

Marco Spruit is an assistant professor in the Organisation & Information research group at the Institute of Information and Computing Sciences of Utrecht University. His information systems research revolves around Knowledge Discovery processes to help achieve organisational goals through Data Mining techniques, Business intelligence methods, Linguistic Engineering techniques and Web 2.0 technologies. Additionally, he investigates Information Security models and Cloud Computing frameworks as infrastructural safeguards and enablers for Knowledge Discovery processes. Marco initiated his Knowledge Discovery research agenda while performing his Ph.D. in Quantitative Linguistics at the University of Amsterdam. In 2005 he was awarded an ALLC Bursary Award for this work.

Michael Rocha was Executive Vice President, Global Support Services and Platform Technology at Oracle Corporation from 2000 to 2005. In this position, he managed a $5.5 billion business, and was responsible for support, platform technologies, On Demand and corporate IT. He reported directly to the CEO and was a member of Oracle's Executive and Product Division Management Committees. Mike enjoyed a 16-year career in Oracle's product division.

Pallipuram V. Kannan is a co-founder and CEO of 24/7 Customer. Kannan is a well-known thought leader in the field of global sourcing. He is featured in a variety of publications, including Tom Friedman's "The World is Flat", "Outsourcing Thought Leaders" by Booz Allen Hamilton, and in Fortune Magazine. Kannan has a number of U.S. and international patent filings to his credit. Prior to 24/7 Customer, Kannan was an officer and VP at Kana Software. In 1995, he founded Business Evolution (BEI), which was acquired by Kana Software. Prior to BEI, Kannan worked in U.S. and Europe in various leadership roles overseeing IT projects. Kannan holds professional degrees in accounting and finance.

Paul G. Sorenson is professor emeritus of Computing Science at the University of Alberta. He has previously held positions of Department Head in Computer Science at the University of Saskatchewan and Department Chair of Computing Science at the University of Alberta. He has been Associate VP (Research) and Vice-Provost and Associate VP (Information Technology) at the University of Alberta. Recently his research interests have focused on service systems delivery, management and quality. He collaborated in the development O-O framework methods and technologies that led to the creation of two spin-off companies Avra Software Lab and Onware Software Systems. He is currently co-chair of the Alberta IBM CAS (Centre for Advanced Studies).

Rajesh Kumar Tyagi is an assistant professor at the HEC Montreal, Department of Logistics and Operations Management. Professor Tyagi teaches Service Operations, Operations Management, and Quality Management. Earlier, Dr. Tyagi has taught service operations and operations management at Kellogg School of Management, Northwestern University and at DePaul University, College of Commerce. He has over 12 peer review publications in scientific and technology journals and has presented at various national and international conferences. He is the co-author of Six Sigma for Transactions and Service and A Complete and Balanced Service Scorecard.

Ravi Vijayaraghavan is a vice-president at 24/7 Customer Innovation Labs. His organization builds data-driven solutions that enhance customer acquisition, service and retention through online and offline channels. Prior to this, Vijayaraghavan was at Ford Motor Company. His contributions were in the applications of computing and mathematical modeling to design and optimization of business and engineering systems. He was the recipient of a Henry Ford Technology award – the highest technical recognition at Ford. Vijayaraghavan has several patent filings, refereed publications and invited presentations at international conferences. Vijayaraghavan holds a bachelor's degree from Indian Institute of Technology, a Ph.D. from University of Wisconsin-Madison and an MBA from Ross School of Business, University of Michigan, Ann Arbor.

Renu Agarwal is a senior lecturer and a research director (faculty of business) at the University of Technology Sydney. Renu has extensive industry experience where she held senior management positions at the State Rail Authority of NSW, Telstra Corporation and its joint venture global company REACH. Dr. Agarwal was awarded the "ANZAM Best Doctoral Dissertation Award 2008" for her research on "Drivers and outcome of elevated service offerings in a collaborative organisational environment". Renu's research expertise lies in innovation through capability building in collaborating service organizations and assessing the impact of management practices on firm performance in the manufacturing and hospitals sectors.

Sam Albert is a senior manager at 24/7 Customer Innovation Labs. He has innovated, architected and developed several text mining solutions for customer acquisition and service. Albert started his career as a systems analyst where he designed and developed automation solutions for businesses. Before joining 24/7 Customer, Sam was teaching Computer Science at Karunya Technical University. Albert has patent filings and research publications to his credit. Albert holds a Ph.D. in Computer Science and a Masters in Computer Applications from Bharathiar University. His has his B.S. degree from Madurai Kamaraj University.

Steve Baron is professor of Marketing and Director of the Centre for Experiential Consumption Studies at the University of Liverpool, and was chair of the AMA Servsig International Research Conference in 2008. His current research interests include the understanding of service experiences from the consumer perspective, and communities of service and social practice. He has publications in services, marketing and management journals, including Journal of Service Research, European Journal of Marketing, Journal of Services Marketing, International Journal of Market Research and Journal of Business Research. He is co-author of 'Services Marketing: Text and Cases', published by Palgrave in 2009.

Sudhendu Rai is a principal scientist at the Xerox Research Center in Webster, New York. He received his Ph.D. from MIT (1993), M.S. from Caltech (1989), and B.Tech. from IIT, Kanpur (India) in 1988 – all in Mechanical Engineering. He is the lead inventor of the LDP Lean Document Production® solution that was a finalist at the 2008 Franz Edelman competition. He holds 18 patents with 40 additional pending. He is a member of ASME, INFORMS, IIE and a senior member of IEEE. He was a finalist for the Rochester Engineer of the Year award in 2007.

Thomas J. Buckholtz helped pioneer information technologies, led a $1 billion business unit, led a company's innovation program, pioneered the enterprise software license, led the team that started a United States nationwide grassroots endeavor to improve governmental service to the public, served as co-chief information officer for the U.S. federal government's Executive Branch, and has been a corporate officer for startups. Based on his suggestions, people created a shoreline preserve, a Rotary International Service Program, and an American political party's grassroots program. Buckholtz earned a physics Ph.D. (University of California, Berkeley) after receiving a mathematics B.S. (California Institute of Technology).

Tim S. Baines specializes in the realization of competitive manufacturing operations. At Cranfield, he is the head of the Manufacturing Systems Centre, leads the Product Service Systems (PSS) theme of the Innovative Manufacturing Research Centre, and is a co-creator and technical director of the Boeing Centre in Integrated Vehicle Health Management (IVHM). Professor Baines works extensively across disciplines, is highly active in post-graduate and executive teaching and supervision, has a strong track record of raising research funding, and has consistently published his work in the leading journals of his field.

Timothy Chou was president of Oracle On Demand from 1999 to 2005. During his tenure Oracle On Demand was the fastest growing business in Oracle, providing applications on demand for more than 250,000 corporate users globally. He has served on several corporate boards, has authored multiple publications, including the books The End of Software and Cloud: Seven Clear Business Models. He has been a lecturer in computer science at Stanford for more than 15 years, where he launched the first course in Software as a Service and cloud computing.

Vikas Krishna is a senior technical staff member and manager at the IBM Almaden Research Center in San Jose, CA, USA. He leads a team of service researchers and engineers focussing on innovative solutions and service systems for IBM's global services business to provide higher personnel productivity, enabling service personnel to work and deliver service smarter, and higher client value propositions. Since joining IBM in 1997, he has led the design and development of systems for net mining, web-based service delivery, business-to-business information exchange, integrated analysis of text and data, managed business processes services, and next generation contact centers holding several patents in these areas. He is also the recipient of several awards for his outstanding innovative and technical contributions to IBM's services business and that of its clients. He received his Bachelor of Technology degree from the Indian Institute of Technology, India, an M.Eng. degree from Memorial University, Canada and his M.S. degree from Syracuse University, USA.

Vinod Kumar Singh is Senior Analytics Consultant at 24/7 Customer Innovation Labs. His expertise is in building predictive models using structured and unstructured data. His research areas include machine learning techniques, text mining and natural language processing. Prior to 247customer, Vinod was with IBM. He holds a Masters degree from Indian Institute of Technology, Kanpur in Industrial and Management Engineering. As a part of his academic research, he developed a methodology for auto classification of patent documents.

Willem Selen is professor of Management (Supply Chain Management and Logistics) at the United Arab Emirates University. He obtained his Ph.D. in Business Administration from the University of South Carolina (1982). His broad research interests span the (service) operations management-, supply chain-, and e-business areas, and he has published in leading journals, including Decision Sciences, International Journal of Production and Operations Management, International Journal of Logistics Management, International Journal of Physical Distribution and Logistics Management, Journal of Operations Management (guest editor). Willem has also been active in short course delivery in operations and supply chain management to leading companies worldwide.

Wout Hofman is a senior innovator at TNO Information and Communication Technology, the Dutch knowledge institute for applied research. Wout has been active in modelling complex service systems, especially in trade, transport, and customs, e.g. the EU New Computerised Transit System. His focus is currently enterprise interoperability. His Ph.D. thesis (Technical University of Eindhoven/ Erasmus University Rotterdam, 1994) was on the design of a system to support customized process configuration. He is author of several books and over 50 articles.

Yao-Hua Tan is professor of Information and Communication Technology at Delft University of Technology and part-time professor of Electronic Business at the Vrije Universiteit, Amsterdam. He was also Reynolds visiting professor at the Wharton Business School of the University of Pennsylvania. He is coordinator of the EU-funded integrated research project ITAIDE on IT innovation to facilitate international trade. His research interests are service engineering and governance; ICT-enabled electronic negotiation and contracting; multi-agent modeling to develop automation of business procedures in international trade.

Testimonials

"This text seamlessly links the nascent field of services science with application, design and case study oriented services research. It illuminates pathways through the value and measurement of service system productivity, and for good measure, provides a powerful blueprint for next-gen service delivery models and their implementation."
Andrew Dingjan
Leader of Services Science Network
The Commonwealth Scientific and Industrial Research Organisation
Melbourne Area, Australia

"Companies have known for decades how to invest smartly in product development. Now, thanks to Service Systems Implementation, they know how to do the same for services. And since services are the largest and fastest growing markets for many of these companies, the opportunities for innovation and shareholder value creation are huge. It is about time."
J.B. Wood, President and CEO
Technology Services Industry Association
USA

"The books are filled with rich fundamental concepts and noble ideas that leverage government officials, policy researchers, and scholars toward the development of new service R&D and service science related policy to enhance the international competitiveness of advanced countries as well as developing countries."
Suk Joon KIM, Ph.D.
The President of Science & Technology Policy Institute
South Korea

"This is an invaluable handbook that illustrates the scope of the service system concept in practice and the rich array of functional tools available to improve the design and delivery of services."
Michael Lyons, Ph.D.
Chief Researcher of Service Systems
British Telecom Innovate & Design
London, United Kingdom

"An abstract understanding of service systems has little value without concurrent tools, frameworks, and methods for implementation. This volume takes the necessary first steps toward developing a language and dialog for service systems implementation."

"This volume presents valuable frameworks, tools, and techniques aimed at effective service system implementation in a variety of industry and discipline contexts."

Mary Jo Bitner, Ph.D.
PetSmart Chair in Services Leadership
Professor and Academic Director
Center for Services Leadership
W. P. Carey School of Business
Arizona State University, USA

"This landmark volume showcases the application of research methods and case studies to help us understand actual service systems, their performance and behavior. The key implementation dimensions of people, information, technology and value propositions are effectively integrated throughout the papers."

Stephen W. Brown, Ph.D.
Edward M. Carson Chair in Services Marketing
Professor and Executive Director
Center for Services Leadership
W. P. Carey School of Business
Arizona State University, USA

"The second volume brings service science theory into practice, providing a selection of case studies that cover a wide array of technologies and socio-technical issues arising in the current practice of service design and implementation. It offers a rich source of contrasted ideas to think smarter about service design."

"The book provides a catalogue of lessons learned about service systems practice that can hardly be found elsewhere, with a coherent grounding on the emergent theory of service science."

Miguel-Angel Sicilia, Ph.D.
University of Alcala at Henares, Spain
Editor in Chief of International Journal of Service Science, Management, Engineering and Technology

"The service science research and innovations (SSRI) are, in my opinion, still in an infant stage. This volume provides stimulating case studies of many service systems, and I am certain that it will contribute to the SSRI growth and advancement."

Kunihiko Niwa, Ph.D.
Principal Fellow of Center for Research and Development Strategy
Japan Science and Technology Agency, Japan

Introduction of Service Systems Implementation

Haluk Demirkan

Arizona State University, Tempe, AZ, USA

James C. Spohrer and Vikas Krishna

IBM Almaden Research Center, San Jose, CA, USA

1   How to Implement Service Systems?

Services systems can range from an individual to a firm to an entire nation. They can also be nested and composed of other service systems. They are configurations of people, information, technology and organizations to co-create value between a service customer and a provider (Maglio et al. 2006; Spohrer et al. 2007). While these configurations can take many, potentially infinite, forms, they can be optimized for the subject service to eliminate unnecessary costs in the forms of redundancies, over allocation, etc. So what is an ideal configuration that a provider and a customer might strive to achieve? As much as it would be nice to have a formula for such configurations, experiences that are result of engagement, are very different for each value co-creation configurations. The variances and dynamism of customer provider engagements result in potentially infinite types and numbers of configurations in today's global economy.

This book, *Service Systems Implementation*, intends to stimulate discussion and understanding by presenting application-oriented, design science-oriented (artifacts building: constructs, models, methods and instantiations) and case study-oriented research with actionable results. This will illustrate how the techniques described can be employed in large scale, real world examples that are developed to match the theoretical and practical presentation. Furthermore, the case studies will help visualize service systems along the four key dimensions of people, information, technology and value propositions which can help enable better integration between them towards higher value propositions.

The papers that we have chosen for this book examine a wide range of substantive issues and implementations related to service science in various industries. The authors' results in all of the articles have implications for service science and systems that go beyond the immediate application settings on which they report. These papers also showcase the application of an array of research methods, including

H. Demirkan et al. (eds.), *Service Systems Implementation*, Service Science:
Research and Innovations in the Service Economy, DOI 10.1007/978-1-4419-7904-9_1,
© Springer Science+Business Media, LLC 2011

surveys, experiments, design science, case studies and frameworks. Given that, what we have striven to do in this volume is compile a series of service system implementations, frameworks and tools that help understand real world services systems, their performance, and their behaviors upon introduction of changes, and hopefully provide the reader with insights and guidelines to help in building their own service systems towards a more favorable service experience as viewed by the customer and the provider. In the remainder of our Editors' Introduction, we will briefly discuss each of the articles in the book to identify their main thrust of the authors' investigation and the relevant findings for research and practice.

Our goal in this volume is not to present the end product, a fully formed science of service systems, but instead to present a useful beginning and process to make progress. The process consists of connecting people with diverse backgrounds, who all appreciate the opportunity at hand. The opportunity is to contribute to an emerging systematic understanding of service and service systems. We hope this admittedly humble beginning and simple process will inspire others to contribute to this emerging area.

In the next chapter, Rai in "Data-Driven Simulation-Enhanced Optimization of People-Based Print Production Service" presents a discrete-event simulation based solution utilizing autonomous cells and hierarchical scheduling to optimize service systems that exhibit significant variability and complexity. The solution demonstrates that abstraction, generalization and automation of the simulation technology to model many service center operations using a common framework and software toolkit is an enabler to deployment of this methodology by a wide range of analysts and consultants. The process for deploying the solution was also discussed in the context of the DMAIC process used in industries. The impact of utilizing this approach by Xerox Corporation is summarized.

Krishna, Bailey, and Lelescu in "Intelligent Document Gateway: A Service System Case Study and Analysis" describe the fast paced world of processing business documents expediently, accurately, and diligently. They evaluate a B2B order placement service system that allows clients to place orders for products and services over a network. They describe the order placement service before and after deploying the Intelligent Document Gateway (IDG), a document-centric business process automation technology from IBM Research. Using service science perspective and service systems frameworks, they provide an analysis of how IDG improved the value proposition for both the service providers and service clients.

Tan, Hofman, Gordijn, and Hulstijn in "A Framework for the Design of Service Systems" develop two conceptual modeling support tools and illustrate their use: the Service Innovation Aspects Model (e3-value) and the Service Innovation Life Cycle Model (e3-control). They try to answer the question about the types of models and tools that exist to support the re-design of Business-to-Business (B2B) and Business-to-Government (B2G) service systems. To validate the adequacy and usefulness of the models and tools, they conducted an extensive case study, the BeerLL, of the redesign of services in international trade, under the influence of technological innovation (TREC device) and a new governance approach (AEO certification).

Rocha and Chou in "Surviving Nuclear Winter: Towards a Service-Led Business" present a case study of Oracle's ambitious plan to build an integrated suite of applications software. It took many years and thousands of developers to build. By early 2000, the company launched the product and started upgrade their entire customer base. Unfortunately, the "tech bubble" burst and the economy went into recession. Oracle's business changed overnight. Their product business declined by 19% over the next 3 years, and the consulting and education businesses further eroded by 33%. Oracle's service business became the engine that powered the company. Based on this experience, they discuss three fundamentals of a service-led business: Service is Information, Personal to You; Service Connects You to Your Customer and Service is Specialization.

Baines and Lightfoot in "Towards an Operations Strategy for the Infusion of Product-Centric Services into Manufacturing" studies the process of creating value by adding services to products, the so called servitization or servicizing process. A science of service systems will need to explore the evolution of different types of service systems. These authors examine the phenomena whereby a portfolio of services are formed and integrated to support product availability and use. Examples in practice are Rolls-Royce's 'Power by the Hour' and their more inclusive 'TotalCare' contracts. These demonstrate how traditionally based manufacturing companies have moved their position in the value-chain from product manufacturers to providing customers with 'desired outcomes' through integrated solutions that may also include the use of multi-vendor products. The specific question underpinning this chapter is "what general form should an operations strategy take to support a manufacturer in the efficient and effective delivery of integrated products and services?" They consider that an operations strategy should be defined in terms of 12 sets of characteristics, namely, Process and Technology, Capacity, Facilities, Vertical Integration, Product Range, Planning and Control, Human Resources, Quality Control, New Product Introduction, Performance Measurement, Supplier Relations, and Customer Relations.

Ricketts in "Theory of Constraints for Services: Past, Present, and Future" extends TOC (Theory of Constraints) to the domain of service systems – specifically Professional, Technical, and Scientific Service (PTSS) businesses. He shows how to apply TOC to PTSS businesses using a five step process: (1) identify the constraint, (2) exploit the constraint, (3) subordinate everything else, (4) elevate the constraint, and (5) repeat. TOC is a well-known management practice. Yet it has been relegated mostly to manufacturing and distribution. With the introduction of TOC for Services (TOCS), however, this body of knowledge is now applicable across the full range of services. TOCS includes standard applications for Resource Management, Project Management, Process Management, and Measurement. It also includes nonstandard applications for Marketing, Sales, Strategy, and Change.

Nieuwerth, Spruit and Zijlstra in "An Assessment Tool for Establishing Infrastructure as a Service Capability Maturity" examine the adoption and integration of Infrastructure-as-a-Service (IaaS) by organizations, and more generally the way service systems are transformed by advancing information technology (IT). They describe the lack of awareness and fear of implementation failures associated with Infrastructure-as-a-Service (IaaS). They define IaaS as an entirely virtualized information technology infrastructure with scalable storage on demand, in combination with either database(s) or computing capacity on demand, or both. There is little scientific information available about the IaaS concept, let alone knowledge on how to deal with the adoption and integration. Their research focuses on IaaS as a strictly defined cloud computing environment. They present a tool to aid in the decision making process by identifying the state of adoption readiness of organizations. Because of rapid advances in IT capabilities, IT service management is an important area of research for the development of a science of service systems.

Luftman, Balaji and Brown in "Customer–Provider Strategic Alignment: A Maturity Model" present a new model called Customer–Provider Strategic Alignment Maturity Model (CPSAM). A science of service systems should inform the way complex entities interact, including their outsourcing decisions. The model presented in this paper aims to improve IT outsourcing success rates, by providing a metric-based framework for assessing the maturity of customer–provider strategic alignment. The most common reasons for an outsourcing engagement to fail include not only the overall strategy, selection process, and contract negotiation, but also implementation, post-implementation, and management of the customer–provider relationship.

Sorenson in "CIO in a Service Economy" explores the impact of the growth of the service economy on the traditional role of CIO (Chief Information Officer), both for today's enterprise and the enterprise of the future. He examines the major elements of a service system (technology, people, organization and shared information) and the impact the CIO must have on each of these elements pertaining to activities such the strategic planning, governance and operations management of information technology services. With the increased emphasis on service-oriented architectures and the ability to interact with stored information anywhere at any time via a web browser, the decisions of what services to support and how they should be supported (internal, outsourced or subscribed) are becoming increasingly complex.

Den Hartigh and Zegveld in "Service Productivity: How to Measure and Improve It?" examine the way some businesses as service system entities focus on flexibility in order to offer a broad portfolio of service offerings that serve different groups of customers. To maintain efficiency, such businesses will often choose to modularize their offerings, so that the different service modules can be configured in many different ways. In a sense, they do not offer predefined services to customers, but they offer their customers a solution space.

Baron and Warnaby in "Value Co-creation from the Consumer Perspective" present a case study of a specific organization, the British Library (BL), which is the national library of the UK. Their paper addresses value co-creation and value-in-use from the consumer perspective. They explore how consumers integrate their resources by engaging in experiences, and how consumers may perceive organizational operant resources. Working on the premise that individual consumers as well as whole organizations are service systems, the paper offers insights into the consumers' processes of valuing. Although the word 'resource' is used many times about the BL itself in their data, the operant resources (physical, social, cultural) at the disposal of BL consumers are quite diverse and non-obvious.

Buckholtz in "Metrics that Matter: Measuring and Improving the Value of Service" constructs two measuring scales that can be used by practitioners when designing new service systems or transforming existing service systems. The first scale is used to assess service functionality (realizing, accomplishing, planning, understanding, marshaling), while the second is used to assess service proficiency (obviated, routine, experimental, ad-hoc, pending). He illustrates the use of the two scales in the context of US government transformations that in the 1980s mandated opening up and improving information access capabilities across multiple agencies.

Wilkins, Laragy and Zadeh in "Succeeding Through Service Innovation: Consumer Directed Care in the Aged Care Sector" begin with the observation that the World Health Organisation (2008) has nominated the growing challenge of age-ing populations as a key global issue for struggling health systems. Consequently more customized and sustainable service models should be of particular interest to those responsible for funding and maintaining services for ageing populations. Consumer Directed Care (CDC) represents one such innovative service delivery system with increasing take-up across industrialized societies in Europe, the United States and Australia. CDC opens up possibilities for re-defining consumer expecta-tions, prompting change in how service providers such as government agencies and not-for-profit organizations (NFPs) operate. However the current literature on CDC implementation has not yet produced an acceptable analytical framework and evaluation system. To fill this gap they propose a recent adaptation of the European Commission policy impact as assessment approach for reviewing specific CDC implementations.

Tyagi in "Measurement in Service Businesses: Challenges and Future Directions" develops a conceptual framework for measurement called the Service Scorecard Architecture. The importance of measurement models and key performance indica-tors appropriate to service businesses is explored. In product businesses, a firm faces variability primarily in the production process. In service businesses, customers introduce additional variability as customers are often integral part of the production process. In this chapter, a clear distinction is made between service processes, a providers' perspective, and a service experience, an end users' perspective.

Agarwal and Selen in "An Integrated View of Service Innovation in Service Networks" develop a conceptual framework to better understand how service innova-tion may be achieved in service networks. They develop the RARE (Resources, Activities and Routines configured and reconfigured through Entrepreneurial actions) strategic framework. Co-evolutionary adaptation of the capabilities of entities occurs in service networks as a result of positioning, leveraging, opportunity creation, expe-riential learning, and customer engagement mechanisms. Each mechanism is devel-oped as a strategic and/or economic logic employed by stakeholders in the network.

Phang and Kankanhalli in "A Service Systems Perspective of E-government Development" go beyond businesses as service systems, to explore governments as service systems. They note the increasing efforts by governments worldwide to innovate public service delivery, one of the means being through e-government. However, the mixed success of e-government initiatives highlights the need to better understand citizens' requirements and engage them in the development of e-government service offerings. In response to this need, they propose a service systems perspective to analyze a participatory e-government service system based on the key resources of people, organizations, shared information, and technologies. By doing so, this study bridges the gap in existing research that has separately examined the different resources without considering their inter-relationships in a systematic manner. Overall, the application of a service systems perspective to e-government service development reinforces the paradigm of viewing citizens as customers.

In the last chapter, Vijayaraghavan, Kannan, Albert and Singh in "Predictive Systems for Customer Interactions" provide a frame-work for managing customer–provider service interactions across the life-cycle of the customer. The framework promises potential gains relative to the current state of customer service, in each of the three dimensions, efficiency, effectiveness and sustainability. Key components of this framework include the ability to integrate structured and unstructured data from different customer interaction channels and the competency to build predictive systems that enable a proactive interface with the customers. In addition, given the dynamic complexity of this system, it is important to be able to measure the impact of changes created by these proactive strategies on customer experience so that the system learns and evolves over time as customers and their engagement mode with the provider changes. They also indicate that future work should measure the dynamic adaptability of the approach as customers' channel preferences evolve, new channels get introduced and other channels become obsolete. For practitioners, this work provides tools and strategies for managing customer contact in a manner that improves customer experience and their life-time value to the provider while driving down costs.

2   Concluding Remarks

As we conclude this project, we recognize that the research and practitioner work that we have included in this edited volume only scratches the surface of the issues that need to be studied and practices that need to be presented. We expect researchers and practitioners to pursue interdisciplinary research agendas in service science and service systems. We expect them to produce rich fundamental and applied work that leverages organizational and behavioural, economics and management science, and technical and design science research approaches toward the development of new managerial knowledge for service systems. If, as our colleagues at IBM, Jim Spohrer, Paul Maglio, and others have averred, we truly are moving to a world involving a "new science for services" for organizations large and small, then the time that we have spent will be a sentinel effort for what is to come. By participating in the beginning of the development of a new paradigm, we – authors, editors and readers alike – will have front row seats at the "table of innovation."

We know the importance of having to start "somewhere" to get the new ideas moving, and finding the appropriate collaborators to make some initial steps and advances in new knowledge possible. The editors would like to thank the Series

Editors of the Service Science: Research and Innovations in the Service Economy Series, Bill Hefley and Wendy Murphy, and the Springer Senior Editor, Melissa Fearon, for their encouragement and guidance for development of this volume. We actually had 80 articles and extended abstracts submitted on the topics of *"The Science of Service Systems"* and *"Service Systems Implementation"* for these two inter-related volumes of the Service Science: Research and Innovations in the Service Economy Series (SSRI). With so many submissions reflecting the interest of these topics among scholars and practitioners in our community, it was necessary for us to make some tough decisions as to papers to accept for further development, and those to pass back to submitting authors with indications of the work that they needed to do to put themselves in a better position to contribute to the service science literature. The articles in these volumes issue went through a three-cycle "review and revise" process. These two inter-related peer reviewed volumes of SSRI on Advancement of Services Systems ("The Science of Service Systems" and "Service Systems Implementation") are very specific in nature. The Science of Service Systems intends to stimulate discussion and understanding by presenting theory based research with actionable results. Service Systems Implementation intends to stimulate discussion and understanding by presenting application-oriented, design science-oriented (artifacts building: constructs, models, methods and instantiations) and case study-oriented research with actionable results.

We include total 34 chapters (17 chapters in each book) that represent research and practices from almost 20 countries including Amsterdam, Australia, Canada, China, Cypress, Germany, India, Ireland, Italy, Mexico, Netherlands, Singapore, Spain, Taiwan, Turkey, United Arab Emirates, United Kingdom, United States of America, and many others. These researches represent studies and practices from many universities, companies, government offices and public and private institutions.

We would especially like to acknowledge the anonymous reviewers, who so generously offered their time, effort and helpful insights for us to make the hard choice and for helping us with development and constructive reviewing that led to the final products that you see in the present edited volume. Finally, we thank the authors, including those whose works we accepted, and those whose efforts did not permit their research and practices to go the final distance to publication. They all were diligent and careful, and gave us private lessons along the way about what vibrant and creative research on service systems. We look forward to the "next generation" of service science and service systems research and practices.

References

Maglio, P. P., Srinivasan S., Kreulen, J. T. and Spohrer, J. (2006). Service Systems, Service Scientists, SSME, and Innovation. Communications of the ACM, Volume 49, No. 7, July 2006.

Spohrer, J., Maglio, P., Bailey, J. and Gruhl D. (2007). Steps Toward a Science of Service Systems. IEEE Computer, Volume 40, January 2007, pp. 71–77.

Editors

Haluk Demirkan is a Professor of Information Systems and a Research Faculty of Center for Services Leadership. His doctorate is in Information Systems and Operations Management from University of Florida, and his research in service science, and service-oriented management and technology solutions have included recent industry-sponsored research projects with American Express, Intel, IBM, MicroStrategy and Teradata. His research appears in a number of journals, including Journal of Information Management Systems, Journal of the Association for Information Systems, Journal of Service Research, European Journal of Operational Research, IEEE Transactions on Systems, Man and Cybernetics, Electronic Commerce Research and Applications, Communications of ACM, and many other leading journals. He has authored or co-authored almost fifty articles in refereed journals or conference proceedings. He has fifteen years of consulting experience in the areas of service-oriented information systems and technology solutions, information supply chain, business intelligence and strategic business engineering with Fortune 100 companies. He is the recent recipient of the IBM Faculty Award for a research project titled "Design Science for Self-Service Systems."

James C. Spohrer is a Director of IBM Global University Programs since 2009, Jim founded IBM's first Service Research group in 2003 at the Almaden Research Center with a focus on STEM (Science Technology Engineering and Math) for Service Sector innovations. He led this group to attain ten times return on investment with four IBM outstanding and eleven accomplishment awards. Working with service research pioneers from many academic disciplines, Jim advocates for Service Science, Management, Engineering, and Design (SSMED) as an integrative extended-STEM framework for global competency development, economic growth, and advancement of science. In 2000, Jim became the founding CTO of IBM's first Venture Capital Relations group in Silicon Valley. In the mid 1990's, he lead Apple Computer's Learning Technologies group, where he received the DEST (Distinguished Engineer Scientist and Technologist) award. Jim received a Ph.D. in Computer Science/Artificial Intelligence from Yale University and a B.S. in Physics from MIT.

Vikas Krishna is a senior technical staff member and manager at the IBM Almaden Research Center in San Jose, CA, USA. He leads a team of service researchers and engineers focussing on innovative solutions and service systems for IBM's global services business to provide higher personnel productivity, enabling service personnel to work and deliver service smarter, and higher client value propositions. Since joining IBM in 1997, he has led the design and development of systems for net mining, web-based service delivery, business-to-business information exchange, integrated analysis of text and data, managed business processes services, and next generation contact centers holding several patents in these areas. He is also the recipient of several awards for his outstanding innovative and technical contributions to IBM's services business and that of its clients. He received his Bachelor of Technology degree from the Indian Institute of Technology, India, an M.Eng. degree from Memorial University, Canada and his M.S. degree from Syracuse University, USA.

Data-Driven Simulation-Enhanced Optimization of People-Based Print Production Service

Sudhendu Rai

Xerox Research Center Webster, MS 128-51E, 800 Phillips Road, Webster, NY 14580, USA

Abstract This paper describes a systematic six-step data-driven simulation-based methodology for optimizing people-based service systems on a large distributed scale that exhibit high variety and variability. The methodology is exemplified through its application within the printing services industry where it has been successfully deployed by Xerox Corporation across small, mid-sized and large print shops generating over $250 million in profits across the customer value chain. Each step of the methodology consisting of innovative concepts co-development and testing in partnership with customers, development of software and hardware tools to implement the innovative concepts, establishment of work-process and practices for customer-engagement and service implementation, creation of training and infrastructure for large scale deployment, integration of the innovative offering within the framework of existing corporate offerings and lastly the monitoring and deployment of the financial and operational metrics for estimating the return-on-investment and the continual renewal of the offering are described in detail.

Keywords Service science, service systems, process optimization, people-based services, simulation, analytics

1 Introduction

Many industries are transitioning from being manufacturing-focused to becoming more service-oriented. The nature of service operations can be "equipment-based" or "people-based" (Thomas 1978). People-based service businesses rely on unskilled labor, skilled labor or professionals for their service production. Equipment-based businesses are further classified as being automated, monitored by relatively unskilled operators, or operated by skilled operators. The focus of this paper is on people-based service.

H. Demirkan et al. (eds.), *Service Systems Implementation*, Service Science:
Research and Innovations in the Service Economy, DOI 10.1007/978-1-4419-7904-9_2,
© Springer Science+Business Media, LLC 2011

It has been observed that while the service business can lead to growth in revenue, the gross margins are lower than the equipment business. At IBM the service business units accounted for roughly 55% of the total revenues in 2005, while hardware and software products accounted for the rest. In comparison, however, service business units contributed only about one-third of the company's total profit (Wladaswky-Berger 2006). Services are more labor-intensive, less amenable to economies of scale, exhibit higher quality variations and are generally less productive and profitable compared to the hardware/software business. Improvement of the productivity of the service business is therefore a key imperative for these industries to make the transition successful.

The general idea of improving the productivity of service business is not new. Leffingwell (1917) was one of the early researchers who applied Taylor's Principles of Scientific Management (1911) to the activities of service industries such as banks, insurance companies, accounting firms and mail-order firms. The goal of this effort was to set up routines that once learned and remembered could govern every aspect of office life. Healthcare was another sector where ideas of industrial engineering were applied early on. For example, Barnes' Motion and Time Study (1937) describes "Operating-room setup showing tables for instruments and supplies designed to facilitate the work of the surgeon, his assistant and the nurses". Walt Disney Corporation has utilized industrial engineering techniques and principles of service operations at their theme parks. Chase and Apte (2007) discuss McDonald Corporation as one of the best-known examples where successful application of scientific management to every aspect of restaurant operation was the key factor underlying McDonald's success. The main principles embodied in McDonald's operation include: (1) standardizing and reducing variety of products; (2) simplification, standardization and automation of processes so that workers with limited skills and training can reliably produce quality products and deliver high quality service offerings; (3) monitoring and control of process performance. Levitt (1972, 1976) describes how companies could apply the production-line approach to service business and further suggests that companies can substitute "technology for people and serendipity", and apply three types of technologies – hard, soft, and hybrid – to industrialize service offerings. Most attempts at industrializing a service on a large geographically distributed scale remains focused on achieving standardization and developing cookie-cutter approaches (e.g. McDonald's) or the notion of applying industrial engineering and operations research techniques on a large industrial scale to improve service operations (e.g. Disney).

Unlike the McDonald's model, there are service operations that are geographically distributed within an enterprise but exhibit significant output variety across each operations center. An example comes from document outsourcing business. A service provider such as Xerox Corporation can manage thousands of print production facilities worldwide on customer premises where the output of one print service center can be significantly different from another. The corresponding service processes that deliver this output are also different. The standardization that McDonald's has achieved is not possible because every customer's document production needs are unique and the service provider has to offer variety in order to be competitive. At the same time, the scale of operations at each service center is not large enough to justify a business case for local "Disneyfication".

The challenge is to develop a methodology that can improve the productivity and profitability of distributed people-based service operations on an ongoing basis while maintaining or improving the variety of the service offering to the customer. The improvement methodology should be sufficiently standardized and supported by automated (or semi-automated) software tools, platforms and processes so that it can be deployed profitably across a distributed enterprise. The work should provide insights for innovations across a broader array of service offerings (Jong and Vermeulen 2003) as well as new service-oriented technology and management frameworks of the future (Demirkan et al. 2008).

2 Optimizing Service Operations and Delivering Business Results for Locally Variable Operations

In this paper I describe a methodology for optimizing service operations on a large distributed scale. By applying this methodology to the printing industry, I demonstrate how high business value can be generated. The printing industry reveals that the methodology can address a high level of the local operational variety (i.e. the optimized solution is tailored to meet the needs of the specific customer), can be deployed profitably across hundreds or possibly thousands of service operations using a cost-effective and standardized process and can be adapted over time to changing customer requirements.

The focus of this improvement methodology is on improving the actual dynamic actions associated with providing the service offering i.e. the provisioning of the offering such that the customer has a better service experience in terms of faster cycle times, lower cost and improved quality. The marketing messages to customers have been reinforced with the improvements resulting from the application of the methodology. This has resulted in several existing service contracts getting renewed and new business being secured. It is worthwhile to note that in most cases, the service contracts are renewed or acquired not because new printing technology (i.e. goods) is introduced but because the design and execution of the existing service operation is significantly improved. This also supports the dominate logic view for marketing proposed by Vargo and Lusch (2004), one in which service provision rather than goods is fundamental to economic exchange.

This methodology is presented as a six-step process, each step of which is described in a section of the paper. Section 3 describes high-level characteristics of a specific service domain, the market size and a categorization of the service business. Section 4 motivates the data-driven simulation-based methodology and describes the key innovations embedded in the service optimization solution. Section 5 highlights the key human factors that have to be considered in order to ensure that the optimization solutions can be successfully deployed. Section 6 describes the tools, training and support infrastructure required for a large scale rollout. In particular this section will discuss a seamless, integrated and automated simulation-based toolkit and a scalable process for deployment of the service on a large distributed scale. Section 7 discusses the integration of process optimization solution within existing corporate processes to enable their institutionalization. Section 8 describes how business results have been delivered on a large scale. The paper concludes with some remarks on a service innovation process where researchers and customers work together to develop the innovation.

3   Step I: Identify a Service Operations Domain and Scope the Opportunity

Enterprises and businesses deliver multiple service offerings and it is not clear at the outset which service operations business has significant opportunity. Before too much effort is put into developing a solution, it is important to develop an understanding of the workflows associated with the service operations, scope out the market size and develop a segmentation of the service operations to understand the types of solutions that will be required to address the entire opportunity.

In the printing industry example, I led a team to optimize the productivity of print shops operated by Xerox via a four step procedure: Firstly we modeled individual print shops to convince ourselves that restructuring the work flow from the traditional departmental organization to cellular configurations offered the possibility of substantial productivity improvement. Secondly, working in partnership with the Xerox service delivery organization, we tested and refined these models in a variety of different print shops to demonstrate that the expected improvements were achievable in practice. We further used this opportunity to perfect techniques for marketing these transformational engagements to the various key audiences required to implement them. These efforts led us to market segmentation and to productivity results that enabled us to establish the business value to Xerox of a corporate-wide roll out of the methodology. Thirdly, in partnerships with the appropriate Xerox service and engineering organizations we developed a roll out plan that included the development of the training, tools, support-infrastructure and marketing collaterals necessary for Xerox service personnel to deliver the transformational engagements to Xerox customers. Fourthly, we marketed this plan to appropriate management in the involved organizations in order to obtain the commitment and funding and authorization to implement it. By conceiving and implementing these four steps over a period of 3–4 years, we identified and scoped a highly profitable service offering for Xerox, and secured authorization for its implementation.

Our point here is to emphasize that identifying the service opportunity in some detail, performing enough exploratory applications to establish its implementation and profit parameters, and preparing an actionable implementation plan for corporate management are indispensable initial steps in creating a new profitable service business based on work process optimization. In the remaining Section 3.1

I describe the work flow characterization, market size, and market segmentation used in the original implementation proposal to management.

3.1 Characterization of Workflow in Print-Service Center Environments

Print service center can be classified into three categories based on the activity that they perform – transaction printing, on-demand publishing, or a combination of both. A transaction-printing environment produces documents such as checks, invoices, etc. Each document set is different. Mail metering and delivery are part of the workflow. On-demand publishing environments focus on producing several copies of identical documents with more finishing options such as cutting, punching and binding. Examples of such products include books, sales brochures and manuals. Other environments perform both types of document production simultaneously with varying emphasis on each one.

The document production steps associated with print jobs are indicated in Fig. 1. Typically print service centers have departments that support individual steps of this workflow. Each department supports many different types of internal workflows resulting from the use of different types of software tools, printing machines types (e.g. offset, digital) and a variety of finishing equipment (such as cutting, binding, laminating, shrink-wrapping).

Each of the six generic steps in the print production workflow is associated with a department:

> *Customer service and production planning department* works with the print service center customers to handle incoming requests, negotiate price and due dates, provide tracking and notification, and work with production department to plan and schedule delivery.
> *Graphics design department* designs the content of the document.
> *Pre-press department* performs tasks such as inspection of incoming print jobs, editing jobs for color quality and accuracy, creating proofs and working with the customer service and printing department to coordinate production.
> *Printing department* prints the document. For offset printing, these activities include performing setups on the offset (lithographic) presses, loading

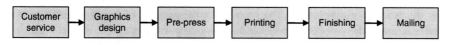

Fig. 1. A print production workflow showing the various production operations

paper and ink, performing runtime color corrections, offloading printed material and transporting it to the finishing department. For digital printing, the input to printers is an electronic print stream and the output consists of printed documents. Digital printing is used for short-run-length jobs and when the variable content is high. Digital printing technology is differentiated by low setup, simpler interfaces and smaller equipment size. The job input is a digital data stream ("digital masters") rather than hard-copy masters ("mechanicals"). The generation of these data streams creates major changes in the work content of the departments that precede the printing step in the overall workflow.

Finishing department takes as input printed material and performs a variety of finishing operations such as folding, cutting, saddle-stitching, binding and packaging.

Mailing department packs and labels the finished goods and ships them to customers.

Offset printing is the dominant printing technology used today (US Census Bureau 2008). More than 98% of print production revenue is associated with offset and offset-like technology. Nevertheless, customer demand for more personalized documents, quicker turnaround time, lower overhead and set-up costs, and geographically distributed printing has led to the migration of offset workflows to on-demand digital printing workflows for monochrome printing. As color digital systems that produce print quality equivalent to or better than offset print quality at competitive costs are developed, the same migration is expected to occur for color documents. For the foreseeable future both of these workflows are expected to co-exist within the printing industry.

3.2   Market Size

The printing industry is large and fragmented. The North American Industrial Classification System (NAICS) code for "printing and related support activities" is 323. In 2005, the total value of print shipments corresponding to code 323 was $97.095 billion with an annual payroll of $24.893 billion (U.S. Census Bureau 2008). The industry employed 642,300 employees with the payroll per employee of $38,753. An estimate of $100,000 in annual sales per employee is remarkably accurate in determining a commercial printer's annual sales (The Industry Measure 2007). Changes over time in the numbers of small (1–9 employees), medium (10–49 employees), and large (50+ employees) establishments provide a measure of industry dynamics. Figure 2 shows the number of print service center grouped by the number of employees. The increase in the number of larger establishments and decline in the number of small and medium service center reveals that business is moving from small and medium sized service center to large service center.

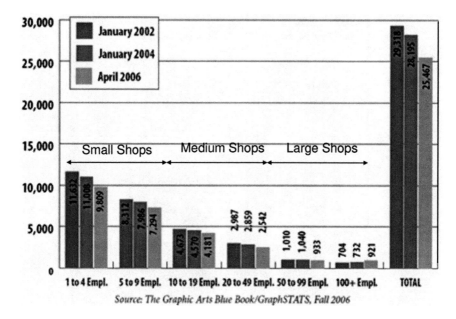

Source: *The Graphic Arts Blue Book/GraphSTATS, Fall 2006*

Fig. 2. Commercial, quick printers by employee size, 2002 vs 2004 vs 2006
(The Industry Measure 2007)

3.3 Print Production Service Categorization

There have been various taxonomies proposed for classifying service systems. Hayes and Wheelwright (1979) proposed taxonomy based on two dimensions, product or market variety (ranging from high to low) and type of production system (ranging from job shop through batch production, flow line to continuous process). Chase (1978) proposed a classification based on the extent of customer contact in service creation. Shostak (1987) proposes a taxonomy that uses two dimensions: degree of complexity of the service delivery structure and degree of divergence allowed at each process step. Wemmerlov (1990) proposes a similar taxonomy using two dimensions namely, degree of divergence and degree of customer contact. Schmenner (1986) also proposes a taxonomy using two dimensions: degree of labor intensity and degree of customization or interaction. Buzacott (2000) developed a categorization of service system structures based on an analysis of their relative performance and how this performance is affected by the nature of the tasks that have to be performed.

Because of the great diversities in print service centers, a categorization scheme has been developed that allows the development of optimization tools and techniques for various segments of the print service center market. Based on the experience from early engagements, the print service center market segmentation matrix

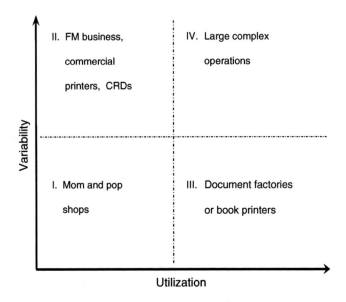

Fig. 3. A segmentation of print service centers within the printing industry (FM designates facilities management. CRD designates corporate reprographics department)

shown in Fig. 3 was developed. Print service centers are characterized based on the job variability (characterized by job mix, job size distribution and job inter-arrival time distribution) and resource (equipment and manpower) utilization levels.

Segment I encompasses service centers that operate individually to produce a few types of products on as-needed basis (e.g., store-front print service centers for convenience document production). Segment II encompasses service centers that are moderately sized (e.g., corporate reprographics departments), produce several different types of job types (typically less than 40), and are challenged with delivering high quality of service such as turnaround time and print quality at competitive costs. Segment III encompasses service centers that typically specialize in a few different types of workflows to create products that are manufactured in high-volumes (e.g., large book manufacturers). Typically these service centers are found to operate at higher levels of resource utilization than print service centers found in segments I and II. Segment IV contains service centers that manufacture a wide array of documents often within a specific industry segment such as financial or healthcare, are large in size (e.g., over $50 million of annual revenue), and exhibit leveraged economies of scale in production processes to achieve better utilization of resources than the service centers in segments I and II. This classification enabled the development of customized solutions that address print shops in each of these segments.

4 Step II: Characterize, Model and Optimize the Service Environment

This section discusses the specific characteristics of a service environment that exhibits high variety and multiple sources of variability and motivates the need for a simulation-based methodology. It further motivates the structure of the solution and the operating policies.

4.1 Characterization of the Service Environment

Print service centers experience many sources of variability. Segment II and IV especially exhibit high levels of task size and routing complexity that makes them hard to optimize (Fig. 3). These service centers are primarily make-to-order service systems that cater to specific requests of each incoming customer. The incoming service requests have random arrival and due-date requirements that vary from job to job and often exhibits variability within the same job-type. The size of the jobs is often characterized by highly non-normal distributions as shown in Fig. 4 and sometimes fat-tail distributions (Rai 2008).

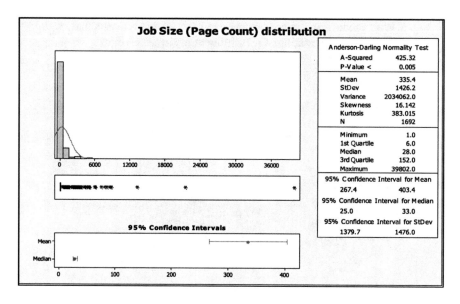

Fig. 4. A histogram of the job size distribution in print production service center can exhibit highly non-normal and long-tail characteristics

Job variety is also high as shown in Fig. 5 and many different product types (i.e. multiple routings) may simultaneously be in the service center at any given time.

Depending on the day of the week or month of the year, the demand is different leading to high demand variability as shown in Fig. 6.

The simultaneous existence of these multiple sources of variability makes it difficult to model, predict and optimize the performance and cost structure of these

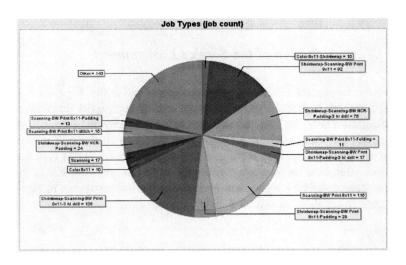

Fig. 5. Print production service centers can have several requests that require multiple routings for fulfillment at any given time

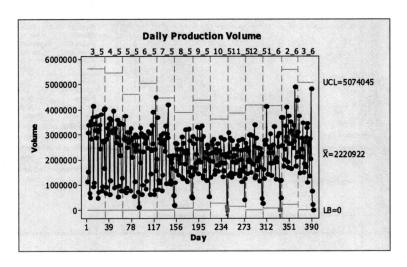

Fig. 6. Print service centers can exhibit very high fluctuation in the volume of incoming print requests

service centers. Discrete-event simulation models can be constructed but they require time and expensive resources and require data collection and validation. Since the conditions of the service center change with time (non-stationary processes), the models need to be updated with time adding additional complexity and cost. Compared with a standardized McDonald's type model, the modeling complexity can be quite high.

An enterprise can take the McDonalds approach and limit the type of document service offerings it provides and create a cookie-cutter operation. While this approach may be applicable to some service centers, the document service variety is determined by the requirements of the document production needs of the enterprise which varies widely across industries and even within industries. The capability to effectively offer document production service offerings requested by the enterprise is one of the key requirements for gaining market-share within the outsourcing business. The ability to handle variety cost-effectively is a key differentiator. Suppliers and vendors that are seen as incapable of offering this variety get excluded from outsourcing consideration.

4.2   Data-Driven Modeling of Service Operations

There are three approaches to model and analyze service processes namely, analytical modeling, direct experiments and simulations.

4.2.1   Analytical Models

These are the best class of models if they can be developed to describe the process at hand. They are usually computationally fast and give good insight into the process. They can also be used to understand how the model variables affect the outcome(s) being studied and perform fast sensitivity and optimization analyses. Analytical models are built on abstractions of the real world process and often make assumptions to get analytical solutions. If the process being modeled is sufficiently complex (which often is the case for real-world service operations), the assumptions that are made to develop the analytical models often make them less useful as predictors of actual system behavior.

4.2.2   Direct Experiments

A second approach is to deploy data collection tools within the service process and then develop analytical tools to analyze and optimize the process. While this is a useful approach, it is limited by the ability to collect data from the processes in an unobtrusive manner without affecting system behavior. Data collection can also be expensive and is often viewed as a non-value added activity unless the data analytics can demonstrate additional value. However, if data can be collected inexpensively on an ongoing-basis, this approach can be effective in assessing and optimizing the performance of service operations. The use of this approach in automated service offerings (ones that require minimal or no people involvement) is well-known. Companies such as Amazon, Google, Yahoo, E-Bay and many others regularly collect service data and use analytics to improve their service offerings.

4.2.3 Simulations

Simulations are used when the process being modeled is complex and not easily amenable to analytical modeling or direct experimentation. It enables the study of the interactions within large systems to get insights into the critical factors that affect desired performance. It can be used to improve and optimize these systems through analysis of numerous what-if scenarios. It can also be used to train personnel without disrupting the actual operations. In many instances simulations are used to establish the validity of analytical models. Simulations are also used with direct experiments and data collection to make them significantly more powerful and useful (Banks et al. 2004).

Advancements in simulation methodologies and increase in available computational power has increased its usage in performing large systems and process analysis. Even though simulation appears to be the most general methodology to model and optimize complex service operations it has two drawbacks namely:

- Simulation models can take a long time to build especially as the process complexity increases.
- The skill level, time and cost required to build simulation models for complex and varying service processes is sufficiently high to inhibit wide-scale deployments of this methodology.

There are many classes of service offerings whose overall operating framework can be represented within a generalized framework but whose specific instantiations have sufficient variability that a single parameterized model is not sufficient to capture the overall complexity. For example, a corporate reprographics department providing print production service can all be described at a high level by a general workflow as shown in Fig. 1. Jobs arrive at the customer service department, are moved to the print area, then to the finishing area and finally to the delivery area. However, when one looks more deeply at the specific instances of these print service centers, one can experience a wide variety. For example, one service center may accept jobs electronically, another may received hard-copy paper documents; the printing area can use digital equipment and/or offset equipment; the finishing area can have automated and/or manual finishers with differing labor requirement. Labor may have different characteristics such as those characterized by skill variations or by their employment category (e.g. permanent or temporary with corresponding wage differences). When one looks at the permutations of these differences, many different process instantiations are possible. While each one can be modeled using any one of the discrete-event simulation packages available in the market, the cost and time associated with building these models can be prohibitive to enable their wide-scale and ongoing use to analyze and optimize these service operations.

Many industries deliver service offerings where people are an intrinsic part of the delivery process. Well known examples include grocery stores, departmental stores, print service outlets, retail banking outlets, restaurants, hospitals, government offices, repair shops and many others. It is not hard to convince ourselves that we live in a primarily service economy if we look at the numerous service industries that surround us and are an integral part of daily life. Owners of these service businesses have long tried to differentiate themselves based on content and quality of the output. However, very few but extremely large franchise owners have applied simulation and modeling tools to optimize the way they deliver these service offerings. Some large franchises (e.g. McDonald's) have tried to achieve process efficiencies by standardization of processes and creating an optimized instantiation of these standardized models. But that also limits their ability to offer wider variety to their customers. On the other hand, specialized restaurants may offer a wide variety of options but cannot typically match the price points of the franchise owners.

Within the print production service space, enterprise clients often demand wide variety in print production that is typical to the document needs of the enterprise. Thus to be a preferred on-site service provider, the print service center has to deliver the required document variety but has to do so at a cost that makes it profitable for them as well. The trade-off between output variety and profitability is a difficult one to manage and if not done effectively can lead to unhappy customers or unprofitable operations.

Since a simulation model is built using abstractions of real-world processes, a key issue to resolve is to determine how much effort is spent in capturing the process details within the model and the accuracy of the prediction that is required. Focusing too much on non-essential details can add unnecessary complexity to the simulation without improving the value it provides while ignoring critical elements can adversely affect its utility and insights it gives. The purpose of the simulation models discussed in this paper is twofold; the first is to provide guidance to make changes to the structure of current state of service operations to improve several productivity metrics and second is to validate that the model-based predictions of the improvements are observed in the re-structured service operations. The emphasis is on capturing the essential elements of the service processes (related to both structural and control aspects) that provide good directional and quantitative guidance on what needs to be changed and how.

The simulations models discussed in this paper are directly driven by data collected from the service operations. The current state metrics are assessed and then changes are made to the structure and control policies within the simulation model to evaluate how productivity metrics can be improved. The improvements are further validated through data collected from the actual re-structured service operations and compared to original state metrics to validate that the model-based changes actually delivered real-life improvements. The combination of data-driven simulation-based modeling and empirical validation of tangible productivity improvements through real-life data collection reinforces the power of this methodology for optimizing service operations. The approach presented in this paper consists of two distinct components. The first is the development of an optimization toolkit based on the rapid modeling and simulation of a service operations center. These models can then be utilized through a series of what-if analysis scenarios (using automated and semi-automated approaches) by relatively low-skilled personnel to optimize the specific operation. The second is the development of a process to deploy this solution cost-effectively on a large distributed scale to multiple service centers within the industry.

This paper presents the solution within the context of the print production service domain. While the domain of application is specific to the printing industry, the solution proposed and learning from this endeavor can be generalized to a wide range of people-based service offerings.

4.3   Service Structure and Process Optimization

The cost and performance of print production service is a function of both the process structure (labor, equipment, facilities layout) and operating policies. To optimize the productivity of the systems it is always necessary to make tradeoffs in system design between the effectiveness in coping with internal and external variability and the efficiency, speed and cost of providing the service.

Most traditional print service centers are functionally organized. All equipment that performs one type of function is located in one area. For example, all printers are located in a print room. Finishing devices such as inserters are located in a separate room. These centers are more akin to job shops that have high levels of flexibility in terms of using equipment for different jobs. Incoming work flows from one department to another until the service request if fulfilled in its entirety.

In the next section, a structure for redesigning the traditional service centers into more efficient and cost-effective operations is proposed.

4.4   Structure Design of Print Service Centers Using Autonomous Cells and Hierarchical Scheduling

Business process innovation or reengineering received much attention in early 1990s. Two books written for business audience (Hammer and Champy 1993; Davenport 1993) attracted wide interest. Hammer and Champy proposed a set of "Commonalities in Reengineered Business Processes" shown in Table 1.

Table 1. Commonalities in reengineered business processes
(Based on Hammer and Champy 1993, Chapter 3)

1. Several tasks are combined into one
2. Workers make decisions
3. The steps in the process are performed in a natural order
4. Processes have multiple versions
5. Work is performed where it makes the most sense
6. Checks and controls are reduced
7. Reconciliation is minimized
8. A case manager provides a single point of contact
9. Hybrid centralized/decentralized operations are present

Buzacott (1996) has evaluated the structure of reengineered (and primarily transaction-processing) systems using formal system models from queuing theory to develop insights about the conditions under which such radical changes of system structure are likely to be appropriate. The basis of comparison are performance measures that can only be evaluated using stochastic models, such as the level of work-in-process or the time a transaction spends in the system (where Little's Law $L = \lambda W$ means that it is only necessary to explicitly consider the level of work-in-process). Two systems are compared namely,

> *Series systems*: Here the total work content is subdivided among m facilities arranged in series with each facility dedicated to a single task.
>
> *Parallel systems*: The parallel system has n identical facilities at any of which all required tasks can be performed on a job one after the other without interruption and with little changeover or setups between task.

Using queuing models developed by Harrrison and Nguyen (1990) and Buzacott and Shantikumar (1993), he concludes that moving from a series (flow-line) type structure with division of labor to parallel systems, depends critically on the processing time variability. If the tasks are such that they are the same for all customers and have relatively low complexity, the series service structure can be quite effective. However, high task processing time variability (resulting from task size or task complexity variation) makes it attractive to move to parallel systems. In addition, different types of allocation strategies such as random allocation, cyclic allocation and single queue are explored.

To address the complexity of operations associated with the print production processes, the service center resources are organized in autonomous cells (Rai et al. 2000). As a result, the most common jobs can be finished autonomously inside (at least) one of these cells. Figure 7 shows how traditional print service centers are organized based on a departmental structure operated by specialized workers and

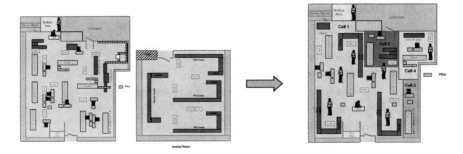

Fig. 7. Figure showing how a departmental configuration of a print service center is transformed into a structure utilizing autonomous cells

compares it to the redesigned operational framework based on autonomous cells where diverse pieces of equipment are collocated and operated by cross-trained workers. This organization into autonomous cells is a key concept of the proposed solution to optimize these print centers, offering the advantages of lowering product transportation times, reducing complexity associated with interaction of large number of job types, easing quality and production control while managing resources more effectively and avoiding congestion. Inspired by the goal of lean production (Womack and Jones 2003) to achieve a waste-free highly efficient document production service center, Xerox coined and trademarked the solution as LDP Lean Document Production®.

To orchestrate the flow and control of jobs through the parallel hierarchical cell structure, the Lean Document Production Controller (LDPC) uses a 2-level architecture (Rai and Viassolo 2001) shown in Fig. 8 for production management. The LDPC has:

- A service center controller module (*Service centerCM*) – high-level controller, in charge of global service center management
- Several cell controller modules (*CellCMs*) – low-level controllers, in charge of local management inside cells

Detailed descriptions of these controllers and the algorithms can be found in the Rai et al. (2009).

The solution requires structural design of efficient autonomous cells (right type, number and configuration of equipment, people and layout) as well as determination of efficient routing and scheduling policies that achieve significantly improved performance over the current state. This is accomplished via the use of discrete-event simulation methodology for evaluating the design and operational efficiency of the restructured process.

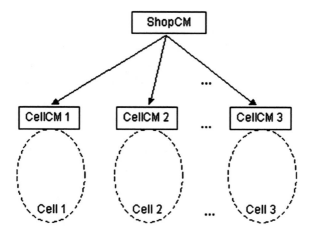

Fig. 8. Two-level architecture for the Lean Document Production Controller

5   Step III: Develop Effective Human Factors Practices

One of the most important and often-ignored aspects of people-based service operations are people who operate and manage them. While data analysis and simulations can provide useful insights into redesigning efficient service operations, ignoring the human factors can prove costly and in some instances nullify the effect of the optimization effort.

From this standpoint, it is necessary to consider both management whose primary focus is to make sure the financial viability and profitability of the operations and the operational staff who are involved in executing and delivering the service on a day-to-day basis. Management needs to be convinced that the simulation-based restructuring will improve profitability and grow revenue and the operational staff needs to believe that this effort will help them deliver better service and improve their future professional prospects.

Conducting experiments on the service operations by restructuring sample jobs based on simulation models and showing before-and-after metrics can be utilized to instill confidence that the simulation predictions can drive tangible benefits to the operations. This can be done prior to performing full-scale simulation and optimization of the entire operations. Testimonials should be gathered from successful engagements and then utilized to build confidence during the course of future engagements.

Since the re-structuring of the operations often requires changes to the facility (such as layout and electrical) that implies cost, management has to be convinced that it is worthwhile to make these investments. A return-on-investment analysis associated with the cost of performing these re-design and the benefits achieved is also critical to getting buy-in. Instituting reward policies that recognizes improvements in operator productivity as a result of re-structuring is also important for the success of the overall optimization effort. It also needs to be emphasized that the re-design effort is not treated as a one-time effort but that the operations needs to continually (or the very least, periodically) assess and improve the structure and control processes.

6   Step IV: Develop Tools, Training and Support Infrastructure for a Large Scale Rollout

This section discusses how the simulation tools were automated and a process developed for large scale rollout of the optimization service.

6.1   Automation of the Simulation Software Toolkit

The benefits of simulation automation are twofold – both technological and economical. Automation enables faster, less error-prone simulations and exploration of a larger design space leading to better solutions. It also allows deployment of this service by less skilled and less expensive personnel improving the economics of the deployment process.

Discrete-event simulation is an established methodology for studying the behavior of a system as it evolves over time. It is frequently used for process modeling in a wide variety of service offerings and industries when direct experimentation or analytical modeling is impractical. Many discrete event simulation software tools (Arena® Simulation Software 2010; ProModel 2010) are available in the market. These tools provide a (graphical) programming interface and basic primitive constructs for model building. The traditional approach to construct a discrete event simulation model is to employ a highly skilled modeler who would typically take significant amount of time (days, weeks or months depending on the size and complexity of the operations) to gather process information data, construct the model and iterate through the design.

However, scaling this methodology to a large scale using available discrete event simulation tools requires major cost investment, infrastructure development, training and periodic refresh to account for changing conditions. There is often sufficient variability in the models that depends on the modeler thereby creating challenges in standardization. This issue can be addressed if a solution can be developed that has a generalized modeling framework that captures essential characteristics of the class of service operations being modeled but has enough flexibility to capture the variation inherent in the specific instantiations within the particular industry. If this problem can be solved, then a modeling solution can be developed that can be scaled and replicated at multiple service center operations. Further, if the process of model building can be automated, it can reduce the time required to build the model and also reduce the errors and associated variations inherent in constructing these models.

To automate a process, it is necessary to understand it in sufficient detail and develop abstractions which are complete enough so that specific instances of the print service operations can be modeled using it. The automated modeling solution should also integrate various aspects of the model building process (e.g. data collection, definition of various elements, process design, planning, scheduling and simulation) to produce a seamless experience for the user. Further, the software toolkit should be embedded in a process improvement framework so that the user can systematically execute the tool effectively and in a replicable manner for optimizing the service centers.

A document production service enterprise may consist of thousands of small on-site operations. Each operation may have few pieces of equipment (e.g. less than 30 machines including computers and printing and finishing equipment) operated by less than 10 service center personnel. The annual revenue being generated from one of these sites may range from $250,000/year to $5 million/year. A service that assesses and optimizes these operations has to be cost-effective to be widely deployable so that it does not negatively impact the profit margins of the operations. Yet the optimization service should be capable of modeling variety and variability discussed earlier.

The approach proposed in this paper to make the simulation capability easier to use is to develop a structure for building the simulation model and automate the time-consuming steps. Instead of working with general purpose primitives available in the simulation model, the service environment is abstracted. Objects and processes that were unique to the document production service industry are modeled as constructs that are recognizable by the industry personnel. An easy-to-use software interface is created to allow the properties and capabilities of the service center to be defined within the simulation tool using these high-level constructs. A range of operating policies, patented process algorithms (e.g. split large jobs into small optimized batches) can be selected and applied to the model. Once the model is defined using a declarative interface using high-level constructs, it is checked for accuracy. Subsequent to that a simulation model is constructed automatically which is then used to optimize the center.

The high-level constructs pertinent to a document production service center consists of equipment, operators, shop schedule, autonomous cell, operating and sequencing policies and service requests. These objects have to be parameterized in a sufficiently generic manner so that specific unique instances can be realized. For example equipment can be described through the specification of its capabilities, setup characteristics, speed, failure and repair time distributions and operator requirements to operate it. While this is a general specification of printing equipment, different values and data sets associated with the individual parameters can readily capture the specific equipments in the shop. Table 2 shows the various objects that are used to characterize the print production service center.

Table 2. A list of objects and their attributes that are required
to define a print production service center operation

Objects	Components and attributes
Service center	Autonomous cells, equipment, operators, schedule, operating policies
Autonomous cell	Operators, equipment, schedules, cell operating policies
Operator	Skills, schedule
Equipment	Function capabilities, schedule
Function capability	Speed, setup requirements, variability, operator requirements, status (up or down)
Job	Job structure, quantities at each node, arrival, due, completion and intermediate events (e.g. start, stop at individual steps)

It is useful to remark here that the development of a complete set of these abstractions is a pre-cursor to automation of the modeling process. The specific objects described in Table 2 are specific to the print production service business and will require adaptation for extensions to other industries.

Once a complete set of abstractions to model the service operations has been developed, the next step is to develop the algorithms that will be used to optimize the center. Depending on the approach, these algorithms could be focused on optimizing the structure of the operation and/or the operational controls used to improve the efficiency. For optimizing the print production service centers, three classes of algorithms were developed, namely – methods to design autonomous cells, scheduling policies for routing incoming requests to the cells and operating policies for splitting large jobs and processing them within the cells. There may be many algorithms that can be effective for each of these classes. The automation goal is to allow the user to select them and automatically build simulation models with those algorithms imposed on the models (Jackson and Rai 2000). This automation vastly improves the speed of modeling and reduces the number of errors in the model.

Other aspects of simulation automation require streamlining the various steps of the optimizing process such as data collection, data analysis and reporting, simulation and modeling, scheduling and monitoring so that the user can easily exchange data from one phase of the analysis to another.

Analysis and optimization of such operations involves a large number of choices that manifest themselves as discrete categorical, continuous variables and constraints that are quite complex and requires many trade-offs to be made. The automation of the simulation process of modeling the autonomous cell architecture with hierarchical scheduling enables an exhaustive search of the design space and allows the user to iterate through multiple scenarios. The generalized framework also allows the tool to capture the variety and variability inherent in these service processes and suggest ways to optimize the operations without necessarily reducing the service capability. For more details on the algorithms and modules of the software tool, the reader is referred to Rai et al. (2009).

6.2   Process for Solution Deployment

The process of optimizing the print service center using the solution and tools developed above is broken down into multiple steps as shown in Fig. 9. These are pre-engagement process, assessment, recommendations, implementation and monitoring.

> *Pre-Engagement*: The service center management team is engaged and through the use of demonstrations and presentations, the solution methodology is explained to the service center personnel. The goal of this step is get concurrence from management to initiate the optimization engagement.
>
> *Assessment*: The assessment phase begins with a survey whereby information relating to operational issues is collected using standardized templates. An approach that has proven useful is to demonstrate some of the key aspects of the optimized solution (such as small batch cellular processing and scheduling) on some sample service requests and measure

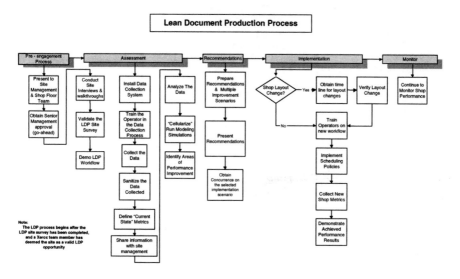

Fig. 9. A multi-step view of how the simulation-based optimization solution is deployed in print service centers

improvements. It is important to address the skepticism of employees at this stage of the engagement and the demonstration exercise is intended to dispel these concerns and prepare them for the step of data collection. Special purpose data collection systems (as discussed in Rai et al. 2009) are installed to collect information. The service center personnel are trained in the use of the data collection tools. The data that is acquired in this phase is periodically checked for quality and consistency and appropriate feedback is provided to the personnel as needed. The data is analyzed to generate current state metrics of the operations and establish a baseline. These include service request lateness, operator and equipment utilization, types of service requests, work-in-process, demand rate profiles and financial metrics (e.g. cost and margins).

Subsequent to developing an understanding of the current baseline metrics, the service center is redesigned into autonomous cells. The software toolkit is used to develop the structure of the cell (equipment, people and their respective skills, layout) by iterating through multiple configurations and scheduling policies. The automation embedded in the modeling and simulation toolkit enables a quick search and iteration over a large number of scenarios as shown in Fig. 10 to develop solutions that demonstrate significant quantitative productivity improvements over the current state. The iterations are performed over both discrete categorical as well as continuous

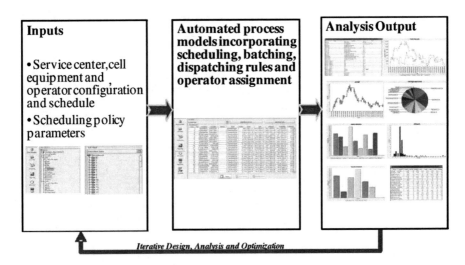

Fig. 10. The figure shows the three steps of optimizing the service center by iterating through defining the service center, automated process modeling and simulations and output analysis

variables such as multiple cell configurations, machine speeds, scheduling policies, skill mix and operations schedule (e.g. one-shift or two-shift operations), variations in request mix and quantity and the like. The innovation and automation embedded in the software enables a much richer and data-driven quantitative analysis and optimization of the process than more qualitative or focused process improvement approaches that are successful in operations with lower variety, variability and uncertainty.

Presentation of Recommendations: The results of the simulation and optimization studies are presented to service center management. A key element is a return-on-investment (ROI) analysis to insure that the approach has business justification. If management accepts the solution, a transition plan for implementing the solution to the new cellular configuration is developed.

Implementation: In this phase, the service center migrates to the new cellular layout. The operators are trained in the new workflows including new scheduling policies. New operational data is collected to fine-tune the operations and demonstrate improvement with respect to the baseline state.

Monitoring: The service center productivity metrics are tracked on an ongoing basis to ensure that the gains continue to be realized from the reengineered process.

7   Step V: Integrate with Related Corporate Processes

7.1   DMAIC and Simulation-Based Optimization

Several companies are utilizing the DMAIC framework (George 2002) for service process improvement. While the DMAIC process is a powerful framework for process improvement, it lacks the use of rigorous discrete-event simulation and optimization tools. Thus if the service operations have significant variety and complexity associated with job mix, non-normal distributions, random failures and repairs, the current set of Lean Six Sigma tools cannot adequately model and analyze the consequences of these interactions.

However, institutionalization of the DMAIC process within an organization leads to a large number of green belt and black belt personnel focused on process improvement initiatives. By training these personnel in the use of the modeling and simulation toolkit and process described earlier, their capabilities are significantly enhanced. These black belts can utilize these tools to optimize the service centers. Within Xerox Corporation, a significant number of black belt personnel were trained in this methodology. This led to a wide-scale deployment of the process optimization methodology (Fig. 11) and toolkit within the printing business.

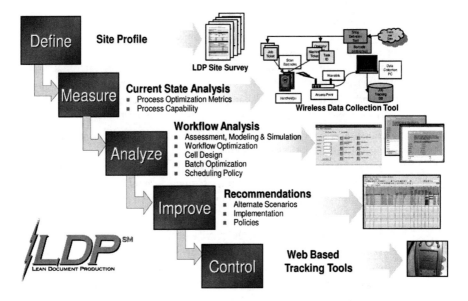

Fig. 11. A mapping of the various tools and analysis steps of the LDP Lean Document Production® solution to the DMAIC process

8   Step VI: Deliver Business Results on a Large Scale

Quantitative measures of improvements resulting from the utilization of the productivity optimization solution averaged over 17 sampled service centers, include labor savings of 20%, productivity (measured as revenue/cost) improvement by 40%, cycle time reduction of 80%, revenue increase of 17%, and annual profit increase of 20% of the revenue of the shop prior to the LDP implementation. Since 2003 it has been widely implemented in the field via the Xerox Corporate Lean Six Sigma (LSS) Black Belt program utilizing the DMAIC process outlined above. A sample of over 80 service centers yields average cycle time improvement of 50% and on-time-performance improvement of 11%. Over 80 consultants have undergone training in the use of these tools and over 100 print production service centers have been optimized using this methodology.

The cumulative value delivered by these engagements is over $250 million across the Xerox customer value chain. In addition, the higher quality and faster delivery enabled by the LDP solution provide strategic competitive advantages to print service centers. Xerox also has filed 64 patents applications related to this solution and 15 have been granted so far.

The LDP innovation was a runner-up at the 2008 Franz Edelman competition (Edelman 2008) sponsored by INFORMS.

9   Remarks on the Service Innovation Process

The service innovation discussed in this paper followed a process that is different from the traditional product innovation. The value chain for delivering a new offering typically involves the conception of the offering by a product team, which then acquires new technology from research and development, develops and tests the offering, and delivers it to the sales and service forces via a structured, phase-gate product development process. In contrast, this invention as described in this paper was developed at customer sites by a team of researchers working in partnership with the sales and service personnel who serviced the sites. This team, in collaboration with an engineering team, created the tools and training that were used to roll out the offerings to sales and service. It drove the planning and implementation of the rollout process, establishing new linkages between the engineering and service organizations. The team established the entire value chain for delivery of the offering in real time, concurrently with the creation of the offering itself, the underlying technology, the toolkit, and the infrastructure needed to deliver the offering to the field.

As emphasized above, our method of service innovation described in this paper can be described as a six-phase process.

I.   The innovative concept is co-developed and tested in partnership with customers. At this stage, algorithms and intellectual property are developed and proof-of-concept prototypes are conducted. The scope of the market is established and a market segmentation is constructed.

II.   Once the domain and scope of the concept are established the (hardware and software) tools used to implement the innovation concept are developed.

III.   Subsequently, the work processes and practices in which the tools are utilized are established. This involves proposing, testing and refining the work process used to engage the customer to implement the service.

IV.   Having developed the service and its implementation plan, the next step is to roll out the service to customers more broadly than the initial test prototypes. This involves creating the personnel, training, and infrastructure needed to deliver the service to customers.

V.   Typically, the new service offering does not stand alone but must be integrated with other corporate offerings, especially in a large firm like Xerox. This in turn involves the development of more training and infrastructure materials and possible minor adaptation of the original deployment processes.

VI.   Finally, the pay off from the large scale implementation must be monitored and financial metrics for its return on investment implemented and tracked. Continually improving the offering is also essential in this step both to improve continually the productivity of the delivery process and to renew the offering so that it is addresses emerging customer needs.

This approach for service innovation has similarities to that proposed by Selden and MacMillan (2006) where they argue a disciplined process of customer R&D at the front lines will turn wishes into an enduring competitive edge and growing market cap. When a service offering gets commoditized, this approach to innovation helps companies generate increasingly tempting value proposition avoiding the trap of having to compete on price. This process also enables one to avoid the pitfalls of innovation (Selden and MacMillan 2006).

10   Conclusions

In this paper, a discrete-event simulation based solution utilizing autonomous cells and hierarchical scheduling is proposed for optimizing a service offering that exhibit significant variability and complexity. Trade-offs exists in the optimization of these processes that can effectively be made by creating simulation models and using them to analyze the interactions. The solution proposed in this paper demonstrates that the abstraction, generalization and automation of the simulation technology to model many service center operations using a common framework and software toolkit is an enabler to wide-scale deployment of this methodology by a wide range of analysts and consultants. The process for deploying the solution was also discussed in the context of the DMAIC process used in industries. The impact of utilizing this approach by Xerox Corporation was briefly summarized.

While this methodology has been demonstrated within the context of the print production service business it motivates thinking relative to the applicability of this methodology for other people-based service businesses that exhibit high variability and variety across multiple instances. A realization of this approach across a broad set of services execution and delivery instances has the potential of significantly improving the productivity of several people-based service businesses while keeping profit margins high without compromising on the variety of service offerings. The methodology presented in this paper provides a structured and replicable approach towards service innovation focused on improving people-based services. It supports the emerging view that services systems innovation can be studied and developed as a science (Spohrer et al. 2007). This should further motivate both researchers and practitioners alike to broadly think on how new innovations leveraging process improvement methodologies, simulation and optimization techniques and emerging computational and IT infrastructures can deliver the next generation of highly efficient, responsive and adaptive people-based service systems.

References

Arena® Simulation Software (2010). Rockwell Automation. http://www.arenasimulation.com

Banks, J., Carson, J., Nelson, B.L., Nicol, D. (2004). *Discrete Event System Simulation* (5th Edition). Prentice-Hall International Series in Industrial and Systems, New Jersey.

Barnes, R.M. (1937). *Motion and Time Study*. Wiley, New York.

Buzacott, J.A. (1996). *Commonalities in reengineered business processes: Models and issues.* Management Science 42(5).

Buzacott, J.A. (2000). *Service system structure.* International Journal of Production Economics 68.

Buzacott, J.A., Shantikumar, J.G. (1993). *Stochastic Models of Manufacturing Systems.* Prentice-Hall, Englewood Cliffs.

Chase, R.B. (1978). *Where does the customer fit in a service operation?* Harvard Business Review 56(6), 137–142.

Chase, R.B., Apte, U.M. (2007). *A history of research in service operations: What's the big idea?* Journal of Operations Management 25.

Davenport, T.H. (1993). *Process Innovation; Reengineering Work Through Information Technology.* Harvard Business School Press, Boston.

De Jong, J.P.J., Vermeulen, P.A.M. (2003). *Organizing successful new service development: A literature review.* Management Decision 41(9); ABI/INFORM Global.

Demirkan H., Kauffman, R.J., Vayghan, J.A., Fill, H., Karagiannis, D. (2008). *Service-oriented technology and management: Perspectives on research and practice for the coming decade.* Electronic Commerce Research and Applications 7.

Franz Edelman. Award for Achievement in Operations Research and Management Sciences (2008). http://www.informs.org/index.php?c=401&kat=Franz+Edelman+Award.

George, M. (2002). *Lean Six Sigma: Combining Six Sigma Quality with Lean Production Speed.* McGraw-Hill, New York.

Hammer, M., Champy J. (1993). *Reengineering the Corporation: A Manifesto for Business Revolution.* Harper Business, New York.

Harrrison, J.M., Nguyen, V. (1990). *The QNET method for two-moment analysis of open queuing networks.* QUESTA, 6.

Hayes, R.H., Wheelwright, S.C. (1979). *Link manufacturing processes and product life cycles.* Harvard Business Review 57 (1), 133–140.

Jackson, W.B., Rai, S. (2000). *System and method for converting print jobs stored in printshop job description language files into printshop workflow.* US patent 7,064,848, filed December 12, 2000, issued June 20, 2006.

Leffingwell, W.H. (1917). *Scientific Office Management.* A.W. Shaw Publishing, Chicago.

Levitt, T. (1972). *Production line approach to services.* Harvard Business Review 50(5), 41–52.

Levitt, T. (1976). *Industrialization of services.* Harvard Business Review 54(5), 63–74.

ProModel (2010). http://www.promodel.com/

Rai, S. (2008). Fat-tail inputs in manufacturing systems. J. Fowler, S. Mason, eds. *Proceedings 2008 Industrial Engineering.* Research Conference, Vancouver, Institute of Industrial Engineers, Norcross, GA.

Rai, S., Viassolo, D.E. (2001). *Production server architecture and methods for automated control of production document management.* US patent 7,051,328, filed January 26, 2001, issued May 23, 2006.

Rai, S., Godambe, A.V., Duke, C.B., Williams, G.H. (2000). *Print shop resource optimization via the use of autonomous cells.* US patent 7,079,266, filed November 3, 2000, issued July 18, 2006.

Rai, S., Duke, C.B., Lowe, V., Quan-Trotter, C., Scheermesser T. (2009). *LDP Lean Document Production – O.R.-enhanced productivity improvements for the printing industry.* Interfaces 39.

Schmenner, R.W. (1986). *How can services businesses survive and prosper?* Sloan Management Review 27(3).

Selden, L., MacMillan, I.C. (2006). *Manage customer-centric innovation systematically.* Harvard Business Review 84(4), 108–116.

Shostak, G.L. (1987). *Service positioning through structural change.* Journal of Marketing 51(1).

Spohrer, J., Maglio, P.P., Bailey, J., Gruhl, D. (2007). *Steps toward a science of service systems.* IEEE Computer Society 40.

Taylor, F.W. (1911). *Principles of Scientific Management.* Dover, Minneola, Paperback Reprint (1998).

The Industry Measure (2007). *Printing Market Demographic Profiles. The Industry Measure Updated Snapshots of the Print and Prepress Markets.* January 2007. Reed Business Information.

Thomas, D.R.E. (1978). *Strategy is different in service businesses.* Harvard Business Review 56(4), 158–165.

US Census Bureau (2008). http://www.census.gov/

Vargo, S.L., Lusch, R.F. (2004). *Evolving to a new dominant logic for marketing.* Journal of Marketing 68(1).

Wemmerlov, U. (1990). *A taxonomy for service processes and its implications for system design.* International Journal of Services Industry Management 1(3).

Wladaswky-Berger, I. (2006). *Services, Markets, People, Complex Systems and Related Subjects,* downloaded on November 29, 2009 from http://irvingwb.typepad.com/blog/2006/07/services_market.html

Womack, J.P., Jones, D.T. (2003). *Lean Thinking: Banish Waste and Create Wealth in Your Corporation.* Simon & Schuster, London.

Intelligent Document Gateway: A Service System Case Study and Analysis

Vikas Krishna and Ana Lelescu

IBM Almaden Research Center, 1063 Minoru Drive, San Jose, CA 95120, USA

John Bailey

Abstract In today's fast paced world, it is necessary to process business documents expediently, accurately, and diligently. In other words, processing has to be fast, errors must be prevented (or caught and corrected quickly), and documents cannot be lost or misplaced. The failure to meet these criteria, depending on the type and purpose of the documents, can have serious business, legal, or safety consequences. In this paper, we evaluated a B2B order placement service system that allows clients to place orders for products and services over a network. We describe the order placement service before and after deploying the Intelligent Document Gateway (IDG), a document-centric business process automation technology from IBM Research. Using service science perspective and service systems frameworks, we provide an analysis of how IDG improved the value proposition for both the service providers and service clients.

Keywords Service systems, intelligent document gateway, service science, customer service representative, B2B gateways

1 Introduction

To succeed in a global economy, enterprises need to exploit their own competencies and to develop strong relationships with suppliers, customers and external business service providers to co-create value they could not produce on their own. Recent economic reports and studies (ILO 2007; NAE 2003) indicate that the global economy is actually a "large service system in need of innovation to grow" (Maglio et al. 2006). A service system comprises service providers and clients working together in complex networks or chains to co-create value for all stakeholders, with value creation being realized by the transformation of something owned or controlled by the client (Spohrer et al. 2007). Additionally, complex service system compositions include people (e.g., individuals, teams, organizations), technology (e.g., information processing, communication, self-service), and

H. Demirkan et al. (eds.), *Service Systems Implementation*, Service Science:
Research and Innovations in the Service Economy, DOI 10.1007/978-1-4419-7904-9_3,
© Springer Science+Business Media, LLC 2011

business management processes all interconnected by value and information networks, resulting in observable dimensions or characteristics.

Richard Norman refers to a "new" global economy in which an "elevated level of value creation" is made possible by new technological breakthroughs associated with the ability to effectively reconfigure resources inside, and especially outside, the corporate boundaries (Norman 2004). Value is then created as a result of better use and deployment of resources. The Intelligent Document Gateway (IDG) is a breakthrough information technology for document-centric business process automation based on key concepts from the emerging field of "document engineering" (Glushko and McGrath 2005) that offers corporations the opportunity to reconfigure its resources in ways that were not possible before.

In this paper we provide an analysis in terms of service systems of a recent successful IDG engagement with IBM's B2B order placement service hosted by e2Open gateway (Krishna et al. 2004). The B2B order placement service allows business clients, procurement analysts or approved employees to place orders over the internet using a web-based or installed application user interface. The order typically includes information such as product or service selections, part numbers, payment information, contract numbers, billing address, shipping address, and shipping preferences. Orders are submitted and routed to the appropriate fulfillment system. However, because orders often contain invalid part numbers, special handling requirements, or custom requests, a large percentage of the orders required manual processing by a Customer Service Representative (CSR). The CSRs are located globally in 35 countries, including Brazil, China, and India. They report into Customer Service Organizations (CSOs), where due to competitive job markets, management struggles with high turn-over rates.

In fall of 2004 researchers in Almaden Services Research met with leaders in IBM.COM worldwide sales and distribution to discuss issues they were facing with the existing B2B order placement service. IBM.COM described their problem in terms of lost orders, ones submitted by IBM clients that were not completed or acted upon by Customer Service Representatives (CSRs). IBM Research proposed an approach based on IDG for intelligent routing of orders that they believed could both completely eliminate lost orders as well as route them more efficiently. The engagement began with several meetings to discuss the proposed solution, gathering of requirements, refinements of the requirements, followed by a 6 month period of active research and development. Following the development phase, IBM Research and IBM.COM engaged on a 6 month deployment activity. Deployment involved Customer Support Organizations (CSOs) around the world, technical support teams, process owners, and content management experts in addition to the researchers.

In the remainder of this paper, we describe the original order placement service before IDG, followed by a high-level description of the IDG framework architecture, and then a description of the new B2B service system after IDG. We then provide an analysis of the order placement service in terms of a service system, followed by a summarization of the case in the conclusions.

2   B2B Order Placement Service Before IDG

In the original order placement system, business rules for routing orders to the appropriate CSR were implemented using Notes agents. The agents routed the orders by sending them to the CSRs as an email. Business process owners updated the routing rules daily using a basic text entry interface. A Lotus system administrator would shut down the order placement system, load the new rules, and then restart the system for them to take effect (see Fig. 1).

This approach had a number of drawbacks:

- *Incorrectly routed orders.* In many cases the orders were sent to the wrong CSRs, who didn't know what action to take. Thus, orders would be left open indefinitely.
- *Lost orders.* Since orders were stored in a Notes email folder, the organization and tracking was idiosyncratic to each individual CSR. When a CSR resigned, there was no easy way to ascertain the number and state of the orders they owned. Relatedly, because there was no central repository for orders, CSO managers were unable to track orders or generate reports. Finding and transferring incomplete orders to another CSR took a long time, or in some cases, they were never recovered. These accountability problems affected 8–10% of the manually processed orders.
- *Routing rules update.* The text based rule entry was time consuming and error prone. Because there were no rules checking capabilities, semantic and syntactic errors were sometimes not discovered until the Notes servers were restarted.

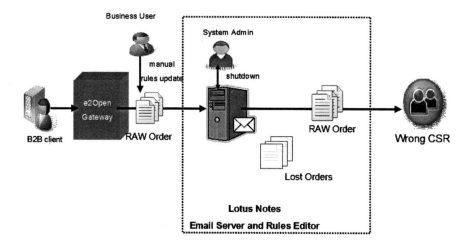

Fig. 1. B2B placement service before IDG

- *System availability*. When the Notes servers were restarted to activate the updated routing rules, order placement service was interrupted. If there were errors in the updated rules, service may be degraded until the errors could be corrected.

3   B2B Order Placement Service After IDG

This section describes the generic IDG framework architecture and provides a graphic of the order placement service after deploying IDG. The core of the IDG framework (see Fig. 2) consists of a Document Gateway component that automatically parses the incoming purchase order, extracts metadata, classifies, and converts the orders depending upon each order type. The data either provided by a business user or automatically extracted by the gateway is sent to a Business Rules Engine component that determines the action to be taken for the order. An example of such action could be notifying via email the appropriate CSR for handling the order.

The following example illustrates a rule in the IBM.com order placement business scenario in which the raw purchase orders must be routed to the appropriate CSR in multiple countries:

If customer name contains the string "AA1" and the country code is in the set {UK, FR} then notify by email the following CRS as follows:

To: johndoe@uk.ibm.com
Cc: aa@fr.ibm.com
Bcc: customer_support@ibmc1.pe.e2open.net

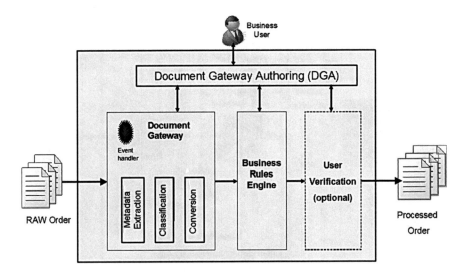

Fig. 2. IDG architecture

Rules are expressed in MS Excel spreadsheets enabling business users to author and update them using an easy and familiar paradigm. The IDG framework provides business users with a Document Gateway Authoring (DGA) tool. This is an intuitive user interface that allows business users to edit and create new business rules along with on-the-fly configuration of the runtime system. All rule updates are automatically and securely delivered to the document gateway component while still in service, ensuring zero system downtime. This is done with on-the-fly syntactic and semantic error checking. If any new rules or updated ones contain anomalies, IDG notifies the business users that authored the rule via email alerts with a suggestion for an appropriate fix. An optional User Verification application is also provided for human verification of the processing output of the system.

4   B2B Order Placement Service Reconfigured

The proposed infrastructure (see Fig. 3) replaced the Lotus Notes agents with the Intelligent Document Gateway (IDG) framework for automating and streamlining document-centric business processes (Krishna et al. 2004).

As illustrated in Fig. 3, the original (i.e. raw) purchase orders were picked up from the e2Open B2B gateway and processed in real-time by the IDG. The new processed order is then stored into the central Content Management repository after ensuring that each order is persisted until a subsequent sub-component of IDG takes ownership of the order. The Content Management system was deployed as part of the IBM WebSphere™ Application Server and provided the backend layer to a web based workflow application that allowed CSRs to get detailed views of the pending orders.

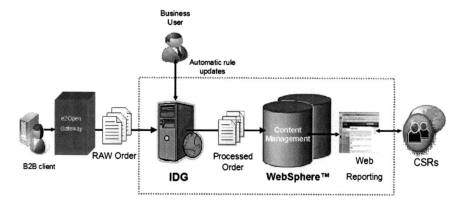

Fig. 3. B2B placement service after IDG

5   Analysis

A typical B2B order placement service comprises a service provider, service client, and a service target that is being transformed as a result of the service (see Fig. 4). These elements and relationships are one useful way to describe a service system (Gadrey and Gallouj 2002). However, there are several alternatives which are not described in this document, including service blueprint (Zeithaml et al. 2006), a framework for services marketing strategy (Lovelock and Wirtz 2004), and the Unified Services Theory model (Sampson 2001). Additionally, there are a number of dimensions or characteristics along which a service system can be evaluated. This analysis is not intended to provide an exhaustive review, rather to introduce some prominent dimensions and illustrate how they can be applied in an analysis.

Using an adaptation of Gadrey's model (Gadrey and Gallouj 2002), the service provider is IBM, the service clients are IBM B2B clients located in 26 countries, and the target being transformed is the clients order information. When the clients enter their order information into the ordering application and submit it, the order service acts upon that information, resulting in the transfer of goods or services from the provider to the client. Thus, information is transformed into a completed transaction.

When using this model, the service system boundaries can be drawn at different places. We approached this mapping by using tangible, easily observed and measured constructs. For example, we determined that what was being transformed

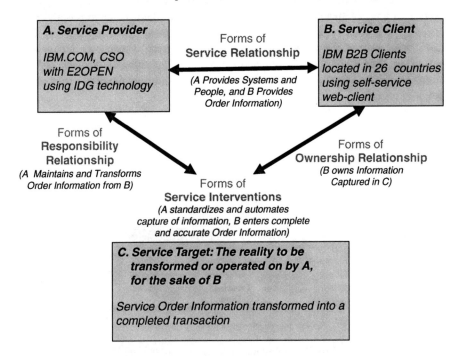

Fig. 4. Order placement service system

was the order information supplied by the B2B client. However, you might imagine that what is actually being transformed is something less obvious, such as ability to compete in a certain marketplace.

This example is much more difficult to study because it is further away from the actual transaction, just one determinate factor of many, and thus more difficult to assess or measure. The approach that we took in drawing the boundaries might be considered first order, since we were driven mostly by the desire to understand the tangible and immediate effects of deploying a new technology. Our choice should not be considered the best approach, nor should choosing less obvious boundaries be dismissed. Indeed, less obvious boundaries may lead to the most unexpected and valuable insights. However, given the more immediate, tangible impacts of IDG, the analysis boundaries that we selected have provided actionable insights.

Next, we evaluate several distinguishing attributes of service systems, considering both before and after deployment of the IDG technology.

5.1 Service Systems Should Satisfy All Stakeholders

In the simplest interpretation of a service system, there are two stakeholders – a single service provider and a service client. It is one person doing something of value for another person. In a complex service system there are many different stakeholders, each with different expectations, arising from their relative needs and goals. Complex service systems are often nested and recursive, with each instance of sub-service systems serving both internal and external stakeholders. Thus, a challenge in analyzing complex service systems is to evaluate them from the perspective of all service stakeholders. In this paper, we chose to simplify the assumptions by not overly emphasizing the service sub-system of IBM research providing a service to IBM. COM, a different IBM business unit, even though in reality there are significant implications to this arrangement. The stakeholder's interests are summarized in Table 1.

5.2 Service Systems Should Adapt

Service systems can be adaptive in the short term, adapting to fluctuations in demand or usage patterns. This kind of adaptability is similar to the ideas of resiliency and agility. Service systems should also be adaptive over the long term, becoming more efficient and effective, utilizing feedback from within and outside the system to guide adaptations (Spohrer et al. 2007). The ability to update the rules that check the order forms and determine routing for manually processed forms can be considered a kind of adaptability. In the original system, updating rules was slow, cumbersome, and potentially risky. After IDG was deployed, updating rules without a restart and built-in semantic and syntactic checking were major advances in the ease with which

Table 1. Stakeholders before and after IDG

System stakeholders	Challenges (before IDG)	Benefits (after IDG)
IBM.com	• 8–10% order loss • Service interruption	• Significant additional revenue /year • Improved reliability • Improved customer satisfaction • Increased customer loyalty, and potentially increased demand
IDG	• Understand business and technical requirements • Provide the technical solution and expertise	• Increased credibility in its value proposition to prospective clients • Great platform for further IDG based innovation and transformation of the ibm.com business
Business user (a.k.a. process owners)	• Manual rule updates	• Improved productivity as they benefit of easier rule updates • Reduced errors in rules due to syntax an semantic checking • Reduced update cycle time due to eliminating requirement to reboot
CSO mangers	• No way to easily track orders • Turn-over problems amplified by poor order accountability	• More productive in their jobs as they no longer have to track unfulfilled orders from CSRs emails • Increased productivity
CSRs	• No order management and accountability	• Lower turnover rate: likely to stay longer due to more user/ worker-friendly toolset
Customers	• Poor service • Misrepresentation	• Orders always processed in short time • No false indicators of order being processed • Eliminate time avnd frustration in tracking down orders

the system could adapt to changing business and demand characteristics. These changes allowed the business process owners to more easily make error free changes to rules, and activation of rule updates did not affect service by reboots.

5.3 Service Systems Should Account for People and Technology Related Costs from a Provider and Client Perspective

In this analysis, we've considered the cost of the IDG intervention not only in terms of the hardware and labor required to deploy and maintain IDG, but also in the terms of training service providers and clients.

On the service provider side, CSR's had to learn the new web-based client for managing their orders, business rules architects had to learn to how to change rules using the MS Excel spreadsheet, a content management specialist and support personnel had to be trained and staffed. CSO managers also had to be trained to use the new content management capabilities. On the client side, there were no changes imposed by IDG. The procurement analysts that place orders using the network-based ordering applications did not have to change anything or learn anything new.

In service systems, the value is co-produced by the service provider and service client during production of the service. The work to improve the IBM order placement service took place on the service provider side of the equation, with the IBM client not being required to learn anything new or change the way they were submitting their orders. Thus, the nature of the co-production relationship in terms of inputs into the system was not changed from the clients' perspective. Because there is a cost to the service client in changing, and any changes that become cumbersome or increase work might result in the client defecting to another provider, the ability to improve service by changing the provider side of the service system is extremely valuable. In this case, the client sees only that the order placement system is more responsive and reliable; likely improving their satisfaction and potentially increasing the number of orders they place (effectively growing demand).

5.4 Service Systems Should Become More Efficient by Standardizing Client Inputs

The unified services theory states that a service involves a provider and client working together to transform the clients inputs during performance of the service (Sampson 2001). Service efficiencies can be realized by standardizing client inputs. The network-based ordering application is a way of standardizing how B2B clients provide their order information to the service provider. The introduction of IDG did not change anything in what the client was required to do, rather it added an extra layer of standardization (orders are analyzed, formatted, saved and routed better) after the clients have completed their part of the co-production relationship.

5.5 Service Systems Should Employ Self-Service and Automation Technologies to Lower Cost and Improve Service

Self-service and automation, used appropriately, can decrease cost to both the service provider and client, while simultaneously improving service for the client. The use of ATM machines is one example of successfully combining self-service and automation to improve availability and speed of conducting simple banking transactions. In this case, the original service system was already a self-service system, which mitigated traditional constraints on order placement such as business hours or salesperson availability, but IDG added an extra layer of automation on the backend. The automation lowered costs by eliminating the need to restart the systems during routine updates to order routing rules, and it resulted in better routing and persistence of the orders. Also, orders were no longer lost, thus eliminating provider work in manually tracking, transferring, and reprocessing them.

5.6   Service Systems Should Scale to Greater Service Capacity at Declining Costs to the Service Provider

Service systems that require equal increases in labor to achieve equivalent growth in service capacity do not yield increasing profits. In this case, it is difficult to determine whether IDG will also contribute towards lowering costs while increasing capacity. Will it require less CSR's per order placed by service client? It is too early to tell, but it is logical to assume that it will have some positive effect. However, larger impacts on this metric might require a different kind of focus, such as interventions that reduce the large number of orders requiring manual processing. Building real-time auto-correction mechanisms for invalid orders is a future direction for IDG.

5.7   Service Systems Should Appear to Be Customized to the Client to the Degree That It Is Equivalent to Cost

A service client will reasonably expect to pay more for a customized service. In this case, IDG did not change the perception or reality of how customized the order service appeared to the client. However, since this is a globally deployed order placement system, it is reasonable to expect that there is some opportunity to customize the order forms or processes to better accommodate local practices or conventions.

5.8   Service Systems Should Provide Evidence to the Client That a Service Has or Is Being Performed

While the service itself is often evidence enough, service satisfaction usually benefits from multiple forms of evidence. The evidence informs and reinforces to the client that a service has been or is being performed. Evidence can also convey as sense of value. When orders were lost in the original placement service, the clients would eventually notice a lack of evidence that their order was being processed. By insuring that all orders are processed, IDG insures that clients receive evidence via CSR phone calls or email. Furthermore, in the original system, a confirmation email sent to the B2B client confirming that the order was received would be misleading in the event that their order was lost. This unfortunate combination would predictably result in service clients wasting time trying to track down orders that they submitted, causing frustration and potentially impacting their business. Eliminating lost orders corrects the problem of misleading evidence.

5.9   Service Systems Should Support Transparency to the Degree That It Enhances Value for the Service Client and Preserves Value for the Service Provider

Transparency is a way for service providers to share production information with the service client. It might also be considered a kind of evidence that the service is being performed. An example of transparency is the UPS or FedEx package tracking capabilities. When a client ships a package, they receive a shipping number, and then can track the package using a web-based service. This allows them to see the progress of the service as it happens. Transparency that divulges competitive trade secrets or submits the client to useless or damaging internal workings should obviously be avoided. Transparency is also bidirectional. Services often require transparency into the service client. Note that IDG did little to change transparency between the provider and client. However, it did significantly change an internal transparency factor between the CSO manager and the CSRs work on orders. This improved effectiveness of the CSO managers.

6   Conclusions

We have described an order placement service system, the problems, and interventions used to address the problems. We then analyzed the system in terms of a service system framework.

The results of this internal service engagement, Almaden Services Research providing technology and expertise to IBM.COM, has exceeded expectations. IBM clients in 26 countries now enjoy an order placement service that is more reliable and responsive, while IBM enjoys a substantial increase in order generated revenue.

In summary, the research and IBM.COM teams that developed and deployed the IDG solution achieved the above results by:

1. Virtually eliminating the 8–10% loss of manually processed orders
2. Eliminating the need to restart routing systems for routine business rule updates
3. Improving syntactic and semantic checking of order routing business rules
4. Providing superior order retention, tracking, and reporting capabilities

Table 2. Service systems attribute analysis summary

Service system distinguishing attribute	IDG
Service systems should satisfy all stakeholders	To some extent
Service systems should adapt	Yes
Service systems should account for people and technology related costs from a provider and client perspective	To a great extent
Service systems should become more efficient by standardizing client inputs	Yes
Service systems should employ self-service and automation technologies to lower cost and improve service	Yes
Service systems should scale to greater service capacity at declining costs to the service provider	Potentially
Service systems should appear to be customized to the client to the degree that it is equivalent to cost	To some extent
Service systems should provide evidence to the client that a service has or is being performed	Yes
Service systems should support transparency to the degree that it enhances value for the service client and preserves value for the service provider	To some extent

We also analyzed the IDG service system along the key nine distinguishing attributes a service system as listed in Table 2.

Additional benefits, less direct but arguably most important, include potentially improving client satisfaction, increasing demand, and lowering client defection rates. Additional interventions as described in the analysis, such as decreasing the percentage of orders requiring manual interventions and customizing the ordering experience, should result in even better overall service system performance.

The IBM.COM order placement document-centric service system was dramatically improved by IDG. However, this is just one example of where IDG has provided value, other document-based domains that could potentially benefit from IDG include immigration, healthcare, finance, and import/export, and global expense reimbursement.

Acknowledgements The authors thank Jim Spohrer and Paul Maglio for insightful discussions and background material on service systems. They also thank Savitha Srinivasan and Jeanette Blomberg for raising questions that further helped shape this study.

References

Gadrey, J. and Gallouj, F. (2002). *Productivity, Innovation and Knowledge in Services, New Economic and Socio-economic Approaches.* Edward Elgar, Cheltenham.

Glushko, R.J. and McGrath, T. (2005). *Document Engineering: Analyzing and Designing Documents for Business Informatics and Web Services*. MIT Press, Cambridge.

ILO (2007). *International Labor Office*, Global Employment Trends Brief, January, http://www.ilo.org/public/english/employment/strat/download/getb07en.pdf

Krishna V., Srinivasan, S. and Deshpande, P. (2004). *Towards Smarter Documents*, CIKM.

Lovelock, C., and Wirtz, J. (2004). *Services Marketing, People, Technology and Strategy*. Pearson Prentice Hall, New York.

Maglio, P., Srinivasan, S., Kreulen, J. and Spohrer, J. (2006). Service Systems, Service Scientists, SSME and Innovation, *Communications of ACM*, vol. 49, no. 7.

NAE (2003). *The Impact of Academic Research on Industrial Performance*. U.S. National Academy of Engineering Report.

Norman, R. (2004). *Reframing Business – When the Map Changes the Landscape*. Wiley, New York.

Sampson, S.E. (2001). *Understanding Service Businesses: Applying Principles of Unified Services Theory* (2nd ed.). Wiley, New York.

Spohrer, J., Maglio, P., Bailey, J. and Gruhl, D. (2007). Steps Towards a Science of Service Systems, *IEEE Computer*, vol. 40, no. 1, 71–77.

Zeithaml, V.A., Bitner, M. and Gremler, D.D. (2006). *Services Marketing, Integrating Customer Focus Across the Firm*. McGraw-Hill, Boston.

A Framework for the Design of Service Systems

Yao-Hua Tan

Department of Technology, Policy and Management

Delft University of Technology, Delft, The Netherlands

Wout Hofman

TNO Information and Communication Technology, Delft, The Netherlands

Jaap Gordijn

Department of Computer Sciences, Vrije University Amsterdam, Amsterdam,

The Netherlands

Joris Hulstijn

Thaurus and Delft University of Technology, The Hague and Delft, The Netherlands

Abstract We propose a framework for the design and implementation of service systems, especially to design controls for long-term sustainable value co-creation. The framework is based on the software support tool e^3-control. To illustrate the framework we use a large-scale case study, the Beer Living Lab, for simplification of customs procedures in international trade. The BeerLL shows how value co-creation can be achieved by reduction of administrative burden in international beer export due to electronic customs. Participants in the BeerLL are Heineken, IBM and Dutch Tax & Customs.

Keywords Service science, service systems, value co-creation, service innovation lifecycle, e^3-control, e^3-value

H. Demirkan et al. (eds.), *Service Systems Implementation*, Service Science:
Research and Innovations in the Service Economy, DOI 10.1007/978-1-4419-7904-9_4,
© Springer Science+Business Media, LLC 2011

1   Introduction

Over the past decades, services have become the most important part of economies (Heineke and Davis 2007). Basically, the service economy refers to the service sector. It leads to more sophisticated forms of cooperation, or what is called value co-creation (Spohrer and Kwam 2009). As Spohrer also points out, service systems are dynamic configurations of resources that interact via value-proposition-based interactions with governance mechanisms. Basic questions in this respect relate to *Service Science, Management, Engineering and Design* (SSMED). We focus, in particular, on the value co-creation in the setting of services that are offered by a service system; i.e. where a composed service is offered by a provider to an individual customer based on outsourcing parts of the composed service. An example of such a service offering is the mobile services that are offered to individual customers on their mobile phones, which is typically offered by a mobile operator, various content providers and a billing organization. Up till now most attention in service systems was focussed on analysing value propositions in a bi-lateral relation between customer and service provider, whereas we will argue that there is also a second important dimension to value propositions, namely in the collaboration between organizations to produce a joint value offering to a customer.

Our basic research question in this context is:

Which conceptual models and tools can be used for (re)design Business-to-Business and Business-to-Government services in service systems?

To answer this question, we present in this chapter a coherent framework for the design of service systems from a business perspective, which consists of two models for the conceptual part of the design process, and two tools that support the actual service system design, in particular in a network setting. We perform an extensive case study of service redesign in international trade to demonstrate that both the models and the tools of our design framework are useful and adequate for answering our research question.

This chapter is structured as follows. First we present both models, namely the *Service Innovation Aspects Model* and the *Service Innovation Life Cycle Model*. Subsequently, we present the two conceptual modelling support tools, e^3-value and e^3-control. The case study elaborates on the application of these models and tools to service redesign in the Beer Living Lab. The chapter ends with a discussion of research implications and conclusions.

2   Service Innovation Aspects Model

The Service Innovation Aspects Model addresses the conceptual aspects of the design process such as coordination and governance between the business analysis of services and identifying IT services to improve value exchange in a service system (Fig. 1). We distinguish the following aspects in this model:

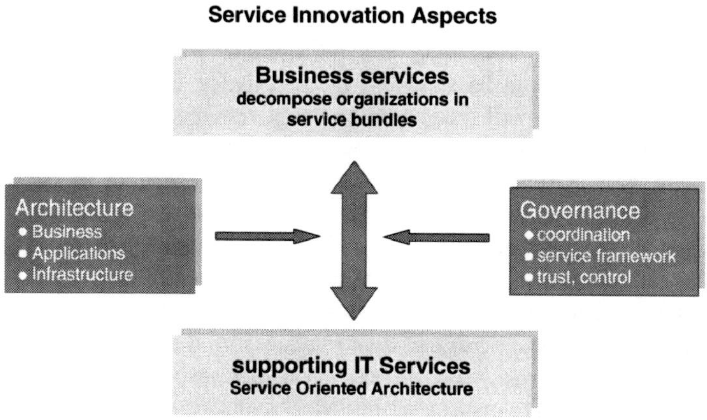

Service Innovation Aspects

Fig. 1. Service Innovation Aspects model

- *Services*: The actual publication of value propositions with their conditions defined by parameter values. Typically, these services can be composed dynamically to meet customer requirements.
- *Supporting IT services*: Design of IT services for value exchanges, technically realized by for instance Web services according to a Service Oriented Architecture (SOA).
- *Governance*: Coordination and alignment of business and IT services, performance and service level agreements at business and IT level, trust and control mechanisms for fair distribution of value co-creation.
- *Architecture*: A conceptual approach to IT service modelling to support value exchange.

Service is the key concept to support value propositions of actors in an organizational network, since this concept only specifies (part of) the behaviour of an actor that is externally visible to other actors. 'Service' as such should not only constitute value propositions, but also requires governance mechanisms for uncertainty reduction (Spohrer and Kwam 2009). The service concept abstracts from internal resources of a service provider to meet customer requirements. A service provider can autonomously allocate its internal resources meeting a customer requirement and outsourcing part of the required service. A service should also refer to policies and performance metrics. A *policy* refers to conditions and assumptions under which value can actually be exchanged. *Metrics* of a service refer to aspects like availability and performance and the basis for Service Level Agreements (Spohrer and Kwam 2009). To support a value proposition, interaction behaviour for actual value exchanges, interaction semantics, reachability (technical communication protocols, etc.), and non-functional properties need to be specified. We will call actual value exchanges according to a predefined interaction behaviour and semantics *business transaction*. Thus, we distinguish between a value proposition published as a service and its actual value exchange by a business transaction.

Non-functional properties of IT services supporting value propositions include aspects like availability, reliability and performance. These non functional IT service properties that can be specified by an existing framework influence the metrics of a service. We will focus here on the governance of service systems and architectural aspects of those systems, since much research has already been done on the other two aspects of our Service Innovation Aspects model. We will especially discuss the impact of these changes to government authorities.

Governance comprises not only issues like open standards and security, but also services for discovery of value propositions with their related IT services, for example, auditing actors in a service system for applying controls according to agreed governance mechanisms, etc. *Open standards* and their semantics need to be globally accepted to implement a service system at a global scale. Trade and transport are examples of global service systems that require open standards. Most probably, semantics differs for each actor in such a (global) service system and additional mediation functionality is required. Standards and their semantics have to be available to all actors, either for free or at reduced (administrative) costs. *Security* is a second aspect of governance. In a setting of a (global) network of organizations, a federated security mechanism must be offered since not all actors will use the same security provider. One must be able to validate the identity of actors in an open environment like the Internet, where each actor can choose its preferred identity provider. A mechanism where these identity providers can be trusted needs to assure that identity of actors can be validated. *Service discovery* of business and IT services is a third aspect of governance. Although standards have been developed for IT service discovery (e.g. Fensel et al. 2008, Quartel et al. 2007), discovering services is still complicated, because commercial issues are at stake. Careful consideration needs to be given on how to structure service discovery results. There are best practices that show how to offer the results, e.g. the airline booking systems, see (Petzinger 1995). *Auditing*, a fourth aspect of governance, could be implemented by periodic or behavioural auditing, e.g. behavioural auditing might be supported by monitoring and analysing the actual behaviour of a service system based on, for instance, process monitoring (Aalst et al. 2007). Behavioural auditing adds trust to service systems, since it will immediately detect flaws in the system. Auditing firms could be actors that play an important role in auditing service system. Finally, one of the most important aspects of governance is the *fair distribution of co-created value* between all actors in a service system. A fair win-win situation must be created, otherwise partners of the service system will drop out, and the service system will not be sustaible. We use e^3-control to model processes for sustainability of value co-creation with a fair win-win situation for all actors in a service system.

Architectural aspects of service systems are related to concepts such as 'business process', 'business service', 'resource allocation', and 'transaction protocols' as the basis for *IT services* (Lankhorst 2005). With these concepts, we are able to build a model that allows us to distinguish services from a business and IT perspective for value propositions and introduce the concept of business transaction for actual value exchanges. It allows us to align business and IT services. We will elaborate on these concepts in more detail and argue that proper definitions are a prerequisite for service systems. As we have stated before, *business services* are the publication of a value proposition by a service provider. Value propositions can be expressed in different ways that need to be recognized by both customers and a service provider, e.g. a joint goal like the transportation of cargo. Different approaches like Spohrer and Kwam (2009), and Fensel et al. (2008) use different terminology and define these terms loosely, or not at all. For instance, Spohrer and Kwam (2009) mentions business goals, whereas Fensel et al. (2008) introduce the concepts of 'goal' and 'capability', meaning that a goal denotes a customer requirement and a capability the offering by a service provider. These two concepts, goal and capability, can be applied to both business and IT services. Since a joint business goal is the basis for service discovery or mediation between a goal and a capability (Fensel et al. 2008), these concepts have to be defined unambiguously. Basically, a *value proposition* not only encompasses a business activity that can be performed by a service provider, but also prices, conditions and IT services with their non-functional requirements for actual value exchange. An example of a business activity is 'transport' that is supported by a business process offering a variety of business services like express transport (individual cargo items that have a maximum weight and are transported by air) or container transport. To be able to perform a particular business activity, resources may have to be allocated. A service provider has to allocate resources (Spohrer and Kwam 2009), e.g. a production line for beer production, to produce value for a customer. A customer should only be aware that a service provider is committed to a value exchange for a particular service. Each actor of a service system should implement a coordination mechanism over resources that are under its control.

Resource allocation to meet customer requirements is based on negotiation between that customer and a service provider and relates to a value proposition. A *negotiation mechanism* comprises various aspects of a value proposition, e.g. costs, duration, start and ending time, and places or stages. During negotiation, both actors try to reach an agreement resulting in a contract as a commitment for actual value exchange. Dietz (2006) defines negotiation as a coordination act with an intention and a proposition. Coordination acts are supported by a transaction protocol. A basic protocol consists of 'request', 'promise', 'state' and 'accept', needs to be implemented by IT services, and can be decomposed in different phases: information or service discovery phase, negotiation phase which can lead to a contract, delivery phase in which value is actually exchanged based on the result of the negotiation phase, and a cancellation phase required for cancelling a contract and its agreed value exchange. A negotiation may lead to a commitment for value exchange of a service provider based on an existing service, which implies that that provider is actually willing to allocate resources. After a customer has accepted that proposition, resources have to be allocated according to the proposition. Support of a transaction protocol by IT services allows us to transform value propositions directly into IT services. We still have to extend this modelling approach with rules for internal orchestration. McGovern et al. (2006), Hofman (1994) already introduced a set of rules based on the coordination of distributed resources.

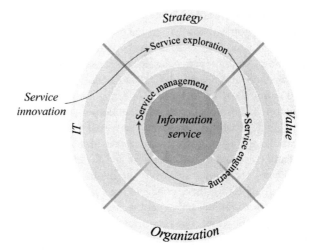

Fig. 2. Service Innovation Life Cycle

3 Service Innovation Life Cycle Model

Service innovation considers reorganizing (parts of) a service system with the objective to obtain business advantages with respect to value exchanges by introducing new services. In fact, service innovation implies a new value proposition (Edvardsson and Olsson 1996). Service innovation can be classified by introducing new services, improving the operation, or increasing growth of services (Curtis and Henderson 2006). Other business improvements like logistics improvement can also be expressed as value co-creation for a service system. Service innovation starts with one particular actor of a service system that wants to introduce a change for improving operations. Existing value exchanges are reconsidered to express business advantages in terms of cost reduction in the service system under consideration (service operation innovation). An innovation life cycle model is required to gradually introduce changes in the total system. The Service Innovation Life Cycle model presented here discusses the introduction of changes in existing service systems with respect to the introduction of new services. The model (Fig. 2) presents a number of phases that have to be taken into consideration for service innovation.

The model consists of three phases in which alternative solutions are evaluated before the actual implementation will take place. The phases are:

- Service Exploration: Possible scenarios are generated and considered to analyze changes from a business strategy viewpoint.
- Service Engineering: One or more options are explored in more detail. Their value is considered in the context of the value exchanges in which an organization operates. Cost/Benefit analyses are made on the basis of the value analysis and changes in processes are explored. Governance

and control mechanisms are developed to guarantee a fair distribution of benefits in the network, and hence a sustainable network.

- Service Management: IT Infrastructure and testing phase. One of the options is developed in more detail and tested in practical situations. Processes and information exchange are defined, tested, and managed (change management, operational management, etc.).

Before actually implementing service systems it must be understood – on a high level – what the system will do and how this will impact its individual actors. This is vital since mistakes made in the early phases of service system design can have large (financial) consequences later on (see further Gordijn and Akkermans 2003; Yu 1995). Another consideration is that in the initial phase one wants to abstract as much as possible from implementation details in order to facilitate an open-minded approach and out-of-the box thinking. This latter consideration holds, in particular, for business analysts (and even top-level management) who typically do not have a very technical background. So, the first step is to explore how an actor of a service system will interact with other actors in the same service system from various perspectives (see outer circle alignment model). In particular, the analysis of value exchanges between partners is essential to identify value proposition. Only after the exploration phase is completed, further design (and alignment) should be considered; these additional steps are however outside the scope of this paper.

To explore the interaction of a system/organization with its environment four different perspectives are taken into consideration. Considering various perspectives on a system to separate concerns is well-known in traditional requirements engineering (e.g. Nuseibeh et al. 1994). Although each perspective takes a different viewpoint, they all view the same phenomenon, which is in our case the interaction within a service system. We consider the following perspectives to be relevant:

- The business perspective that encompasses the business strategy perspective, which considers how other actors influence the strategic position of an actor, and also which collaborations in a network setting might be used to jointly offer a bundled service, and the value creation perspective, which considers how value is created by the service system in which the actors operates
- The computational perspective encompassing the process perspective, which considers the cross-organizational coordination processes to support the value creation, and the IT perspective, which considers information systems that interact with their surrounding to exchange information with a variety of technology, e.g. portal technology and web services

We must note that stakeholders decide which perspectives are actually explored. Stakeholders can find perspectives irrelevant, simply because they are at that point not (yet) interested in the specific concern explored by a perspective.

A consequence of having multiple perspectives on a service system and its interactions is that each perspective should be properly aligned with the others. However, alignment between the perspectives should not only be intra-organizational, which considers alignment decisions between perspectives within a single organization; alignment should also be created between organizations leading to truly co-created value for all partners. This results in two more alignment issues: (1) inter-organizational alignment within a perspective, which considers alignment decisions per single perspective but between multiple organizations (e.g. interoperability between cross-organizational IS), and (2) inter-organizational alignment between perspectives, which considers alignment decisions between perspectives and between multiple organizations (e.g. value co-creation based on alignment of business – and IT services).

A naive way to reason about alignment is to use a kind of top-down or "waterfall" approach as known from traditional software engineering methods. Each perspective would then be developed sequentially, and in a top-down way. This is, at least for the exploration phase, not a realistic approach. In the numerous case studies that we conducted (Derzsi and Gordijn 2006), innovative ideas came from the IT service perspective (e.g. new technologies), process perspective (e.g. process optimization) or value co-creation perspective (e.g. joint business opportunities). Also, the service system is continuous and fast moving in terms of enterprises, services, and technologies. So, we consider the alignment process a continuous and iterative "tuning" between the four perspectives within an organization and between organizations.

The business strategy and the IT perspective are considered most relevant, since the stakeholders require an IT service design in a service system to improve processes from a business perspective. Value exchange analysis in service systems is a well-known construct for both understanding the business strategy of an actor (see e.g. Porter 1980) and information systems (see e.g. Wieringa 2003). To this end we make both the "business strategy" and "IT" operational in terms of interactions of actors in a service system, resulting in interactions at strategic and IT level.

3.1   Software Support Tools: e³-Value and e³-Control

To develop service systems, the tools *e³-value* and *e³-control* can model different aspect of those systems. Whereas e³-value can be used to model and analyze value exchanges in service systems, e³-control is used to make the value co-creation in a collaborative environment sustainable by modelling processes in more detail. Process modelling in service systems presents safeguards to sustainable value co-creation for all actors involved. This section discusses both tools, and their applicability is illustrated in the next section by the Beer Living Lab case study.

3.2   Value Co-creation Modelling: e³-Value

A first step in service system (re)design is the development of a value model, focusing on value creation (Porter 1980), distribution and consumption. The *e³-value* methodology and its supporting tools can be used to support design of a value model of a service system. The e³-value methodology differs from other business modelling languages, because it focuses not on the modelling of business processes or very high-level strategic issues, but rather on the modelling of value exchanges between actors in the economic sense (Anderson et al. 2006).[1] This modelling of value exchanges is, in particular, useful for analysing value co-creation among business partners of a service system in a network setting. The *e³-value* methodology (Gordijn and Akkermans 2003) can be used to construct a value model, representing it graphically in a structured way, and performing an economic sensitivity analysis of this model. The *e³-value* methodology provides modelling concepts for showing which parties exchange resources of *economic* value with whom, and expect what in return. The methodology has been applied in a series of case studies including media, news, banking and insurance, electricity power, and telecommunication companies to design value models of network organisations (Gordijn and Akkermans 2003).

Most of the currently available design methodologies lack a value-based view representing *what* the value proposition is; rather they focus on business processes representing *how* a value proposition is implemented. There are a few value chain design methodologies, which provide concepts for describing value constellations in service systems settings, for example the AIAI Enterprise conceptual framework (Uschold et al. 1998) or the Resource Event Agent (REA) (Geerts and McCarthy 1999) conceptual framework. However, these frameworks only focus on the description of the final result, and do not support the value chain design process itself. Other business modelling methodologies (see Pateli and Giaglis 2004 for an overview) offer only generic conceptual frameworks, and do not provide software tools to support the actual modelling in a proper analysis. Tapscott et al. (2000) offer a graphical diagramming approach to represent economic exchanges between enterprises, however, compared to *e³-value*, it has several drawbacks; e.g. it has no notion of economic reciprocity, economic activity, it does not allow the profitability assessment of individual organisations, and lacks the proper level of formality.

Figure 3 shows in the upper part the legend of e³-value constructs used in the example in the lower part. For instance, 'actor' is represented by a square and has a name like 'buyer'. We explain the concepts of the *e³-value* methodology the simple example, e.g. a buyer obtains goods from a seller, offers money in return, and according to the law, a seller is obliged to pay the value-added tax (VAT). This is conceptualised by the following *e³-value* constructs:

- *Actor*. An actor is perceived by its environment as an independent economic (and often legal) entity. In a sound, sustainable, business model *each* actor should be capable of making profit. The example shows a number of actors: a *buyer*, a *seller*, and a *tax administration*.

---

[1] For further info on the tool see www.e3value.com, where also free demo versions of the tool can be downloaded.

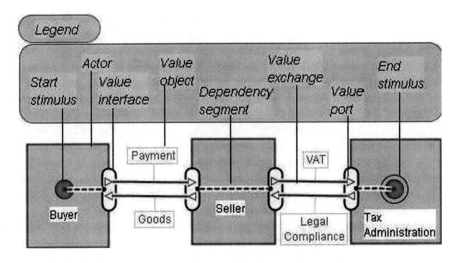

Fig. 3. e^3-*Value* model of a purchase with tax payment

- *Value Object.* Actors exchange value objects, which are services, products, money, or even consumer experiences. The important point here is that a value object is *of value* for one or more actors. *Good* and *payment* are examples of value objects, but *legal compliance* to pay tax is also a value object.
- *Value Port.* An actor uses a value port to show a value proposition to its environment. The concept of port enables to abstract away from the internal business processes.
- *Value Interface.* Actors have one or more value interfaces, grouping reciprocal, opposite-directed value ports. A value interface shows the value object an actor is willing to exchange, *in return for* another value object via its ports. The exchange of value objects is atomic at the level of the value interface.
- *Value Exchange.* A value exchange is used to connect two value ports with each other. It represents one or more *potential* trades of value objects between value ports.

These concepts show bilateral links between customers and service providers, but cannot yet show value chains in which more than two actors are involved. For this purpose *dependency paths* (based on Buhr 1998) between value interfaces are introduced: a dependency path connects the value interfaces in an actor and represents triggering relations between these interfaces. A dependency path consists of dependency nodes and segments:

- *Dependency Node.* A dependency node is a stimulus (represented by a bullet), a value interface, an AND-fork or AND-join (short line), an OR-fork or OR-join (triangle), or an end node (bull's eye). A stimulus represents a consumer need; an end node represents a model boundary.

Value Interfac	Value Trans	Occurrence	Valuatio	Value	Total
{MONEY,GOOD}		10		100	
	MONEY	10	10	100	
	(all transfers)	10	0	0	
INVESTMENT				0	
EXPENSES				0	
total for actor					100

Fig. 4. Example of a profitability sheet

- *Dependency Segment.* A dependency segment connects dependency nodes and value interfaces. It is represented by a link.
- *Dependency Path.* A dependency path is a set of dependency nodes and segments that leads from a start stimulus (*consumer need*) to an end stimulus. The meaning of the path is that if values are exchanged via a value interface, then other value interfaces connected by the path also exchange values.

Additionally, profitability sheets are used to support cost-benefit analysis for each individual actor (Fig. 4). The advantage of *e³-value* is that it contains a *minimal* number of basic constructs, which makes it easy to understand and apply, even for non-technical marketers or business analysts.

It is important to understand that an *e³-value* model *only* models an ideal situation with a given structure. The *Principle of Reciprocity* as defined in *e³-value* is the requirement that if an actor offers something of value to someone else, this actor always gets in return something what s/he wants. Hence, it assumes that *all* actors behave correctly. The violation of the principle of reciprocity (e.g. an actor receiving something without returning another service for it) can be seen as a violation of an obligation, which would lead to incorrect *e³-value* models with a value interface with only one incoming or outgoing value object; e.g. delivering goods and not receiving a payment in return.

3.3 Sustainability: e³-Control

Even the most profitable business models will not be adopted by a company, if their interests in the business model are not properly safeguarded, and if there are no control mechanisms in place that will guarantee that they will obtain a fair share of the profits or benefits. e³-control provides sustainability of value co-creation by focussing on the design of inter-organizational controls. It is a methodology for control procedure analysis and redesign (Kartseva et al. 2004, 2005, 2006, 2010; Tan and Gordijn 2005; Liu et al. 2006, 2007, 2010) based on the key ideas of (1) structured modelling approach, (2) process-based analysis, and (3) value-based analysis. It has been shown that structured modelling approaches can be used as a means to solve complex inter-organizational problems (e.g., Baida 2006; Franken and Janssen 1998; Gordijn and Akkermans 2003; Janssen et al. 2006). Process-level analysis of control issues follows ideas of other researchers (e.g., Chen and Lee 1992; Weigand and De Moor 2003), building on previous research (e.g., Arens and Loebbecke 1999; Bons et al. 1999; Geerts and McCarthy 1999) and best practices that consider control as a process element (COSO 1992). The main reason for using a process-level analysis is that the large knowledge base on designing controls, which is the basis of e³-control, focuses on analyzing operational tasks, or business processes (Bons et al. 1999; Chen and Lee 1992), and describes control with checking procedures based on the (electronic) exchange of business documents as a process. A broad consensus exists in the literature that the design and analysis of control is about identifying actors, activities and exchanges of business documents, and in particular the interdependencies between these concepts. Control principles are rules prescribing these interdependencies. A well-known control principle is Segregation of Duties, which states that when an activity is checked in an organization, the actor checking the activity should be different from, and socially detached from, the actor that is executing the activity. If this principle is not complied with, then likelihood of fraud in the checking is high. By applying control principles from auditing and accounting literature to process models (e.g. Romney and Steinbart 2003; Starreveld et al. 1994), we are able to identify control flaws, and to propose control mechanisms to handle these flaws. For a detailed description of e³-control's process level analysis, we refer to Liu et al. (2006, 2007). Finally, e³-control uses also a value model analysis to reason about controls (Kartseva et al. 2005), to model the value that can be lost by some actor in a network, if no controls are implemented. The e³-value methodology is used in e³-control to model this value analysis. We refer to the value model as *ideal model*, meaning that it reflects the situation when all actors fulfil their obligations. The ideal situation can be violated in the *sub-ideal* situation, which is the case that a value exchange does not hold reciprocally; e.g. in the purchase example the seller commits fraud and does not pay VAT accordingly. The e³-control methodology is visualized in Fig. 5.

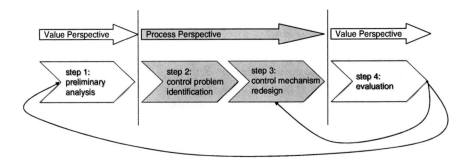

Fig. 5. *e³-Control*: value and process perspectives combined into a redesign method

The key ideas of e³-control are applied as follows:

1. A value analysis using e³-value is performed to understand the existing business model and to identify which value exchanges between actors in a service system are at risk.
2. Once the weak points in a value model have been identified, a process-level analysis of these points follows. It facilitates an understanding of how – in the business processes – value can be lost by actors.
3. The next step in process analysis is the development of corrective measures, i.e. new governance and control mechanisms, resulting in revised business processes.
4. Finally, the new business processes and control mechanisms may alter the business model; in particular require new control services and actors that provide these services. Therefore in the final step the value analysis is redone and it is investigated how the suggested changes influence the business model, and it is evaluated whether the new business model is feasible for the actors involved.

As Fig. 5 shows, evaluation can be followed by redesign of control mechanisms or even restarting at the preliminary analysis in accordance with the Service Innovation Life Cycle Model discussed earlier. After evaluating one possible solution, alternative solutions may be investigated. Thus, e³-control is a support tool for a specific step in the Service Innovation Life Cycle Model, in particular in service engineering. To perform the analysis in steps 2 and 3 the Unified Modelling Method (UMM) is applied.

3.4   Beer Living Lab

The Beer Living Lab, abbreviated to BeerLL, is a living lab case study that was conducted in 2006–2007 as part of the research project ITAIDE.[2] Participants in the BeerLL were Heineken NL, a large Dutch beer producer, Heineken UK, an independent company that buys beer from Heineken NL, a UK retailer, the Dutch Tax Administration, IBM as a service provider and the VUAUniversityAmsterdam for project management, analysis, and redesign. In the BeerLL innovative IT was piloted to replace paper-based control procedures by electronic customs procedures to improve security and efficiency of international supply chains in the beer industry. This pilot was conducted with real container shipments of beer to England and the United States.[3]

---

[2] The ITAIDE project is funded by the 6th Framework IST Programme of the European Commission, for further information see www.itaide.org.

[3] Heineken ships on average 40,000 (!) containers to the US, so the potential benefits of simplification of customs procedures are very significant for Heineken.

This section explains the current As-Is situation of doing business with paper-based customs procedures, with its potential risks. Subsequently, the proposed To-Be situation is presented based on IT innovations. Finally, we illustrate how our framework was used in the BeerLL to design the new electronic customs procedures.

3.5   Current As-Is Situation

The current As-Is situation is as follows. Within the European Union (EU), goods (and people) can move freely from one EU Member State to another. In case these goods are imported from a country outside the EU, import taxes have to be paid in the Member State where these goods are becoming EU goods and can move freely. Similar procedures and excise payments are applicable to exporting goods to countries outside the EU. When goods are produced and sold in the EU, a producer needs to pay excise in the EU Member State where the goods are actually consumed. Hence, if a Dutch beer producer exports beer to a retailer in the UK, that sells the beer to English consumers, the excise has to be paid by the English retailer to the UK Tax office and the producer has to offer proof of excise payment. These goods can already be physically located in that country, without paying excise in a so-called excise warehouse. Excise has to be paid when these goods leave the excise warehouse and are to be consumed. The so-called *Administrative Accompanying Document* (AAD) is the core document for excise-free export within the EU. The document provides shipment data for customs personnel and is proof that, after the document is signed by a tax office in the country of consumption, excise has been paid. This paper-based control procedure with the AAD is known to be vulnerable for fraud since it requires a paper-based administration by all parties involved. It could operate correctly if one AAD always relates to one container for which excise is paid at once. However, a container may contain a variety of consumer products, potentially with different excise percentages. Furthermore, as the transport between EU Member States increases, the number of AAD's received increases and Dutch Tax will not have sufficient personnel to validate all AAD's.

3.6   Proposed To-Be Situation

The To-Be situation of the BeerLL describes how the paper-based procedure could be replaced by a completely paperless procedure by introducing two IT innovations, namely smart container seals for real-time monitoring of beer containers and services for sharing information. First of all, we present both IT innovations and, secondly, show how risk reduction is achieved applying these innovations.

The *smart container seal* is a tamper proof seal developed by IBM (TREC device) for container tracking and tracing with GPS, detection of unauthorized opening of a container, and monitoring the physical condition of the container content (e.g. temperature and humidity). It can be programmed with business rules; e.g. it can give periodic alerts with respect to its position. The seal's unique reference number is linked to a Movement Reference Number identifying shipment data from customs perspective. The seals need to be managed by a service provider; they need to have a unique identification number and reverse logistics has to be in place. This service provider needs to be trusted to cater for the security issues of the seals.

Introduction of *services* for sharing information between business partners and customs authorities is the second IT innovation piloted in the BeerLL. Services provide customs authorities access to shipment data stored in a companies' ERP system, and whenever any governmental agency – whether dealing with export, excise, VAT or any other regulation – wishes to obtain data concerning a shipment, it can retrieve – or "pull" – this data from that system. Services were implemented using (1) standards for product descriptions, such that information from Heineken's system was interpretable for Dutch Tax, and (2) standards for the implementation of services. Each organization in the BeerLL had its own database which contains a replication of (part of) the data of its internal IT system. Discovery services are required to interactively retrieve data from various databases and present the results to an end-user. Whilst a harmonised data structure is used, the data retrieved from different databases is always presented in the same way.

Figure 6 shows Heineken, which replicates its purchase order data to a database (EPCIS), Dutch customs that replicates reports and alert data to their database, which is accessible to UK Customs, and Safmarine, a subsidiary of the Maersk container shipping line. Safmarine replicates the Bill of Lading into their EPCIS. The Bill of Lading contains all relevant shipment data for transport purposes, like container size and type, container number, weights, temperature, and parties

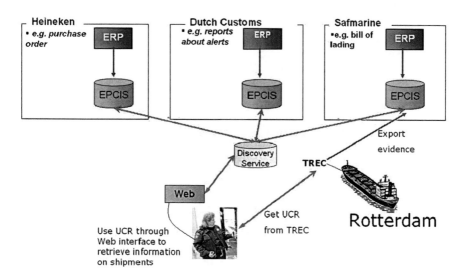

Fig. 6. Service-oriented architecture applied in the BeerLL

involved in the shipment. Furthermore, data in the EPCIS database of Safmarine is enriched with container tracking and tracing and physical status data gathered and generated by TREC alerts. A device independent portal with integration functionality (the *Shipment Information Sharing Services* (SISS) developed by IBM) provides an actor specific discovery service for secure data access based on a unique seal number. In this way, customs can for instance access the data stored by Heineken and Safmarine in the EPCIS databases of these two companies. EPCGlobal (see www.epcglobal.org), a subsidiary of GS1 (see www.gs1.org), provided the IT service specifications for communication between the portal and the EPCIS databases and the harmonised data structure of the EPCIS databases.

With these two innovations, Dutch and UK Customs have access to all container movements and their excise status, which makes the AAD obsolete. Shipment declarations are no longer required, since all transport movements are transparent to customs authorities. Control procedures are improved, because tracking and status information of containers is always accessible to customs authorities. Customs authorities have to take the initiative for monitoring transportation and assurance of excise payment. This differs from the current procedure, in which Heineken NL has to present, upon request from Dutch Customs, an AAD as evidence of excise payment.

3.7   Analysis of the BeerLL with e³-Control

The applicability of our framework and tools is illustrated by a value – and process level analysis of BeerLL (see Beer Living Lab 2007; Baida et al. 2007, 2008) as discussed hereafter. A value-level analysis, yielded the following insights:

- Understanding of the BeerLL by analysing value exchanges between actors in the service system.
- Exploration of weak points in the business model.
- Understanding changes of the existing business model by introduction of the two IT innovations.

This chapter only provides a few insights and examples of value models. First of all, we present the value models of the As-Is and To-Be situation and, secondly, we present the process analysis.

Figure 7 is one of the value models that we developed in Step 1 of modelling the Beer Living Lab with e³-control. It shows the network of actors that participate in the value chain where Heineken NL sells beer to Heineken UK and consumption of the beer by end consumers. Actors (visualized as rectangles) exchange (visualized as blue lines) objects of economic value (text labels). The value chain starts at the start stimulus of the actor "Consumer UK" and follows the scenario along the value exchanges (blue lines) and dependency paths (dashed lines). The figure shows two sub paths:

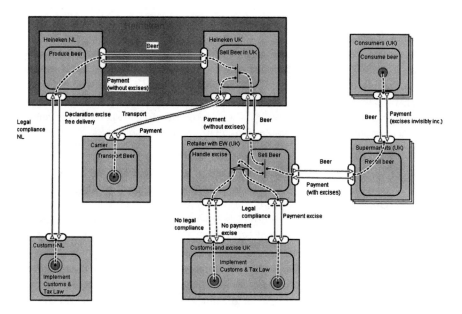

Fig. 7. e³-Control As-Is model of the BeerLL

- A value exchange between Heineken UK and a carrier, where Heineken pays a fee in return for transport services.
- A value exchange between Heineken UK and Heineken NL: Heineken NL sells beer to Heineken UK. Following this dependency path, we can see that in order to be exempted from excise payment in the Netherlands, Heineken NL has to provide Dutch Customs export (data) evidence about the excise free shipments.

In case the beer is transported from an excise warehouse to the supermarket, two sub paths represented by an OR gate are feasible:

- The UK-based retailer in its role of Excise Warehouse pays excise to the UK authorities.
- The UK-based retailer defaults and does not pay excise duties for the beer that it sold to the UK-based supermarkets. This sub path represents a fraud case.

Whilst these sub paths are modeled by an OR gate, only one of the sub paths will be executed. A sub-ideal situation exists, which cannot be modeled by e³-value. The e³-control modelling tool allows modelling sub-ideal situations to identify possible problems with respect to control. This is indicated by the value exchange with dotted lines; i.e. "No Legal Compliance" and "No Payment Excise". Modelling of sub-ideal value exchanges is an extension in e³-control to e³-value to enable modelling of control flows.

The second part of e³-control is modelling the To-Be situation (step 4 of e³-control, Fig. 8). The major difference between this and the previous value model is the introduction of a new actor – TREC service provider – to cope with the control problems we have mentioned. As we have described before, a TREC service provider supports the logistics of the seals and, in the BeerLL, hosts the portal and the EPCIS databases. This will give the following opportunities:

1. Since TREC can monitor the state of a container and the TREC service provider provides sufficient monitoring and control to Dutch Customs, Dutch Customs has proof of excise payment in the UK.
2. TREC service provider offers and extra control by submitting information (automatically generated by TREC) to both Dutch Customs and UK Customs that can be used to match excise payment.
3. Heineken NL is able to provide all relevant accountability data to qualify as an AEO (Authorised Economic Operator), which leads to considerable benefits and cost reductions to Heineken.
4. TREC service provider is able to improve the supply chain management of the beer transport for the carrier, which has immediate benefits and cost reductions also for Heineken NL and Heineken UK.

By comparing the To-Be model with the As-Is of step 1, the value of performing step 4 becomes visible. First, we identify changes in actors and in linkages between actors. Secondly, the To-Be model also supports a profitability (cash flow) and business analysis: (1) reduction of administrative burden of all private parties and (2) fraud reduction for customs authorities. The total profitability depends on the business model of the new services required by the introduction of both IT innovations and their adoption by all stakeholders. The seal service provisioning is a typical example of a networked service offering. Various services have to be bundled, which refers to the governance aspects of our Service Innovation Aspects Model. First, there should be a seal provision service offered by an actor, including seals logistics. Secondly, there should be a mechanism to process and store seal data linked to a container number and a Movement Reference Number. Third, the services have to be implemented and published by companies and a service discovery portal is required according to agreed standards and semantics. This requires services of a standardization body, like GS1 and EPCglobal. Finally, there should be federated security service providers, because the distribution and use of digital certificates has to be at a global scale and there exists no globally acting Certification Authority (CA). Most governments issue their own digital certificates and act as a CA. Hence, federation is needed to provide global coverage. An additional complexity of this network formation is that for each of these services the investment profile is quite different. For example, consider millions of container movements with relative less investment for TREC devices compared with investments for developing a CA

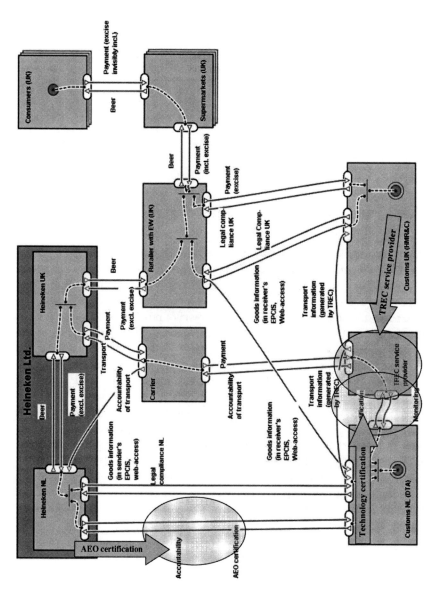

Fig. 8. e³-Value To-Be model of BeerLL

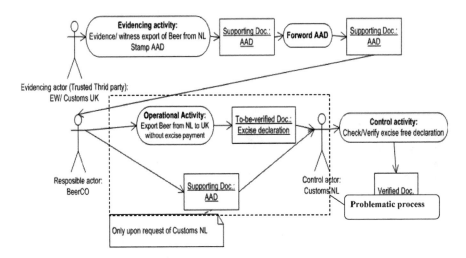

Fig. 9. Step 2 of e³-control: process model of the BeerLL As-Is situation

federation to provide global security coverage and operating the complete service system. The value modelling and underlying profitability analysis was used extensively to make a detailed scenario-based analysis of the profitability for each of these services, and to determine which actor was most likely to provide these services. One of the solutions is that container owners provide the seal services as built-in functionality of their containers. The value analysis for a seal service showed that these services are primarily profitable for the transport of high-value goods (mobile phones, electronic components etc.). For commercial reasons we are unable to provide more details about these more detailed value models for seal services.

Steps 2 and 3 of e³-control consist of a process-level analysis focussing on the business processes that realize the As-Is and To-Be business models. A process analysis is required for value co-creation sustainability by all actors involved. Figure 9 shows the highest level As-Is process model that was constructed in Step 2 of the BeerLL. It illustrates the basic principles of the paper-based AAD approach and is refined in various steps to, for example, use case diagrams and activity models that include swim lanes for each actor, using the Unified Modelling Language (UML).

Process analysis specifies how processes are affected by the introduction of the a container seal and the TREC service provider. Detailed models can be found in (Beer Living Lab 2007). Process analysis yielded the following insights (Fig. 10):

- Based on a combination of IT innovations such as the TREC smart container seal and services, paper-based administrations become obsolete.

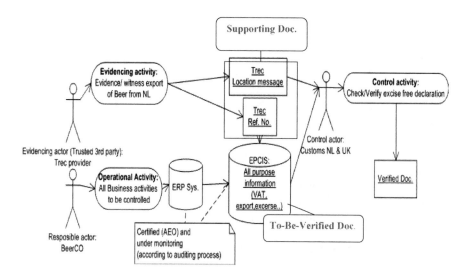

Fig. 10. Step 3 of e³-control: process model of the To-Be situation

- Current EU procedure for export and intra-community supplies of excise goods based on a paper document does not comply with control principles and is therefore vulnerable to fraud and misuse.
- The BeerLL concept complies with audit and control principles and solves the control risks that we identified for the paper-based customs procedure.

Figure 10 shows the To-Be process of Step 3 of the BeerLL redesign, where all the evidence of movements of beer containers is stored in EPCIS databases that are accessible to Dutch and UK customs authorities. The database contains all relevant data for customs purposes, which is also present at the AAD document. In particular, a TREC can be programmed to send a signal when it crosses the Dutch border, which is an automated export evidence for Dutch Customs. The data stored in the EPCIS database of Heineken NL replaces the role of the To-Be-verified paper export declaration.

4   Conclusions

In this paper we have discussed two models, the Service Aspects model and the Service Innovation Life Cycle Model, and two conceptual modelling tools, e³-value and e³-control to support the re-design of Business-to-Business and Business-to-Government services. To validate the adequacy and usefulness of the models and tools, we have conducted an extensive case study, the BeerLL, of the redesign of value chains in international trade with the introduction of two IT innovations (smart seals and services). The BeerLL case study provides a clear example of what we called the second dimension of value propositions in service systems, namely that services are typically offered by collaborative service system of service providers. First of all, it is clear that no single actor is able to provide seal services, so it is a truly networked service offering. Secondly, to design the seal service, it appears to be essential to find a service system setting that is not only profitable as a whole, but profitable for every partner participating in the service system. The most complicated part of a seal service is to determine the value co-creation among the actors in the service system. In particular, to determine for each actor (1) the profitability of the value model of his own service contribution, and (2) to design controls that guarantee for each actor the fair distribution of profitability of the total service system to each of the actors in that system. In both steps the tools e^3-value and e^3-control are proving to be useful for analysis and design. Regarding the research question, we can now say that applying these tools in practice enabled us to model weaknesses in control procedures and to redesign these procedures by introduction of extra controls based on new technology that is provided as a networked service offering provided by a service system. In other words, the tools have been adequate for the redesign task and have provided useful insights.

We expect the research to have the following implications. Regarding theory, the combination of value-based modelling (e^3-value and e^3-control) and service oriented models (Service Aspects model and the Service Innovation Life Cycle Model) has proved beneficial. It provides another step towards reconciling these mutually beneficial modelling perspectives for service design. Regarding practice, we expect that these insights will help practitioners to better understand the impact of regulation change on service redesign. In future research, we will further investigate the separation of the design phase and operational phase in the life-cycle of service systems, and further define the underlying concepts of this contribution.

Acknowledgments This research was partially supported by the integrated project ITAIDE (Nr.027829), which is funded by the 6th Framework IST Programme of the European Commission (see www.itaide.org).

References

Anderson, J.C., Narus, J., Narus, A., and van Rossum, W. (2006). Customer value propositions in business markets. *Harvard Business Review*, 84(3), pp. 90–99.

Arens, A. and Loebbecke, J. (1999). *Auditing, an Integrated Approach*, 8th edition, Prentice Hall, Englewood Cliffs.

Baida, Z. (2006). *Software-aided Service Bundling – Intelligent Methods and Tools for Graphical Service Modeling*, Ph.D. thesis, Vrije Universiteit Amsterdam, The Netherlands.

Baida, Z., Rukanova, B.D., Wigand, R.T., and Tan, Y.H. (2007). Partnership: The story of how Heineken's supply chain benefits from tight collaboration with government. *Supply Chain Management Review*, 11(7), pp. 11–12.

Baida, Z., Rukanova, B., Liu, J., and Tan, Y.H. (2008). Preserving control in trade procedure redesign – The Beer living lab, electronic markets. *The International Journal*, 18(1), 53–64.

Beer Living Lab (2007). Beer Living Lab, Final Report, D5.1:5, ITAIDE.

Bons, R.W.H., Lee, R.M., and Wagenaar, R.W. (1999). Computer-aided auditing and interorganizational trade procedures. *International Journal of Intelligent Systems in Accounting, Finance and Management*, 8(1), pp. 25–44.

Buhr, R.J.A. (1998). Use case maps as architectural entities for complex systems. *IEEE Transactions on Software Engineering*, 24(12), pp. 1131–1155.

Chen, K.-T. and Lee, R. M. (1992). *Schematic evaluation of internal accounting control systems* EURIDIS Research Monograph, Erasmus University Rotterdam.

COSO (1992). *Internal Control-Integrated Framework*. The Committee of Sponsoring Organizations of the Treadway Commission, New York.

Curtis, K. and Henderson, A. (2006). Hiding in plain sight: service innovation – a new priority for chief executives. *IBM Institute for business value*. Somers, New York.

Derzsi, Z. and Gordijn, J. (2006). A framework for business/it alignment in networked value constellations. In T. Latour and M. Petit, editors, *Proceedings of the Workshops of the 18th International Conference on Advanced Information Systems Engineering (CAiSE 2006)* Namur University Press, Namur, B, pp. 219–226.

Dietz, J.L.G. (2006). *Enterprise Ontology – Theory and Methodology*, Springer, Berlin.

Edvardsson, B. and Olsson, J. (1996). Key concepts for new service development. *The Service Industries Journal*, 16(2), pp. 140–164.

Fensel, D., Kerrigan, M., and Zaremba, M. (eds.) (2008). *Implementing Semantic Web Services – The SESA framework*, Springer, Heidelberg.

Franken, H. and Janssen, W. (1998). Get a grip on changing business processes: Results from the Testbed project. *Knowledge and Process Management*, 5(4), pp. 208–215.

Geerts, G. and McCarthy, W.E. (1999). An Accounting Object Infrastructure for Knowledge-Based Enterprise Models. *IEEE Intelligent Systems and Their Applications*, 14(4), pp. 89–94.

Gordijn, J. and Akkermans, H. (2003). Value based requirements engineering: Exploring innovative e-commerce idea. *Requirements Engineering Journal*, 8(2), pp. 114–134.

Heineke, J. and Davis, M. (2007). The emergence of service operations management as an academic discipline. *Journal of Operations Management*, 25, pp. 364–374.

Hofman, W.J. (1994). *A conceptual model of a Business Transaction Management System*, Ph.D. thesis, Uitgeverij Tutein Nolthenius, The Netherlands.

Janssen, M., Gortmaker, J., and Wagenaar, R.W. (2006). Web service orchestration in public administration: Challenges, roles and growth stages. *Information Systems Management*, 23(2), pp. 44–55.

Kartseva, V., Gordijn, J., and Tan, Y.-H. (2004). Value-based business modelling for network organizations: Lessons learned from the electricity sector. *Proceedings of the 12th European Conference on Information Systems (ECIS'04)*, Turku.

Kartseva, V., Gordijn, J., and Tan, Y.-H. (2005). Towards a modelling tool for designing control mechanisms for network organisations. *International Journal of Electronic Commerce*, 10(2), pp. 57–84.

Kartseva, V., Gordijn, J., and Tan, Y.-H. (2006). Inter-organisational controls as value objects in network organisations. *Proceedings of the 18th Conference of Advanced Information Systems Engineering (CAiSE06)*, Springer Verlag, Berlin pp. 336–350.

Kartseva, V., Hulstijn, J., Gordijn, J., and Tan, Y.-H. (2010). Control patterns in a healthcare network. *European Journal of Information Systems*, 19, 320–343.

Lankhorst, M. (2005). *Enterprise Architecture at work*, Springer, Heidelberg.

Liu, J., Baida, Z., Tan, Y.-H., and Rukanova, B. (2006). Designing controls for e-government in network organizations. *Proceedings of the 13th Research Symposium on Emerging Electronic Markets*, September 23–25, Stuttgart, Germany, pp. 22–36.

Liu, J., Baida, Z., and Tan, Y.-H. (2007). e-Customs Control Procedures Redesign Methodology: Model-Based Application. *Proceedings of the 15th European Conference of Information Systems* (ECIS 2007), St. Gallen, Switzerland.

Liu, J., Higgins, A., and Tan, Y.-H. (2010). IT enabled redesign of export procedure for high value pharmaceutical product under temperature control: the case of drug living lab. *Proceedings of the 11th Annual International Conference on Digital Government Research (DG.O 2010)*, ACM International Conference Proceeding Series.

McGovern, J., Sims, O., Jain, A., and Little, M. (2006). *Enterprise Service Oriented Architectures – Concepts, Challenges, Recommendations*, Springer, Dordrecht.

Nuseibeh, B., Kramer, J., and Finkelstein, A. (1994). A framework for expressing relationships between multiple views in requirements specification. *IEEE Transactions on Software Engineering*, 20(10), pp. 760–773.

Pateli, A.G. and Giaglis, G.M. (2004). A research framework for analysing business models. *European Journal of Information Systems*, 13(4), pp. 302–304.

Petzinger, T. Jr. (1995). *Hard Landing: The Epic Contest for Power and Profits That Plunged the Airlines into Chaos*, Times Books, New York.

Porter, M.E. (1980). *Competitive Advantage. Creating and Sustaining Superior Performance*, The Free Press, New York.

Quartel, D.A.C., Steen, M.W.A., Pokraev S., and Sinderen M.J. van (2007). COSMO: A conceptual framework for service modelling and refinement. *Information Systems Frontiers*, 9(2–3), pp. 225–244.

Romney, M.B. and Steinbart, P.J. (2003). *Accounting Information Systems*, 9th edition, Prentice Hall, New Jersey.

Spohrer, J. and Kwam, S.K. (2009). Service Science, Management, Engineering and Design (SSMED) – An emerging discipline – Outline and references. *International Journal on Information Systems in the Service Sector*, 1(3).

Starreveld, R.W., de Mare, B., and Joels, E. (1994). *Bestuurlijke Informatieverzorging, Deel 1*, 4th edition, Samsom, Alphen aan den Rijn (in Dutch).

Tan, Y.H. and Gordijn, J. (2005). A design methodology for modeling trustworthy value webs. *International Journal of Electronic Commerce*, 9(3), pp. 31–48.

Tapscott, D., Ticoll, D., and Lowy, A. (2000). *Digital Capital – Harnessing the Power of Business Webs*, Nicholas Brealy Publishing, London.

Uschold, M., King, M., Moralee, S., and Zorgios, Y. (1998). The enterprise ontology. *The Knowledge Engineering Review*, 13(1), pp. 31–89.

van der Aalst, W.M.P., Reijers, H.A., Weijters, A.J.M.M., van Dongen, B.F., Alves de Medeiros, A.K., Song, M., and Verbeek, H.M.W. (2007). Business process mining: An industrial application. *Information Systems*, 32(5), pp. 713–732.

Weigand, H. and De Moor, A. (2003). Workflow analysis with communication norms. *Data & Knowledge Engineering*, 47, pp. 349–369.

Wieringa, R.J. (2003). *Design Methods for Reactive Systems*, Morgan Kaufman, San Fransisco.

Yu, E. (1995). Models for supporting the redesign of organizational work. In COCS '95: *Proceedings of Conference on Organizational Computing Systems*, ACM Press.

Surviving Nuclear Winter Towards a Service-Led Business

Michael Rocha and Timothy Chou

Openwater Networks

Abstract During the tech-led recession in 2001 a little known transformation occurred at the world's largest business software company. This transformation was led by a realization that existing customers of mature software need service of the products they purchased more than just purchasing new products. Organizing around the installed base of customers both defined new organizations, as well as new technology to power the specialists. This paper both gives a glimpse of the Oracle transformation as well as lays out some fundamental tenants of anyone interested in a service-led business.

The U.S. economy is over 80% a service economy and much of the rest of the world is headed that way. While we all know this to be true, our common perception is that service means flipping burgers at McDonald's. Nothing could be farther from the truth. Instead,

- Service is information, personal to you.
- Service connects to the customer. Nothing could be more obvious in a post-Internet world.
- Service is specialization.
- Service is information + specialists.

Today, from technology to healthcare, from automobiles to books corporations are striving to differentiate based on service. We think this paper will help all of you.

Keywords Service systems, service networks, search-based applications, product support, Product Service, Oracle, service clouds, maintenance

H. Demirkan et al. (eds.), *Service Systems Implementation*, Service Science: Research and Innovations in the Service Economy, DOI 10.1007/978-1-4419-7904-9_5, © Springer Science+Business Media, LLC 2011

1   Introduction

When the tech bubble burst on March 10, 2000 many technology companies faced tough times. Today as a second nuclear winter has arrived many more will face the same challenges. But perhaps all is not gloom and doom. White House Chief of Staff Rahm Emanuel told the New York Times: "You don't ever want a crisis to go to waste; it's an opportunity to do important things that you would otherwise avoid." Perhaps this is an opportunity for many companies to make a transition from the traditional product-led business to a service-led business.

We say this because in 2000 Oracle began a little known transformation towards a service led business. Oracle's approach allowed the company to exit the downturn acquiring companies that didn't have the size, couldn't change fast enough or worse yet didn't have the wherewithal to change. Table 1 tells the story in numbers of a

Table 1. Oracle financial performance

	2000	2001	2002	2003	2004	Change	Change (%)	Corporate highlights
New software	4,315	4,584	3,441	3,270	3,541	(774)	−18	• Product support and advanced Product Services revenue grew sharply
Product support	2,978	3,571	3,836	3,929	4,529	1,551	52	• All other product and services revenue declines
Product revenue	7,293	8,155	7,277	7,199	8,070	777	11	• Corporate profitability increased 25%
Consulting	2,293	2,257	1,982	1,761	1,589	(704)	−31	• Product services hdcnt declined 10%, expenses declined 15% and profit contribution increased 76% – 11 pts
Advanced product services	132	137	96	257	258	126	95	• Product services became a differentiator winning innovation awards and playing a critical role in product marketing
Education	411	411	317	258	239	(172)	−42	
Other services	2,836	2,805	2,395	2,276	2,086	(750)	−26	
Total revenue	10,129	10,960	9,672	9,475	10,156	27	0	

company that improved its income statement, balance sheet and market position in the worst of times.

The audience for this chapter is anyone in a traditional product business who sees that the way forward is not just more of the same. While many of our examples are from the world of business software we believe the lessons learned here have broader application. The first section gives you a more detailed view of a transformation of Oracle's business. Led by your two authors it is many of the lessons learned firsthand in this endeavor that lead us to describe some fundamental principle of a service-led business. We hope you'll take some of these fundamentals as use the opportunity at hand to change businesses for the twenty-first century.

2 Surviving Nuclear Winter: The Oracle Case Study

During the late 1990s, with strong demand for its products and services, Oracle launched an ambitious plan to build an integrated suite of applications software. It took many years and thousands of developers to build. By early 2000, the company launched the product and started to upgrade their entire customer base. Unfortunately, the "tech bubble" burst and the economy went into recession. Oracle's business changed overnight. The new product business declined by 19% over the next 3 years, and the consulting and education businesses further eroded by 33%. Oracle's product service business became the engine that powered the company.

Historically software product support and service was an after-thought. It was delivered over the phone by local organizations. With an expanding product line and increasingly global customers, this model broke down. It was extremely difficult and expensive to put the right product skills in every region, and it was no longer possible to operate in local time zones. A complex application migration and the "tech bubble" recession forced a complete re-engineering. Not only did this result in redeployment of the human labor but also an early idea of the technology needed to power such a transformation. There were several elements to the story

- Customer information (e.g., service contracts) was fragmented in local databases. Oracle deployed a single contract base to understand its obligations and service its customers globally.
- Oracle's information, which explained how to use, configure and maintain its software, was built and deployed to provide direct access to clients globally.
- Technical specialists were reorganized. Developers and service personnel became responsible for closing service requests. Technical service engineers were organized into global support centers to provide global standards for problem resolution. Furthermore, Oracle invested in local resources to manage services for key accounts.

- Decommissioned local and line of business-specific applications for incident tracking and escalation management, and standardized on global systems and a single global work queue.
- Created tools and infrastructure to standardize methods for capturing customer configuration information.
- Created new personalized support programs to provide improved services and take more responsibility. These new services were critical to development of its entire business.

The results were impressive. Oracle's service business grew 61% from fiscal year 2000–2004. Oracle's Advanced Product Service business grew 116% during the same time period. All of this growth was organic, pre-acquisition. Amazingly, at the same time, Oracle's support delivery costs actually shrank by 11% in real dollars.

Ultimately, this growth in the Product Service business meant that Oracle's corporate revenue remained flat, and its profits increased during the industry downturn. By 2004, Oracle received many awards for the quality and innovative service it supplied. In fact, service had become a strategic differentiator and served as a platform for the next phase of Oracle's growth – acquisition. By mid-2009 Oracle's service revenue from all of its acquisitions topped $12B, exceeding the size of the entire company in 2004.

3   Service Economy

The U.S. economy is a service economy. Figure 1 shows how dramatically the shift from manufacturing and agriculture to services has been over the last 50 years.

The service economy accounts for 80% of the US GDP. Financial services, healthcare, education, IT services, software are all industries which don't manufacture

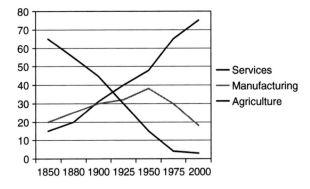

Fig. 1. U.S. economy

High-skill Autonomous	40%	Executive, Scientist
Semi- Autonomous	30%	Admin, Manager
Labor Intensive	25%	Maid, Child Care
Tightly Constrained	5%	Call Center, Fast Food

Fig. 2. 1996 census

or grow a single thing. Furthermore, contrary to conventional wisdom, this shift has not been an increase in the number of kids flipping hamburgers. Instead 70% of the service employment has been for highly skilled people. This includes executives, scientists, and administration and management functions. Figure 2 shows the results of the 1996 census.

While service may be seen as non-manufacturing oriented labor, over the past 20 years computers have replaced much of the repetitive work. Transaction processing changed the way we bank and has enabled tremendous efficiencies in back-office automation. No one has been more focused on transaction efficiency than the mega retailer Wal-Mart. But more supply-chain efficiency is not the key to their future. A recent Time magazine article noted: "The Company's cult like focus on supply-chain logistics grinds away at costs but doesn't allow it to know the neighbors. The new strategy tries to make that connection – editing for the area, offering a point of distinction." The article goes on to quote then CEO Castro-Wright: "It's going to tell the customer that we understand what they need. We not only understand what you need, we respect your point of view. We want to be your store of choice because we understand you better than anyone else in the market-place." Said another way – they've done a great job at their transaction systems – their challenge is how to make a connection to their customers.

Another leader has a similar point of view. Bharthi Enterprises is India's leading telecom conglomerates, but you'd be surprised to know they focus on the customer and outsource just about everything else, including all the IT equipment and the even the network itself. "The customer, not the technology, is the heart of my business" says Sunil Mittal, Chairman of Bharthi Enterprises. So what are the important principles for any service-led business whether you're a retailer, a telecom provider or a high technology product company? We think there are four fundamentals: Service is Information, Personal to You; Service Connects You to Your Customer and Service is Specialization.

4   Service Is Information, Personal to You

Ten years ago if you were interested in a book you went down to your local bookstore, found a parking space and then waited patiently to talk to Jack, the bookstore owner. You might have asked him "Do you have the book Blink?" or "Do you have the new book by the author of The Tipping Point?" or "What book would be best to read and understand viral marketing?" Between his store inventory system running on his PC, Books in Print, and access to the Prentice-Hall computers, he might have been able to answer your question. If you went on to ask, "What do people in Northern California think of this book?" or "Is there a review in the New York Times?" Jack would probably have looked at you and thought – why do you think I would know? And, if you went further and said "Do you think I would like this book?" He would probably have walked away muttering – who is this person?

Of course, today, we do not think twice about logging on to Amazon and having all information instantly. More importantly, Amazon knows your name and tries to deliver personal and relevant information to me before you search for it. You can access this information from the comfort of your hotel room in Shanghai and have the book delivered to your house in Hillsborough. As is the case with many organizations, it's not that Jack didn't want to answer all of my questions, it's that Amazon is using the information they have about YOU to deliver a more targeted and useful experience than Jack could ever provide.

So what does this mean to the world of business software? Most of us think paying for software support or maintenance is paying for bug fixes. Of course early versions of any software have high change rates because they are feature incomplete and require constant changes (upgrades) to meet users' demands. As a result early in the life of a piece of software most of the money and effort is spent providing new features and fixing bugs from these major and minor changes. But over time as the software matures the challenges are no longer about bug fixing, but rather how to optimally use the software. In other words, people who support the software require more education about how to deploy and use the software and the surrounding business processes. Essentially, customer service and support transitions from code level defect support to configuring for better performance, or managing the implementation of a new business process. Nowhere is this more obvious than in a slide presented by Michael Rocha, then Executive Vice President of Global Product Service and Platform Technology at Oracle, at Oracle's 2004 investor conference (Fig. 3).

The slide is a result of a year long study documenting the nature of 100 million requests customers files with Oracle Support. Bottom line, Oracle received 100 million requests for service in its fiscal year 2003 and less than 0.1% of those requests resulted in a new "code fix" for their software. 94% of the requests were managed directly by the knowledge base. 6% (six million) were filed as service requests. In other words, the library of information could not directly answer six million requests. Interestingly, by integrating a knowledge base with the process for filing a service request, 56% of actual service requests were also handled without human-intervention. In total 97% of all requests were managed directly by the knowledge-base without human intervention.

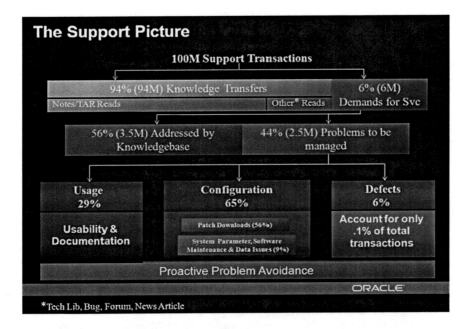

Fig. 3. 2004 Oracle investor conference

Of the 3% of total requests (which amount to 2.5 million issues) 29% were closed as usage related issues, 65% were closed as configuration related and only 6% resulted in new software fixes. An analysis of the 2.5 m tickets discovered: 29% were closed as usage related, 65% were closed as configuration issues and only 6% resulted in new software fixes. In other words, of the 100 million requests over a yearlong period, just one-tenth of 1% of the requests actually resulted in any new software fixes; *99.9% could be answered by information in a library or in people's heads*. It should be noted that this analysis aggregates database, middleware and application related software. Given that application software was changing far faster than database software, if we were to be able to separate out the database software statistics, we could imagine that 99.99% of the requests could be answered by known information stored on computers or in people. Furthermore we should realize that if 100 million transactions reached Oracle, there are easily 10 times the number of requests occurring inside each corporation that is managing the Oracle software. Service is indeed information.

5 Service Connects You to Your Customer

For those of you who buy lots of shoes Zappos.com will need no introduction. For the rest of us, Zappos is a nearly $1B e-retailer whose corporate culture is to exceed a customer's expectations for service. They start by offering free shipping both ways with a 365-day return policy. Zappos promise customers you'll get their shoes in four to five business days, but actually, for most they do a surprise upgrade to overnight shipping. They run their warehouse 24/7, which traditional warehouse managers will tell you isn't the most efficient, but it gets the orders out to customers as quickly as possible.

Traditional call centers have this concept of average handle time, which is all about how many customers a day each agent can talk to – and the more the better. But Tony Hsieh, CEO, says that just ends up translating into, "How quickly can we get the customer off the phone?" At Zappos everyone is trained so if their customer is looking for a specific pair of shoes, and they're out of stock they'll search the web for someone who can provide the shoes and direct the customer to that web site. All of this has led to a company that grew to $1B in just 9 years. One of Tony's favorite expressions is "Customer service is not a department."

In most companies the customer support people are trying to get off of the phone and never talk to a customer; while on the other side of the building the inside sales people are desperately trying to get you to pick up the phone. And even when we are willing to connect to the customer we don't take advantage of the tremendous amount of information available to us. In enterprise software it's often the case the computer knows what the software configuration, when it was last modified and the last three times a patch failed. But rather than connect to the computer we interview the person and typically make them repeat the information as we forward them up the call tree. We often know more about our customers when they are prospects, than after they have purchased. And while we sell products that are many times more expensive than a pair of shoes, as customers we have learned not to expect more. Shouldn't this change?

6   Service Is Specialization

Read Jared Diamond's (2005) bestseller *Guns, Germs and Steel: The Fates of Human Societies* and you may see the world a little differently. Diamond's book centers around answering a question asked by his New Guinea friend Yali: "Why is it that you white people developed so much cargo [goods] and brought it to New Guinea, but we black people had little cargo of our own?" The essential answer is due to many local conditions in a few isolated places in the ancient world, some peoples began to produce food either through herding large mammals or growing crops. The lucky ones had the right circumstances to do both. Being a food producer meant that the population could grow. Having the ability to store food meant that the society could develop specialization. Specialization meant technology could develop. Some people could make weapons, others could grow food, and still others could build buildings.

While this idea is in many ways not new, how much have we applied it to our new service economy? Conventional wisdom is that a service-business is low margin and that a product business is high margin. Furthermore, none of us want to be in a low margin business. But what is a product business and why is it high margin? A product business is simply any business where I can create something enough people want, where the product is standard, and can be repetitively manufactured. If the product must be changed for every customer, or where the manufacturing line must be re-tooled for each product, then there is no way to get a high margin product business.

Now why can't a service be a product business? The short answer is it can. Let's focus on an area where a lot of money is being spent on traditional services: the service of software. By this we mean the human labor devoted to managing the security, availability, performance and change in any business software. From large ERP applications to managing an Exchange server most CIOs will tell you they spend four times the purchase price of the software per year – and that's every year. The end result has been many IT shops have large budgets but little to no discretionary spend. The traditional answer to the problem has been to outsource the tasks to low cost labor countries – hence the rise of the Indian outsourcing business.

But there is a better way. If I can standardize the service then I can produce the service repetitively ultimately reducing cost and improving quality. But this is not a particularly unique idea. The key to excellence in anything is born of standardization, specialization and repetition. This is true for all human endeavors. Swimmers swim thousands of laps to perfect a stroke, a student recites multiplication tables to learn to multiply, and a great surgeon performs hundreds of surgeries to master her craft. A neurosurgeon, said, "You don't want to be the first guy to get your cabbage worked on." Yes, but in most IT departments today, complex surgeries are done for the first time by people who read the book the night before.

A simple question posed to surgeons, the research shows, can often separate the talented from the average: How often do you do this? Research has established that busy hospitals generally deliver better care. But recent work adds more detail, citing the specific risks patients face in the hands of low-volume surgeons, who don't frequently and regularly perform certain procedures. "It is now a very legitimate question to ask a surgeon: How much experience with a procedure do you have? What are your complication rates?" Do we ask the same of our operations staff? How many times have the operations staff upgraded from Release 1 to Release 2?

Some surgeons are convinced that measuring patient volume alone is too crude a measure for grading surgeons. But increasingly, the profession sees constant repetition as key to mastering complex surgeries. "The more often I do a procedure, the more I fall into a standard routine," said a vascular surgeon who performs a procedure to clear a key artery of blockages. "Then, if I encounter something out of the ordinary, I'm quicker to recognize it and correct it." Many studies of recovery from computer outages show the outage is often extended because the operator has seen something out of the ordinary. Since it may be the first time they've seen the issue, they don't know how to react.

So what's a high degree of repetition? In one recent study high volume meant 40 or more surgical procedures annually. Consider a corporation's system, network, and database and application operations teams. How many times a week have they performed a particular procedure? Is the procedure even written down? Can it be repeated? The good news is that if a process can be repeated hundreds of times it can be automated. And computers are far better and lower cost than people. But it all starts with specialization.

7 Current Technology

While transaction processing has automated many back-office functions what is the technology we've applied to our all-important service businesses? Simple answer: Phone a Friend. How many times have any of us started with the help desk, been put on hold, routed to another person, repeated our requests, put on hold again as the individual goes to phone a friend – hoping to find the information – and remember 99.9% of the time the information is there. What we're using is the usage of a human network to find fragmented pieces of information – sometimes successfully, sometimes not (Fig. 4).

The business community has identified this same fragmentation problem. In Larry Ellison's Oracle OpenWorld 2004 keynote address, he noted the irony that for just $19 per month that you can subscribe to a news service and get information from as far away as Iraq at your fingertips, but you may "spend seven-hundred million on your business systems, and you can't get basic information on your business" such as "how much you sold yesterday," or "how many customers" you have or "how

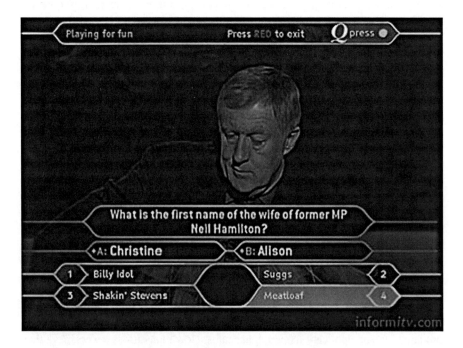

Fig. 4. Current technology: phone a friend

much did I spend yesterday?" Larry concluded that "the data fragmentation problem was the biggest problem we faced," with our data residing on many different databases. While creating single data schemas, warehouses, or data marts are a partial solution to the problem, the Internet has shown us the power of search, while not precise enough to process transactions, can change the way we service customers.

8   Towards a Service Cloud: Search Not SQL-Based Apps

The first generations of business software have delivered enormous value in reducing the cost of transaction processing. But transactional systems are a small part of our world of work. In fact, most transactional systems automate those simple tasks easily done by computers (e.g., purchase-to-pay). But the hard tasks of diagnosing a problem, making a recommendation, or tuning a solution is today supported by very little software. To comprehend the scale of the solution required – take a look at the Amazon.com website and see how much of the site is devoted to transaction processing. Hint: it's the little shopping cart in the upper right hand corner. If service is information, and service is about delivering known information in a personalized way – then search will play an important role

Today's surface Web (which Google, Yahoo and others have indexed) is thought to contain ten billion pages; or somewhere on the order of 25–50 terabytes of information. But this surface Web of less than 100 terabytes pales in comparison to the deep Web of information contained in every business. How deep is it? Consider that 1,030 petabytes (a petabyte is 1,000 terabytes) of hard disk capacity was shipped in the fourth quarter of 2006. The simple math says the deep Web is, at a minimum, 10,000 times the size of the surface Web. Sales, support, HR, purchasing, and manufacturing information are all locked up in relational databases, document management systems, and file systems all around the world. While seeing or indexing the information is one thing, the challenge is finding the relevant information. Eric Schmidt, CEO of Google, speaking at the annual conference of the Association of National Advertisers said it could take "300 years to index all the world's information and make it searchable".

The opportunity to mine this deep Web has not been lost on numerous companies. Google launched their Enterprise Appliance in 2002 and, every year since, has produced a major new release. Today they are deployed in over 9,000 sites around the world. Independent companies like Fast, which was acquired by Microsoft for over $1B, and Autonomy, have both focused on the challenges of enterprise search. While these efforts have all been successful, enterprise search in 2009 is today probably only a $500M business. This is small when compared to the SQL database business, which today exceeds $10B annually. So why is there such a big gap? Perhaps the answer lies in tracing the history of SQL. Oracle was the most successful at commercializing SQL and by 1987 was generating $100M a year.

But relational database technology has no intrinsic business value (it's just cool technology) and it wasn't until the advent of enterprise SQL-based applications like

Remedy, Peoplesoft, SAP, Siebel, and many more to make the technology useful to business.

So if the pattern is to repeat itself, we need to understand what it means to have search-based applications. John Lervick, who founded FAST, said "Google has been good and bad for search. Good because they made search important; bad because they've made everyone think it's a search bar. Search can be so much more if you think of it as a technology platform." So what might these search-based applications look like?

Just like SQL-based applications attempt to standardize business processes, search-based applications will need to standardize language. While finding known information in the Deep Web would be difficult assuming you had to index and search the entire Deep Web, a search-based app could segment just a portion of the network and thru explicit and implicit means establish a language. Anyone who's joined a new group or a new company knows the first 6 weeks is spent trying to figure out acronyms and common terms that are used in a unique way with your team, group, or tribe. Once we know the key concepts, words and phrases we become part of the tribe and can collaborate and contribute. Search based applications establish a language usage can improve.

Information we make available and the powerful languages we develop using search based applications are critical enablers - but, as we have also learned, service is also about specialization and expertise. The quality, currency and relevance of information and ultimately the service we deliver depends on the contribution of experts. John Lervick's point is that Google leads people to conclude that search is passive. Service isn't. Therefore, while our applications need be organized around information that's personal and provide a language to connect to our customers, they must also be write enabled.

Therefore, while it is critical to understand that 90% of the time we are spent searching, we also need to participate using the same processes and system. Therefore, this class of service must integrate read and write.

9   Service Is People + Information

As most business software has been transactional by nature, people are often on the sideline, perhaps clicking an approval button or filing a document, but rarely contributing or qualifying information. But a service-centric business needs to find a way to bring people and information together. Systems like this have the capability to be extremely powerful. Again, we'll draw on an example from the consumer Internet: Flickr (www.flickr.com). Flickr with no photos, no information, is just a random chat room. Flickr with no people would just be a photo repository. But Flickr is much more because it was engineered to bring people and information together.

This particularly relevant in business software. Early on in the life of business software, two conditions exist: the software is changing frequently to repair defects

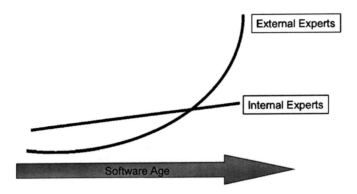

Fig. 5. Number of internal versus external experts as software ages

and provide enhancements; and second, the expertise in how to fix a defect or how the business process works exists only inside the group or organization that created the software. While this might be true in year one, by year five, the world is different. As software matures, there are fewer meaningful defects and little need for new enhancements. In addition, as software matures, all of the expertise migrates outside the organization that created the software to users who know the challenges of servicing and using the software. In addition, as software matures, all of the expertise migrates outside the organization that created the software to users who know the challenges of servicing and using the software as shown in Fig. 5.

The point where external and internal expertise intersects is a tipping point that moves power and information from a small internal community to the much larger external community located around the world. To turn this into numbers consider that the number of experts registered on Oracle's Technology Network exceed 5,000,000 – that's easily 1,000 times more people than the number of experts inside of Oracle. With the Internet we have the ability for people to be known, to be notorious. Nowhere has this been more evident than in the explosive growth of Facebook – the first application where we can be known. But this is only the beginning. In the future each of us a simple LinkedIn resume will be a simple representation of our skills. Instead there will be many more ways in which you can judge my work and my skills based on my contributions. Whether this becomes videos, blogs, tweets, webinars, podcasts or other vehicles we will all value an individual by the contributions they make and their ability to communicate those contributions in the context of their specialization.

Furthermore as software matures, defect rates fall and service information related issues increase as software transitions through a typical lifecycle as shown in Fig. 6. This must be the pattern for successful software. Consider at this stage of its maturity the Oracle DBMS has very few defects, but given its wide deployment there are millions of questions regarding how to use and configure the software for optimal performance, security and reliability.

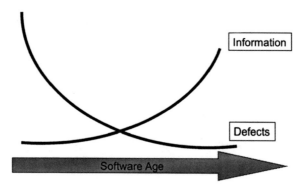

Fig. 6. Software defect and information requests vs. software age

10   Summary

The Great Depression lasted between 5 and 10 years. While we all hope this recession will be short it indeed may have presented us with an opportunity to transform product-led business to service-led business. For the first time, with the advent of the ability to bring large amounts of high quality information and experts together on the Internet (aka cloud), we can change how everything from software to health care may be serviced. Service is not the execution of repetitive tasks, better performed by computers. Service is information. Service is information, relevant to you. Service is bringing the right specialists together with the right information at the right time. We have the technology; we have the lessons from the Consumer Internet. If we can bring the components together into service networks and systems every business can be re-shaped for the twenty-first century. To borrow the words of the ancient Roman philosopher, Horace: "Adversity has the effect of eliciting talents, which in prosperous circumstances would have lain dormant". Will you now take your talents in this nuclear winter and move your business to a service-led business?

References

Diamond, J. (2005) Guns, Germs, and Steel: The Fates of Human Societies, Norton, W. W. & Company, New York

Towards an Operations Strategy for the Infusion of Product-Centric Services into Manufacturing

Tim S. Baines

Aston University Business School, Birmingham, B4 7ET

Howard W. Lightfoot

Innovative Manufacturing Systems Centre, Cranfield University, Cranfield MK43 0AL, UK

Abstract The work in this chapter is concerned with product-centric servitization. This is where a portfolio of services are formed and integrated to support product availability and use. Such servitization can be a valuable source of revenue for a manufacturer, yet little attention has been given to the configuration of the wider operations strategy that needs to be in place to deliver integrated products and services successfully. Therefore, the purpose of this chapter is to put forward a generic set of characteristics for such operations. Our intention is that these characteristics will be valuable to practitioners contemplating sophisticated forms of servitization, as they suggest the likely and significant changes that will be needed to the operations strategy of a conventional manufacturing organisation.

Keywords Servitization, service operations, service marketing, service systems, operations management, framework, service science

1 Introduction

Servitization, or servicizing as it's sometimes referred to (White et al. 1999), is now widely recognised as the process of creating value by adding services to products. Our particular interest in this chapter is product-centric servitization. This is the term we give to the phenomena where a portfolio of services are formed and integrated to support product availability and use. Examples in practice are Rolls-Royce's 'Power by the Hour' and their more inclusive 'TotalCare' contracts. Although such servitization can be a valuable source of revenues for a manufacturer, and can be somewhat more resilient to economic downturns, full attention has yet to be given to the configuration of the wider operations strategy needed to deliver integrated products and services successfully. Indeed, servitization by a conventional manufacturer principally presents challenges for service design, organisation strategy and organisation transformation (Vandermerwe and Rada 1988; Wise and Baumgartner 1999; Oliva and Kallenberg 2003). Unfortunately, the research covering the transition from pure producer to product-service provider in business markets is still immature and in need of more empirical research (Jacob and Ulaga 2008). Therefore, this chapter considers the implementation of Service Systems and puts forward a framework which captures the key practices of a generic operations strategy for the efficient and effective delivery of integrated products and services.

Some specialised frameworks already exist that deal with combining products and services. In the PSS literature, for example, authors such as Mont (2000), Tukker (2004) and Wong (2004) propose classification frameworks with, pure product manufacture being positioned at one end of a continuum, which moves through various forms of product-service systems, to the opposite extreme of pure service provision. Similarly, Shostack (1982) uses a framework with pure product and pure service at the extremes with the 'middle' ground being various combinations of product and service mix. The framework proposed by Tukker (see Fig. 1) is typical of these forms of framework, focusing on the features and examples of various product-service combinations, and so helping to illustrate the alternatives available. Limitations only become apparent when manufacturers seek to understand in detail how best to configure production and support operations for a combined product-service offering.

Detailed frameworks do exist for production and support operations independently. Production centred frameworks are typified by, for example, Hayes and Wheelwright (1984) and Hill (2000), who illustrate how a jobbing production

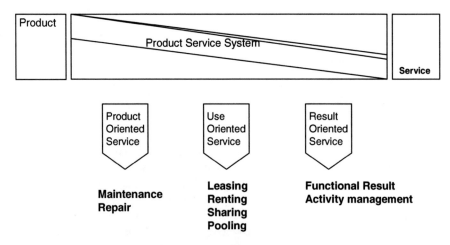

Fig. 1. PSS classifications (Tukker 2004)

structure should differ from project, batch, line or continuous processing. Likewise, the service operations literature suggests a number of frameworks for classifying services (see Cook et al. 1999 for a review). These are typified by Collier and Meyer (1998) who propose a Service Positioning Matrix (SPM) to establish a delivery system based on the nature of the required customer service. To a manufacturer such frameworks provide a relatively detailed description of the required configuration for either product or service delivery, but offer little guidance for those concerned with delivering an effective and efficient integrated product and service offering. Here, there is insufficient detail about the integration of production and support operations (see Heineke and Davis 2007).

The research in this chapter therefore questions what form a generic operations (production and support) strategy should take for a manufacturer to be successful in delivering integrated products and services. Through a synthesis of existing literature, and an in-depth case study of a leading manufacturer, we propose a framework that posits an appropriate set of operations practices. Such a framework should help manufacturers to fully appreciate the likely implications of servitization on their own internal organisation and immediate supply-chain. However, much is still to be done to improve the reliability and resolution of this framework, and so our hope is that we will also help to stimulate and guide further research into the operations strategy for servitized manufacture. This chapter is structured to first set out the key definitions and literature directly associated with servitization of manufacturing. We then begin to develop our framework by exploring how to best categorise the key characteristics of an operations strategy, and this subsequently leads to populating our structure with evidence from theory and practice. The framework itself is then presented. Finally, the contribution of this chapter is summarised and directions for future research are laid out.

Section 2 considers the emergence of the research on the provision of services by manufacturers and looks at five clusters of research communities. Section 3 explains the methodology for the development of the framework structure and the selection and design of the case study work used to populate some areas of the framework. Section 4 considers the structural and infra-structural characteristics of an operations strategy to deliver product-centric services. Section 5 considers the framework that posits the characteristics of a successful operations strategy that complements a servitization strategy and comments on its novelty and limitations.

2 The Emergence of Research on the Provision of Services by Manufacturers

There are five key clusters or communities of researchers currently addressing the servitization of manufacture. To provide a suitable context for our operations strategy framework, we start by providing a short summary of the activities in each of these communities.

2.1 Servitization Community

The first use of the term servitization in a context of manufacturing operations was by Vandemerwe and Rada in a 1988 European Management Journal article titled 'Adding Value by Adding Services'. They defined servitization as "the increased offering of fuller market packages or 'bundles' of customer focussed combinations of goods, services, support, self-service and knowledge in order to add value to core product offerings" (p. 314). Here, it is important to distinguish between manufacturers who offer services reactively, as a necessity in their markets (services as order qualifiers), and services that proactively form the basis of value creation within a manufacturers competitive strategy (services as order winners). It is only this latter case that we term servitization.

Since the term servitization was first coined, there has been a growing output of articles/papers addressing the 'servitization' of businesses in managerial, business practitioner and operations literature. These have addressed areas such as service business expansion (e.g. Wise and Baumgartner 1999; Martin and Horne 1992; Oliva and Kallenberg 2003; Gebauer and Friedli 2005), solutions provision (e.g. Galbraith 2002; Miller et al. 2002; Windahl and Lakemond 2006; Davies et al. 2006), after-sale marketing (e.g. Cohen et al. 2006; Cohen 2007), service profitability (e.g. Samli et al. 1992; Anderson and Narus 1995; Gebauer et al. 2006 and new business models (Edvardsson et al. 2008).

Servitization is frequently purported to come about in an attempt to satisfy financial drivers. The provision of services is seen to induce repeat-sales by intensifying contact opportunities with the customer and also put the supplier in the right position to offer other products or services (Mathieu 2001; Malleret 2006). Finally, by offering services, companies gain insight into their customers' true needs and are able to develop more tailored offerings. Examples in the literature of leading practice in the adoption of servitization are focused on larger companies supplying high-value capital equipment such as Alstom and ABB (Miller et al. 2002; Davies 2004), Thales Training and Simulation (Mulholland 2000; Davies et al. 2004) and Rolls-Royce Aerospace (Howells 2000; Baines et al. 2009). These demonstrate how traditionally based manufacturing companies have moved their position in the value-chain from product manufacturers to providing customers with 'desired outcomes' through integrated solutions that may also include the use of multi-vendor products.

2.2 Product-Service Systems Community

The term Product-Service System (PSS) originated in Northern Europe, principally The Netherlands and Scandinavia, in the late 1990s (Goedkoop et al. 1999). A PSS is a specific type of value-proposition or business model that inherently focuses on fulfilling a final need, demand or function (Tukker and Tischner 2006). It is a special case in servitization, which values asset performance or utilisation rather than ownership (Baines et al. 2007). A PSS achieves differentiation through the integration of product and services that provide value in use to the customer and can release the customer from the responsibilities of asset ownership (Mont 2001).

A successful PSS needs to be designed at the systemic level from the client perspective, requires early involvement with the customer and changes to the organisational structures of the provider (Mont 2000; Manzini et al. 2001). While some methods and practices are proposed for designing and operating a PSS (Luiten et al. 2001; Maxwell and van der Vorst 2003), these tend to lack the pedigree that is formed through careful evaluation in practice The principal barriers to the adoption of PSS are positioned at both sides of the dyad: customers may not be enthusiastic about ownerless consumption (Meijkamp 2000; Mont 2003; Wong 2004), and manufacturers may be concerned with pricing, absorbing risks and changes to the organisation (Goedkoop et al. 1999). A diverse range of PSS examples can be found in the literature with some demonstrating economic success but most tending to emphasise potential environmental and social gains (Oman 2003).

2.3   Services Marketing Community

In the first issue of the Journal of Marketing, a review of research being undertaken at that time indicated that much of the work focussed upon the exchange and distribution of commodities (Taylor 1936). Over the intervening years the emphasis of marketing moved from economic exchange to marketing management with a focus on 'satisfying the customer' coming to the fore (e.g. Drucker 1954; Levitt 1960). In the following decade the marketing mix (e.g. Kotler 1967) – or the 4Ps – of product, price, place and promotion added further granularity to the way in which a firm could adjust its offering independently of market factors to satisfy their customers. In the late 1970s there was acknowledgement that the marketing of services was different to products (Shostack 1977). Furthermore, products and services are often inseparable and the sale of a product would lead to a relationship where services could be sold over an extended period of time (Levitt 1983) moving marketing from transactional to relational exchange and an acknowledgement that goods and services needed to be treated differently.

The work of Shostack (1977) and Levitt (1983) acted as the precursors of two new streams of marketing – services marketing and relationship marketing. Services marketing scholars argued that the marketing of goods and services is different as services are intangible, heterogeneous, inseparable and perishable, IHIP (Fisk et al. 1993). Conversely, the relationship marketing literature is founded on the premise that competition is between firms and that exchange between actors increasingly has a temporal, relational dimension as opposed to being solely about discrete transactions (Morgan and Hunt 1994). In the early twenty-first century, the validity of the 4Ps was being challenged for its lack of recognition of marketing as an innovating and adaptive force Lovelock and Gummesson (2004) challenged the use of IHIP as a core paradigm for service marketing and offered the alternative perspective that marketing exchanges not resulting in the transfer of ownership from seller to buyer are fundamentally different from those that do, and that these services offer benefits through access or temporary possession not ownership. At the same time a service-centred dominant logic was proposed (Vargo and Lusch 2004), based on the exchange of intangibles, specialist skills, knowledge and processes where value is defined by and co-created with the customer rather than embedded in output. Ambler (2005) considers the propositions from Vargo and Lusch and Lovelock and Gummerson simply as alternative perspectives on marketing.

2.4   Service Operations Community

In the paper 'The Industrialisation of Services' (1976) Theodore Levitt points out that, even at that time, the service sector of industrialised nations had been in the ascent for almost three quarters of a century. He describes service industrialisation through hard technologies, soft technologies and hybrid technologies. Sasser (1976) at this time points out that the balancing of service supply and demand is not easy and that success is achieved through managing capacity. The 'Service Factory' concept (Chase and Garvin 1989) is seen as a key contribution in reversing the trend in operations management literature, which focussed on manufacturing based concepts in a services environment (Voss 1992). The 1980s focus on the quality of products and service resulted in goods quality being measured by marketers but quality in service was largely undefined and so SERVQUAL emerged as a survey instrument to measure service quality in marketing and operational contexts (Chase and Apte 2007). The classification, positioning and delivery strategy for services has been addressed by authors. For example Schmenner (1995) suggests a matrix based on customer interaction and labour intensity; Silvestro (1999) propose service positioning along a process diagonal; Collier and Meyer (1998) use four service quadrants based on labour intensity and customer contact and Kellog and Winter (1995) introduce a service process/service package (defined by the degree of customisation) positioning matrix. Heineke and Davis (2007) discuss the emergence of service operations management and, go on to argue, that applying manufacturing operations concepts to the management of service operations is limiting and that there is a need for a trans disciplinary approach appropriately suited to the characteristics of services industries, Chase and Apte (2007) expect that in the future "Operations Management concepts will be applied to service settings rather than the factory" (p. 384).

2.5   Service Science Community

Originating in the IT sector, service science is a relatively new interdisciplinary concept for services. It sets out to embrace and integrate all communities that deal with services. Service science, aims to create the basis for systematic service innovation by combining organization and human understanding with business and technological understanding to explain the origins and growth of service systems (Cesborough 2005). Hence it focuses, not merely on one aspect of service, but rather on service as a system of interacting parts that include people, technology, and business (Chesborough and Spohrer 2006). Service Science is the study of service systems and the co-creation of value in complex configurations of resources (Vargo et al. 2008). It is a melding of technology with an understanding of business processes and organisation. As such, service science draws on ideas from a number of existing disciplines including computer science, engineering cognitive science, economics, organizational behaviour, human resources management, marketing, and operations research. It aims to integrate them into a coherent science of service. Spohrer et al. (2007) suggest that service systems could provide theory and practice around service innovation. Vargo et al. (2008) see an intersection between service science and service-dominant logic. This growing stream of marketing thought is seen by them as foundational to service science and to the study of value creation in service systems.

3   Methodology for Framework Development

The specific question underpinning this chapter is "what general form should an operations strategy take to support a manufacturer in the efficient and effective delivery of integrated products and services?" This has been addressed through two stages of analysis. First, the general structure of the framework has been established through reflection on previous contributions by researchers. Then, this structure has been used to guide the collection and synthesis, of data from literature and practice, and so form the completed framework. Our knowledge of practice has been gained through an in-depth case study of a leading servitized manufacturer. In this section we describe the process of structuring the framework, and then provide an overview of the case study methodology.

3.1   Developing the Framework Structure

Our approach to establishing the constructs of the operations strategy framework was done in three parts. First, the scope of the framework was decided upon. Existing frameworks, such as those provided by Hill (2000) and Hayes and

Wheelwright (1984), all illustrate the importance of having a clearly defined target and purpose. For example, Hill's framework is only relevant when positioning differing production demands (e.g. low, medium and high volume) against types of production system (e.g. jobbing, batch, line). The target for our framework is operations strategy for the integrated delivery of products and services. For example, in the aerospace sector we would see Rolls-Royce' with their 'TotalCare' offering as a typical audience. This helps to illustrate the distinction between the servitization framework developed here and general production operations and service operations. However, difficulties can arise because each of these categories can themselves be subdivided. For example, under the production category we can have batch, mass, etc. (Hayes and Wheelwright 1984; Hill 2000). Likewise, under services we can have professional, service shop, mass, etc. (Silvestro 1999; Collier and Meyer 1998). We have therefore been mindful to position our framework at a level of abstraction that allows a distinction between pure service and production operations, but not to be so detailed as to attempt to delve into the more subtle differences between mass production and mass services. Such detail would be too complex with the current knowledge of this topic.

Armed with a clear understanding of the scope, the second part in the development process came about by reflecting on the literature about strategy formulation. It is apparent that from Ford (1922), through to the work on Lean systems (Womack et al. 1990), the starting point of operations strategy formulation is to understand customer value requirements. Researchers such as Schroeder and Lahr (1990), Mills et al. (1996) and Hill (2000), all propose processes that begin with customer value dimensions using measures such as cost, quality and timeliness. Hence, understanding the differing dimensions of value was a key stage in developing the framework. Some broad appreciation of how value propositions differ is gained by reflecting on how businesses create value. Thompson (1967) suggests that value can be created through transformation (e.g. raw material), problem solving (e.g. consulting) and mediation (e.g. banking). Thus value creation can be both transactional and/or relational. Here, customers of a pure product may value the ownership of the artefact, whereas customers of a pure service may, on the other hand, tend to value the functional result. For a product-centric offering the focus is likely to be a blend of transactional activities (to deal with the initial sale of the product) and customer relationship activities to deal with the initial product design, use, and return at end of life. Further refinement in understanding the value proposition is gained through the work of Hill (2000) who emphasizes the importance of order winning criteria. Products tend to win or lose orders on measures such as product specification, quality conformance, and delivery, whereas services tend to be more biased toward relationships and speed of response. For a servitized product offering, the measures become a subtle blend, changing from transactional as a product is initially sold, to relationship as the product is supported in use.

The final part was then to decide upon the range of characteristics that an operations strategy should cover. An indication of the appropriate categories is again provided by reviewing existing classification systems for manufacture (e.g. Hayes and Wheelwright 1984; Hill 2000). There are a number of these, with little to suggest that any one classification is more rigorous and complete, but agreement is generally high amongst them (Anderson et al. 1989). This led us to consider that an operations strategy should be defined in terms of 12 sets of characteristics, namely; Process and Technology, Capacity, Facilities, Vertical Integration, Product Range, Planning and Control, Human Resources, Quality Control, New Product Introduction, Performance Measurement, Supplier Relations, and Customer Relations.

The outcome of this development process was the basic structure of the framework. We had established that the scope should be on integrated product-service offerings, that the value proposition for these is based on both transaction and relationship dimensions, and that the associated operations strategy can be expressed in terms of 12 characteristics. Completion of this framework required these 12 characteristics to be determined, yet there is limited evidence within the existing literature of the form these should take. Therefore, our approach has been to study, in depth, an organisation that succinctly fits the scope of our framework, and then by contrasting their practices against lessons in the wider literature, establish the required characteristics. The following section describes the chosen case study.

3.2   Case Study Design and Selection

A detailed understanding of practice has been gained through an in-depth study of an organisation that designs, builds and delivers integrated product-service offerings. A semi-structured data collection protocol was developed, and this focussed on determining how and why the case company had begun to deliver servitized offerings and the challenges this was posing for their manufacturing and wider operations. A series of guiding interview questions were identified. Typically these were centred on:

- How does your company do business, and what do your customers value?
- How is this value measured, and what performance is key to success?
- How have you organised your operations to deliver this performance?
- Has such a strategy caused issues to arise, and what are they?

The choice of case company was critical to this study. We sought to investigate a manufacturer who has a track-record of achieving business success through providing a portfolio of product related services. Therefore, the case study organisation is a UK based OEM that designs and manufactures high value capital equipment for the power, defence and aerospace markets. For reasons of confidentiality and in order to give us greater freedom to discuss our results and findings, we refer to the company as 'ServitCo'. The company, which operates globally, today generates over 50% of revenues from the provision of services that are closely coupled to its products.

Data collected was based on interviews across the organisation. These included personnel from Design Engineering, Global Component Repair, Service Innovation/ Marketing, Projects, After Market Services, Global Component Repair, Manufacturing Operations, Customer Services and Supply chain. Each interview lasted between 2 and 3 h and was recorded and subsequently transcribed. The interviews were then coded and analysed by the same team of researchers and, in this way, the practices that the organisation used to deliver its integrated product and service offering was reliably established. The final stage of analysis was to contrast these practices against those given in the literature, and to reason the most appropriate practice for each of the 12 sets of operations characteristics. The following section of this chapter describes the process.

4   Formation of Operations Strategy Characteristics

The framework is intended to capture the general characteristics of product-centric servitized operations strategy (see Table 1). To illustrate these characteristics, we have shown them along side production operations and service operations. Production operations focus on the physical transformation of materials into tangible goods and tend to be configured on conventional manufacturing principles. Service operations focus on delivering experiential transformation for the customer through facilitation and mediation. However, for product-centric servitization, the operations strategy will require a subtle combination of these two extremes across the structure and infrastructure of an organisation. We consider these in terms of 'Structural' charac- teristics of facilities, capacity, process technology, planning/control, and supply chain positioning, together with the 'Infra-structural' characteristics of product/ service range, new product/service introduction, quality control, human resources, performance measurement, customer and supplier relations. For each our unit of analysis is the Strategic Business Unit (SBU).

4.1   Structural Characteristics

The choice of the facility in manufacturing operations typically includes the type of production site, its location and specialisation. This topic has been considered widely, from Henry Ford in the early part of the twentieth century (see Ford 1922), through to the work of Toyota in the 1990s (see Womack et al. 1990). When con- sidering such contributions, the popular production operations strategy is to exploit economies of scale by bringing together and centralising manufacturing activities in large factories. These are located to exploit resource availability. Service opera- tions differ. In answer to Chase's question in his article of 1978, "where does the customer fit in a service operation?", the facilities for service operations tend to focus more on accommodating customer's expectations, physical and

Table 1. Framework for production, product-centric servitized and service operations

Characteristics		Type of operations		
		Product focussed operations	Product-centric servitized operations	Services focussed operations
	Unit of Analysis	*SBU*	*SBU*	*SBU*
	Type of company being considered	Larger and somewhat conventional volume production	Product sold with platform of bespoke services	Larger and somewhat conventional services
	Examples of associated products and services	Bosch, Goodrich, Smiths Medical	Lexus, Rolls-Royce (TotalCare), Toshiba Medical	Hertz, Easyjet, BUPA
	Principal delivery system	Product focused delivery system	Integrated product and service delivery system	Services focused delivery system
	Nature of the delivery system	Tends towards physical transformation of materials into tangible goods	Tends towards physical transformation of materials into tangible assets, sold along with support services, to deliver functional capability to the customer	Tends towards creating experiential transformation through facilitation and mediation
Scope	Typical scope and capabilities of the delivery system	Design, development, procurement, production, test and distribution	Design, development, production, test, monitoring, maintenance, repair refurbishment, upgrading, and disposal	Design, co-development, delivery, facilitation and evaluation

(continued)

Table 1. (continued)

Characteristics		Type of operations		
		Product focussed operations	Product-centric servitized operations	Services focussed operations
Characteristics of value	Business model: *how the company tends to do business*	Tends towards transactional based:	Tends to be based on a blend of transactional and relationship:	Tend towards relationship based:
		Focusing on producing and selling material artefacts	Focusing on providing an integrated product and service offering that delivers value in use	Focusing on delivery of services
	Value Proposition: *what the customer tends to value*	Tends to focus on the ownership of an artefact	Tends to focus on product availability, performance, along with risk and reward sharing	Tends to focus on the delivery of functional result
	Order winning criteria of the customer	Features of product	Features of product and service	Features of services
		Purchase cost of product	Total cost of ownership	Cost of services
		Specification and Quality conformance	Availability of product and capacity to deliver services	Quality conformance of services
		Delivery of product		Delivery of services
	Typical value metrics for the internal delivery systems	Cost of production	Product life-cycle costs	Cost of service delivery
		Product conformance	Product conformance and service delivery	Conformance to customer requirements
		Delivery performance	System responsiveness	Availability and service delivery performance

(continued)

Characteristics of operations				
Structural	1. Process and technology	Tend to exploit automation to deliver high levels of product conformance and volume with minimal worker intervention	Tend to exploit a range of technologies, throughout operations, to achieve efficiency in production and effectiveness in service delivery	Tend to exploit largely information technologies, such as databases and Integrated communications, to enhance customer interaction
	2. Capacity	Tend to match capacity to demand, controlling and balancing, in order to maximise utilisation of expensive resources	Tend to experience varying demand signals at multiple customer 'touch points' and so need to operate with differing levels of capacity utilisation	Tend to accommodate fluctuations in demand by running at lower levels of capacity utilisation
	3. Facilities	Tend to be large factories, arranged around similar product to exploit economies of scale, and often located to exploit resource availability	Tend to combine both centralised manufacture, but mainly focusing on product final assembly and test, along with multiple field facilities for maintenance and repair located close to market	Tend to be smaller, multiple facilities, that are client friendly, located close to market, and help to impress and reinforce relationships
	4. Supply chain positioning	Tend to be vertically integrated where such control can help to maximise quality conformance and minimise cost	Tend to retain vertical integration in product manufacture and a range of closely integrated partners to deliver services	Tend to focus on only the brokerage of knowledge and capacity necessary to respond to customer requirements
	5. Planning and control	Tend to focus on replenishment systems, sometimes large and complex, that minimise stock holding costs	Tend to focus on the optimisation of product availability	Tend to rely on project management techniques and individuals themselves to provide responsive service to customer

(continued)

Table 1. (continued)

Infrastructural	6. Human resources	Tend to use lower skilled workers through minimisation of intervention and well defined production routines	Tend to need workers with high levels of product knowledge and relationship development capability	Tend to be highly skilled workers with particularly good communication skills with which to demonstrate value to customer
	7. Quality control	Tend to have systems that measure and monitor quality conformance throughout production in order to minimise scrap materials and components	Tend to use product assurance methods combined with customer satisfaction assessments	Tend to rely on individuals developing acceptability criteria and judging performance against these
	8. Product/service range	Tend to vary in size, though smaller product ranges are preferred to help maximise production efficiencies	Tend have limited product range combined with 'bundles' of supporting services	Tend to vary in size, though smaller ranges of services are preferred to help maximise delivery efficiencies
	9. New product/ service introduction	Tend to use centralised capabilities to fully design and test new products, prior to their entry into production, in order to minimise in-market 'disturbances'	Tend to used centralised capabilities for product design, taking particular account of maintenance and repair, and that complement services co-created with the customer	Tend to be co-created, tested and refined, with customers in the field
	10. Performance measurement	Tend to use parameters such as - 'to specification', 'to cost' and 'on time' delivery	Tend to use product availability, response time and customer satisfaction	Tend to use customer satisfaction metrics
	11. Supplier relations	Tend to apply direct and forcefully leverage to suppliers to minimise input costs	Tend to integrate internal and external supply chains into the delivery process to achieve cost effective flexibility in supply	Tend to expect same level of responsiveness and commitment from suppliers as they would give to their own customers
	12. Customer relations	Tend to have limited interaction with customers choosing, instead, to invest energies internally to improve efficiencies	Tend to have strong interaction with customers through relationships based on product availability and performance	Tend to invest heavily in developing and maintain relationships with customers

psychological needs, and enhancing the customer experience. Product-centric servitized operations appear to be a hybrid of these two strategies. Evidence from case study work suggests that these organisations need to locate themselves to be, primarily, responsive to customer requirements, but then also be efficient in product manufacture. This can be achieved through a combination of centralised manufacturing focusing on product final assembly and test, along with multiple field facilities for maintenance and repair, located close to the customer's operations.

Capacity in production operations, should be matched to demand, in order to ensure the effective utilisation of expensive resources. However, lower capacity utilisation is accepted within service operations in order to be able to meet peak demand in high contact systems or conversely to 'chase demand' in low contact ('service factory') situations. Sasser (1976), highlights the complexity of the matching of supply and demand in service industries. Case study work of Product-centric servitized operations, indicates that demand signals emanate from multiple customer 'touch-points', each potentially generating varying capacity demand and requiring differing forms of response from the service delivery organisation (see Fig. 2). For example, maintenance and repair activities need to be configured to respond to unscheduled demand, such as unforeseen component failures, and so lower levels of capacity utilisation are necessary to deal with variability. Whereas, in the traditional product build and test organisation, which experiences more stable demand cycles, a greater level of capacity utilisation is achievable.

The automation of processes in order to reduce worker intervention and achieve high levels of product conformance is a common theme in manufacturing system design for conventional production operations. However in service operations, processes embody the use of intensive, mediating and long-linked technologies and use IT systems to enable higher levels of customer optimisation with minimal customer influence. Authors such as Quinn et al. (1990) suggest that in product centric

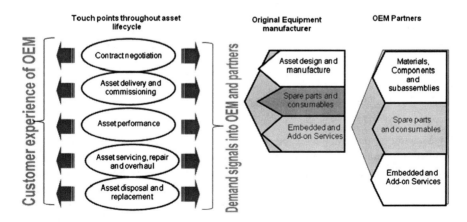

Fig. 2. Lifecycle touch points and demand signals within a servitized manufacturer

operations, processes and technologies should be built around service delivery requirements. These should be facilitated through good integrative information systems to allow enhancement of company knowledge and management processes for best practice.

Automated master production scheduling, planning and control systems that are linked to markets and processes for effectiveness (Hill 2000) are generally used in production operations. In contrast in service operations, forecasting is short-time or long-time output oriented (Chase 1978) and relies on individuals and project planning techniques to respond to customer requirements. Case study work indicates that the service organisations within product-centric servitized operations recognise that, when the emphasis is on product availability and delivery of functionality to the customer then the need to be 'more joined up' between the delivery arm, commercial arm and the customer service groups becomes much more imperative. Here, operations planning and control systems encompass hardware manufacture and maintenance, service processing and data storage, and decision making.

Davies (2004) notes that successful providers of integrated product-service solutions are becoming less dependent on broad based in-house capabilities. Producing the Model T earlier in the twentieth century, Henry Ford used a vertically integrated organisation to maximise quality conformance, minimise cost, and ensure control over material supplies. Nowadays improvements in supplier capabilities, a focus on core competences and greater use of outsourcing (Baines et al. 2005) has changed the apparent structure of supply chains. None the less the underlying concerns with cost and quality have largely endured in traditional manufacturing organisations. However, service operations tend to focus more on providing a platform of capabilities that deliver a complete solution to the customer. Case study work suggests that product-centric servitized operations use a combination of practices, where the manufacture of products still reflects a desire to control costs and quality, and so that part of the organisation remains relatively vertically integrated. However, to achieve effective and efficient service delivery, organisations realise the need to change the way that they interrelate (internally and externally) and as a result engage with partner organisations to assist in the delivery of services.

4.2   Infra-Structural Characteristics

Manufacturing efficiencies are best preserved by producing higher volumes of a limited product range. However, Hill's work on production operations (2000) shows that typically product ranges may vary greatly, from large in the case of project type build, to very narrow in mass production systems. In both production and service operations, organisations, therefore, tend to favour less variety. The extant literature in this area provides little guidance as to what to expect in a product-centric servitized operation. Case study work suggests that in this type of organisation we would tend to find a limited range of physical products that are closely combined with varying 'bundles' of supporting services, This 'menu' approach to service innovation can create problems since customers who remove service elements from a 'total package' are likely to expect some reduction in service charges, even though this potentially reduces the scalability of the service offering and can add to the overall cost of service delivery.

Typically traditional manufacturers decentralise product design activities into business units and use new product introduction methodologies such as set based, point based or concurrent engineering. Before release into the market place, new products are thoroughly designed and tested. In contrast, for service operations, Levitt (1981) argues, services can seldom be tried out, inspected or tested in advance of their introduction to the market and requires the development of customer trust and an understanding of customer habits and behaviour. Here, new services will be highly tailored to customer expectations and often co-developed with the customer. For product-centric servitized operations Miller et al. (2002) highlights the importance of the NPI process being client centric with solutions tailored to desirable client outcomes, Case study work showed that although a similar process to that in more conventional production is followed there is an increased emphasis on those design aspects impacting on service activities (e.g. maintenance and repair), which are integral to the overall product-service offering. This forces the organisation to think a lot more about products, their predictability and how they can be designed so that they are more customer friendly and meet the customer's expectations.

The most efficient production operations have introduced Lean Manufacturing techniques (Womack et al. 1990), where quality control is focussed on achieving product conformance and the minimisation of waste in materials and resource usage by using techniques, such as Statistical Process Control, Statistical Quality Control, Quality Circles, and Poke Yoke. Quality control systems in service operations need to cope with customers having a set of intangible requirements, which may exist at a range of levels of consciousness, forming part of the customer perception of an acceptable service (Morris and Johnson 1987). Measurement tends to be through individuals developing appropriate criteria and subjectively judging performance against these or in some cases surveying the customer. Through case study work, it appears that in product-centric servitized operations, the physical product quality tends to be controlled using traditional production techniques. However, service quality is a measure of a products availability to deliver functional performance for the customer and a product that is reliable, easy to maintain and quickly repaired is essential to the delivery of the level of service quality expected by customers.

In Ford's revolutionary approach to automotive manufacture, which has prevailed in large right up to the present day, the tasks of the assembly worker were de-skilled through the sub-division of labour and strictly defined and controlled production routines. This use of highly procedural production activities is evidenced in Toyota, widely recognised as the leading manufacturer of automobiles world-wide. In service operations, where there is high customer contact, value tends to be delivered through skilled workers who have good customer interface and communication capabilities. The workforce is a major part of the service product and the credibility of its expertise is fundamental and people must be able to identify with individual customers (Vandermerwe and Rada 1988). Case study work reveals that managers responsible for service provision within product-centric servitized operations consider that delivering services is difficult and requires people training, especially when services are linked to complex products. It needs people who are customer focussed and processes that work smoothly. Appropriate resources are not necessarily available internally and acquiring the expertise from outside the organisation is often necessary in order to take on more service [business] from customers. Workers are required who have both high levels of product knowledge and an ability to manage and develop ongoing customer relationships.

Performance measurement in traditional product operations uses criteria such as 'to cost', 'to specification' and 'delivery on time'. In contrast to service operations will tend to use criteria such as customer and employee satisfaction and business success. Morris and Johnson (1987) suggest that the perception of acceptable service varies from one customer to another since the customers view consists of many different interactions (service encounters) and each must be measured separately, and each depends on whether it is environmental, transactional or assistance-based. In product-centric servitized operations (Lewis et al. 2004) suggests that effective performance can be measured against criteria such as customer expectations of service (and hence product availability), co-location and speed of response. This view is supported by case study work where the organisation uses a 'disruption index' as measure of product availability and a 'resolved customer incidents' as a measure of speed of response and considers problem resolution to be a measure of agility and responsiveness. In addition its service operations units are located close to its customer's operations centres.

The relatively limited interaction with end customers in manufacturing operations is a consequence of the transactional nature of the business. In service operations, customer relationships do not begin and end with a single transaction and there is a stronger need to invest in developing and maintaining relationships with customers. Customer Relationship Management enables the building of stable, iterative and long term relationships. For product-centric servitized operations Davies (2006) suggests that customer facing units are necessary in these organisations having strong interactions with customers. Evidence from case study worked shows that at the interfaces between the company and the customer there was increasing evidence of responsive and agile service-centred behaviour.

'Partnering', although considered in many organisations as critical for efficient and effective production operations, faces challenges to its relative benefits (Lamming 1993) and power (Cox et al. 2001). The 'partnership' goal often adopted in service operations (Windahl et al. 2004) can however, generate an expectation that suppliers will provide the same responsiveness and commitment to the service provider as that received by service customers. Case study work highlighted problems in aligning the supply chain in a product-centric service provider to what the customer really wants. Aligning supplier relations in both internal and external supply chains and to partner with suppliers on a win/win basis was important to the effective delivery of the service offering. Internal 'functional silo' behaviours, along with a tendency to adopt forceful corporate leverage with external suppliers, however, had the potential to adversely impact their success.

5   Concluding Remarks

Servitization is now widely recognised as the innovation of a manufacturer's capabilities and processes to move from selling products and a few essential services, to competing on the basis of integrated products-service offerings. This chapter has formed a framework that posits the characteristics of a successful operations strategy that complements such servitization.

In summary, the framework illustrates that if a manufacturer, who has been traditionally production centric, chooses to follow a path towards product-centric servitization many of their practices are likely to need to change. First, their behaviour with customers will blend of both transactional (around the initial sale of the product) and relationship (around services supporting the use of the product). To support this, the internal operations will need to focus on; integration in the design of products and services; development of tightly focused advanced manufacturing systems; exploitation of global and transnational supply chains; novel practices in service delivery; and innovative support technologies. As our framework in Table 1 illustrates, at a general level the associated practices will include; centralised product assembly and configuration, with test and repair capabilities located near to customers; a focus on response time, with planning and control systems set-up to optimise product availability and use; and employees having high levels of product knowledge, but balanced with customer management and relationship development skills.

The novelty of our framework lies in the bridging of the gap between (1) detailed frameworks that focus exclusively either on production or service operations, and (2) abstract frameworks that integrate product and services. The resultant contribution to practitioners is that the framework suggests the likely practices that will be necessary to support a relatively sophisticated servitization strategy. Consequently, it will allow a more informed assessment as to whether a servitization strategy is achievable by a manufacturer and the associated implications throughout their operations.

The findings of our work should, at this stage, be treated as indicative rather than absolute. In forming the framework we have sought to balance abstraction (so it can be widely applied) against detail and relevance (so it useful to practitioners). Such a balance is fraught with difficulties, and having completed this research, it is now apparent that further work is needed to enhance the resolution and reliability of this framework. In particular, we suggest delving further into the types of servitization, in this chapter we have focused on product-centric, but this may be too abstract. For example, do other bundles of services naturally fit together? Likewise, the reliability of the framework can only be confirmed as, over time, it is tested and refined. This is clearly on opportunity for further work. Although these avenues for further enquiry are apparent, the framework presented in this chapter nevertheless makes an important contribution to understanding servitization, and moving this whole topic forwards.

Acknowledgements We would like to acknowledge the support of EPSRC via the Cranfield Innovative Manufacturing Research Centre programme for providing the funds for this research. We would also like to thank our anonymous reviewers for their constructive and insightful comments.

References

Ambler, T. (2005), A long perspective on marketing, *European Business Forum*, 21, 50–53

Anderson, J. and Narus, J. (1995), Capturing the value of supplementary services, *Harvard Business Review*, Jan–Feb, 75–83

Anderson, J. et al. (1989), Operations strategy: A literature review, *Journal of Operations Management*, 8(9), 133–157

Baines, T. et al. (2005), Strategic positioning – An integrated decision process for manufacturers, *International Journal of Operations and Production Management*, 25(2), 180–201

Baines, T. et al. (2007), State-of-the-art in product-service systems, *Proceedings of the Institution of Mechanical Engineering (Part B), Journal of Engineering Manufacture*, 221(10), 1543–1552

Baines, T. et al. (2009), Servitized manufacture: Practical challenges of delivering integrated products and services, *Proceedings of the Institution of Mechanical Engineering (Part B), Journal of Engineering Manufacture*, 223, 1207–1215

Cesborough, H. (2005), Toward a science of services, *Harvard Business Review*, 83, 16–17

Chase, R. (1978), Where does the customer fit in a service operation, *Harvard Business Review*, 56(6), 137–142

Chase, R. and Apte, U. (2007), A history of research in service operations: What's the big idea? *Journal of Operations Management*, 25, 375–386

Chase, R. and Garvin D. (1989), The service factory, *Harvard Business Review*, 67(4), 61–69

Chesborough, H. and Spohrer, J. (2006), A research manifesto for services science, *Communications of the ACM*, 49(7), 35

Cohen, M. (2007), Power by the hour: can paying only for performance redefine how products are sold? www.knowledge.wharton.upenn.edu Accessed 25 June 2008

Cohen, M. et al. (2006), Winning in the aftermarket, *Harvard Business Review*, May, 129–138

Collier, D. and Meyer, S. (1998), A service positioning matrix, *International Journal of Operations and Production Management*, 18(12), 1223–1244

Cook, D. et al. (1999), Service topologies: A state of the art review, *Production & Operations Management*, 8(3), 318–338

Cox, A. et al. (2001), Supply chains and power regimes: Toward an analytic framework for managing extended networks of buyer and supplier relationships, *Journal of Supply Chain Management*, 37(2), 28

Davies, A. et al. (2004), Moving base into high-value integrated solutions: A value stream approach, *Industrial and Corporate Change*, 13(5), 727–756

Davies, A. et al. (2006), Charting a path towards integrated solutions, *MIT Sloan Management Review*, 43(7), 39–48

Drucker, P.F. (1954), The Practice of Management, *Harper & Row, New York*

Edvardsson, B. et al. (2008), Initiation of business relationships in service-dominant settings, *Industrial Marketing Management*, 37(3), 339–350

Fisk, R. et al. (1993), Tracking the evolution of the services marketing literature, *Journal of Retailing*, 69(1), 61–103

Ford, H. (1922), My Life and Work, *Kessinger Publishing*, LLC, 2004

Galbraith, J. (2002), Organising to deliver solutions, *Organizational Dynamics*, 31(2), 194–207

Gebauer, H. and Friedli, T. (2005), Behavioural implications of the transition process from products to services, *Journal of Business & Industrial Marketing*, 20(2), 70–80

Gebauer, H. et al. (2006), Success factors for achieving high service revenues in manufacturing companies, *Benchmarking, An International Journal*, 13(3), 374–386

Goedkoop, M. et al. (1999), Product Service-Systems, Ecological and Economic Basics, *Report for Dutch Ministries of Environment (VROM) and Economic Affairs (EZ)* Dutch Policy Document on Environment and Economy

Hayes, R. and Wheelwright, S. (1984), Restoring Our Competitive Advantage Through Manufacturing, *Wiley, New York*

Heineke, J. and Davis, M. (2007), The emergence of service operations management as an academic discipline, *Journal of Operations Management*, 25, 364–374

Hill, T. (2000), Manufacturing Strategy, *Palgrave, Great Britain*

Howells, J. (2000), Innovation and Services, *UMIST Internal Publication, Manchester*

Jacob, F. and Ulaga, W. (2008), The transition from product to service in business markets: An agenda for academic inquiry. *Industrial Marketing Management*, 37(3), 247–253

Kellog, D. and Winter N. (1995), A framework for strategic service management, *International Journal of Production Management*, 13, 323–337

Kotler, P. (1967), Marketing Management Analysis, Planning and Control, *Prentice-Hall, Englewood Cliffs*

Lamming, R. (1993), Beyond Partnership – Strategies for Innovation and Lean Supply, *Prentice Hall International, London*

Levitt, T. (1960), Marketing myopia, *Best of Harvard Business Review*, July/August 2004, 138–149

Levitt, T. (1976), The industrialisation of service, *Harvard Business Review*, 54(5), 63–74

Levitt, T. (1981), Marketing intangible products and product intangibles, *Harvard Business Review*, May–June, 92–104

Levitt, T. (1983), After the sale is over, *Harvard Business Review*, 61(5), 87–93

Lewis, M. et al. (2004), Beyond products and Services: opportunities and threats in servitization. *IMS International Forum, Italy*

Lovelock, C. and Gummesson, E. (2004), Whither services marketing? In search of a new paradigm and fresh perspectives, *Journal of Service Research*, 7(1), 20–42

Luiten, H. et al. (2001), Source: Sustainable Product Service-Systems: The Kathalys Method, *Proceedings Second International Symposium on Environmentally Conscious Design and Inverse Manufacturing*, 190–197

Malleret, V. (2006), Value creation through service offers, *European Management Journal*, 24(1), 106–116

Manzini, E. et al. (2001), Product service-systems: using an existing concept as a new approach to sustainability, *Journal of Design Research*, 1(2)

Martin, C. and Horne, D. (1992), Restructuring towards a service orientation, *International Journal of Service Industry Management*, 3(1), 25–38

Mathieu, V. (2001), Product services: From a service supporting the product to service supporting the client, *Journal of Business & Industrial Marketing*, 16(1), 39–58

Maxwell, I. and van der Vorst, R. (2003), Developing sustainable products and services, *Journal of Cleaner Production*, 11, 883–895

Meijkamp R. (2000), "Changing Consumer Behaviour Through Eco-efficient Services: An empirical study of car sharing in the Netherlands". Delft University of Technology: 296

Miller, D. et al. (2002), The problem of solutions: balancing clients and capabilities, *Business Horizons*, Mar–Apr, 3–12

Mills, et al. (1996), A framework for the design of manufacturing process strategies, *International Journal of Operations and Production Management*, 15(4)

Mont, O. (2000), Product Service-Systems, *Final Report for IIIEE*, Lund University

Mont, O. (2001), Introducing and Developing a PSS in Sweden, *IIIEE Reports 2001:6* Lund University, Sweden

Mont, O. (Intl. Inst. Indust. Environ. Econ., Lund University); Lindhqvist, T. The role of public policy in advancement of product service systems. Source: Journal of Cleaner Production, v 11, n 8 SPEC., December, 2003, p 905–914

Morgan, R. and Hunt, S. (1994), The commitment-trust theory of relationship marketing, *Journal of Marketing*, 58(3), 20–38

Morris, B. and Johnson R. (1987), Dealing with inherent variability: the difference between manufacturing and service, *International Journal of Operations and Production Management*, 7(4), 13–22

Mulholland, D. (2000), Technology threatens sector's profits, companies need to shift business to service, upgrade sales, *Defence News*, Feb 7

Oliva, R. and Kallenberg R. (2003), Managing the transition from products to services, *International Journal of service Industry Management*, 14(2), 1–10

Oman I. (2003), Product Service-Systems and their impacts on sustainable development – a multi-criteria evaluation for Austrian Companies. Frontiers

Quinn et al. (1990), Beyond products: services-based strategy, *Harvard Business Review*, Mar–Apr, 58–67

Samli et al. (1992), What pre-sale and post-sale services do you need to be competitive, *Industrial Marketing Management*, 21, 33–42

Sasser, E. (1976), Match supply and demand in service industries, *Harvard Business Review*, Nov–Dec, 133–140

Schmenner, R. (1995), Service Operations Management, *Prentice-Hall, Englewood Cliffs*

Schroeder, R. and Lahr, T. (1990), Development of Manufacturing Strategy – A Proven Process, *Proceedings of the Joint University Conference on Manufacturing Strategy*, Michigan

Shostack, G. (1977), Breaking free from product marketing, *Journal of Marketing*, 41(2), 73–80

Shostack G., (1982), "How to design a service", *European Journal of Marketing*, 16(1), 49–63

Silvestro, R. (1999), Positioning service along the volume-variety diagonal, *International Journal of Operations and production Management*, 19(4), 399–420

Spohrer et al. (2007), Steps toward a science of service systems, *Computer*, 40, 71–77

Taylor, M. (1936), Progress in marketing research, *Journal of Marketing*, 1(1), 56–64

Thompson, J. (1967), Organizations in Action, *McGraw-Hill, New York*

Tukker, A. (2004), Eight types of product service system; Eight ways to sustainability? Experiences from SUSPRONET, *Business Strategy and the Environment*, 13, 246–260

Tukker, A. and Tischner, U. (2006), New Business for Old Europe, *Greenleaf Publishing, Sheffield*

Vandermerwe, S. and Rada J. (1988), Servitization of business: adding value by adding services, *European Management Journal*, 6(4), 314–324

Vargo, S. and Lusch, R. (2004), Evolving to a new dominant logic for marketing, *Journal of Marketing*, 68, 1–17

Vargo, S. et al. (2008), On value and value co-creation: A service systems and service logic perspective, *European Management Journal*, 26, 145–152

Voss, C. (1992), Applying service concepts in manufacturing, *International Journal of Operations and Production Management*, 12(4), 93–99

White, R. et al. (1999), Servicizing: The Quiet Transition to Extended Product Responsibility, *Report from Tellus Institute*

Windahl, C. and Lakemond N. (2006), Developing integrated solutions: The importance of relationships within the network, *Industrial Marketing Management*, 35(7), 806–818

Windahl, C. et al. (2004), Manufacturing firms and integrated solutions: characteristics and implications, *European Journal of Innovation Management*, 7(3), 218–228

Wise, R. and Baumgartner, P. (1999), Go downstream: The new profit imperative in manufacturing, *Harvard Business Review*, Sept–Oct, 133–141

Womack, J. et al. (1990), The Machine That Changed the World, *Maxwell MacMillan International, New York*

Wong, M. (2004), PSS in the Consumer Goods Industry, *Ph D Thesis, Cambridge University*

Theory of Constraints for Services: Past, Present, and Future

John A. Ricketts

Two Lincoln Centre, IBM Corporation

Oakbrook Terrace, IL 60181, USA

Abstract Theory of constraints (TOC) is a thinking process and a set of management applications based on principles that run counter to conventional wisdom. TOC is best known in the manufacturing and distribution sectors where it originated. Awareness is growing in some service sectors, such as Health Care. And it's been adopted in some high-tech industries, such as Computer Software. Until recently, however, TOC was barely known in the Professional, Scientific, and Technical Services (PSTS) sector. Professional services include law, accounting, and consulting. Scientific services include research and development. And Technical services include development, operation, and support of various technologies. The main reason TOC took longer to reach PSTS is it's much harder to apply TOC principles when services are highly customized. Nevertheless, with the management applications described in this chapter, TOC has been successfully adapted for PSTS. Those applications cover management of resources, projects, processes, and finances.

Keywords Theory of Constraints, constraint management, professional, scientific, and technical services, service science, service systems

1 Introduction

Service sectors comprise about 75% of mature economies today, and services are the fastest growing sectors in many emerging economies. Yet most service enterprises are still managed according to conventional wisdom with its roots in the Industrial Revolution. There are ways, however, that service enterprises can break the bonds of conventional wisdom.

If your main concern is services, Theory of Constraints – or just TOC as it is commonly known – is possibly the most famous paradigm you've never heard of. It's famous in manufacturing and distribution sectors because its unconventional approach yields results well beyond the ordinary. On the other hand, TOC is almost unheard of in service enterprises.

H. Demirkan et al. (eds.), *Service Systems Implementation*, Service Science:
Research and Innovations in the Service Economy, DOI 10.1007/978-1-4419-7904-9_7,
© Springer Science+Business Media, LLC 2011

TOC has been directly applied in service enterprises that sufficiently resemble manufacturing and distribution enterprises, and as expected, the results are beyond what can be attained with conventional wisdom. So there's ample incentive to make TOC work across the board in services. Unfortunately, the same TOC methods that work so well in manufacturing, distribution, and repeatable services generally cannot be applied directly to highly customized services.

TOC for Services is a recent innovation that makes TOC applicable to a wider range of service enterprises. This chapter covers what TOC for Services is at a high level, ways practitioners can get started with it, how researchers can contribute to it, and what students should be expected to know about it.

1.1   Why Do Constraints Matter?

Picture a dozen machines in a factory manufacturing products, or picture a dozen people in an office delivering a service. All these elements are arranged in a row. Designate the one on the left as the entry point in this system. Designate the one on the right as the exit point. Now picture arrows connecting the elements in a series.

Assume that each machine or person accepts work from its predecessor and passes work to its successor, where it sits until the successor has time to perform its task. To keep this illustration really simple, assume all the work flows in one direction, without looping back to a previous element. Also, assume there's enough demand to keep the system busy. Finally, assume that each batch of work has its own due date, so some batches need to be done sooner than others, no matter when they start. In other words, this is an extremely simple system, but it is just what we need for illustration purposes.

Now, take this test: *Where is the constraint?* Stop and think about it. Think hard.

Give up? You're probably thinking you don't have enough information to tell where the constraint is – and you're right. However, most workers and managers in systems managed the conventional way have lots of information about their own system, yet they seldom know where the constraint is – because they aren't looking for it. Tell the truth: Did you wonder about the constraint in this system before starting this test?

Here are a couple bits of information to help you take the next part of this test. To keep things really simple, assume that every element in this system can produce 100 units/hour – except the constraint, which can only produce 90. And after some investigation, you locate the constraint as a specific machine or person somewhere in the middle of this system.

Now, take the second part of this test: *What happens if you run this system at maximum capacity?* How much work goes in? How much work comes out? What happens to the work in between?

Since the system has enough demand to keep busy, and the entry point can produce 100 units/h, most people say they would start 100 units/h. If we do that, however, will we get 100 units out of the system? No, because the constraint can only do 90 units, every one of its successors can only do 90 units, and the system overall can only do 90 units. So what happens to the other 10 units? They pile up ahead of the constraint. That's why the constraint matters. The constraint governs what the system as a whole can produce.

But there's a bigger problem here because the system promised 100 units of work/h to customers, yet actually completes only 90. So not only is the system filling up with partially completed work, some customers are probably wondering why their work isn't done on time.

Thus, this problem cannot go on indefinitely. If available cash doesn't limit the inventory, the walls or fence around the factory will. Likewise, the in-boxes or computers of office workers will limit work-in-process. More importantly, however, customers whose work is chronically late, tend to take their business elsewhere. At this point, the system is probably in chaos, workers have a hard time comprehending priorities, and managers have an even harder time setting them.

Next, take the third part of this test: *What is the utilization of each machine or person – the percent of time that machine or person is productive – and why should you care?*

Well, if elements ahead of the constraint can and do produce 100 units/h, they are 100% utilized. Likewise, if the constraint can produce only 90 units, and that's what it actually does, it too is 100% utilized. However, if elements after the constraint could produce 100 units but the constraint passes them only 90 units, they are only 90% utilized – and 10% of their productive capacity apparently goes to waste.

If you're the factory manager or the office manager, you care about this because the reports your boss sees says you are wasting capacity. Or if you're one of the factory workers or office workers who are less than fully utilized, you care about this because it says other people are more productive than you are. But is that right? All the elements in this system have exactly the same capacity except the constraint, yet some are fully utilized and others are not.

So, take the final part of this test: *How would you optimize what this system can produce?* Think hard.

Would expediting solve this problem? No, because no matter how hard we push work into or through the system, the constraint and any of the elements after it can only produce 90 units. The most an expediter can do is ensure that work with the closest due date is done first.

Would more capacity solve this problem? It might, but only if it expands in the right place. If you were following conventional wisdom and didn't know where the constraint is, you wouldn't know where additional capacity would help.

Would scheduling solve this problem? It might, but only if the scheduling takes the constraint into account. Unfortunately, Enterprise Resource Planning (ERP) software generally does not recognize constraints, let alone schedule around them. On the other hand, that's precisely what TOC software does.

Hence, the ultimate solution to this problem is not expediting, capacity, or scheduling. The solution is understanding causes and effects – and changing assumptions about how things work. TOC does this through a set of principles that run counter to conventional wisdom. For example, most managers assume that optimizing every element by getting it to 100% utilization will optimize the system as a whole. But as we just saw, that's not what actually happens, and the push for high utilization everywhere creates undesirable effects.

In a nutshell, the *TOC Focusing Steps* that would optimize this system are:

1. *Identify the constraint.* That's the first thing we did in this test, even though it's not what conventional wisdom says we should have done.
2. *Exploit the constraint.* That means making sure the constraint almost never runs out of work from its predecessors. It also means making sure downtime on the constraint itself is minimized.
3. *Subordinate everything else.* In this test, that would mean starting work according to the constraint's capacity, not the entry-point's capacity. This keeps the predecessors as well as successors working at the same pace as the constraint, which prevents the build-up of work-in-process that ties up cash and ultimately leads to chaos.
4. *Elevate the constraint.* In this test, that could be done many ways, such as overtime on the constraint or adding another machine or person to perform the constrained task.
5. *Repeat.* Whenever the constraint moves (due to an increase or decrease in capacity), production has to be rescheduled around the new constraint. Ideally, the new constraint's capacity is higher than the old, and the whole system ratchets up to a higher level of productivity.

Thus, constraints matter because they govern what a system can produce. This happens even when workers and managers are unaware of it. It happens even in systems more complicated than the one in the test, such as those with multiple paths, loops, widely variable capacities, or complex topologies. And it doesn't matter whether the system has 10 elements or 10,000: Most systems have just one active constraint at a time.

Constraints also matter because they are where process improvements must be focused. Improving a non-constraint, as local optimizations do, has no effect on what the system overall can produce.

1.2   What Is Theory of Constraints?

Theory of Constraints (TOC) is a body of knowledge that has fostered dramatic gains in productivity and sales for industrial and distribution companies. TOC accomplishes this by giving its practitioners, researchers, and students a set of guiding principles that run counter to considerable conventional wisdom about best practices.

For example, as we just saw, conventional wisdom says every resource in a system should be as highly utilized as possible because lower utilization represents a lost opportunity for production. In other words, conventional wisdom says that the best way to optimize a system is to optimize every element because local optimizations add up to global optimization. TOC, however, demonstrates that that's just not so.

In every real system there is one element – a person, a machine, a task – that cannot produce as much as the other elements. That's the constraint, and it governs what the entire system produces. When every individual element produces as much as it can, the non-constraints overwhelm the constraint to the point that they further diminish its productivity. Thus, the unintended consequence of pushing more jobs into a manufacturing shop to keep utilization high is productivity of the shop overall declines and inventory rises markedly.

In contrast, the *TOC Production Principle* says the constraint should be utilized as much as possible – but every other element should be subordinate to the constraint. That is, no non-constraint should produce more than the constraint can produce. Once this is accomplished, every increase in productivity at the constraint translates into increased output for the system as a whole. This simple change in perspective has astounding benefits: Lead time can drop by as much as 70%, inventory by 50%, and on-time delivery can increase over 40%.

Once a manufacturing enterprise enjoys such gains, however, the system constraint typically moves outside, into the market. That is, manufacturers who adopt the TOC production principle quickly discover that they can actually produce more than their customers will buy – sometimes much more. For the company to grow, it thus has to figure out how to generate more sales.

Conventional wisdom says inventory should be pushed in large batches through the distribution chain until it reaches retail stores because that's where sales are made and distributing large batches is most efficient. TOC, however, demonstrates that that's just not so. The unintended consequence of filling a distribution chain with inventory is it still experiences high stock-outs and returned merchandise, because at the same time some retailers are out of stock, others may have it stacked to the ceiling.

In contrast, the *TOC Distribution Principle* says the best place to hold most inventory is centrally, rather than at retail locations, because aggregation reduces volatility. Likewise, the best way to distribute inventory is in small amounts, not large batches, because small amounts can be distributed more readily to the right place, at the right time. In other words, retail stores should hold the smallest possible inventory, and that inventory should be replenished frequently based on actual sales. This simple change in perspective has astounding benefits: Stock-outs drop as much as 15%, while inventory drops 66%.

These two examples illustrate why TOC is highly regarded in the manufacturing and distribution industries. Nevertheless, attempts to generate comparable gains for service companies have met with mixed results. Where services sufficiently resemble manufacturing and distribution, the standard TOC solutions work fine. For instance, a restaurant is enough like a factory that the TOC production principle can be applied. However, restaurants differ from factories because they do not stock finished goods inventory. Thus, a restaurant that produces more than its patrons will eat winds up discarding (or donating) uneaten meals. Perishability is thus a key difference between goods-based and services-based industries.

Nowhere among services-based enterprises is the contrast with manufacturing and distribution more stark than in *Professional, Scientific, and Technical Services (PSTS)*. Professional services include accounting, law, engineering, and consulting. Scientific services include basic and applied research. Technical services include development, testing, installation, operation, maintenance, diagnosis, and repair. How TOC principles could be applied in enterprises delivering such services is seldom obvious – yet it can be done. *TOC for Services* thus extends this decades-old body of knowledge for the current services-based economy.

1.3   What Is the Theory in Theory of Constraints?

"In theory, there is no difference between theory and practice; but in practice, there is," said Yogi Berra. That saying rings true to anyone who has seen a theory crack and crumble when confronted with reality – and the social sciences have more than a few idle theories.

In the tradition of the hard sciences, however, the theory in Theory of Constraints is founded on observations of the real world. Anything that doesn't work in practice is not admitted into TOC. Thus, TOC has a tight connection between theory and practice.

Here are the fundamentals of the theory behind TOC:

1. The way to maximize what a system as a whole produces is to maximize what its constraint produces.
   (a) Attempting to maximize what every element of a system produces causes the non-constraints to overload the constraint, and this prevents the system overall from producing as much as it could.
   (b) The nature of the system dictates how its constraint should be managed, so there are various methods of constraint management for various system types, yet they follow the same principles.
2. Complex systems require simplifying, holistic solutions.
   (a) By subordinating non-constraints to the constraint, even the most complex systems need just a few well-chosen control points.
   (b) Holistic solutions cover the system well enough to avoid unintended consequences.
3. A system with more than one goal has to be sub-optimizing most of them, if not all of them.
   (a) Most things perceived as goals are actually necessary conditions for achieving the real goal.
   (b) Every goal has a set of sufficient conditions that must be satisfied: Anything less is insufficient.

4. Measurements drive behavior, so if you measure things wrong, you get the wrong behavior.
   (a) The strongest drivers of behavior require the fewest measurements.
   (b) The measurement system has to be internally consistent to drive consistent behavior.
5. Pushing a system requires constant steering, but a system designed to pull steers itself toward the goal.
   (a) A minimal set of control points creates leverage because there are fewer ways for the system to stray from its goal.
   (b) Solutions designed to pull a system toward its goal change management's role from supervisor and rescuer to visionary and designer.
6. People will change when presented with an alternative that they recognize as superior and attainable.
   (a) Individuals have to recognize the problem before they can accept the solution.
   (b) The biggest inhibitor of change is not the change itself but how and when it is presented.

In a nutshell, here's how the theory behind TOC applies to service systems. First, there are separate TOC for Services (TOC$_S$) applications for optimizing each type of service system within Professional, Scientific, and Technical Services (PSTS). Those applications interlock, but they can be implemented sequentially or concurrently.

Second, TOC$_S$ is holistic because it has applications for critical management functions, including management of resources, projects, processes, finances, sales, marketing, strategy, change, technology, and implementation. Despite this breadth, the solutions are simpler than service systems based on conventional wisdom.

Third, the goal is typically maximization of net profit, but it can be another goal for non-profit or governmental units, such as pro bono professional cases closed, scientific research studies completed, or technical innovations created. Client satisfaction is a necessary condition, however, not a goal. And client satisfaction is not a sufficient condition when other stakeholders, such as employees and shareholders, must be satisfied as well.

Fourth, measurements do not contradict one another. For instance, if project managers are complaining about lack of skilled resources, the measurements will not say resources and projects are both on target to achieve the goal.

Fifth, buffers provide an unambiguous indicator of whether the service system is pulling itself toward the goal. For instance, when a resource buffer drops too low, it triggers resource replenishment; and when it rises too high, it triggers resource redeployment. Likewise, when a project buffer is being consumed faster than tasks are being completed, it reminds the project team to perform like runners in a relay race because that's what keeps the project from falling too far behind to finish on time.

Finally, when properly presented, the logic behind TOC is compelling. Hence, resistance to change turns into pressure for change once the solutions are seen as better and attainable. Experience has shown that senior executives can take less than a week to embrace TOC and establish the vision for TOC implementation in their enterprise – and the initial benefits can begin to flow within weeks. However, it can take a year to implement the full vision throughout a large enterprise.

2   A Brief History of Theory of Constraints

Although all great ideas require an incubation period, most practitioners trace the founding of Theory of Constraints (TOC) to publication of *The Goal* (Goldratt and Cox 1992). Publication of subsequent TOC books are milestones marking eras when various TOC applications had been refined enough for public consumption.

The Goal is a best-selling business novel about a beleaguered factory manager and his mentor, Jonah, who guides him to solutions for seemingly unsolvable production problems. To this day, TOC practitioners are known as Jonah's.

It's Not Luck (Goldratt 1994a), the sequel, follows the newly promoted factory manager as he hones his thinking process on seemingly unsolvable problems in marketing, sales, and distribution. Even though the constraints are different, TOC principles still apply.

The Haystack Syndrome (Goldratt 1994b) and *The Theory of Constraints and Its Implications for Management Accounting* (Noreen et al. 1995) are tutorials that tackle measurement systems. They show how Cost Accounting drives enterprises to maximize utilization and build unnecessary inventory while TOC-based measures minimize inventory and maximize throughput.

Critical Chain (Goldratt 1997) is a business novel that covers the TOC approach to project management for single projects. *Project Management in the Fast Lane* (Newbold 1998) and *Critical Chain Project Management* (Leach 2004) are tutorials that extend it for multiple projects.

The World of the Theory of Constraints (Mabin and Balderstone 2000) is a literature review covering hundreds of articles, books, and dissertations. It summarizes benefits attained during TOC implementations as well as insights gained through research and teaching.

The Logical Thinking Process (Dettmer 2007) is a tutorial that explains how to create various diagrams that TOC practitioners use to understand and communicate the current situation, the desired future state, and how to get there. The emphasis on cause and effect rather than conventional wisdom requires TOC practitioners to think differently – and to teach others how to think differently, too.

Necessary But Not Sufficient (Goldratt et al. 2000) is a business novel that shows how to turn technology from an impediment to a springboard for TOC implementation. Thinking differently is necessary but not sufficient if software perpetuates conventional wisdom.

We All Fall Down (Wright and King 2006) is a business novel that applies TOC principles to the Health Care industry. It shows how the TOC thinking process and production application improve health care processes.

Agile Management for Software Engineering (Anderson 2004) is a tutorial that applies TOC principles to the Software industry. It shows how TOC project management and accounting applications improve software development processes.

Reaching the Goal (Ricketts 2008) is a tutorial that applies TOC principles to Professional, Scientific, and Technical Services. It shows how the full spectrum of TOC applications improve PSTS processes.

The Choice (Goldratt 2008) is a set of conversations between the author and his adult daughter. This book applies TOC principles to life philosophy.

The aforementioned books are just a sample from over 100 books in print about TOC. In addition to publications, one organization is especially notable. The Theory of Constraints International Certification Organization (TOCICO) was founded to standardize the practice, research, and teaching of the TOC body of knowledge. That knowledge can be organized into four parts: the TOC Thinking Process, applications, principles, and implementation.

2.1   TOC Thinking Process

At its most fundamental level, the TOC Thinking Process starts with a goal, such as optimizing what a system can produce, and then answers these questions:

1. What to change?
2. What to change to?
3. How to cause the change?

The Thinking Process thus identifies the core conflict standing in the way of achieving the goal. For example, in the test at the beginning of this chapter, we saw a conflict between the desire for high utilization of every element in the system and the goal of maximizing what the system can produce. Through a Conflict Resolution Diagram, also known as an Evaporating Cloud, the Thinking Process reveals that an invalid assumption creates this conflict. Once it becomes clear that the assumption that high utilization on every element does not in fact optimize the system, the conflict evaporates and attention can shift to the TOC Focusing Steps seen earlier at the conclusion of the test.

In support of the TOC Focusing Steps, the Thinking Process provides several additional diagram types:

- Current Reality Tree
- Future Reality Tree
- Prerequisite Tree
- Transition Tree

These diagrams are called trees because they are drawn as boxes, arrows, and other symbols that show cause–effect relationships. Careful analysis of cause-and-effect is what distinguishes TOC from conventional wisdom, where cause-and-effect are rarely questioned.

As the names imply, the Current Reality Tree and Conflict Resolution Diagram answer "What to change?" The Future Reality Tree answers "What to change to?" And the Prerequisite Tree and Transition Tree answer "How to cause the change?"

Details of these diagrams are beyond the scope of this chapter, but they are well covered in books devoted entirely to the TOC Thinking Process. These diagrams are mentioned here because they are an essential part of every TOC practitioner's toolkit. They are not, however, what distinguishes TOC for Services.

2.2   TOC Applications

TOC applications are well thought-out solutions to thorny problems in specific domains. These applications can be divided into two categories. Standard applications embody fundamentally the same design across all implementations. Nonstandard applications follow TOC principles, but the design of each implementation is unique in some way because the core problem afflicting the system is unique in some way.

Drum-Buffer-Rope (DBR) is the standard TOC application for production. It is the one that would be applied to the system described in the test you took earlier. In DBR the *drum* is the constraint because it sets the pace for non-constraints. The *buffer* is work anywhere ahead of the constraint. By managing the buffer, DBR keeps the constraint fully utilized because the entire system depends on it. The *rope* is an information system that connects the constraint to the entry point and connects the exit point to the constraint. The entry-point connection subordinates upstream elements to the constraint so that they don't overload it and create unnecessary work-in-process. The exit-point connection ensures the constraint works on the highest priorities, which leads to on-time delivery of finished goods or services.

Replenishment is the standard TOC application for distribution. As explained earlier in the "What is TOC?" section, Replenishment distributes goods in small batches at frequent intervals, even though this is counter to the conventional wisdom that distributing large batches is more efficient. When the impact that large batches have on over-stocks and stock-outs is considered, their supposed efficiency on shipping costs is usually revealed as false economy. So rather than pushing inventory out to retail locations where demand is most volatile, Replenishment holds most inventory at a central warehouse where aggregated demand is least volatile. This allows manufacturing to produce large batches infrequently while distribution ships small batches frequently, thus resolving a core conflict between these functions. Buffer management is what triggers Replenishment. That is, when a *retail buffer* (inventory level) drops below a predefined threshold, this triggers a replenishment order at the warehouse. Likewise, when a *warehouse buffer* drops below a predefined threshold, that triggers a manufacturing order at the factory.

Critical Chain (CC) is the standard TOC application for projects. Though CC originated for engineering projects in a manufacturing environment, it has been used on all kinds of projects, including software development and information technology implementation. CC alters how projects are planned, executed, and measured. During planning, CC removes contingency typically embedded in task estimates and instead creates a project time buffer that protects the entire project. During execution, CC changes work rules to prohibit multi-tasking – working on more than one task at once – because it is one of the main causes of late task completion. CC further changes work rules so that projects are executed like a relay race, with each task starting as soon as its predecessors are complete rather than waiting for the planned task start date. This eliminates the tendency for late task completions to accumulate until the project itself is late. Finally, during measurement, CC measures progress in terms of project buffer penetration because the project will finish on time if that buffer is not fully consumed. Consequently, even though CC project schedules are usually shorter, CC projects finish on time more often than conventional projects.

Throughput Accounting (TA) is the standard TOC application for measurement. In this context, "Throughput" means revenue minus totally variable cost, which is also known as contribution margin. TA is a radical alternative to Cost Accounting (CA) in many ways. For instance, CA uses standard costs to infer which products or services are profitable, but cost allocation schemes distort the analysis, so TA does not use standard costs. Consequently, CA and TA typically lead to different product mix or services mix decisions, with TA always finding the mix that maximizes profit. Furthermore, TA makes Throughput the top management priority and cost reduction a lower priority, which is the opposite of what CA does. Also, CA promotes universally high utilization, while TA drives high utilization only on the constraint, for reasons explained earlier. Finally, CA inadvertently creates powerful incentives to build excess inventory, while TA intentionally creates powerful incentives to minimize inventory. Overall, TA drives higher revenue and profit for the enterprise at the same time it manages the enterprise's cash buffer.

In addition to standard applications, TOC has nonstandard applications for Marketing, Sales, Strategy, and Change. These applications are nonstandard because every implementation is unique in some way. That stands to reason because a successful marketing program for one company is not likely to be the best marketing program for another company, even if they are arch competitors. And since Sales depend on the offerings prepared by Marketing, Sales also require nonstandard TOC applications. Nevertheless, TOC principles guide even nonstandard applications.

2.3   TOC Principles

TOC principles underlie both the Thinking Process and TOC applications. That is, these principles guide investigations of cause-and-effect as well as the design of solutions to core problems. Here is a sample of TOC principles.

The *Weakest Link Principle* is based on the observation that a chain is only as strong as its weakest link, and so it is with constraints in systems for production, distribution, engineering, and other business functions. That's why every TOC application manages constraints. It doesn't matter how strong the other links are if the weakest link governs what the system overall can produce. Ironically, conventional wisdom says managers should strive for balanced capacity on the assumption that will eliminate the weakest link, but this just makes it impossible to locate the constraint because it floats around. In contrast, TOC strives for unbalanced capacity because managing the constraint then optimizes the entire system.

The *Pull Principle* is based on the observation that systems are also like chains in the sense that pulling is a lot more effective than pushing. Yet pushing is what conventional wisdom calls for. Orders get pushed into production. Inventory gets pushed through the distribution network. Projects get pushed for delivery. Workers get pushed for utilization. Customers get pushed for orders. And so forth. Contrast that with what TOC does. DBR pulls orders into and through production based on the pace set by the constraint. Replenishment pulls inventory through supply chains based on actual sales, not forecasts. CC pulls projects to completion via better estimating, work rules, and measurements. And TA tells managers which products or services to pull in order to achieve the enterprise's goal.

The *Optimization Principle* is based on the observation that local optimizations do not add up to global optimization because improving a non-constraint has no effect on the system as a whole. Yet this is what conventional wisdom assumes when it drives every element of a system for high utilization. In contrast, TOC uses the Focusing Steps to drive global optimization directly, even if that means non-constraints have less than full utilization.

The *Aggregation Principle* is based on the observation that the more things are aggregated, the less variable they become because deviations in one direction are more likely to be offset by deviations in the opposite direction. In contrast, forecasts for individual products, services, sites, or periods are notoriously inaccurate, yet that is what conventional wisdom calls for because it says managers need forecasts to push work through systems.

The *Core Problem Principle* is based on the observation that one core problem is usually the cause of many undesirable effects. Yet conventional wisdom says solutions should treat every pain point, even if it makes those solutions complicated and expensive. In contrast, TOC recognizes that pain points often arise from conflicts, such as the big batch versus small batch conflict described earlier. TOC therefore uses cause-and-effect investigation to solve core problems with the knowledge that one carefully crafted solution will eliminate multiple pain points by resolving the conflict.

The *Policy Constraint Principle* is based on the observation that physical constraints, such as how much a machine can produce, are easier to break than policy constraints, such as a rule that says every machine should be utilized as much as possible. For instance, this physical constraint can be broken just by scheduling an extra shift or buying another machine; but this policy constraint can only be broken by getting executives, managers, and workers to buy into the Optimization Principle explained above. Ironically, most TOC strategy applications are designed to break policy constraints because that creates sustainable competitive advantage.

2.4   TOC Implementation

Though TOC principles are durable, TOC applications are not easy to implement. Virtually all enterprise-level TOC implementations begin with executive workshops led by experienced TOC consultants because buy-in at the senior level is necessary to dislodge conventional wisdom. Then the implementation can proceed top-down from a vision shared by all C-level executives.

Bottom-up TOC implementation is also possible, but on a much smaller scale, and virtually never enterprise-wide. Recent college graduates exposed to TOC and recently certified TOC practitioners can be anxious to apply their new skills. And they can do so on individual projects if they are the project manager, but it is far harder to do on a large scale because conventional wisdom tends to squelch new paradigms.

Each of the TOC applications explained earlier has a solution design in *Reaching the Goal* (Ricketts 2008). And the steps needed to implement the solution designs are explained as well. Details are beyond the scope of this chapter, however.

3   Current Innovations in Theory of Constraints

Current innovations in TOC are defined here as those that are relatively recent, and therefore have not yet been adopted by the majority of enterprises using TOC. Nevertheless, they illustrate the state of the art. As in previous sections, the examples covered here are representative but not comprehensive.

3.1   TOC for Goods

Simplified DBR (SDBR) recognizes that maximizing what the constraint can produce does not always address market priorities (Schragenheim et al. 2006). In other words, even when an enterprise has an internal production constraint that should be managed, achieving the enterprise's long-term goal sometimes requires it to accommodate orders that do not maximize what the constraint, and therefore the system, can produce. In basic terms, SDBR connects the shipping rope (ordinarily between the exit-point and the constraint) directly to the entry-point where jobs are released into production. SDBR thus uses one rope where conventional DBR uses two, and SDBR manages the shipping buffer instead of the constraint buffer.

Synchronized Replenishment (SR) combines Replenishment with DBR for an integrated production management solution (Constraints Management Group 2008). In other words, instead of using Replenishment just for distribution, SR also uses Replenishment to manage parts within the manufacturing process itself. By placing parts buffers strategically within that process, work-in-process inventory is reduced and so are production times. That is, rather than requiring every order to start at the first task, some orders can be accommodated much more quickly by starting them at the latest upstream task with a sufficient parts buffer ahead of it. Thus, an order that might requires 30 tasks end-to-end, might only require five tasks to complete because the first 25 tasks had already been completed before those parts were placed in the buffer. This gives the enterprise a competitive advantage in speed.

3.2   TOC for Software

Agile Management (Anderson 2004) adapts TOC applications for software projects. For example, unlike the physical inventory that is central to TOC for Goods, the "inventory" in a software project is mostly intangible because it consists of requirements, designs, test cases, computer programs, and user documentation. The paper or computer media that contain those ideas are like bins in a factory: It's what's inside the containers that really matters.

Nevertheless, Critical Chain and Throughput Accounting do apply. Software projects can be managed according to CC just like any other project. And although some of the measures in TA have to be adapted for software projects because software is not physically consumed with each sale, the underlying TOC principles are exactly the same.

3.3   TOC for Services

TOC applications originally devised for manufacturing and distribution have been used largely unchanged on repeatable services such as lawn care, food service, and health care. Though services themselves are consumed as they are delivered, and therefore cannot be produced in advance and saved as inventory, repeatable services often do consume physical inventory at time of delivery, such as fertilizer, vegetables, or medications. Thus, TOC applications designed to manage inventory do play a role when used on repeatable services. For instance, Replenishment works fine on the physical inventory associated with repeatable services. And DBR or CC work fine for services scheduling, so long as customers are willing to wait for service.

Of course, not all services are repeatable, and not all clients are willing wait for service. Professional, Scientific, and Technical Services (PSTS) are the extreme example. Such services are highly customized, they often consume no physical inventory whatsoever, and clients expect services to be delivered on demand. All these factors make direct adoption of TOC applications by PSTS enterprises problematic. For example, the traditional Replenishment application is irrelevant if there is no physical inventory to manage. Likewise, traditional DBR and CC assume clients will wait for service if necessary, which is incompatible with service on demand. Nevertheless, there is no reason to believe that TOC principles do not apply to PSTS.

TOC for Services (TOC_S) therefore adapts TOC applications for the PSTS sector (Ricketts 2008). By making TOC usable in the services sector most different from manufacturing and distribution, TOC is now usable across the entire services spectrum.

Replenishment for Services (R_S) is the TOC_S application for resource management. Professional, Scientific, and Technical Services are predominantly labor-based because those services require expertise to meet unique customer requirements. Thus, resource management is a critical function in every PSTS enterprise. The core problem that R_S solves is how to acquire resources at just the right time and in just the right amount to meet market demand. Conventional wisdom dictates that managers should either hire-to-plan or hire-to-deal. But hire-to-plan requires a forecast, and forecasts are notoriously inaccurate, while hire-to-deal means that managers often scramble to find capable resources in time to launch projects on demand.

R_S solves this problem via hire-to-buffer. That is, R_S determines the right number of resources to have on the bench in each skill group, ready to deliver services on demand for clients. Time on the bench is not wasted, however. It's used, for instance, to get training or to work on internal projects. And when resources come off the bench, thereby depleting the resource buffer, R_S replenishes that buffer.

Critical Chain for Services (CC_S) is the TOC_S application for project management. For individual services projects, the traditional Critical Chain application works fine. However, service providers in the PSTS sector often perform multiple projects concurrently. The traditional CC application for multiple projects schedules those projects around availability of the enterprise constraint by staggering their schedules. For example, on aircraft maintenance projects, if hangar space is the constraint, aircraft must wait for service until a hangar is available. On PSTS projects, however, the constraint is usually a specific skill. For instance, on information technology (IT) projects, the constraint is often information technology architects, and clients are unlikely to wait for their project to start. They can just find another service provider.

CC_S solves this problem by using resource management for leverage on project management. That is, because R_S can provide resources on demand, CC_S can start projects on demand. This requires coordination between these TOC_S applications, but that can be done manually on a modest number of projects or it can be built into computer software used to manage a large portfolio of projects.

Drum-Buffer-Rope for Services (DBR_S) is the TOC_S application for process management. Whereas PSTS projects are unique, PSTS processes are somewhat repeatable even though they require expertise. For example, preparing tax returns, performing statistical analysis, and doing technical support are PSTS services that aren't amenable to project management because they are each comprised of a small number of tasks with relatively short duration and simple precedence relations.

The traditional DBR application would release work into the process based on availability of the constraint, of course, but that's problematic when clients expect services on demand. Indeed, many service providers have service level agreements (SLAs) with their clients that dictate the speed, cost, and quality of service.

DBR_S solves this problem by replacing buffer management with capacity management. In this case, the drum is still the constraint, and a rope still connects the system exit-point – the attained service levels – to the drum, but rather than connecting the drum to the system entry-point, the second rope connects to a capacity management function that increases or decreases capacity of the entire process as needed to meet the SLAs.

Throughput Accounting for Services (TA_S) is the TOC_S application for measurement. Like the traditional TA application, TA_S makes Throughput a higher priority than cost reduction, and TA_S has no standard cost construct. However, TA_S uses financial measures suited to PSTS. For instance, rather than generating Throughput via sale of goods, TA_S recognizes PSTS enterprises generate Throughput via project deliverables and process service levels. And rather than investing in physical inventory, PSTS enterprises invest more in intangibles, such as skills and intellectual capital. Just as traditional TA supports optimal product mix decisions, TA_S supports optimal service mix decisions. The place where traditional TA and TA_S depart most is in the measurement of inventory. Inventory minimization is a central concern of traditional TA, while TA_S instead minimizes excess resources.

Although the adaptation of TOC applications for PSTS occurred over a period of several years, publication of TOC_S is recent. Hence, it is still rightfully considered a nascent area for TOC.

4   The Future of TOC for Services

Collectively, service sectors are larger than the manufacturing and distribution sectors where TOC began – and that's true for both mature and emerging economies. Thus, TOC for Services (TOC_S) roughly doubles the number of enterprises which could adopt TOC.

Nevertheless, TOC remains controversial. For example, here are a few notions from TOC that newcomers usually find hard to believe:

- Emphasis on cost reduction decreases the revenue an enterprise can generate.
- High utilization everywhere decreases what a system can produce.
- Distributing large batches is less efficient.
- High-margin products can be less profitable.

TOC_S creates some controversy of its own. For instance, traditional TOC classifies constraints as *internal* (inside the enterprise) or *external* (in the market). With an internal constraint, the enterprise cannot produce as much as the market demands. With an external constraint, the market will not buy everything the enterprise can produce.

TOC_S adds a third class of constraints, however. *Interface* constraints are neither external nor internal. They exist literally at the interfaces between a service provider and its clients or its subcontractors. An interface constraint occurs when something at an interface, such as a service level agreement or a regulation, prevents the provider or its subcontractors from delivering more service, and thereby prevents the client from consuming more service than it otherwise would.

Adding a third class of constraints is controversial among practitioners of traditional TOC because the long-standing dichotomy between internal and external constraints has served them well in manufacturing and distribution settings. For TOC_S practitioners, however, interface constraints are a perennial problem.

The future of TOC in general and TOC_S in particular depends on getting buy-in to controversial ideas such as these. Conventional wisdom is difficult to overcome, but it can be done.

4.1   Ways Practitioners Can Get Started with TOC_S

The easiest way to get started with TOC is to read. A simple web search will find all the books mentioned earlier – and more. The average number of books purchased per year by practitioners in the information technology field rounds to zero, however. So it doesn't take much to stand out.

The largest source of new TOC practitioners is colleges and universities because TOC has been widely incorporated into textbooks and curricula. Unfortunately, graduates with TOC knowledge have little opportunity to practice their skills in enterprises bound by conventional wisdom. So, recent graduates are a frequently overlooked source of TOC knowledge.

Certification is another way to get started because it requires completion of formal training as well as exams. It has the additional benefit of demonstrating a level of proficiency beyond what can typically be attained on the job or through independent study.

Other ways to get started with TOC are hire an experienced Jonah or engage TOC consultants. These alternatives can provide deep skills quickly, which may be exactly what's needed for buy-in.

4.2   How Researchers Can Contribute to TOC_S

Empirical studies are an obvious research contribution. Though simulation studies are common, field studies and case studies have the advantage of observing TOC in practice.

Literature reviews are another potential contribution. The TOC literature is scattered across several fields and many journals, so the most effective literature reviews are broad.

One of the biggest challenges researchers face in an applied field such as TOC, however, is making their research consumable by practitioners. TOC has its own jargon, little of which has been included in this chapter. When combined with scientific jargon, the result can be incomprehensible to many readers. Researchers are advised, therefore, to make their research comprehensible to practitioners as well as other researchers – and comprehensible to both novices and experts in TOC.

4.3   What Students Should Know About TOC_S

Students need to know about TOC principles, applications, and the Thinking Process. The more hands-on their education is, they more likely they are to retain that knowledge. Thus, simulation games in which students assume roles and play out scenarios based on TOC are a staple of TOC education. But there's no substitute for seeing TOC in practice.

Students also need to know about the TOC Buy-In Process, which is what TOC practitioners use to help others understand and adopt TOC. Obstacles to TOC adoption are many, so students equipped only with a toolkit of TOC applications will run headlong into opposition.

5   Conclusion

Theory of Constraints is a venerable set of management practices. Yet it has been relegated mostly to manufacturing and distribution. With the introduction of TOC for Services (TOC_S), however, this body of knowledge is now applicable across the full range of services.

TOC_S includes standard applications for Resource Management, Project Management, Process Management, and Measurement. It also includes nonstandard applications for Marketing, Sales, Strategy, and Change.

Individually, TOC applications each solve a thorny management problem in an elegant manner. Collectively, TOC applications eliminate conflicts that plague conventional management methods.

References

Anderson, D. (2004). *Agile Management for Software Engineering: Applying the Theory of Constraints for Business Results*. Upper Saddle River, New Jersey: Prentice-Hall.

Johnson, P. (2008). Beyond MRP: Meeting the Current Materials Synchronization Challenge. *Case Study of LeTourneau Technologies.* Constraints Management Group User Conference, Enumclaw, Washington.

Dettmer, H. W. (2007). *The Logical Thinking Process: A Systems Approach to Complex Problem Solving.* Milwaukee, Wisconsin: ASQ Quality Press.

Goldratt, E. (1994a). *It's Not Luck.* Great Barrington, Massachusetts: North River Press.

Goldratt, E. (1994b). *The Haystack Syndrome.* Great Barrington, Massachusetts: North River Press.

Goldratt, E. (1997). *Critical Chain.* Great Barrington, Massachusetts: North River Press.

Goldratt, E. (2008). *The Choice.* Great Barrington, Massachusetts: North River Press.

Goldratt, E. and Cox, J. (1992). *The Goal: A Process of Ongoing Improvement,* 2nd Revised Edition. Great Barrington, Massachusetts: North River Press.

Goldratt, E., Schragenheim, E. and Ptak, C. (2000). *Necessary but Not Sufficient.* Great Barrington, Massachusetts: North River Press.

Leach, L. P. (2004). *Critical Chain Project Management,* 2nd edition. Boston, Massachusetts: Artech House.

Mabin, V. and Balderstone, S. (2000). *The World of the Theory of Constraints: A Review of the International Literature.* Boca Raton, Florida: St. Lucie Press.

Newbold, R. C. (1998). *Project Management in the Fast Lane.* Boca Raton, Florida: St. Lucie Press.

Noreen, E., Smith, D. and Mackey, J. T. (1995). *The Theory of Constraints and Its Implications for Management Accounting* (pp. 20–23). Great Barrington, Massachusetts: North River Press.

Ricketts, J. A. (2008). *Reaching the Goal: How Managers Improve a Services Business Using Goldratt's Theory of Constraints.* Upper Saddle River, New Jersey: IBM Press.

Schragenheim, E., Weisenstern, A. and Schragenheim, A. (2006). What's really new in Simplified DBR? *TOCICO Conference Proceedings,* Miami, Florida.

Wright, J. and King, R. (2006). *We All Fall Down: Goldratt's Theory of Constraints for Healthcare Systems.* Great Barrington, Massachusetts: North River Press.

An Assessment Tool for Establishing Infrastructure as a Service Capability Maturity

Justin Nieuwerth

Department of Information and Computing Science, Utrecht University,
Padualaan 14, 3584 CH Utrecht, The Netherlands

Marco Spruit

Department of Information and Computing Science, Utrecht University,
Padualaan 14, 3584 CH Utrecht, The Netherlands

Danny Zijlstra

Accenture, Gustav Mahlerplein 90, 1082 MA Amsterdam, The Netherlands

Abstract The concept of using IT services 'out of the cloud' is relatively new, let alone having an entire infrastructure in that same cloud. The technological advancements in virtualization technology have brought organizations to the point where they have the opportunity to outsource their entire IT infrastructure and use it as a service, out of 'the cloud'. This phenomenon is known as a specific form of 'cloud computing' called 'cloud architecture' or Infrastructure-as-a-Service (IaaS). Adoption of IaaS has a massive impact throughout all layers in the entire organization.

This research is focused on examining where the adoption of Infrastructure-as-a-Service, as it is defined in this research, might impact and what factors pose an important role for successful IaaS adoption. It presents an assessment framework that measures the maturity of these factors, which are grouped together in seven different aspects (referred to as Adoption Capability Aspects in this research) and were identified by explorative expert interviews combined with a literature study. The framework consists of around 80 statements derived from several established frameworks and assessments. The purpose of the framework is to identify the maturity and state of readiness of an organization with regard to the adoption of IaaS, thereby aiding in the decision making process.

The concept of IaaS architectures is yet to gain more attention and maturity, but will also prove to be interesting and show its potential in the near future. The framework proposed in this research will contribute to the IaaS adoption maturity of organizations

H. Demirkan et al. (eds.), *Service Systems Implementation*, Service Science:
Research and Innovations in the Service Economy, DOI 10.1007/978-1-4419-7904-9_8,
© Springer Science+Business Media, LLC 2011

and attempts to increase awareness of IaaS as an emerging IT infrastructure architecture, as well as its most influencing aspects.

Keywords Infrastructure-as-a-Service, cloud computing, cloud architecture, service Science, service Systems

1   Introduction to Service Systems and Infrastructure-as-a-Service

To relate the subject of this book to the subject of this research, a definition of the term *Service System* and *Service Science* in general needs to be provided. According to Spohrer et al. (2007): "A *service system* comprises people and technologies that adaptively compute and adjust to a system's changing value of knowledge. A *science of service systems* could provide theory and practice around service innovation." With the research described in this chapter, the authors attempt to provide some of this theory and practice by proposing an assessment framework which will hopefully add value to future (cloud) *Service Systems.*

Undoubtedly, the greatest revolution in the history of *Service Systems* after the introduction of the PC, was the rise of the internet. It is a development that changed the way we live and we have become dependent on it. The same applies for businesses all around the world as the internet opened the doors for fast, cheap and generally reliable and around-the-clock information exchange. Not surprisingly, a lot of companies took advantage of the opportunities this relatively new medium offered and so the "internet-boom", caused by the extremely rapid increase in availability of internet providers and web-browsers, soon enabled the following "off-shoring-boom" in the mid-1990s which enabled companies to do their business 24 h a day, save costs and focus more on their core-businesses. This concept is described in (Gupta and Seshasai 2007) as the "24-hour knowledge factory". A direct consequence of offshoring part of your company is that process streamlining to allow working in a uniform way, worldwide, is difficult to achieve due to the large distances between offices (Metters 2007). Of course, the internet acts as an enabler when it comes to solving this issue (Gupta and Seshasai 2007) and many companies already use various web-based applications to synchronize their work on a global scale. However, the amount of data that needs to be shared and synchronized is ever increasing and as a result, internal information networks tend to grow large, inefficient and require a lot of maintenance.

In the meanwhile, technology also evolved and concepts such as desktop virtualization, cloud computing and Software-as-a-Service (SaaS), emerged as answers to these growing issues. By separating software possession and ownership from its use, these technologies follow an entirely new software paradigm focused on describing and delivering a service (Turner et al. 2003).

A "service" can be described as the following definition:

> An act or performance offered by one party to another. Although the process may be tied to a physical product, the performance is essentially intangible and does not normally result in ownership of any of the factors of production (Lovelock et al. 1996).

Software-as-a-Service is often seen as the first major step towards what in 2004 was already described as 'service based computing' (Shipley 2004). The SaaS concept is receiving widespread attention with Salesforce.com and IBM establishing themselves as major providers and market leaders. With bandwidth ever increasing as a result of rapid advances in hardware virtualization, IT automation, and usage metering and pricing, the SaaS concept later evolved and extended to include infrastructure components like storage and computational resources, cleverly coined 'Hardware-as-a-Service' (HaaS) by Carr (2006). The term HaaS has since been superseded by Infrastructure-as-a-Service (IaaS), which has been introduced by the first emerging providers offering this concept (e.g. Bluelock.com, Tier3.com).

Lack of awareness and fear of implementation failures result in that even today there are still not many organizations making the decision to adopt these technologies and analyst firms state that a distinct market and market leaders will not emerge for at least another year in the IaaS market (Fenn et al. 2008). This is the reason that there is little scientific information available about the IaaS concept, let alone knowledge on how to deal with the adoption and integration. This research attempts to provide some of that information. It focuses on IaaS as a strictly defined cloud computing environment (see definition in Sect.1.2). The mission of this research is to increase awareness of the factors that play an important role in the adoption process and provide a tool to aid in the decision making progress by identifying the state of adoption readiness to ease the (perhaps inevitable) transition to an IaaS architecture in the future.

The research attempts to fulfill this mission by accomplishing a number of goals, which will subsequently be covered in the next sections:

- Identification of factors that pose a significant risk to the adoption and implementation of IaaS
- Identification of factors having specific requirements with regard to IaaS
- Identification of processes in existing frameworks covering these risks
- Mapping of risk factors to adoption aspects
- Development of an assessment tool measuring aspects of adoption readiness
- Development of a matching maturity model covering the most important aspects

1.1   Research Approach

The first step in conducting this research is the determination of the research method. Because the subject of the research is new and there is little to no literature at all available to extract information from, the first stage of the research conducted in this thesis, the definition of the Adoption Capability Aspects, can be classified as explorative (qualitative) research as described in 't Hart, H and Boeije (2005), amongst others.

The second phase, the actual construction of the assessment framework, can be classified as design science. The choice for this method is that 'design-science research addresses important unsolved problems in unique or innovative ways or solved problems in more effective or efficient ways.' Design science is a problem solving process in which problems are considered to have the following characteristics (Hevner et al. 2004):

- Unstable requirements and constraints based upon ill-defined environmental contexts
- Complex interactions among subcomponents of the problem and its solution
- Inherent flexibility to change design processes as well as design artifacts (i.e., malleable processes and artifacts)
- A critical dependence upon human cognitive abilities (e.g., creativity) to produce effective solutions
- A critical dependence upon human social abilities (e.g., teamwork) to produce effective solutions

One might argue that most, if not all of these characteristics apply in this research and thus making it a justified research approach for designing an assessment construct for Infrastructure-as-a-Service adoption capability.

1.2   What Is Infrastructure-as-a-Service?

In order to begin with the research as proposed in the previous section, a proper definition for the concept of Infrastructure-as-a-Service had to be established. Available literature does mention that Infrastructure-as-a-Service is an emerging development based on the service delivery paradigm (e.g. Software as a Service, Platform as a Service). It is sometimes also referred to as *cloud computing* or, more specifically, *cloud architecture*. However, as there is no standard terminology (yet) to strictly define Infrastructure-as-a-Service, this research defines the Infrastructure-as-a-Service as:

An entirely virtualized information technology infrastructure with scalable storage on demand, in combination with either database(s) or computing capacity on demand, or both.

These services are limited in terms of available database-versions, CPU types, etc. Additional generic services such as internet access, monitoring services, network security (e.g. intrusion detection systems) are optional as well as integration with the customer's own generic services. Application and OS (Operating System) hosting is managed by the provider, where the applications are provided and maintained by the customer for optimal configurability. The provider is not responsible for functional

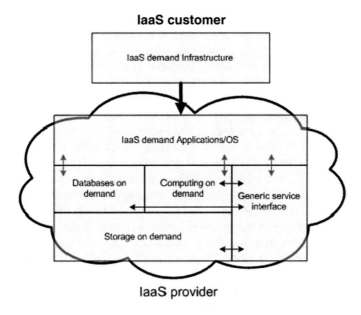

Fig. 1. IaaS visual representation

or technical management of hosted applications but solely provides the OS environment. Furthermore, end user support responsibility remains with the customer.

Access is possible via public networks by a variety of hardware (thin clients, desktop and laptop computers, mobile devices, explicitly not using its own local storage but solely operating via a virtual environment provided by the IaaS architecture).

A visual representation of the Infrastructure-as-a-Service definition as described in the previous section can be seen in Fig. 1.

2   Research Execution and Framework Development

In this chapter the research approach and the subsequent development of the framework will be described in detail.

2.1   *Phase One: Literature Study and Explorative Interviews*

The first research phase was twofold, a literature study was conducted to identify risks, requirements and characteristics of technologies closely related to Infrastructure-as-a-Service (IaaS); and explorative interviews with eight experts, functioning in the financial services and communications and high tech business segments, were held to identify risks and requirements directly related to IaaS.

For the literature study, technologies such as desktop virtualization, Software as a Service and IT outsourcing were studied to determine what benefits these technologies have to offer and, more important, what challenges they have overcome or still face. This was done to identify potential challenges that IaaS may inherit through the evolution of these technologies. This literature study thus resulted in the theoretical perspective of potential IaaS challenges.

The goal of the expert interviews was to gain as much information about IaaS adoption in practice as possible. A semi-structured approach was chosen as interview strategy to leave room for improvisation when the opportunity would arise to gain more detailed information about the subject. The structured part of the interviews consisted of questions about the current trends of infrastructure outsourcing, success rate of previous IaaS initiatives, and most importantly, risks and requirements that would apply to IaaS implementation from their business point of view, resulting in the practical perspective of potential IaaS challenges.

Originally, experts from two different business segments were interviewed to examine if there was substantial difference in the answers or if business specific challenges would be mentioned. Interview results did not provide suggestions that this was the case, hence the assumption was established that the assessment framework could function for both the financial services and the high tech business segment, and could possibly also function for other business segments.

The two perspectives combined provided a base of information to identify certain aspects of an organization that have an essential role in the adoption of an IaaS architecture. Interview results were listed, made consistent, sorted, compared to- and supplemented with the information gathered during the literature study. This process eventually resulted in the seven Adoption Capability Aspects (ACAs) that form the dimensions of the assessment framework:

- IT Infrastructure Complexity – *measures current state of IT infrastructure complexity*
- IT Infrastructure Health – *measures current state of IT infrastructure health factors such as hardware age, performance*
- Cost & Benefit – *identifies current control over IT costs to measure the ability to achieve ROI*
- Governance – *measures the condition of the governance function*
- Capacity Management – *measures the ability to effectively monitor and forecast capacity usage*
- IT Service Management – *measures the condition of several IT service management related processes*
- Security & Compliance – *measures the condition of security & compliance processes and regulations*

These ACAs would form the seven dimensions of the assessment tool to be constructed. In the later stages of the research the ACAs were validated during a second interview round and considered useful and satisfactory complete by experts within the IaaS provider market. The identification of the ACAs concluded the first phase of the research, they would be given mass in the development phase.

2.2   Phase Two: Assessment Development

For the development of the assessment framework, the *design science* method described by Hevner et al. (2004) proved to be a suitable research method, as the situation complied with most of the characteristics mentioned earlier.

To provide the Adoption Capability Aspects with units of measure that would accurately reflect the state of maturity for the concerning aspect, several well established frameworks such as the IT Infrastructure Library OGC 2007 and the COBIT best practice framework ITGI 2007 were consulted to study process descriptions that were directly or indirectly relevant to the identified aspects. The ITIL and COBIT process descriptions proved to contain detailed information including a description how the process should look like in an ideal situation, process metrics and maturity level descriptions. This information was used to establish measureable statements that cover the ACAs. Additionally, the Infrastructure Assessment Toolkit was used to derive statements and maturity descriptions.

In Fig. 2, the derivation method is visualized. This method was used to provide the ACAs with metrics.

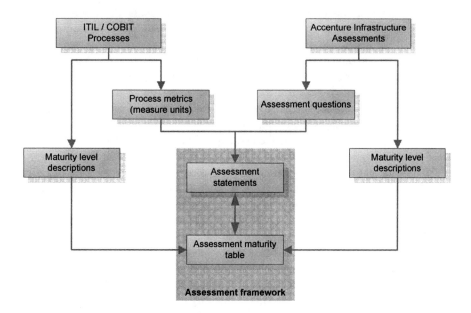

Fig. 2. Assessment framework compilation

The Infrastructure Assessment Toolkit (IAT) consists of predefined assessment questions instead of process metrics so these questions were derived from the IAT directly rather than interpreted from the process descriptions in the ITIL and COBIT frameworks. Therefore, the derivation method is slightly different and is visualized apart from the ITIL and COBIT framework.

The IAT was used to incorporate Accenture's existing view on how to assess IT infrastructures in the framework, although it must be stressed that the final framework is absolutely not restricted to internal usage.

3   Adoption Capability Assessment Framework

The Infrastructure-as-a-Service (IaaS) adoption capability assessment framework is the primary result of this research. The framework consists of seven Adoption Capability Aspects (ACAs) which were identified through expert interviews. The ACAs form the dimensions of the assessment framework and were given mass by means of analyzing existing frameworks and technologies and deriving measurable statements from the process descriptions and assessment questions from these frameworks. The maturity level descriptions in the assessment maturity model are derived in a similar way as the assessment statements, as the frameworks from which the statements originate, all offer accompanying maturity descriptions with its process descriptions.

ACAs are subdivided into factors which in their turn contain a varying number of five point Likert-scale based statements. Each statement has a 1–5 output score which will be used to determine the maturity level for the concerning aspect. The maturity level outcome resembles a state of maturity described in the maturity table and for each ACA there is a minimum state of maturity concerning IaaS adoption. Using a spider graph to visualize the assessment result, an organization is able to identify which aspects are sufficiently mature for the adoption of an IaaS architecture, and which aspects still need attention.

An overview of the ACAs and factors, along with the original sources that were used in the derivation of the assessment components is provided in Table 1.

To further clarify the derivation of the assessment statements and maturity descriptions from the sources mentioned in Table 1, see Fig. 2 in the previous chapter. An excerpt from the actual assessment is provided in Fig. 3.

Figure 3 shows the contents of the IT Infrastructure Complexity aspect. This ACA consists of the factors *Integration* and *Compatibility* which are measured by five and ten statements, respectively. The statements are designed so that position 5 on the Likert scale always resembles the most ideal situation, and thus a positive score on Infrastructure-as-a-Service adoption maturity. For each specific factor, five maturity descriptions are described in the maturity table. To determine the maturity score on the factor, the average score resulting from its statements is used. The

Table 1. Overview of sources used for assessment factors

ACA	Factor	Source
IT Infrastructure Complexity	Integration	IAT[a]
	Compatibility	IAT
IT Infrastructure Health	Legacy	IAT
	Performance measurement	COBIT
Cost & Benefit	TCO	Gartner TCO
	ROI	Explorative interviews
Governance	Control	COBIT
	Outsourcing	Explorative interviews
Capacity Planning and Management	Monitoring/availability	ITIL
	Forecasting/planning	ITIL/IAT
IT Service Management	Support	ITIL
	Changes	ITIL
	Third party management	ITIL
Security & Compliance	Security	IAT/COBIT
	Compliance	COBIT

[a] Infrastructure Assessment Toolkit developed by Accenture for internal use

maturity score on the ACA is subsequently determined by the average score of all of its statements.

Upon completing the assessment, all ACA maturity scores are plotted into a spider graph, clearly indicating the organization's maturity in contrast to the minimum maturity score required for proper IaaS adoption. An impression of the spider graph result is provided in Fig. 4. This result will help organizations to identify the factors that need improvement before an IaaS architecture can be adopted.

4   Conclusion

The Infrastructure-as-a-Service (IaaS) Adoption Capability Assessment framework is developed to provide a quantifiable way of identifying the state of readiness of organizations for the adoption of an IaaS architecture. It identifies the maturity of seven aspects within an organization, exposing its strong and weak points concerning the adoption of an IaaS architecture, contributing to the organization's long term (IT) strategy.

While the concept of IaaS is still in its infancy and widespread adoption at least a few years away, the assessment framework contributes in creating awareness of the factors that influence the adoption of this emerging technology which may very well be the future of IT infrastructure.

Applicability	1	2	3	4	5
Integration					
1	Open standards (e.g. open file formats such as PDF, XML) and interfaces are used extensively within the organization					
2	The organization makes extensive use of directory service(s)					
3	The organization makes extensive use of (a) Wide Area Network (WAN)					
4	The organization makes use of a Storage Area Network (SAN)					
5	OS virtualization is extensively used within the current infrastructure of the organization					
Compatibility					
6	The organization limits the number of database vendors to a minimum					
7	The organization limits the number of database versions to a minimum					
8	Dedicated hosting is used for all databases					
9	The organization limits the number of server vendors to a minimum					
10	The organization limits the number of server versions to a minimum					
11	The organization limits the number of vendors of operating systems to a minimum					
12	The organization limits the number of operating system versions to a minimum					
13	The organization limits the number of vendors of storage infrastructure to a minimum					
14	The organization limit the number of storage infrastructure versions to a minimum					
15	The organization only uses commercial off-the-shelf applications					

Fig. 3. Contents of the IT Infrastructure Complexity ACA

4.1   Future Research

Although this is a start in identifying challenges and influential factors that have to be faced and taken into account when adopting an Infrastructure-as-a-Service architecture, there are several opportunities for further research.

In the first place; a case study is desirable for the validation and completeness of this research. Due to the worldwide economic crisis, organizations are not eager to release sensitive information needed to execute the assessment, thus validation

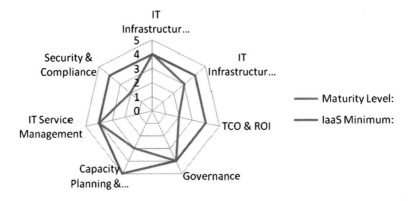

Fig. 4. Assessment spider graph result (impression)

opportunities are scarce. It is for this reason that a case study could not be executed for the validation of this research and a less desirable method (a second round of expert interviews) was chosen for validation purposes instead. Nevertheless, a case study would still be an interesting addition to the research and would provide the opportunity to fully validate the developed assessment tool.

Secondly; quite early in the research an observation was made that there was no significant difference between the interview answers of personnel from financial services and the communications/high-tech business segments concerning specific risks and challenges of IaaS adoption for their department. An assumption was made that the assessment framework did not need to include business-sector-specified statements and could thus be used to assess organizations from different business segments. Future research could further examine this assumption by extending the case studies to other business segments to validate the claim that a 'universal' IaaS Adoption Capability Assessment framework would suffice for every sort of organization.

Thirdly; it might be interesting to extend this research with a second hypothesis examining the relation between the assessment maturity scale and IaaS adoption capability. It was assumed in this research that adoption successfulness was related to the maturity descriptions derived from the varying sources. Further research can examine how adoption successfulness relates to the identified levels of maturity as they are currently described in the assessment framework, and how *individual* statements impact IaaS adoption.

References

't Hart, H. and Boeije, H. (2005). *Research Methods [Onderzoeksmethoden, NL]*, Amsterdam: Boom Education.

Carr, N.G. (2006) *Here comes HaaS*. 'Rough Type' weblog. Retrieved November 5, 2008, from http://www.roughtype.com/archives/2006/03/here_comes_haas.php

Fenn, J. et al. (2008). *Hype Cycle for Emerging Technologies*, July 2008. Gartner Group, pp. 2–3.

Gupta, A. and Seshasai, S. (2007). 24-Hour knowledge factory: using Internet technology to leverage spatial and temporal separations. *ACM Transaction on Internet Technology (TOIT). vol. 7, no. 3.* Social Science Research Network.

Hevner, A.R., March, S.T., Park, J. and Ram, S. (2004). Design science in information system research. *MIS Quarterly. vol. 28, no. 1, pp. 75–105.*

IT Governance Institute. (2007). *COBIT 4.1.* Rolling Meadows: ISACA.

Lovelock, C., Vandermerwe, S. and Lewis, B. (1996). *Services Marketing*, Europe: Prentice Hall.

Metters, R. (2007). A typology of offshoring and outsourcing in electronically transmitted services. *Journal of Operations Management. vol. 26, no. 2, 198–211.* ScienceDirect.

Office of Government Commerce (OGC). (2007). *ITIL Version 3.* London: TSO (The Stationery Office).

Shipley, C. (2004). *The dawn of service-based computing.* NetworkWorld. Retrieved November 30, 2008 from http://www.networkworld.com/columnists/2004/092704shipley.html

Spohrer, J., Maglio, P.P., Bailey, J., and Gruhl, D. (2007). Steps toward a science of service systems. *IEEE Computer. vol. 40, no. 1, pp. 71–77.*

Turner, M., Budgen, D. and Brereton, P. (2003). Turning software into a service. *IEEE Computer. vol. 36, no. 10, pp. 38–44.*

Customer–Provider Strategic Alignment: A Maturity Model

Jerry Luftman and Carol V. Brown

Howe School of Technology Management

Stevens Institute of Technology, Hoboken, NJ, USA

S. Balaji

Bentley University, Waltham, MA, USA

Abstract This chapter presents a new model for assessing the maturity of a customer–provider relationship from a collaborative service delivery perspective: the Customer–Provider Strategic Alignment Maturity (CPSAM) Model. This model builds on recent research for effectively managing the customer–provider relationship in IT service outsourcing contexts and a validated model for assessing alignment across internal IT service units and their business customers within the same organization. After reviewing relevant literature by service science and information systems researchers, the six overarching components of the maturity model are presented: value measurements, governance, partnership, communications, human resources and skills, and scope and architecture. A key assumption of the model is that all of the components need be addressed to assess and improve customer–provider alignment. Examples of specific metrics for measuring the maturity level of each component over the five levels of maturity are also presented.

Keywords Service system maturity framework, IT outsourcing, customer–provider strategic alignment, customer–provider relationship management, collaborative service delivery, IT services alignment

1 Introduction

Recent years have seen enormous growth in the nature and extent of the IT services industry. Far from being considered as just providing automated operational benefits, today the focus has shifted to value co-production (Ramirez 1999)

that provides strategic competitive advantage via a collaborative network of people, technology, and processes (Maglio et al. 2006).

At the same time, the outsourcing of IT services, where whole or part of an IT function is contracted-out to a provider/vendor that is onshore, near shore, or off-shore, has also steadily gained in prominence and become an integral part of the IT strategy of a customer/client.[1] The scope of outsourced IT service offerings has evolved from back office to front office, from operational to strategic.

IT outsourcing also redraws the IT resource portfolio of customer and provider firms; the IT resources and activities now span across organizational boundaries, to not only include the customer and provider entities, but also their external value chains – that is, their own customers or providers. Therefore, customer and provider firms are increasingly faced with a dilemma of not only enhancing the IT service offerings that they co-produce, but also proactively maintaining their evolving roles in a given customer–provider engagement. Given these emerging trends in size and scope for the outsourcing of IT service offerings, the concept of IT–business alignment needs to be expanded to accommodate the evolving world of outsourcing. Specifically, a metric-based framework for assessing *the maturity of customer–provider strategic alignment* is needed.

This chapter will present a new model called Customer–Provider Strategic Alignment Maturity Model (CPSAM). It primarily builds on two prior sources: a model for assessing IT–business strategic alignment (Luftman 2000, 2007) and additional research on managing customer–provider relationships (Balaji 2008). The chapter proposes six overarching components (value measurements, governance, partnership, communications, human resources and skills, and scope and architecture) and the criteria for measuring them over five maturity levels. A key assumption of the model is that all of the components need be addressed to assess and improve customer–provider alignment.

In Sect. 2 we briefly discuss relevant prior research on which we built our model. In Sect. 3 the six components of the model are presented. In Sect. 4 we describe the five levels of maturity and provide examples of metrics for measuring the maturity levels for each of the six components.

2   Prior Literature

Although there are many outsourcing success stories, the anticipated benefits from outsourcing have not always materialized. Over the past decade, many failures have been reported and by 2002 less than two-thirds of outsourcing agreements

---

[1] For the remainder of this chapter we will utilize the term 'provider' to refer to the provider of a service and the term 'customer' to refer to the recipient of the service. The customer and provider firms are both also considered to be 'service entities.'

typically had realized the expected cost savings (Caldwell 2002; Lacity and Willocks 1998; Simhan 2002).Some of the most common reasons for an outsourcing engagement to fail include not only the overall strategy, selection process, and contract negotiation, but also implementation, post-implementation, and management of the customer–provider relationship (Barretto 2004).

Researchers as well as industry surveys have clearly shown that IT outsourcing is not a static phenomenon. Outsourcing engagements can consist of one or more of the following offerings: (1) application development, purchasing, and maintenance, (2) computer and network operations and support, (3) end-user computing support (e.g., help-desk, training), and (4) strategic planning and management. Depending on the overall IT and business objectives, the customer can choose to engage one or more providers for performing important strategic or tactical activities, such as new application opportunities and planning, or more operational activities such as end-user support. Although this type of 'selective outsourcing' is popular, some customers engage in 'total outsourcing,' where all or most of the IS activities are outsourced to one or more providers.

Further, IT outsourcing is an 'intervention' in which the service provider augments the customer's capabilities – sometimes taking responsibility for monthly service-level agreements and year-over-year productivity improvements (Maglio et al. 2006). There are significant investments in time and effort from both the customer and provider perspective, as the requirements for the engagement continue to evolve. Some customer organizations are also reporting a portfolio approach to managing a set of outsourcing providers in which different levels of engagement are contracted for, with different expectations for provider partners versus more "arms-length" engagements (Poston et al. 2009).

As a result, any outsourcing arrangement today probably involves changes for both the customer and the provider. A good relational strategy (e.g., effective communications, partnership, value measurements, and governance process) between the customer and provider therefore becomes essential for any outsourcing engagement for which a long-term customer/provider engagement is envisioned, by either stakeholder. Transitions and transformations in business processes and technologies in competitive environments, as well as changes in economic environments, result in uncertainties that may render original contractual approaches less viable. Thus, it is the customer–provider relationship that becomes the primary success factor.

Of course the importance of achieving alignment between a customer and an IT service provider is not something new. For over 30 years, alignment between an internal IT service unit and the business has been consistently ranked as one of the most important IT management issues in practitioner surveys (e.g., see Luftman et al. 2009). Terms such as harmony, link, fuse, fit, match, meld, converge, interwoven, and integrate are frequently used synonymously with the term alignment. Prior IS researchers who have studied IT–business alignment have drawn upon a rich stream of literature in organization theory and strategic management, and the most commonly referred to strategic alignment models emerged from thought leaders at MIT in the early 1990s:

The inability to realize value from IT investments is, in part, due to the lack of *alignment* between the business and IT strategies of organizations. (Henderson and Venkatraman 1993, p. 4)

However, the definition of IT–business alignment in these studies has for the most part taken on a one-sided view: that is, how IT should be aligned with business. This perspective of alignment becomes especially problematic when applying it to relationships that extend beyond firm boundaries, such as IT outsourcing. When resources are shared across firms, the alignment dimension needs to incorporate perspectives from both firms.

In summary, the strategic alignment maturity model for the outsourcing of IT offerings presented in this chapter fills a critical need for multiple reasons. First, outsourcing relationship models have largely focused on the impact of customer and provider capabilities for outsourcing separately – e.g., managerial capabilities of the customer (Ranganathan and Balaji 2007) or the technical capabilities of the provider. However, this perspective of capabilities falls short of considering the impact of the *joint customer and provider capabilities* required for successful outsourcing. Second, prior research addressing the relationship dimension in outsourcing has, until recently, focused largely on the *management of the relationship* as opposed to the alignment aspect, and thus falls short of examining a full range of potential matches or mismatches between the customer and the provider. A related but important third issue is that the extent of *value co-production*, which is a fundamental basis for competitive advantage from customer–provider arrangements (Ramirez et al. 1999; Vargo and Lusch 2004), has also received little attention. Consequently, an in-depth understanding of the strengths and weaknesses of an outsourcing relationship due to *customer/provider alignment* requires systematic attention and new approaches.

This chapter presents the *Customer–Provider Strategic Alignment Maturity Model* (CPSAM), which captures alignment between the customer and IT outsourcing provider along six key dimensions. The model builds on findings from prior field research by the authors, and has two parts:

- Six components of alignment
- Five maturity levels, with examples of metrics for each component

The components of the alignment for the customer–provider relationship are built heavily on the conceptual and empirical studies by Luftman and his research associates, who have used the SAM model to benchmark IT–business alignment within more than 300 Global 1,000 companies (e.g., see Luftman and Kempaiah 2007). Specifically, the CPSAM maturity model also assesses six alignment components and provides metrics for five maturity levels. The SAM model focuses on the alignment issue from an *internal* customer and provider perspective: how the IT function is aligned with the business and how the business is aligned with IT. In contrast, the CPSAM model presented here seeks to address how the *external* provider is aligned with the customer and how the customer is aligned with the provider. Further, the component descriptions are also based heavily on prior research on customer–provider relationships in IT outsourcing using survey instruments and case studies (Balaji 2008; Ranganathan and Balaji 2007). The CPSAM model also incorporates service management concepts and other recent literature on IT alignment and IT outsourcing relationships.

The central premise of this chapter is that – irrespective of the nature or extent of the IT offerings outsourced – understanding the alignment criteria is critical for both the customer and the provider to realize both strategic and operational benefits from the engagement. In addition, depending on the current *strategic intent*, or type of outsourcing engagement, a given maturity level might be most appropriate. For example, a more passive role for the provider, in terms of meeting the agreed upon SLAs, may be the best option for help-desk activities; help desk personnel may simply be focused on achieving agreed upon SLAs rather than identifying root causes for a given problem that is occurring at multiple points in the organization. This suggests that a different maturity level may be appropriate for providing end-user support than for providing application development services. These types of differences are elaborated on in the maturity descriptions in this chapter.

In the next section, the six components for measuring customer–provider alignment within an IT outsourcing context are presented and summarized (see Fig. 1).

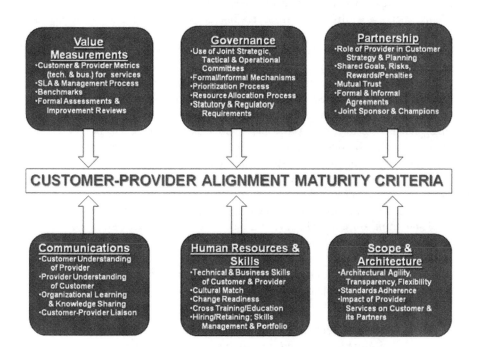

Fig. 1. Six components of customer–provider alignment

The goal is to present a model that can be applied to all types of outsourcing of IT service offerings. Hence, the application of CPSAM is an important tool for improving the harmony among providers and customers, and achieving the performance benefits sought, no matter what type of IT outsourcing is being provided, and no matter how many providers a given customer may be working with (and vice versa). It is essential to assess all six components; there are no silver bullets.

3   The Six Components of Alignment

3.1   Value Measurements

One of the differentiating factors among firms in a competitive environment is the value derived from the provisioning of services (Parasuraman et al. 1988). Service value includes quality, productivity, and sustainable innovation (Spohrer et al. 2008). Differentiation based on value is especially true for IT services (Jia et al. 2008; Kettinger and Lee 1994): unlike commodities, service offerings are customer-centric (Vargo and Lusch 2004).

However, three features unique to services also pose value measurement challenges: their intangible nature, differences in services based on the heterogeneity of customers, and difficulties in separating out impacts due to production and consumption (Parasuraman et al. 1985, 1988). Customer firms therefore need to rely on objective and subjective means to measure service performance and the value of services received.

The Value Measurements component assesses the demonstrable technical and business benefits, accepted by both the customer and the provider, as a means for understanding and tracking the contributions and returns from an outsourcing engagement. Typically, such value measurements are embedded as part of the outsourcing contract between a customer and provider. Such contracts provide a mutually agreed upon platform for specifying a range of accepted behaviors in the arrangement (Poppo and Zenger 2002). They also form the basis for establishing metrics such as quality (Zeithaml et al. 1991) and service-level agreements (SLA) for the engagement. Contracts can be designed to explicitly specify what to measure, how to measure, benchmarks, formal assessments and reviews, and possible penalties for underperformance.

Balaji (2008) found that a higher level of perceived value, as reflected in the contracts, is a significant predictor of outsourcing performance. The items used to capture this value dimension included:

1. Guidelines, such as pricing, data protection, penalties, etc., and SLAs
2. Well-established monitoring of the specified outcomes
3. Comparisons of actual and expected outcomes

In other words, outsourcing engagements that articulated, monitored and measured their value dimension better, had significantly better outsourcing performance.

Customers and providers therefore need to invest in strategic alignment of their value measurements for outsourcing, to achieve the desired level of outsourcing performance. This component captures the importance of the expectations for meeting specific metrics between a customer and provider. When the customer and provider have dissonance in their expectations, the outsourcing engagement tends to fail. Additionally, the processes in place to derive, discuss, learn, adjudicate, and evolve the measurements are fundamental to successful alignment.

3.2   Governance

As entities in the exchange of services, customer and provider firms can often have disputes during their interactions (Spohrer and Kwan 2009). To resolve the disputes, it is imperative to provide effective mechanisms (March 1988; Spohrer and Kwan 2009; Williamson 1999) both before (preventive mechanisms) and after (resolution mechanisms) disputes occur. Management and monitoring structures are therefore an integral part of successful outsourcing engagements (Poppo and Zenger 2002). However, many outsourcing arrangements fail because too often the customer and the provider do not coordinate with an established formal structure and joint review process, which identifies opportunities for improvement and ensures that they are carried out. The customer and provider need to ensure that their oversight and review mechanisms (including appropriate stakeholder representation) are in place at the appropriate strategic, tactical, and operational levels to obtain maximum benefits from their outsourcing arrangements. These mechanisms should also include all suppliers of services, including those that are subcontracted.

The Governance component defines the various structural aspects of the outsourcing arrangement, ranging from the establishment of planning strategies, clear lines of authority, joint committees, and meeting schedules. Active participation from the appropriate stakeholders from both customer and provider organizations is fundamental to ensuring success. Structural mechanisms such as teams, task forces, and committees make decisions about the engagement (e.g., prioritization of initiatives, resource allocation, project reviews) and establish close regular contact between the customer and the provider. In addition, reporting structures are used to clearly define and establish formal lines of authority for escalating concerns or to resolve disputes. These mechanisms help iron-out differences and resolve disputes if and when they arise. Naturally, the need to ensure compliance with statutory and regulatory requirements is also fundamental to the engagement.

The survey findings from the Balaji (2008) study were that firms that invested more in the Governance of the engagement achieved better outsourcing performance. The specific survey items used to capture the governance dimension in this study included (a) the extent to which well-established committees (such as an oversight committee, technical review committee) existed, (b) the extent to which well-defined mechanisms such as escalation paths for conflict resolution were used, and (c) the extent to which a separate outsourcing office and key liaisons (or relationship managers) were used by the customer to coordinate with the provider. Both customers and providers need to invest in *aligning* their structural governance mechanisms for outsourcing to achieve the desired outsourcing benefits.

3.3   Partnership

When IT outsourcing agreements became popular in the early 1990s, starting with the landmark Kodak-IBM outsourcing deal in 1989, the dominant approach was to consider outsourcing providers as 'suppliers.' The IT outsourcing decision was viewed primarily as a make versus buy decision. However, as outsourcing agreements have evolved over the years, customers have increasingly come to view their IT providers as 'partners' rather than suppliers (Willcocks and Kern 1998). The goal of a service partnership is to not just satisfy a customer's needs and maintain a contractual arrangement, but to *enhance* the customer–provider relationship (Johnson and Seines 2004).

As partners in a service exchange, providers and customers can choose to interact formally or informally to establish common goals and achieve value. According to Spohrer et al. (2008), these interactions take place by not only explicit means – such as commitments and contractual promises – but also by implicit means in which social norms 'govern' the relationship. Informal modes of interaction can provide access to resources (access rights), and can significantly impact value co-production (Ramirez 1999).

Consistent with this notion, prior research in IT outsourcing has found that the quality of the collaboration between a customer and provider is a significant predictor of outsourcing success (Grover et al. 1996; Lee and Kim 1999). Establishing effective collaborations between the customer and the provider can also curtail negative effects such as cost overruns and internal resistance (Marcolin 2002).

The Partnership component therefore captures the collaborative aspects of the customer–provider relationship, including trust-forming mechanisms and the extent of informal meetings with key stakeholders. It is measured using the degree of compatibility between customer and provider with respect to values, norms, goals, and objectives. It also includes trust, and the extent of informal meetings with stakeholders, and captures how customers and providers effectively coordinate the informal aspects of their relationship. Having appropriate sponsors and champions from both customer and provider collaboratively involved on a regular basis is fundamental to ensuring the success of the engagement.

The study by Balaji (2008) indicates (a) the extent to which social meetings and informal review meetings were conducted with the provider, (b) the extent to which customer and provider had compatible work cultures, and (c) the extent to which customer and provider had a similar outlook on values, norms, and various issues in the engagement are significant predictors of outsourcing performance. In other words, outsourcing engagements in which providers and their customers had compatible outlooks and work cultures outperformed those engagements that did not. Customers and providers therefore need to invest in *aligning* these collaborative partnering aspects to achieve the desired outsourcing performance, in addition to aligning their formal contractual aspects.

3.4   Communications

The Communications component refers to the extent to which the customer and provider can effectively share information, ideas, and knowledge, and ensure a clear mutual understanding about the status of their respective objectives. Prior research on strategic alliances argues that the sharing of information and knowledge between partners is a significant predictor of alliance performance. In particular, the customers' relevant domain knowledge needs to be shared with the provider, and the provider's perception of the status for meeting the customer's objectives needs to be shared with the customer.

Recent IT outsourcing studies have also shown that the extent and quality of communications and knowledge transfer between the customer and provider are related to outsourcing success. Such sharing of knowledge is extremely important not only for strategic knowledge-intensive application development engagements, but also for complex IT infrastructure outsourcing engagements (Hawk et al. 2009). These authors also argue that investments in knowledge management capabilities, such as devising ways of understanding how best to handle and overcome knowledge transfer challenges in an outsourcing arrangement, are also related to outsourcing success (Hawk et al. 2009). Liaisons facilitate knowledge sharing and effective exchange of ideas.

The study by Balaji (2008) also indicates that greater customer learning in outsourcing engagements leads to perceptions of higher outsourcing performance. The survey items that were used to capture the communications aspects in this study included (a) the extent which the customer learned something new and valuable from the outsourcing engagement, and (b) the measurement of the different types of knowledge – including technical, business, and project management knowledge – regarding the engagement. These results imply that investing in communications for knowledge transfer for outsourcing is crucial for the customer and provider firm, to derive maximum benefits from outsourcing.

3.5   Human Resources and Skills

The Human Resources component includes the hiring, training, motivation, and retaining of people resources that are part of an outsourcing engagement. IT outsourcing involves a complex network of people resources from both the customer and provider organizations. Resources are sometimes even pooled together from both the provider and customer firms, which has direct impacts on the service profit chain of an IT outsourcing engagement (Heskett et al. 1994).

Fast-growing IT outsourcing provider firms can also be faced with different HR challenges than their customers, such as higher turnover rates in provider firms operating in developing countries. Due to such workforce fluctuations, retaining exceptional talent as well as maintaining high motivation levels among employees can be a difficult challenge for providers (Mehta and Mehta 2009). Since employee satisfaction in the provider directly impacts the service value provided to the customer (Heskett et al. 1994), investing in HR practices that develop and retain talent to benefit both the customer and the provider becomes fundamentally important.

Customers and providers in mature relationships therefore engage in personnel development strategies that are not just intra-firm approaches, such as 360-degree feedback, but also customer–provider, cross-firm performance feedback. Rewards for cross-firm learning, the ability to leverage new ideas from a business partner, and the sharing of risks and rewards would also be characteristics of more mature relationships.

The Skills dimension of this component refers to the extent to which the customer and provider provide complementary skills in the outsourcing engagement. Provider and customer firms are constantly faced with having employees with the needed skill sets in rapidly changing IT industry environments. For application development outsourcing, the required skills can be classified under three categories: technical skills, business skills, and project management skills. For example, a strategic engagement to define a new integrated CRM initiative would demand a strong balance of industry, business, process, technical, and project management knowledge, as well as strong interpersonal skills to work with business and IT executives in the customer firm; some of these skills would be much less important for an operational engagement to maintain a VOIP system.

The extent to which distinct skills/resources are brought to the table by the customer *and* the provider characterizes the maturity of the relationship. The survey items that were used to capture the skills aspect in Balaji (2008) included the extent to which the different skills were provided by the customer firm or the provider firm. Analysis of the survey responses for the skills dimension from Balaji (2008) indicates that outsourcing engagements, in which customers and providers *complement* their technical skills and business skills, outperformed those that did not. This implies that, based on the nature of the engagement, both customers and providers need to understand the mix of skills that needs to be brought to the table by the customer and provider – i.e., each service entity needs to understand what type of skills they need to provide, and what type of skills they need to acquire from the other firm. This also has implications for what skills need to be acquired and retained by a customer or provider for future IT outsourcing engagements.

The HR and Skills component is an important alignment dimension for both the customer and provider. If the appropriate people resources cannot be deployed by either the provider or the customer in a given engagement, consideration may also be given to outsourcing to a third party. In a mature relationship, both the customer and provider are continuously assessing the extent to which their people resources are well aligned for current and future engagements.

3.6   Scope and Architecture

The Scope of the outsourced IT offerings and the IT architecture used for the outsourcing engagement has both reach and range characteristics (Keen 1991). Scope refers to the range of IT offerings outsourced and the role expectations for the customer and the provider. For example, operational support functions (e.g., help-desk support and software maintenance activities) are typically associated with a more passive relationship between the customer and the provider. In contrast, strategic initiatives such as defining and designing a new integrated supply chain management system requires more proactive roles on the part of the customer and the provider to develop more customizable solutions and to enable or drive business strategies (Nolan and McFarlan 2005). Further, an application that involves more than an internal customer reach – such as interactions with the customer's customers or other business partners – would require a very mature customer–provider relationship.

Architecture refers to the hardware, software, and networking choices (including standards) used for the outsourcing engagement. In many IT outsourcing engagements, the customer and provider firms have differing perspectives on the nature of the IT infrastructural components to be used in the outsourcing engagement, due to their varied experiences in their own organizations and industries, or with other companies. For example, a customer might prefer a one-part XML-based standard, but an IT provider might prefer a three-part XLSI-based standard to take advantage of multiple layers available for development (Markus et al. 2006). Differing perspectives about the expectations for a specific outsourcing engagement is a characteristic of a less mature relationship.

The extent to which the customer and provider are engaged in strategic (as opposed to operational) initiatives also affects the maturity level that is most appropriate for an engagement. Customer firms need to understand to what extent their outsourcing engagements can help them refocus on their core business, move them from technological obsolescence, and decrease the cost of their products/services. In more mature customer–provider relationships, the provider would typically be expected to work with the customer in defining internal standards, as well as those that extend beyond the customer (to the customer's customers and other business partners). More mature relationships would also be characterized by providers taking a leading role in identifying, evaluating, and applying emerging technologies for the benefit of the customer, as well as providing the means for evolving the customer to a more flexible infrastructure.

4   Five Levels of Alignment Maturity

Like other maturity models (e.g., CMM/CMMI model and People Maturity model from the Carnegie Mellon Institute, SAM model by Luftman 2000), the CPSAM model has multiple maturity levels. The Optimized label is also used in the earlier models to signal the most mature or ideal state. The five levels in the CPSAM model can be described as follows:

1. *Initial/ad hoc*. Customer and provider have low alignment and harmony in their relationship.
2. *Committed*. Customer and provider have strong commitment to align. Some processes are emerging, while some are lacking in improvement.
3. *Established/focused*. Strategic alignment maturity between the customer and provider is established and focused. Most processes show better articulation and implementation; others are evolving.
4. *Managed*. Customer and provider realize value potential from each other's contributions. There is a higher degree of integration and customer–provider participation in each other's business activities.
5. *Optimized*. Customer and provider strategic planning is integrated and co-adapts and co-evolves as needed; there is flexibility to change rapidly to match changing business conditions and learning from each other. Joint value is realized, governance structures are highly adaptive and may be extended to include additional strategic partners, and informal interactions are relied on to be tightly aligned.

4.1   Performing the Assessment

Different scales can be applied to perform the assessment (e.g., qualitative scales such as excellent, good, fair, poor; quantitative ratings, with a midpoint, such as 1–5). Whatever the scale, it is important to evaluate each of the six components with both customer and provider executives, to obtain an accurate joint assessment. The idea is to have the team of customer and provider executives converge on a maturity level with the collaborative goal of achieving an alignment level appropriate for a given customer–provider engagement. The process for applying the strategic alignment assessment to obtain the engagement's maturity score (using the model as a descriptive tool) is a key step for deriving a plan to improve alignment maturity (using the model as a prescriptive tool), as described later in this chapter.

Further, although the maturity model applies to a single customer–provider relationship, pooling together the scores can also provide a basis for assessing the overall maturity of the customer in its multiple outsourcing relationships. As Poston et al. (2009) point out from a customer perspective, for customers with

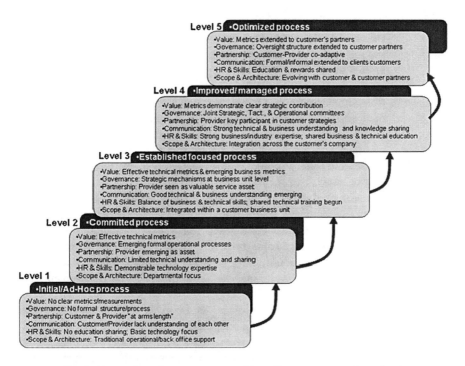

Level 5 •Optimized process
- •Value: Metrics extended to customer's partners
- •Governance: Oversight structure extended to customer partners
- •Partnership: Customer-Provider co-adaptive
- •Communication: Formal/informal extended to clients customers
- •HR & Skills: Education & rewards shared
- •Scope & Architecture: Evolving with customer & customer partners

Level 4 •Improved/ managed process
- •Value: Metrics demonstrate clear strategic contribution
- •Governance: Joint Strategic, Tact., & Operational committees
- •Partnership: Provider key participant in customer strategies
- •Communication: Strong technical & business understanding and knowledge sharing
- •HR & Skills: Strong business/industry expertise; shared business & technical education
- •Scope & Architecture: Integration across the customer's company

Level 3 •Established focused process
- •Value: Effective technical metrics & emerging business metrics
- •Governance: Strategic mechanisms at business unit level
- •Partnership: Provider seen as valuable service asset
- •Communication: Good technical & business understanding emerging
- •HR & Skills: Balance of business & technical skills; shared technical training begun
- •Scope & Architecture: Integrated within a customer business unit

Level 2 •Committed process
- •Value: Effective technical metrics
- •Governance: Emerging formal operational processes
- •Partnership: Provider emerging as asset
- •Communication: Limited technical understanding and sharing
- •HR & Skills: Demonstrable technology expertise
- •Scope & Architecture: Departmental focus

Level 1 •Initial/Ad-Hoc process
- •Value: No clear metrics/measurements
- •Governance: No formal structure/process
- •Partnership: Customer & Provider "at arms length"
- •Communication: Customer/Provider lack understanding of each other
- •HR & Skills: No education sharing; Basic technology focus
- •Scope & Architecture: Traditional operational/back office support

Fig. 2. Examples of customer–provider alignment maturity criteria

multi-provider arrangements, a lack of focus on the portfolio of providers ('vendor set') can lead to sub-optimal outcomes for the customer.

4.2   Component Metrics for Each Maturity Level

The measurement criteria for the five levels of alignment maturity are presented below and summarized in Fig. 2.

Level 1: Initial or ad-hoc processes. Organizations at Level 1 generally have poor communications between customer and provider and also a poor understanding of the value or contribution the other service entity provides. Their relationships tend to be formal and rigid, based on contracts alone, and their metrics are usually technical rather than business oriented. Service level agreements are ad-hoc, not comprehensive. Engagement planning is also ad-hoc. Customers view the provider from a pure cost perspective, and the two entities have minimal trust for their service partners. Little to no HR information and training are shared. The engagement focus is operational, traditional back-office support such as e-mail, help desk, accounting, and HR, with little integration intent. Finally, Level 1 organizations do not have an integrated customer–provider strategy.

Level 2: Committed processes. Organizations at Level 2 have begun enhancing their customer–provider relationship. Alignment occurs for independent functions or geographical locations. However, the customer and provider have limited overall understanding of each others' responsibilities and roles. Provider metrics and service levels are technical and cost-oriented, and they are not linked to other value measurements. The technical skills of the provider are typically the most important for the engagement. Interactions between customer and provider entities tend to be transaction-based rather than partnership-based and perceived provider value relates to basic operations. There is some sharing of education/training between the customer and provider, but investments in developing the customer–provider relationship are limited.

Level 3: Established, focused processes. In Level 3, the customer–provider engagement becomes more integrated enterprise-wide. Key stakeholders (e.g., engagement managers, executives, sponsors, and champions) from the provider understand the customer, and the customer's understanding of the provider is emerging. Service level agreements (SLAs) begin to reflect enterprise-level goals although the results are not always proactively shared or acted upon. Strategic planning tends to be done separately, although some customer–provider planning has begun. The provider is increasingly viewed by the customer as an asset, but engagement prioritization still usually responds to "the loudest voice." Formal governance committees emerge and meet regularly. The provider engagement is still primarily driven by cost versus longer-term contributions, but awareness of the provider's "investment potential" is emerging. The customer is more tolerant of outsourcing risks and is willing to engage in some risk-sharing with the provider. Education/training crossovers and more people resource pooling between the customer and provider occur. Both business/industry and technical skills become important to the relationship. Provider influence is emerging at the enterprise level.

Level 4: Improved, managed processes. Organizations at Level 4 manage the processes they need for strategic alignment. One of the important attributes of this level is that increased provider understanding of the customer and customer understanding of the provider has closed the service gaps. The provider's service offerings reinforce the concept of the provider as a value co-producer, with initiatives to co-produce strategic value and offerings to enhance the customer's business processes for sustainable competitive advantage. Provider influence is demonstrated at the enterprise level. SLAs reflect enterprise-wide customer goals, and benchmarking (and taking action based on benchmarking results) is a routine practice. Strategic customer and provider planning processes are appropriately integrated. Formal governance committees meet regularly and are effective at the strategic, tactical, and operational levels. The customer views the provider as a valued provider and as an enabler (or driver) of change. The customer and provider share risks and rewards. Communications and change management are highly effective. Education/training and IT talent cross-overs between the customer and provider are recognized as effective long-term mechanisms for harmony.

Level 5: *Optimized processes.* Organizations at Level 5 have optimized strategic customer–provider alignment through rigorous governance structures and informal interactions, as well as processes that integrate strategic business planning and provider planning. Alignment goes beyond the specific customer–provider engagement; the provider has extended its reach to encompass the value chains of the client's customers and suppliers; business metrics, provider metrics, and SLAs are also extended to linkages with external partners. Trusted relationships between the customer and provider are reinforced through informal interactions, and new knowledge is regularly shared. Benchmarking and value measurements are routinely performed Strategic customer and provider planning are integrated to ensure business investment decisions that reflect the potential and actual value received from the continuous investment in the customer–provider relationship.

4.3   Strategic Alignment as a Process

The approach applied to attain and sustain customer–provider alignment focuses on understanding the alignment maturity, and on maximizing alignment enablers and minimizing inhibitors. The process includes the following six steps:

1. *Set the goals and establish a team.* Ensure that there is an executive business sponsor and champion(s) for the alignment assessment from both the customer and provider organizations. Next, assign a team of both customer business and IT stakeholders, and provider stakeholders. Obtaining appropriate representatives from the major business units that are impacted by the engagement is critical to the success of the assessment. The purpose of the team is to evaluate the maturity of the customer–provider alignment with the objective of enhancing the of customer and provider relationship. Facilitated assessments can range from 3 to 12 half-day sessions. The time demanded depends on the scope of the

engagement, number of participants, the degree of consensus required, and the extent of the recommendations to carry out.

2. *Understand the customer–provider linkage.* The CPSAM assessment is an important tool in understanding the current status of a customer–provider relationship. The team evaluates each of the six components. Perspectives can be obtained via any combination of interviews, group discussion, or surveys. All of the elements are important – focusing only on one or a subset will likely lead to failure; there is no silver bullet. A trained impartial facilitator can be valuable in guiding the important discussions.

3. *Analyze and prioritize gaps.* Recognize that the different opinions raised by the participants are indicative of the alignment opportunities that exist. Once understood, the group needs to converge on a maturity level (using the model as a descriptive tool). The team must remember that the purpose of this step is to understand the activities necessary to improve the customer–provider linkage. The gaps between where the organizations are today and where the team believes it needs to be are the gaps that need to be prioritized. Knowing where the organizations are with regards to alignment maturity will drive what specific actions are appropriate to enhance customer–provider alignment.

4. *Specify the actions (project management).* Apply the next higher level of maturity as a roadmap to identify what can be done next, thus using the model as a prescriptive tool. Assign specific remedial tasks with clearly defined deliverables, ownership, timeframes, resources, risks, and measurements for each of the prioritized gaps.

5. *Choose and evaluate success criteria.* This step necessitates revisiting the goals and regularly discussing the measurement criteria identified to evaluate the implementation of the project plans. The review of the measurements should serve as a learning vehicle to understand how and why the objectives are or are not being met.

6. *Sustain alignment.* Obtaining customer–provider alignment is a difficult task, and this last step in the process is particularly challenging because business and environmental conditions change. To sustain the benefit from the engagement, an alignment mindset and alignment "behaviors" must be developed and cultivated.

The criteria described to assess alignment maturity provide characteristics needed to improve customer–provider alignment. By adopting an alignment mindset and behaviors, the service entities can increase their potential for a more mature alignment, and improve their ability to gain business value from outsourcing. Taking the necessary actions to improve both customer–provider harmony and the co-production of business value from the engagement is fundamental. However, a *continued focus* on understanding the alignment maturity for a given customer–provider engagement is also a requirement.

5   Conclusions

Achieving and sustaining an appropriate level of customer–provider alignment maturity are essential for successful IT outsourcing. Outsourcing relationships evolve over time, across customers and across providers. The goal of this chapter was to provide a comprehensive model and measurement tool for assessing customer–provider alignment maturity at a given point in time.

Like IT–business alignment, which is a persistent and pervasive challenge, customer–provider alignment is also a persistent and pervasive challenge, especially given today's dynamic business and technical environments. Experience shows that no single activity will enable a firm to attain and sustain IT–business alignment, and the same situation is true for customer–provider alignment. Lack of alignment threatens the achievement of the goals for a specific outsourcing engagement; it also means missed opportunities for value co-production from these types of partnerships.

This chapter described a comprehensive model and measurement tool for systematically assessing the alignment maturity of a customer–provider IT outsourcing arrangement. It is a valuable tool for both customers and providers to evaluate a current IT service relationship and identify what actions to take to attain and sustain alignment as the respective customer–provider engagement evolves. It is also an important tool for identifying the specific actions necessary to ensure future engagements are effective with other IT service entities, as well as to avoid IT outsourcing engagement failures.

This chapter also highlights some future research directions for researchers in the services domain. Effective co-production requires not only relationship management, but also alignment across six components. Further research on the criteria and the application of the CPSAM model are warranted by practitioners, consultants, and researchers alike. The authors' own research intentions are to enhance this alignment measurement tool in collaboration with industry, with a long-term goal of providing a vehicle to benchmark exemplar customer and provider organizations.

6   Appendix: Methodology for Two Primary CPSAM Sources

The Luftman Strategic Alignment Maturity (SAM) assessment has been applied since 2000 to over one quarter of the Global 1,000 companies, as well as hundreds of companies of all sizes. It evaluates six components (the same six described in this chapter) of an organization to identify an alignment maturity score, and more importantly, specific opportunities to improve the IT–business relationship. The instrument is robust and validated (Luftman and Kempaiah 2007; Sledgianowski 2004; Nash 2005; Rigoni et al. 2006). For this research, interviews, group discussions, and questionnaires were administered to over 2,000 business and IT executives from four regions and seven countries.

The Balaji study (Balaji 2008) involved an online survey of members of the Project Management Institute (PMI-ISSIG). Target respondents were specified as IS managers in customer firms responsible for an application development outsourcing engagement. A total of 141 useful responses were obtained from all three rounds of the survey. The profile of the survey respondents who provided demographic data is as follows: 67% were male; 76% were senior IT managers such as at the level of directors, CIO, and/or VP; and the median age was between 40 and 50. The survey data was analyzed using Partial Least Squares (PLS) techniques, to establish instrument validity, obtain construct correlations and to establish causal effects.

References

Balaji, S. (2008). IS Outsourcing Effectiveness: Understanding the Effects of Relationship Diversities, Client Capabilities and Knowledge Capital Gains. Ph.D. Dissertation, Indiana University, Bloomington.

Barretto, C. B. (2004). Weekender: Labor & Management. *Business World*, p. 1.

Caldwell, B. (2002). 2001 Trends in IT Outsourcing Delivery, Solution Development, Marketing, Sales and Alliances. *Gartner Dataquest*. http://www.Itclive.com/e-mail/docs/2001 trendsoutsourcing.pdf. Accessed 18 November 2004.

Grover, V., Cheon, M.J. and Teng, J.T.C. (1996). The Effect of Service Quality and Partnership on the Outsourcing of Information Systems Functions. *Journal of Management Information Systems*, 12(4), 89–116.

Hawk, S., Zheng, W. and Zmud, R.W. (2009). Overcoming Knowledge-Transfer Barriers in Infrastructure Management Outsourcing: Lessons from a Case Study. *MIS Quarterly Executive*, 8(3), 123–139.

Henderson, J. and Venkatraman, N. (1993). Strategic Alignment: Leveraging Information Technology for Transforming Organizations. *IBM Systems Journal*, 32(1), 4–16.

Heskett, J.L., Jones, T.O., Loveman, G.W., Sasser Jr. W.E., and Schlesinger, L.A. (1994). Putting the Service-Profit Chain to Work. *Harvard Business Review*, 72(2), 164–174.

Jia, R., Reich, B.H. and Pearson, M.J. (2008). IT Service Climate: An Extension to IT Service Quality Research, *Journal of the Association of Information Systems*, 9(5), 294–320.

Johnson, M.D. and Seines, F. (2004). Customer Portfolio Management: Towards a Dynamic Theory of Exchange Relationships. *Journal of Marketing*, 68, 5.

Keen, P.G. (1991). Shaping the Future: Business Design through Information Technology. *Harvard Business School Press*, Boston.

Kettinger, W.J. and Lee, C.C. (1994). Perceived Service Quality and User Satisfaction with the Information Services Function. *Decision Sciences*, 25(5), 737–766.

Lacity, M.C. and Willocks, L.P. (1998). An Empirical Investigation of Information Technology Sourcing Practices: Lessons from Experience. *MIS Quarterly*, 22(3), 363–408.

Lee, J. and Kim, Y. (1999). Effect of Partnership Quality on IS Outsourcing Success: Conceptual Framework and Empirical Validation. *Journal of Management Information Systems*, 15(4), 29–61.

Luftman, J. (2000). Assessing Business-IT Alignment Maturity. *Communications of the Association of Information Systems*, 4(14), 1–50.

Luftman, J. and Kempaiah, R. (2007). An Update on Business-IT Alignment: A Line Has Been Drawn. *MIS Quarterly Executive*, 6(3), 165–177.

Luftman, J., Kempaiah, R. and Rigoni, E. (2009). Key Issues for IT Executives 2008. *MIS Quarterly Executive*, 8(3), 151–159.

Maglio, P.P., Srinivasan, S., Kreulen, J.T. and Spohrer, J. (2006). Service Systems, Service Scientists, SSME, and Innovation. *Communications of the ACM*, 49(7), 81–85.

March, J.G. (1988). *Decisions and Organizations*. New York: Basil Blackwell.

Marcolin, B.L. (2002). Spiraling Effects of IS Outsourcing Contract Interpretations. In R. Hirschheim, A. Heinzl and J. Dibbern (Eds.), *Information Systems Outsourcing: Enduring Themes, Emergent Patterns and Future Directions* (pp. 277–311). Berlin: Springer-Verlag.

Markus, L.M., Steinfeld, C.W. and Wigand, R.T. (2006). Industry-wide Information Systems Standardization as Collective Action: The Case Study of the U.S. Residential Mortgage Industry. *MIS Quarterly*, 30 (Special Issue), 439–465.

Mehta, N. and Mehta, A. (2009). Reducing the Client Risks from Human Resource Challenges of Offshore IT Vendors. *MIS Quarterly Executive*, 8(4), 191–201.

Nash, E. (2005). Assessing IT as a Driver or Enabler of Transformation in the Pharmaceutical Industry Employing the Strategic Alignment Maturity Model. Ph.D. Dissertation, Stevens Institute of Technology, Hoboken.

Nolan, R. and McFarlan, F.W. (2005). Information Technology and the Board of Directors. *Harvard Business Review*, 83(10), 96–106.

Parasuraman, A., Berry, L.L. and Zeithaml, V.A. (1985). A Conceptual Model of Service Quality and Its Implications for Future Research. *Journal of Marketing*, 49(4), 41–50.

Parasuraman, A., Berry, L.L. and Zeithaml, V.A. (1988). SERVQUAL: A Multiple-Item Scale for Measuring Consumer Perceptions of Service Quality. *Journal of Retailing*, 64(1), 12–40.

Poppo, L. and Zenger, T. (2002). Do Formal Contracts and Relational Governance Function as Substitutes or Complements? *Strategic Management Journal* 23(8), 707–725.

Poston, R.S., Kettinger, W.J. and Simon, J.C. (2009). Managing the Vendor Set: Achieving Best Pricing and Quality Service in IT Outsourcing. *MIS Quarterly Executive*, 8(2), 45–58.

Ramirez, R. (1999). Value Co-Production: Intellectual Origins and Implications for Practice and Research. *Strategic Management Journal*, 20(1), 49–65.

Ranganathan, C. and Balaji, S. (2007). Critical Capabilities for Offshore Outsourcing of Information Systems. *MIS Quarterly Executive*, 6(3), 147–164.

Rigoni, E., Lunardi, G., Brodbeck, A. and Maçada, A. (2006). Validation of Quantitative Instruments in Information Systems Research: A Study of Strategic Alignment Maturity. *Business Association of Latin American Studies (BALAS)*, http://balas.org/

Simhan, R. (2002). An Inside View of Outsourcing. *Business Line online edition*. http://www.thehindubusinessline.com/ew/2002/10/30/stories/2002103000020100.htm. Accessed 22 October 2005.

Sledgianowski, D. (2004). Identification of Factors Affecting the Maturity of Business-IT Strategic Alignment. Ph.D. Dissertation, Stevens Institute of Technology, Hoboken.

Spohrer, J., and Kwan, S.K. (2009). Service Science, Management, Engineering, and Design (SSMED): An Emerging Discipline – Outline and References. *International Journal of Information Systems in the Service Sector*, 1(3).

Spohrer, J., Anderson, L., Pass, N. and Ager, T. (2008). Service Science and Service-Dominant Logic. *Otago Forum 2 – Academic Papers*. http://www.commerce.otago.ac.nz/marketing/events/OtagoForum/Final%20forum%20papers/Otago%20Forum%20Paper%202_Spohrer.pdf. Accessed 10 October 2009.

Vargo, S.L., and Lusch, R.F. (2004). Evolving to a New Dominant Logic for Marketing. *Journal of Marketing*, 68(1), 1–17.

Willcocks, L.P., and Kern, T. (1998). IT Outsourcing as Strategic Partnering: The Case of the UK Inland Revenue. *European Journal of Information Systems*, 7(2), 29–45.

Williamson, O.E. (1999). *The Mechanisms of Governance*. Oxford: Oxford University Press.

Zeithaml, V., Parasuraman, A. and Berry, L. (1991). Refinement and Reassessment of the SERVQUAL Scale. *Journal of Retailing*, 67(4), 420–450.

CIO in a Service Economy

Paul G. Sorenson

Department of Computing Science, University of Alberta, Alberta, Canada T6G 2E8

Abstract The role of the Chief Information Officer (CIO) has evolved considerably since its inception in the 1980s. This paper begins with a brief review of the evolution of this role and sets the stage for future change brought about by the rise of the service economy. The enterprise of the future is then characterized based on an important global study by IBM. Using this characterization, the future challenges for CIOs in areas such as strategic planning, governance and operations management of information technology services are assessed from the perspectives of the four major elements of a service system (technology, people, organization and shared information). The paper concludes with a summary of the important findings, pointing to the challenge that CIOs of the future must be the leaders in their organizations in the delivery of smarter, on-demand service systems to smarter customers.

This chapter explores the impact of the growing service economy on the role of CIO in both today's enterprise and the enterprise of the future. We begin by reviewing both the changing role of the CIO in Sect. 1 and the rise of services in our modern economy in Sect. 2. We then review an important study on the enterprise of the future in Sect. 3 and use this as a basis for better understanding the future role of the CIO. Next, we examine in Sects. 4–7, respectively, the four major elements of a service system (technology, people, organization and shared information) and the impact the CIO must have on each of these elements pertaining to activities such the strategic planning, governance and operations management of information technology services. Finally, in Sect. 8 we summarize our findings and dangerously distill the results into a final statement that CIOs of the future must be the leaders in delivering smarter, on-demand service systems to smarter customers.

Keywords Service science, service systems, chief information officer, service economy, service innovation

H. Demirkan et al. (eds.), *Service Systems Implementation*, Service Science: Research and Innovations in the Service Economy, DOI 10.1007/978-1-4419-7904-9_10, © Springer Science+Business Media, LLC 2011

1   The Changing Role of the CIO

This section reviews the initial focus of the CIO[1] position in enterprises and how it has changed in the past decade. It sets the stage for later sections by identifying the need for even greater change in the future brought about by the rise of service-oriented systems.

In most enterprises, CIO positions were created by enhancing the Director of IT Services position, which was primarily focused on IT operations, to a position focused on the strategic deployment of IT across the organization. Traditionally the CIO's role dealt with the planning and managing of information systems infrastructure for an enterprise. As the use of information technology grew tremendously in modern enterprises the CIO role became even more strategic. In the past decade, the role has risen in the management hierarchy to the point that in many enterprises it is positioned as a Vice-President (CIO Papers 2009). This change is illustrated by examining the following ordered list of the ten most concerns for CIOs as uncovered by CIO magazine in their 2007 survey of CIOs (CIO 2007).

1. People leadership
2. Managing budgets
3. Business alignment
4. Infrastructure refresh
5. Security
6. Compliance to regulations
7. Resource management
8. Managing customers
9. Managing change
10. Board politics

While some items like 4, 5, 7–9 have operational aspects, all items have significant strategic elements that must be addressed by the CIO.

The strategic nature of this position is further reinforced by a 2008 Centre for CIO Leadership survey in which CIOs worldwide assessed themselves in four categories of core competencies: leadership, business strategy and process, innovation and growth, and organization and talent management. The survey findings revealed "… several areas of opportunity for further advancement in CIO skills and competencies:

---

[1] "Chief Information Officer (CIO) is a job title commonly given to the person in an enterprise responsible for the information technology and computer systems that support enterprise goals. As information technology and systems have become more important, the CIO has come to be viewed in many organizations as a key contributor in formulating strategic goals. Usually, a CIO proposes the information technology an enterprise will need to achieve its goals and then works within a budget to implement the plan" (SearchCIO 2009).

- CIOs are leaders in their organizations and are playing an increasingly important role in leading change, but they are still evolving to be viewed as true trusted advisors by their business colleagues.
- CIOs have a seat at the [Executive] table, but have yet to fully seize the opportunity for participation in developing the business strategy.
- CIOs are emerging as leaders of innovation and bringing new ideas to the enterprise, with a real opportunity remaining to fill the innovation execution gap.
- CIOs know where they need to lead their IT organizations, but continue to wrestle with delegation and with building the next-generation team" (IBM Center for CIO Leadership 2008).

In a study involving people who are not CIOs (CIOInsight 2006), respondents give a less positive view of the leadership abilities of CIOs than CIOs provide in their self-assessment. Specifically, 96% of CIOs rate their leadership abilities as excellent or good, while only 64% of other IT executives, 63% of IT managers and professionals, and 76% of business executives rate CIOs leadership abilities as excellent or good. The primary reason cited for this difference in perception is "... they [CIOs] still haven't mastered key relationship-building skills: dealing with difficult people issues and sensitivity to others... the problem is that some CIOs who think they have a 'logical' leadership style are seen as having a 'commanding' style..."

In the article *Circa 2015: The CIO of the Future* (Cramm 2008) author Susan Cramm lists several changes to the current IT operating model that will transpire if CIOs show the leadership she believes is needed in the next 5–10 years.

1. Enterprises will recognize that IT is an organizational asset, not simply an organization structure.
2. IT will transition from being the sole provider of the asset to enabling IT capabilities of others in the enterprise.
3. IT will shift focus from controlling to defining IT policies.
4. IT will shift from servicing to coaching.
5. IT will shift from providing "point" solutions to providing enabling tools.
6. IT will shift from managing fixed assets to managing *variable, on demand services*.

Cramm (2008) points out that the biggest obstacles preventing CIOs from leading this shift is the lack of time and consultation with other business leaders in the organization. We will revisit Cramm's suggestions for change to the IT operating model later in the chapter when we examine the key elements of IT service systems.

2   The Rise of Services

With the increased emphasis on service-oriented architectures and the ability to interact with stored information anywhere at any time via a web browser, the decisions of what services to support and how they should be supported (internal, outsourced or subscribed) are becoming increasingly complex. This section provides some background to the increase in the service sector of our economy. It also sets the stage for an analysis of both the effects of these changes and the service quality considerations broken down by the major elements characterizing a service system: technology, people, organizations and shared data.

A 2005 OECD Council report reveals "… the services sector now accounts for over 70% of total employment and value added in the OECD economies." Much of this sector growth has been in the past decade with "… services [in particular for markets such as telecom, finance, transport, insurance and business services] accounting for around 60% of all employment created in the OECD" (Meeting of the OECD Council at Ministerial Level 2005). Although this growth is impressive, the report notes that productivity growth in services has been slow in many OECD countries. Some of the important factors affecting success and growth are: open markets and the globalization of services, innovation in services by leveraging information and communication technologies, and the changing nature of organizations and the workforce. The report encourages policy makers to take seven actions related to opening markets, labor and education reform to meet the rapidly changing needs for new skills in the service sector. It also recommends the removal of impediments preventing service firms from seizing the benefits of information and communications technology in support of service innovation.

Studies of the service economy in the United States reinforce this dramatic shift toward services and away from manufacturing. A 2006 study (Tien and Berg 2006) indicates "…services employment in the U.S. is at 82.1 percent, while the remaining four economic sectors (i.e., manufacturing, agriculture, construction, and mining), which together can be considered to be the 'goods' sector, employ the remaining 17.9 percent." This study, along with others (Chesbrough and Spohrer 2006), concludes that the service sector will continue to grow dramatically and both research and education in services systems lag behind the economic development in this sector. Before examining the effect of this growth in detail, we review an important study that provides a vision of what the enterprise of the future will look like.

3   Enterprise of the Future

In past 3 years IBM has undertaken annual Global CEO Studies involving over 1,000 CEOs from around the world. The 2008 study (IBM 2008a) focused on the general question of "what will the Enterprise of the Future look like?" Among the large number of interesting results from this consultation the study concluded that "At its core, the Enterprise of the Future is ... 1) hungry for change, 2) innovative beyond customer imagination, 3) globally integrated, 4) disruptive by nature, and 5) genuine, but not generous." Given the recent downturn in the world economy it may be difficult for enterprises to maneuver as quickly as they would like, but the need for enterprises to be both innovative and globally integrated will only increase in this economic climate.

What are the elements CIOs must take note of in this view of the future? With respect to "hungry for change" the CEOs see three external forces driving change: market factors, people skills and technology. For the CIO this means a focus on adding real value to the products and services of their organization, promoting more knowledgeable employees and keeping abreast of and, as appropriate, adopting technologies that produce real innovation.

More globally available markets and increasingly knowledgeable and demanding customers drive the need for greater innovation in the enterprise of the future. With billion+ customers available over the Internet, huge opportunities exist in new markets many of which either are service-oriented or provide service support for new products that are Internet-based. Again, the CIO can play a huge role in at least two ways: taking on a leadership role in promoting innovation in their enterprise and finding ways to connect the customer to all the important support mechanisms including helpful employees and customer-friendly service systems.

As the world becomes more globally connected CIOs must play a major role in identifying and promoting new sources of expertise and new markets (IBM 2008a). In the IBM study, 85% of CEOs plan to partner extensively to capitalize on global integration opportunities. In most instances effective integration means the formation of and support for global marketing, sales and service team activities – yet another area in which CIOs must provide leadership.

CEOs also indicated "... they are changing their business models because it is increasingly difficult to differentiate based on products and services alone." (IBM 2008a) Among the disruptive nature of change identified by the CEOs, "... 44% are focused solely on enterprise model innovation or are implementing it in combination with other forms of business model innovation."(IBM 2008a) One of the biggest opportunities for major change is by incorporating more services into enterprise offerings and changing from one-time to on-going payment models. This type of change creates important service system delivery challenges for the CIO.

The enterprise of the future must cater to "an emerging generation of socially minded customers, workers, partners, activists and investors..."(IBM 2008a). The demand is for corporate leadership that is genuinely interested in societal issues such as the environmental impact of the enterprise and regulatory compliance satisfying financial reporting, security and privacy legislation. The opportunities for CIOs in improving corporate social responsibility include a greater emphasis on "green computing" (Gingichashvill 2009) and the adoption of best practices in service management (e.g., such as implementing IT service management standards

(Swabey 2008). Determining the advantages and understanding the potential negative impact of social networking systems[2] on an enterprise is another important responsibility for the CIO. In response to the new generation of customers, workers, partners, etc., the enterprise of the future must be prepared to service a smarter and more interdependent world (Spohrer 2008).

We now turn our attention to the service quality aspects CIOs must understand and manage for each of the four components of a service system: technology, people, organization and shared data (Spohrer et al. 2007).

4   Technology

Traditionally, the predominant focus of the CIO has been on technology planning in order to meet the information management needs of an organization. Although many argue that the technology focus will not change substantially, the scope of the technology planning activity will broaden as service systems begin to dominate information management solutions in the future. In this section we examine the broadening that will occur at both the high or macro system level and the low or micro system level. For both levels, planning for technology will be driven by conformance quality considerations such as performance, reliability, and availability.

At the macro system level, new or improved technology is required to achieve higher-level application integration afforded by service systems. Significant advances have been made over the past decade in understanding and delivering on flexible SOA (Service Oriented Architecture) solutions and more user-friendly web service interfaces for applications; nevertheless, many of the existing applications do not integrate well with other applications. Major software vendors, such as Oracle and SAP, are re-architecting their ERP (Enterprise Resource Planning) systems (Oracle Corp. 2009) (SAP 2009) to take advantage of SOA and web service technology, but these are taking more time and money than originally planned. In response to the high cost of maintaining and upgrading existing service system assets, many enterprises are moving some of the non-strategic services to external agencies through outsourcing contracts or more recently using SaaS (Software-as-a-Service) offerings. Most CIOs have experience in outsourcing contracts and are well aware of both the advantages and the pitfalls of external contracting in this manner (ICT Standards 2009). SaaS, on the other hand, is a relatively new option with which few CIOs have direct experience. Because of the expected increase in SaaS use as our service economy expands, a CIO must understand its potential and drawbacks when undertaking service system planning activities.

In simple terms, SaaS is a model of software deployment where an application is hosted as a service provided to customers across the Internet (SaaS.com 2009). By eliminating the need to install and run the application on the customer's

---

[2] Such as Facebook, Twitter, Second Life and YouTube.

computer, SaaS alleviates the burden of software maintenance, ongoing operation, and client support for the customer. Conversely, customers relinquish control over software versions or changing requirements. Costs to use the service become a continuous expense, rather than a single expense at time of purchase. SaaS applications are generally charged on a per-user basis and are shared by multiple independent customers (Lheureux et al. 2006). The biggest apparent benefit for the service customer is access to "best-of-breed" software, with clearly understandable costs, at a contractually defined service level (Waters 2005). The role of the CIO in the deployment of SaaS in a customer organization is to work with the appropriate business unit(s) as an information technology advisor to ensure that a proposed SaaS solution provides real value by applying the following techniques:

- Functional analysis to determine that the requirements of the business unit can be met with the SaaS solution.
- Operational analysis such as determination of appropriate service level agreements (SLAs) related to conformance quality requirements such as responsiveness, reliability and availability.
- Financial analysis such as cost–benefit (Mindtools 2009) or ROI (Return-on-Investment) (CIO Council 2009) approaches.
- Risk determination and analysis (VOSE Software 2009) especially for risks related to data loss, security and privacy.

Although the presence of SaaS vendors is still relatively small and immature, the number of vendors is growing quickly (Alvarez 2008). Perhaps two of the best-known examples are Salesforce.com (2009), an early player in the customer relationship management market, and Google Aps (Google Corporation 2009). One of the largest challenges SaaS vendors have is the integration of their on-demand service with other services many of which might be provided in-house by the customer's IT services unit. More advanced SaaS vendors, like Salesforce, are wisely opening up some of their service system interfaces to third party vendors who can then market their expertise and service add-ons with the SaaS vendor. Effectively, this creates a community of service providers for an SaaS solution.

To assist in benchmarking SaaS capabilities, SaaS maturity models have recently been proposed. Microsoft (Chong and Carraro 2006) has a four level model that primarily focuses on an SaaS application architecture using three key attributes to differentiate capability: configurability, multi-tenant efficiency and scalability. Forrester (Ried et al. 2008) provides a five level model that provides a strategy for software vendors to move from a simple outsourcing capability to the provisioning of a comprehensive application and integration platform on demand, providing multi-tenant support that can be pre-populate with business applications or services. Both of these maturity models focus only on the service provider. In response to this Chen et al. (2010) have proposed a four level QoS (Quality of Service) SaaS evaluation model that takes into account the provider, the customer and the service relationship between provider and the customer. This model assists in defining QoS levels needed in SaaS support as these services become more strategic to a customer organization. Reviewing these maturity models would help a CIO's understanding of planning for SaaS in the future (Chen et al. 2010).

At the lower (micro service) level, new technologies such as server virtualization (like VMware (2009)) are providing tremendous new opportunities for managing services effectively across any organization: local, national or international. Virtualization is at the heart of SaaS deployment in a service infrastructure now commonly referred to as "cloud computing" (Gruman and Knorr 2008). Cloud computing yields scalability, multi-tenancy, reliability, security and sustainability. By leveraging the sharing of the almost unlimited resources in a cloud it is possible to support on-demand, pay-as-you-use services. At the micro system level this provides substantial benefits in terms of low cost, energy efficient solutions and the acquisition of additional service infrastructure on an as needed basis. Of course there are drawbacks to cloud computing that must be understood. These include the need to work with and negotiate suitable infrastructure service contracts with cloud computing service vendors related to performance guarantees and data security and ownership provisions.

5   People

People are ultimately the most important elements of a service system. We build service systems so people can use them effectively in their work and social interactions. Service systems promise more user friendly, responsive and flexible support for people in organizations. This section identifies some of the important issues that must be considered by organizations in general and CIOs in particular to take advantage of these new service system capabilities. We also examine approaches to measuring the impact on customers of service system deployment using gap quality measures. Such measures are needed to improve the overall functionality and quality of service systems.

People who build and maintain service systems are usually from the service provider organization and people who use the service systems are generally from the service customer organization. Although there are exceptions to these two roles, these are the predominant people roles and the two we concentrate on in this section.

As noted in Sect. 1, *People Leadership* is identified as the most important concern for CIOs in the recent CIO survey. People leadership is an issue for CIOs from either service provider organizations or service customer organizations.

For service provider organizations, employing people who are productive and innovative in the deployment and management of service systems is critical to their organization's success. People with strong information technology skills are needed to design, implement, maintain and evolve service systems. CTOs[3] in a provider organization must show leadership in service system innovation, and plan the development and be responsible for the management of a strong group of IT professionals. All IT professionals know they must upgrade their skills continuously. This need has certainly not changed in the past 5 years during which the dramatic increase in the deployment of service systems has occurred. Increased knowledge and use of SOA and web services dominate the recently-needed skills set. Future skills (Erlanger 2008) include new technologies such as virtualization, the unification of communications (in particular, voice, video and data), wireless networking and security, and the development of modern applications that are not just web-enabled, but can be seamlessly integrated (or "mashed-up") with mobile GPS (Global Positioning Services) and sensor-based services.

In addition to individuals with IT skills, there is a growing need for people who understand the use of service systems from an enterprise-wide, business perspective. Skill sets for these individuals have been mapped out in the new emerging area of SSME (Service Science, Management and Engineering). In the article (University of Cambridge and IBM 2008), an interdisciplinary approach is needed in the development new "T-shaped" professionals in SSME who are equipped "… with the concepts and vocabulary to discuss the design and improvement of service systems with peers in other disciplines." The authors believe this approach can lead to (University of Cambridge and IBM 2008)

> [C]urricula, training, and research programs that are designed to teach individuals to apply scientific, engineering, and management disciplines that integrate elements of computer science, operations research, industrial engineering, business strategy, management sciences, and social and legal sciences, in order to encourage innovation in how organizations create value for customers and stakeholders that could not be achieved through such disciplines working in isolation. (US Congress HR 2272, 2007)

It appears that CIOs of the future would also need and benefit from SSME training and skills.

Other areas of the provider organization also need people that better understand service systems in our service economy. In particular, new approaches to marketing (Hirschheim et al. 2006) Internet-based services, financing service innovation, and establishing service supplier chains and partnerships are needed.

There is also a growing need for people with expertise in service systems for organizations that are predominately service customer based. CIOs of customer organizations, working with business area leaders, must establish strategic plans identifying which services will be delivered "in-house" and which services will be contracted externally through arrangements such as outsourcing or SaaS. Critical to any strategic plan is the identification of the people to lead and carry out the plan.

---

[3] The leader overseeing the group of IT professionals in a service provider organization is often called a CTO (Chief Technology Officer). We strongly believe the skills and concerns of the CTO are similar to those outlined for the CIO in most enterprises.

In their Global Human Capital Study 2008 (IBM 2008b), IBM explored "… the challenges companies face as they work to more effectively attract, allocate and invest in their human capital." The study, which involved over 400 HR executives from 40 countries participating in structured interviews, established that over 75% of companies identified the ability to develop future leaders as one of their central capability-building issues. The ability of the CIO to build future leadership skills is important to many of the challenges for the Enterprise of the Future (IBM 2008a) such as expansion into emerging economies, formation of alliances with outside IT partners, and changing workforce demographics of IT professionals. CIOs must also assist HR (Human Resource) executives in finding new employees in all aspects of their enterprise that have a basic understanding of IT and can flourish in a service-centric economy. As stated in (IBM Corporation 2008), HR and IT can assist each other by:

- Developing an adaptable workforce
- Driving growth through workforce analytics
- Recognizing, developing and retaining talent
- Planning for leadership succession

How can we be sure of the effectiveness of those using service systems and those developing and evolving service systems? This is an important question that CIOs need assistance in answering, whether they are part of a service provider or service customer organization. A common approach to determining customer's effectiveness is to gather customer's opinions and performance information of the service quality using survey and performance monitoring techniques. Using gap quality approaches, such as SERVQUAL (Parasuraman et al. 1988), can be helpful in determining the customer's perspective of the delivered service, which provides valuable feedback that can lead to service improvement. To measure the effectiveness of customers requires the establishment of benchmark service scenarios to monitor and then evaluate customer performance and accuracy. The effectiveness of service system support teams can be assessed by tracking problem reports, problem resolution strategies and turnaround time.

6   Organizations

The impact of service systems on how organizations operate will be tremendous in the future. This impact will require the adoption of new approaches to governance and responsibility management that must be well understood and supported by CIOs. More than ever, organizations will be looking for effective approaches to automating or providing better automation support for the key business processes, especially those processes that are shared between organizational units. There will also be a need to plan for and enact effective and efficient processes with business partners

(Business-to-Business) through the use of service systems. As shared service systems adoption increases the need to establish clear measures of the value of the shared relationships in terms of return on investment and risk management becomes a more critical responsibility of the CIO. New approaches to "value quality" assessment and management are needed and are discussed at the end of this section.

Let us begin our discussion with the important, direct question of what has been the impact on organizations during this dramatic growth in services sector? In the past decade most CIOs have invested heavily in both time and resources to improve their service management capabilities. In a recent survey of IT directors (Swabey 2008), the reasons most commonly cited for this investment are configuration management (49%) and compliance with audit requirements and accepted industry standards (46%). The need to focus on configuration management is understandable given the rapid increase in new applications and services and the need to better integrate these with legacy systems at an enterprise level. This is important "housekeeping" that cannot be ignored. With respect to compliance, two important driving forces have pushed compliance regulations. First, Sarbanes–Oxley, Sarbox (or SOX) is the United States federal law enacted in 2002 in response to a number of major corporate accounting scandals from large publicly traded firms including Enron and Worldcom. The most significant aspects of SOX to affect IT service management is the need for well-defined governance, proper internal controls and independent auditing of an enterprise's information systems, especially those dealing with financial accounting. The second major driving force has been the need for better security measures as enterprises conduct more and more of their business on-line using the Internet often through wireless access.

Two predominate approaches have been adopted by organizations to address these challenges. The first approach promotes better practices and guidelines in how IT services are managed in an organization. ITIL (Information Technology Infrastructure Library) (2001) is the most popular set of IT management guidelines, with 58% of the Information Age survey respondents identifying it as their compliance standard (Swabey 2008). Of the ITIL v2 standard recommendations, 77% of respondents identified the service support area as the greatest focus of their IT service management activities. This area, which focuses on service request, incident, problem and change management, is one that most directly supports service customers. Although the adoption of standards like ITIL is not yet universal, its uptake has been significant and the most accepted parts have focused on customer. ITIL promotes a continuous improvement approach to service quality but does not prescribe definitive levels of maturity in an IT service management practice.

The second approach to meet compliance regulations at the organizational level focuses on IT control management by the adoption of a framework that assists in risk identification, mitigation and removal. This approach is adopted in COBIT (ISACA 2009), a framework that assists managers, auditors and customers in understanding their IT systems and deciding the level of security and control that is necessary to protect their organization's assets. COBIT requires a well-defined governance model to oversee the four domains of the COBIT framework: (1) Plan and Organize, (2) Acquire and Implement, (3) Deliver and Support, and (4) Monitor and Evaluate together with their 34 associated IT processes. Given that it is more control-oriented and less service-oriented than ITIL, COBIT has been widely adopted in auditing IT systems and services. The CIOs in some organizations are adopting aspects of both standards: ITIL for service improvement and COBIT for review and audit of service systems (Hill and Turbit 2009).

The previous discussion focused on management practices and frameworks for services that are primarily delivered within an organization. What do these standards have to say about externally delivered services? The service deployment and management issues are "one step removed" from customers when the service is delivered externally. Typically, a customer organization relies on contractual agreements and oversight committees to help ensure the services are delivered and managed properly. While both ITIL and COBIT address these issues generally, external services are not given the same level of treatment as internally delivered services. Best practices or control management guidelines related to service definition and contract management of external services are not provided. This is an area that needs greater attention in the future as organizations rely more and more on externally delivered services.

At the organizational level, what are the key concerns with respect to service quality? Foremost is the value of a service to an organization. With the increased deployment of external service systems such as SaaS new approaches to defining value quality for a service are receiving significant attention. Traditionally, CIOs have used approaches like ROI (Return on Investment) (CIO Council 2009) and Cost-Benefit Analysis (Mindtools 2009) to determine the initial and ongoing value of a service. New approaches based on balance scorecard (Kaplan and Norton 1996) or risk assessment and mitigation (VOSE Software 2009) are being considered. Because service systems are meant to derive co-value for the customer and the provider, new shared-value approaches promoting strategic partnership relationships between customer and provider organizations are being examined (Chen et al. 2010). The issues of managing integrated services and service-chain delivery involving multiple parties are important future challenges for CIOs that need more research.

7   Shared Data

The need within and between organizations to more effectively and actively share data is also growing dramatically. Collaborative activities such as co-design and co-decision that use web 2.0 enabled applications are now important, common day activities. However, the popularity of these activities is causing even greater concerns for the CIO related to security and privacy of data. This, in turn, is leading to the increased need to review, revise and add new policies and procedures in these areas. Service quality approaches that assist in assessing access to and management of shared data repositories are just emerging and these are reviewed in this section.

One of the fundamental definitions from the emerging area of service science (Spohrer et al. 2007) is that a "… service system is a value co-production configuration of people, technology, other internal and external service systems and shared information." For people needing or providing IT services, shared information represents the real value of a service – the technology and service systems are simply the vehicles used to gain access to the shared information. The increased use of personal services, particularly those involving social networking,[2] have created expectations regarding the instant and user-friendly access to shared data from anywhere at any time of the day. Most CIOs have not been able to deploy services within their enterprises that match this level of availability and responsiveness. In fact, CIOs in some organizations are facing challenges in dealing with users who want to employ personal services on a regular basis as part of their job (e.g., creating a social club of organization employees on Facebook, using YouTube to advertise or show certain corporate events, or using Travelocity to book trips that are work related). Some of the social networking services provide or require peer-to-peer access, which can play havoc for enterprise firewalls and create significantly greater security risks. The security issues are so great that in many enterprises that need high security (e.g., military, healthcare, research institutes) will not allow these services on their networks. Over time, however, the challenge of meeting user expectations and supporting these types services may have to be met. When the personal computer (PC) first became popular in the early 1980s for personal use at home their use was banned in many organizations – at least until there was a revolt and user departments started to purchase them with or without the support of central IT services. Are CIOs ready for a similar situation to arise with respect to PS (personal services) or are they already proactively planning for ways to support the use of these new services within their enterprises?

Key to the success of service systems will be the proper planning of access rights management and privacy policies particularly as they pertain to shared data and services. Both activities are and will continue to be a responsibility of the CIO. As enterprise activities become more global, as user become more knowledgeable, and as services become more linked, integrated and mutually dependent, the CIO will require more planning and diagnostic tools to assist in the proper sharing of data within and between enterprises. Many sectors, such as the airline industry, cannot operate effectively, or perhaps at all, without shared data that is secure, reliable, available and correct. These are all important factors affecting the real and perceived quality of service delivered. As such CIOs should ensure they institute a quality measurement program for each service system. Many point to the future Web 3.0 applications that are based on the semantic web (with its meta descriptions of data) as the natural evolution towards "intelligent service systems" – service systems which can continually monitor, report on and potentially self-improve their levels of service. CIOs must become attuned to this prospect and all the challenges and opportunities it brings for their enterprise.

8   Summary and Conclusions

In this chapter, we have described how the traditional activities of the CIO in technology planning, deployment and maintenance must be expanded to consider the other facets in service systems: people, organization and shared information. CIOs must continue to be technology innovators in their organization at the application service level through the evaluation and, as required, the adoption of new service delivery models such as SaaS (Software as a Service) and service supply chain integration. At the technology infrastructure level, CIOs must consider new "greener" approaches to service system deployment such as the use of server virtualization and the installation of low power consumption computing and storage devices.

CIOs must take on a greater leadership role in the attraction and retention of highly qualified people for their enterprise. They must work with the HR (Human Resource) department to provide better service system support for people management and training. They must assist in defining the future skills needed by employees to efficiently and effectively use new service systems. They must plan carefully to develop and retain their own team of highly competent IT experts for deploying and upgrading the service systems of the future. This team may well be quite different from teams in the past. Not all members will be co-located, permanently employed and sharing the same cultural background, but they must work with the same sense of purpose in support of high quality service system delivery. CIOs should also actively support and participate with academic institutions in the development of SSME curricula that will produce the T-shaped professionals needed to develop future service systems and CIOs.

CIOs must take on more responsibility and have greater impact at the highest levels of their organizations. More and more enterprises will be identified by the value quality of the services they deliver. CIOs must provide a leadership role in identifying opportunities made possible by new technologies, improved governance models and quality processes that are enterprise-wide in scope. Strategic planning and plan reviews at the enterprise level will become more important given the need to service smarter customers and form a greater number of strategic partnerships with co-suppliers of services on a global basis. CIOs must investigate and where appropriate adopt the new models that accurately reflect the value quality of service systems.

Finally, CIOs must understand better that the real value of service systems to the customer is not in the technology per se but in the shared information provided by this technology. The traditional, rather narrow focus on technology has been widening in the past decade; the next decade will demand an even greater rate of change, especially as it pertains to the management of shared information. In the near future, this shared information will be defined more rigorously using meta-level (or semantic) information and will hold the true "nuggets" of knowledge and processes of an enterprise that must be used wisely and guarded carefully. The CIO will have a major responsibility in overseeing this change in a timely and effective manner. Ultimately, CIOs must lead the way in delivering smarter, on-demand service systems to smarter customers.

Epilogue and Acknowledgements In preparing this paper I have had many interesting discussions with other CIOs at Canadian companies and universities, with researchers in service systems including several in the Services Science department at the IBM Almaden Research Center, and with several CIOs from Australia Universities that I recently visited. A common question I asked was "Will this rapid change toward the adoption of service systems fundamentally change the role of the CIO?" I did not get a consensus in the responses. Some believe that it will require a fundamental role shift that focuses on thinking exclusively about the services needed and provided by an enterprise with little emphasis on the technology strategy – their view is that the technology is simply a commodity and provides little if any strategic value. Others, in particular, more senior CIOs believe the change is more evolutionary – just as CIOs had to deal with the decentralization of IT systems in the 1990s they will need to address the centralization trends of today and in the near future brought on by service systems. In all cases, it was agreed that in the near future there will be major changes required of the CIO and all currently in this position will be challenged by these changes.

I wish to take the opportunity to thank all those who participated in many interesting discussions with me but in particular Jim Spohrer, Norm Pass and Paul Maglio from IBM Almaden during my visit at Almaden in October and November 2008. I wish to also thank my Ph.D. students Xian Chen and Abhishek Srivastava for assisting me in this research and gratefully acknowledge NSERC (National Science and Engineering Research Council) of Canada for funding support of this research.

References

Alvarez, M. (2008). Gartner Predicts Great Growth in SaaS Adoption, October, http://www.atelier-us.com/e-business-and-it/article/gartner-predicts-great-growth-of-saas-adoption

Chen, X., Srivastava, A. and Sorenson, P.G. (2011). Towards a QoS-focused SaaS Evaluation Model, *Cloud Computing and Software Services: Theory and Techniques,* CRC Press, pp. 389–408.

Chesbrough, H. and Spohrer, J. (2006). A Research Manifesto for Services Science, *Communications of the ACM,* 49(7) 35–40.

Chong, F. and Carraro, G. (2006). Architecture Strategies for Catching the Long Tail," *Microsoft Corporation, Software as a Service Architectural Guidance Series,* April, http://msdn.microsoft.com/en-us/library/aa479069.aspx

CIO (2007). Top Ten Concerns of CIOs, a 2007 CIO Study, http://www.cio.co.uk/concern/

CIO Council (2009). The Value of IT Investments: It's not just Return On Investment, http://www.cio.gov/documents/TheValueof_IT_Investments.pdf

CIO papers (2009). Chief Information Officer: Insights & strategy, http://www-935.ibm.com/services/us/cio/

CIOInsight (2006). CIOs Get Mixed Reviews From Their Most Important Constituents, January 19, http://www.cioinsight.com/c/a/Research/CIOs-Get-Mixed-Reviews-From-Their-Most-Important-Consituents/

Cramm, S. (2008). Circa 2015: The CIO of the Future, September, https://bestpracticeinstitute.org/members/articles/cramm-webinar.html

Erlanger, L. (2008). How to Keep Your Tech Career Afloat, *Infoworld Channels,* September, http://www.infoworld.com/d/adventures-in-it/how-keep-your-tech-career-afloat-262

Gingichashvill, S. (2009). Green computing, *The Future of Things,* http://thefutureofthings.com/articles/1003/green-computing.html

Google Corporation (2009). Google Apps Service Level Agreement, http://www.google.com/apps/intl/en/terms/sla.html

Gruman, G. and Knorr, E. (2008). What cloud computing really means, *InfoWorld,* April, http://www.infoworld.com/article/08/04/07/15FE-cloud-computing-reality_1.html

Hill, P. and Turbit, K. (2009). Combine ITIL and COBIT to Meet Business Challenges, *The Register*, http://whitepapers.theregister.co.uk/paper/view/111/pipm-itil-cobit-english-white-paper-jan-start.pdf

Hirschheim, R. Schwarz, A. and Todd, P. (2006). A Marketing Maturity Model for IT: Building a Customer-Centric IT Organization, *IBM Systems Journal*, Vol. 45, No. 1, 2006, 181–199.

http://www.cs.ualberta.ca/~sorenson/TowardsQoS-FocusedSaaSEvaluationModel.htm

IBM (2008). The Enterprise of the Future, IBM Global CEO Study, http://www.ibm.com/ibm/ideasfromibm/us/ceo/20080505/index.shtml

IBM (2008a). Unlocking the DNA of the Adaptable Workforce: The Global Human Capital Study, http://ibm.com/services/us/gbs/bus/html/2008ghcs.html

IBM Center for CIO Leadership (2008). The CIO Profession: Leaders of Change, Drivers of Innovation, October, http://www-935.ibm.com/services/us/cio/pdf/cio-leadership-white-paper-2008.pdf

IBM Corporation (2008). Creating an adaptable workforce: implications for the CIOs, March, http://www-935.ibm.com/services/us/cio/pdf/ciw03005usen.pdf

ICT Standards (2009). Advantages and Disadvantages of Outsourcing, www.ictstandards.com/Advantages_And_Disadvantages_Of_Outsourcing.htm

ISACA (2009). COBIT standard, http://www.isaca.org

IT Infrastructure Library (2001). Office of Government Commerce, *Service Delivery, IT Infrastructure Library*. The Stationery Office, 2001, http://www.itil-officialsite.com/home/home.asp

Kaplan, R.S. and Norton, D.P. (1996). The Balanced Scoreboard: Translating Strategy into Action, *Harvard Business School Press*, August.

Lheureux, B.J., Desisto, R.P. and Maoz, M. (2006). Evaluating Software-as-a-Service Providers: Questions to Ask Potential SaaS Providers, *Gartner RAS Core Research Note*, April, http://www.gartner.com/DisplayDocument?id=491288

Meeting of the OECD Council at Ministerial Level (2005). Growth in Services: Fostering Employment, Productivity and Innovation, www.oecd.org/dataoecd/36/10/35026756.pdf

Mindtools (2009). Cost/Benefit Analysis: Evaluating Quantitatively Whether to Follow a Course of Action, http://www.mindtools.com/pages/article/newTED_08.htm

Oracle Corp. (2009). Peoplesoft Enterprise Information Portal, www.oracle.com/applications/peoplesoft-information-portal.html

Parasuraman, A., Zeihaml, V.A. and Berry, L.L. (1988). SERVQUAL: A Multi-Item Scale for Measuring Consumer Perception of Service Quality, *Journal of Retailing*, (64)1, 1988, 12–40

Ried, S., Rymer, J.R. and Iqbal, R. (2008). Forrester's SaaS Maturity Model: Transforming Vendor Strategy While Managing Customer Expectations, August, http://www.forrester.com/go?docid=46817

SaaS.com (2009). Improving Human Productivity Through Software as a Service, http://www.SaaS.com

Salesforce.com (2009). Salesforce.com products, http://www.salesforce.com/products/

SAP (2009). SAP Community Network, https://www.sdn.sap.com/irj/sdn

SearchCIO, Definitions (2009). http://searchcio.techtarget.com/sDefinition/0,,sid182_gci213620,00.html

Spohrer, J. (2008). Declaration of Interdependence for a Smarter Planet, SRIC (Service Research & Innovation Community), November, http://forums.thesrii.org/srii/blog/article?blog.id=main_blog&message.id=119

Spohrer, J., Maglio, P., Bailey, J. and D. Gruhl (2007). Steps Towards a Science of Service Systems, *Computer*, IEEE Computer Society, January, 71–77.

Swabey, P. (2008). Service Response, *Information Age*, November 17, www.information-age.com/rss/813802/813797/service-response.thtml

Tien,. J.M. and Berg, D. (2006). On Services Research and Education, *Journal of Systems Science and Systems Engineering*, 15(3): 257–283.

University of Cambridge and IBM (2008). Succeeding through service innovation: A service perspective for education, research, business and government, ISBN: 978-1-902546-65-0, April, http://www.ifm.eng.cam.ac.uk/ssme/documents/ssme_discussion_final.pdf

VMware (2009). VMware Virtualization Technology, http://www.vmware.com

VOSE Software (2009). Introduction to Risk Analysis, http://www.vosesoftware.com/

Waters, B. (2005). Software as a Service: A Look at the Customer Benefits, *Journal of Digital Asset Management,* (1)1, 32–39.

Service Productivity: How to Measure and Improve It?

Erik den Hartigh

Özyeğin University, Kuşbakışı Caddesi no. 2

34662 Altunizade Üsküdar, Istanbul, Turkey

Marc Zegveld

Partner Strategy and Change IBM, Johan Huizingalaan 765, 1066 UA Amsterdam,

The Netherlands

Abstract Productivity is a key performance measure for service businesses and serves as a compass for measuring their innovativeness. In this chapter we present a tool for measuring productivity in service businesses. Improvements in service business productivity do not depend on industry, business size or business growth, but on the specific knowledge and competences of managers. Using case examples we show various ways of how managers can improve the productivity of their service businesses. They can do so by adopting a perspective of standardization, flexibility or individualization. Based on these perspectives, we provide a framework that shows how managers can improve service business productivity by coordinating strategic orientation, value creation and the configuration of business processes.

1 Introduction

Service businesses represent a major and increasing part of the global economy. While in industrial businesses it is common to measure and improve productivity, in service businesses this is less common. While productivity in industry has increased enormously over the past centuries, productivity in service businesses is growing less fast than desirable. The research question of this paper is therefore *"How can service businesses measure and improve their productivity?"* To answer this question we present a tool for measuring service business productivity and we develop a framework to help managers to improve the productivity of their service business.

We start in Sect. 2 by arguing that productivity is an important concept for service businesses. It is a measure of their success and innovativeness. Improvement of productivity is essential for the development of the global economy as well as for the profitability of individual service businesses.

H. Demirkan et al. (eds.), *Service Systems Implementation*, Service Science: Research and Innovations in the Service Economy, DOI 10.1007/978-1-4419-7904-9_11, © Springer Science+Business Media, LLC 2011

Productivity is often associated with mechanization, with working harder and with large-scale dismissal rounds. In Sect. 3 we give a different interpretation: we argue that productivity is mainly a compass to measure innovativeness.

Productivity is often thought to be dependent on the sector in which a business is active, on the size of the business or on the growth of the business. In Sect. 4 we argue that, instead, the growth of productivity is mainly determined by business-specific knowledge and competences. This implies that managers of service businesses are in the driving seat to improve the productivity of their business.

To assist them with this, we show in Sect. 5 how three leading service businesses have improved their productivity. They have done so by adopting a single perspective: standardization, flexibility or individualization. Taking these perspectives, they consistently adjusted their strategies, the ways they create value and the ways they structure their business processes.

To further assist managers of service businesses, in Sect. 6 we present a model with which they can analyze their own business, with which they can identify their productivity growth perspective and with which they can make choices how to further improve their productivity. In Sect. 7 we provide management implications and an outlook for further research.

2   The Importance of Productivity for Service Businesses

Service systems comprise service providers and service clients working together to co-produce value in complex value chains or networks (Tien and Berg 2003; Spohrer et al. 2007). Important characteristics of service systems are their inputs and their outputs (Karni and Kaner 2007). Outputs refer to what is produced, marketed and sold, i.e., service offerings, and the inputs refer to what is required to make this possible, i.e., information, materials, employee efforts and capital. The relationship between the outputs and inputs of an economic system is described by the *production function*. It implies that the quantities and qualities of the outputs are a function of the configuration of the inputs. *Productivity* is the ratio between the outputs and the inputs of the system and is therefore a measure of the success of this production function. Productivity is generally considered as a key performance measure for economic systems, be they countries, sectors, networks or businesses.

We propose to use productivity as a key measure for the success of service businesses, too. Service businesses can be regarded as a specific form of service system. Service businesses are responsible for the larger part of total income and employment in developed countries (Maglio et al. 2006; Spohrer et al. 2007; Demirkan et al. 2008). Moreover, many businesses that are statistically classified as industrial are for a large part service businesses or they add a significant portion of service offering to the goods they produce. In business, it may therefore be difficult to make a precise distinction between "goods" and "services" (see also Araujo and Spring 2006). Whatever the exact figures, it is clear that the global economy is heavily dependent on the prosperity and development of service businesses.

Agricultural and industrial businesses have a long history of measuring, analyzing and improving their productivity. Service businesses do not. Chesbrough and Spohrer (2006) argue that the productivity improvements in the agricultural and manufacturing sectors have greatly enhanced our welfare and wellbeing over the past centuries. They ask whether it is possible to "... *continue rapid productivity advances in a largely services-based economy?*" (Chesbrough and Spohrer 2006, p. 36). Clearly there are reasons to be concerned about this. The question is equivalent to Drucker's (1999) statement that the increase of knowledge-worker productivity is the "*biggest challenge*" for the twenty-first century. These issues are strongly connected because various studies point out that service businesses rely to a large extent on knowledge inputs, and/or on the labor inputs of knowledge workers (Johnson et al. 2005; Spohrer et al. 2007; Boone et al. 2008).

We see that service businesses are improving their productivity at a slower rate than industrial businesses (Bangma et al. 2004). This holds for most developed countries. Still, in our own research we found that many managers of service businesses do not consider productivity as a priority issue (Zegveld and Den Hartigh 2007). Some managers would claim that productivity is not relevant for them, because their business is offering services and not standardized products. In economics, it has long been thought that the inherent nature of service processes made productivity improvements less likely, a conviction that is known as "Baumol's disease" (Baumol 1967; Triplett and Bosworth 2003). And yet, research shows that service businesses *can and do* increase their productivity (e.g., Triplett and Bosworth 2003; Boone et al. 2008). There is also research that shows that productivity is one of the most important factors determining profitability (e.g., Heskett et al. 1994; Zegveld 2000).

Improvement of service business productivity is of the utmost importance for the development of the global economy (Chesbrough and Spohrer 2006) as well as for the profitability of individual service businesses. This brings up the question of *how* the productivity of service businesses can be measured and improved.

3 Productivity as a Compass for Innovativeness

Productivity is often associated with mechanizing production processes, reducing numbers of employees, cutting costs and working harder. This is only part of the truth. Productivity is mainly related to innovation: smarter organization of a service system, i.e., better organizing the ways in which employees and capital are deployed and in which supply and marketing of service offerings are arranged. Innovation in service offerings, improvements in quality and efforts to better match market demands are excellent alternatives to cost-cutting and employee lay-offs. Innovative service providers, like ING Direct (a direct retail bank), Randstad (a temporary employment agency) or Endemol (a TV show producer) are able to realize higher-value outputs with less input because of a smarter organization of employees and capital. *Productivity is therefore a good compass to measure innovativeness in service businesses.*

Productivity is often defined as *labor productivity*: the number of products produced per employee. For service businesses this conceptualization is too limited. Businesses that produce only lumps of cotton or gallons of beer can work with standardized product units and standardized quality. When the deployment of employees and capital for a production process can be exactly determined, it is possible to perform an exact productivity measurement in units: units of outputs divided by units of inputs. When additionally the prices of the outputs and the costs of the inputs can be measured, a distinction can be made between a (physical) productivity effect and a price effect. The (physical) productivity effect is a measure of the efficiency of the internal processes, while the price effect is the result of the extent to which the business can influence prices in the markets where it buys its inputs and sells its outputs.

Service businesses, however, do usually not produce standardized lumps of cotton or gallons of beer. Specifically, service offerings are intangible, heterogeneous, simultaneously produced and consumed, and perishable (De Jong and Vermeulen 2003; Araujo and Spring 2006). Therefore they are difficult to count, difficult to aggregate and it is difficult to establish at which moment they are delivered. The practice of productivity measurement in service businesses along the idealized lines as sketched above is therefore fraught with problems. First, many businesses deliver a very heterogeneous palette of products (goods and service offerings). It then becomes very difficult to correctly determine which input factors contribute to which product. Second, while in economic statistics it is preferred to standardize product categories, businesses try to do exactly the opposite: they try to distinguish themselves in the eyes of the customer by providing goods and service offerings in different qualities, or by developing a brand image to increase their product's prices. Third, many products are amalgamates of goods and service offerings. Take the example of a pizza from the supermarket and a pizza from the pizza courier. Although physically equivalent, the important differences are in the pizza temperature and the way the pizza is distributed. The pizza courier adds a service to the physical product by organizing different value adding activities. Because of this, the price of the delivered pizza differs considerably from the one purchased from the supermarket. We could compare the physical productivity of both processes, but it is clear that we are dealing with different things and that the physical productivity does not provide a meaningful comparison.

Therefore, for service businesses, the most useful concept of productivity measurement is *total factor productivity* (TFP) based on *added value* (Wolff 1999; Diewert 2000; Brynjolfsson and Hitt 2003; Triplett and Bosworth 2003; Van Ark and De Jong 2004; Dorgan et al. 2006). It has two main advantages. First, by defining "output" as "added value", it measures the difference between the prices the business is able to set in the market and the cost has to incur to buy its inputs (e.g., labor, capital). It therefore captures the value that the business adds in the process. Moreover, it also captures innovations and improvements in marketing, brand building and quality: any activity that the business carries out to improve perceived customer value and for which customers a willing to pay the price. Second, with TFP measurement, the outputs are related to multiple inputs, usually employees and capital. Growth in TFP, then, is the consequence of either an increase in added value (see above) or of making smarter combinations of employees and capital (Brynjolfsson and Hitt 2003). For a business, this means that knowledgeable people, new technology, organizational renewal, innovative production processes and new marketing, distribution and sales methods are coordinated in such a way to enable successful development, introduction, marketing and fulfillment of new service offerings.

The growth of the service economy is the result of a co-creation process with a wide variety of intangibles, e.g. the brand or the smartness of the organization. Using the TFP-measure provides us with the opportunity to measure the productivity share of these intangibles. However the different intangibles themselves are neither defined nor measured, the proposed measurement defines the share of intangibles in the productivity growth.

For the measurement of productivity we therefore propose to use total factor productivity (TFP) at the level of the individual business. This measure was originally conceptualized at the macro economic level and at the sector level (Solow 1957), but it was demonstrated to be applicable at the business level as well (Zegveld 2000, 2004). It was also specifically demonstrated to be applicable to service businesses (Zegveld and Den Hartigh 2007). In the TFP-measure, outputs are related to labor and capital inputs. To calculate TFP at the business level, we define output, labor input and capital input by following Zegveld (2004): *output is measured as added value*, i.e., the sum of the operational factor cost (total cost of labor and capital) and net profit; *labor input is measured as the total number of hours worked*, i.e., the number of employees times the annual hours worked per employee; *capital input is measured as depreciation*.

As we are concerned with productivity improvements, it is important to measure the *growth of TFP* of an individual business over a sufficient number of periods. Based on the definitions we specifically calculate *TFP growth* as the change in output per hour worked, minus the capital fraction of output, times the change in capital employed per hour worked (see Fig. 1).

This measurement tool is based on earlier studies have provided a framework for measurement, e.g., Triplett and Bosworth (2003) and Van Ark and De Jong (2004) as well as on our own research (Zegveld and Den Hartigh 2007). It differs from earlier studies in that (1) it is relatively easy to use, (2) it can be applied by using publicly available data of individual businesses, (3) it can be used by service businesses as well as industrial businesses as well as the mixtures of those, and (4) it can be used to compare businesses within and across industries.

$$\text{TFP growth} = \left[\frac{\text{Added Value per hour}_{(T=2)} \ -/- \ \text{Added Value per hour}_{(T=1)}}{\text{Added Value per hour}_{(T=1)}} \right]$$

$$-/- \left[\frac{\text{Capital}_{(T=1)}}{\text{Added Value}_{T=1)}} \right] * \left[\frac{\text{Capital per hour}_{(T=2)} \ -/- \ \text{Capital per hour}_{(T=1)}}{\text{Capital per hour}_{T=1)}} \right]$$

Fig. 1. Calculation of total factor productivity growth

4   Why Do Service Businesses Differ in Productivity Growth?

It is often assumed that productivity growth is dependent on the *sector* in which a business is active. This is a plausible assumption, because in different sectors different types of services are offered, some of which might be more or less suitable for productivity improvement. Furthermore, sectors differ in market size, market growth, competitive intensity, technological developments and customer characteristics. All these factors could cause differences in the possibilities for businesses to improve their productivity.

Alternatively, we could search for explanations in factors related to the business itself, like business size, business growth or business-specific resources and capabilities. *Business size* is a plausible explanation for productivity growth differences, because larger businesses will have more possibilities for standardization and economies of scale. Additionally, larger businesses usually have more market power, which will enable them to increase added value by lowering input prices and increasing output prices.

Business growth is also a plausible explanation for differences in productivity growth. There are different, opposing arguments for this. One argument is that businesses that grow faster will realize higher productivity growth because they profit from dynamic scale and learning effects. The opposite argument is that businesses will realize productivity growth when they become smaller, as their labor and capital efficiency will improve through lay-offs and through the sale of unprofitable business activities.

We investigated to which extent the differences in productivity growth between different service businesses are attributable to the *sector* in which they operate, to their *size* and to their *growth* (Zegveld and Den Hartigh 2007). To do so, we measured the growth of total factor productivity (TFP) as presented above for a research sample of 848 Dutch businesses over a period of 5 years and 319 Dutch businesses over a period of 10 years. We investigated the systematic differences in productivity growth between service businesses in different sectors, size of businesses and growth of businesses on both samples. Our study shows that productivity growth in service businesses is explained only to a very limited extent by the sector in which they are active, by their size, or by their growth. The differences *between businesses* in each sector, each size category and each growth category are magnitudes bigger than the differences between the sectors, size categories or growth categories. The most sensible implication of these findings is that productivity growth in service businesses is mainly the effect of business-specific knowledge and competences. Dorgan et al. (2006) found comparable results. This is good news: it means that managers of service businesses can act to stimulate the productivity growth of their businesses.

These findings confirm the original research of Penrose (1959) who found that even within the same industry, the productivity of businesses differs enormously. Penrose related business heterogeneity to the process of business-specific knowledge accumulation. Within each business three generic processes can be identified.

The first is the process to *form strategic orientation*. It can be defined as the process of forming the *"theory of the business"* (Drucker 1994) or the mental model of the business. This mental model includes perceptions as well as explicit and implicit assumptions concerning environmental change, resources, competencies, assets and positional advantages. Following Prahalad and Hamel (1990), the process of forming strategic orientation is related to the vision of the business and its interpretation as *strategic intent*. Others, like Dosi (1982) and Nelson and Winter (1982), found that the perspective of the business is strongly influenced by business-specific paths, stressing the importance of historical events. Three major perspectives on strategic orientation can be recognized: strategic orientation toward *standardization*, toward *flexibility* or toward *individualization*.

The second is the process to *configure production*. It focuses on turning resources into products (goods and service offerings). According to the industrial organization theory this process involves translating the strategic position of the business into an organizational configuration that includes procurement, technology development and human resource management. Based on the resource view, the process of configuring and facilitating production is oriented towards turning resources into products that fit the formulated vision. The process of production uses primary activities, i.e., inbound logistics, operations, outbound logistics, marketing and sales and distribution (Porter 1985), to transform intermediates into goods and service offerings to gain a sustainable competitive advantage or a defensible position. From the resource perspective, production is defined as a method to exploit core competencies (Hamel and Prahalad 1993). Three attractors of the process to configure production are defined: focus on *homogenous* processes, focus on *heterogeneous* processes or focus on *individualized* processes.

The third is the process to *create value*. It focuses on the orientation of the value creation process and aims to realize success in terms of long-term dominance or profits. For the operational value creation process also three attractors are defined: focus on *volume*, focus on *efficiency* or focus on *differentiation*.

These three generic processes are fully interlinked: choices made in one generic process will affect the other generic processes as well. Through implicit trial and error and explicit choices all three generic processes will create new successful routines and thus new business-specific intangibles. Businesses that actively manage the three different generic processes and the linkages between these different processes are able to increase their productivity as the result of business-specific intangibles. In the next section a qualitative analysis is made on how three service businesses actively steer their productivity.

5   Cases

We illustrate how service businesses can improve their productivity by presenting three cases of service businesses that have done so in different ways: ING Direct, Randstad and Endemol.

5.1   ING Direct (Direct Banking): Productivity Growth Through Standardization

ING Direct actively manages its productivity. In a market in which heterogeneity and differentiation are buzzwords, ING Direct was able to build a business by capitalizing on clients' irritation with existing retail banking service offerings. ING Direct offers limited choice, but focuses on zero mistakes and therefore the market accepts the limited choices that it offers. As a result the service process of ING Direct deviates considerably from that of traditional retail banks. ING Direct has no office network: all transactions go through call centers or through the internet. All work processes are fully standardized with a strong focus to get every transaction right from the beginning. *No-mistake* is the key word.

Through providing standardized, faultless service offerings, ING Direct has been able to gain considerable sales volume and market share. The standardized processes enable an extremely efficient, low-cost operation. As a result of strong growth, ING Direct realizes scale effects, which enable it to reduce costs even further. The low cost advantage, in turn, is used to stimulate further growth. With this alternative business model, ING Direct managed to realize a big impact in the world of retail banking. Productivity is clearly governed by managing the (mutually reinforcing) interactions between standardization, efficiency, scale effects and low cost.

5.2   Randstad (Temporary Staffing Agency): Productivity Growth Through Flexibility

Randstad Callflex is one of the largest operational units within Randstad Netherlands and is focused on the hiring, selecting, training and deploying flexible labor for call centers (call center agents). Since its incubation in 1998 it has grown spectacularly.

The business develops toward a configuration in which it can offer services to different groups of customers in different ways. The boundary condition for this is to keep cost development at bay. To realize this, Randstad Callflex works with a model in which business processes are developed from homogeneous to heterogeneous through the following layers: (1) operational excellence, (2) organic growth and efficiency improvement, (3) copy-paste of successful concepts from elsewhere, (4) new service offerings, and (5) new markets.

Randstad Callflex uses productivity as the compass to steer this: movement towards a new layer will only happen if it increases productivity. Randstad Callflex intends to create value by improving customer value in the market while keeping process cost at the same level. On the one hand this means a broadening of the service offerings by introducing new higher-margin offerings, like managing administrative or planning processes for clients. On the other hand it means changing the structure of the back office processes toward a modular setup. Such a modular setup enables the delivery of different combinations of existing (more homogeneous) and new (more heterogeneous) service offerings in a cost-efficient way. Productivity is clearly governed by increasing customer value in the market while simultaneously modularizing business processes to maintain cost-efficiency.

5.3 Endemol (Television Show Producer): Productivity Growth Through Individualization

In September 1999 the first candidates entered the *Big Brother house* in the Netherlands. They lived with a small group in a luxury but confined environment. Everything they did, every movement they made, every conversation they had, every behavior they showed, and every intimate moment they had was broadcasted: live on web cams through the internet and every evening on TV as a digest of the day's events. It was the talk of the whole country. In the years to follow, Endemol would repeat and extend this formula and sell it to many TV channels in dozens of countries around the world. *Big Brother* became a worldwide hit.

With *Big Brother*, interaction with individual spectators is organized on a massive scale. Spectators were able, for example, to vote by SMS or through the internet which of the candidates should leave the *Big Brother house*, and through this they were able to influence the course of the show.

Big Brother is an example of a format directed toward individualization: to optimally serve the moment-specific desires of individual customers. The business processes of Endemol must be very flexible to enable this. They have to be molded to enable recognizing and fulfilling the wishes of the individual customer. The customer is in the driver's seat and co-determines what the eventual TV show will look like. The marketing process should be able to immediately recognize moment and customer specific value and be able to capture it. The fulfillment process must be able to deliver this moment and customer specific value. The cost of organizing these processes is of secondary importance, as long as the captured customer value is higher than the extra cost incurred. Productivity in this case is clearly governed by capturing individual customer value and by organizing processes in an individualized way.

6 A Model for Improving Productivity

Our research connects to previous studies that have stressed the importance of management action to improve service business productivity (e.g., Van Ark and De Jong 2004; Dorgan et al. 2006). Additionally, we provide a systematic framework

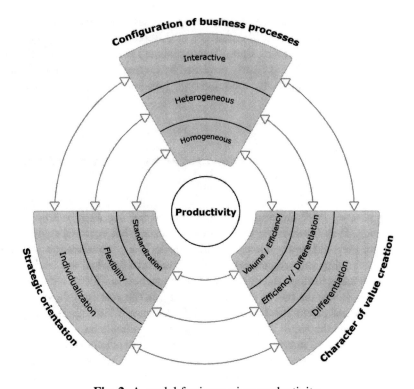

Fig. 2. A model for improving productivity

that helps managers to take such action. From the analysis of the case studies we constructed a model for improving productivity that consists of three concentric rings, or *perspectives*: (1) standardization, (2) flexibility, and (3) individualization (see Fig. 2). Within each of those three perspectives businesses have to choose their strategic orientation, choose how they will create value, i.e., earn their money, and choose how they will design and structure their business processes.

We found that a better alignment of strategic orientation, value creation and business processes is the key to improving productivity.

6.1   *Standardization, Flexibility and Individualization*

Businesses that *standardize* focus on providing a limited portfolio of standardized service offerings in large volumes. Often they will try to become the cost-leader in their market. The design and structure of their business processes is tuned to this: simple, no-frills and no space for specialties. In other words: homogeneous. They have strong governance towards realizing economies of scale, earning their money through increasing their sales volume while simultaneously improving their efficiency.

Businesses that focus on *flexibility* offer a broad portfolio of service offerings to serve different groups of customers. Through differentiating themselves in the market in this way, they try to realize higher prices. To maintain efficiency, such businesses will often choose to modularize their offerings, so that the different service modules can be configured in many different ways. Such a configuration puts specific demands on the design of the business processes, as those processes, too, will have to be modularized. In other words: heterogeneity. In this case, an optimal combination has to be found between the efficiency of providing the individual modules and the flexibility of the whole.

Businesses that *individualize* strive to maximize customer value by offering services that are optimally tuned to the moment-specific wishes of individual customers. In a sense, they do not offer predefined services to customers, but they offer their customers a *solution space* (Van Asseldonk 1998). Within the boundaries of this space, customers can move around and have an infinite choice. Such businesses earn their money by charging high prices for the customer experience that is delivered in this way. The customer's choice is customer-specific and moment-specific and is determined in direct interaction between the customer and the service provider. In other words: interactive. In this perspective there is a strong co-production between the customer and the service provider. This puts very high demands on the provider's ability to build a genuine direct relation with the customer.

In practice, it seems that many businesses do not coordinate their activities in one of the perspectives. Many service businesses seem to be not choosing any strategic focus at all. Rather, they are *capacity businesses*, offering services when the customer asks for them. In this description we recognize the typical corner shop hairdresser or pizza baker. These businesses do neither profit from standardization, nor are they able to realize higher prices for offering better customer solutions. Their processes are not organized in any specific way, save for the capacity they have to provide. Their way to earn more money is to sell more of the same, but as every increase in volume demands an increase in capacity, they will not realize productivity improvements. A way out of this is to *standardize*. For example, standardization is the reason why McDonald's is a successful worldwide operating business while your typical hamburger baker at the corner is still that.

6.2   Analyze Position, Formulate Ambition and Take Action

Businesses can analyze their position in the model presented above and compare this position with their productivity growth (see Fig. 3). In which perspective are they currently positioned? Is this a logical position and are all the choices logically coordinated with this position? A low productivity growth is a sign that something is wrong with the way the strategic orientation, value creation and business processes are coordinated. A high productivity growth creates perspectives for further development.

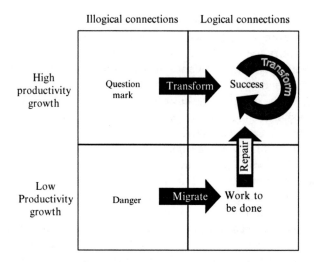

Fig. 3. Analyze position, formulate ambition and take action

Next to the current perspective and current productivity growth, businesses can formulate ambitions, e.g., to optimize within a current perspective, to consolidate within an existing perspective or to transform to a different perspective. Based on their position and on their ambitions, businesses can determine their priorities for action. Of course, the current position puts some limits on the possibilities to realize that ambition.

From a position of "danger", i.e., when the connections between the strategic orientation, the value creation and the business processes are illogical and the productivity growth is low, the best action is to radically improve the logic in the connections and migrate the business towards a logical perspective.

From a "work to be done" position, i.e., when there is a logical connection, and productivity growth is still low, it is not advisable to move to another perspective, as repair work has to be done first. It is advisable to repair the existing connections in small incremental steps and see what the impact is on productivity growth, in other words, to optimize. From the "work to be done" position it is tempting to start up many parallel initiatives to improve productivity. Taking too many initiatives in parallel, however, may lead to a loss of focus, and may cause the business to fall back into a position of "danger".

From a position of "success", i.e., when there are logical connections and productivity growth is high, businesses can either consolidate within their existing perspective or migrate to a different perspective. Consolidation may the best when competitive market pressures are high and all has to be done to ensure that at least maintain current productivity growth can be maintained. Alternatively, transforming to a new perspective may be possible to capture more value from the market. Our case analyses show that such a transformation will only be successful when businesses can build further on their existing capabilities. The layered model explained in the Randstad case is a good example of how this can be done. To transform successfully towards flexibility, the business has to master all the volume and efficiency-generating capabilities and business process configurations of a standardizing business. To transform successfully towards individualization, the business has to master the efficiency and differentiation capabilities and business process configurations of the flexible business.

When a business is in the "question mark" position, i.e., when there is no logic in the connections, but the productivity growth is nevertheless high, this is a sign that something exceptional is the matter. It could be that the business took an exceptional, innovative and successful "quantum leap". The preferred action is then to exploit this success by trying to bring logic into the connections from this new perspective. Another explanation is that the business may be already in a transformation stage, e.g., already aiming to create value from differentiation while the business processes are still configured for standardization. In this case the logical action is to finish the current transformation process until there is again logic in the connections.

Businesses can govern their productivity growth using the presented model by choosing a clear perspective, i.e., position themselves in one of the perspectives, and make or improve the logical connections within that perspective. Managers in service businesses therefore have the possibility to make choices that will impact their businesses' productivity. Possibilities for productivity growth are therefore dominantly determined by the knowledge and competences of the business itself and the quality of its management.

7 Management Implications and Research Outlook

Productivity is a key performance measure for service businesses, measuring the success and innovativeness of the configuration of their business processes. Improvement of productivity is essential for the development of the global economy as well as for the profitability of individual service businesses.

This article dealt with the questions of how productivity in service businesses can be measured and improved.

7.1 Management Implications

We identify four major management implications. First, managers should *measure the productivity* of their service businesses. To help them do so, we proposed the use of total factor productivity (TFP). This instrument best captures customer value (output) as created by service businesses and the smartness of deployment of employee and capital inputs. This tool can be applied using publicly available data, it can be used for industrial as well as service businesses and it can be used to make comparisons between businesses.

Second, managers should act to *improve the productivity* of their service business. Productivity growth in service businesses is mainly the effect of business-specific knowledge and competences and only to a very limited extent by the sector in which the business is active, by its size, or by its growth. This means that managers of service businesses can act to stimulate the productivity growth of their businesses.

Third, to improve the productivity of their service businesses, managers should *choose a clear perspective*, i.e., position their business as standardization, flexibility or individualization. To show how service businesses can do this, we provided three case examples. We showed how ING Direct improves productivity by making a consistent choice for *standardization* and high quality in direct banking, we showed how Randstad improves productivity by orienting itself towards *flexibility* in the temporary staffing business and we showed how Endemol improves productivity by organizing massive *individualized* interaction in television programs.

Fourth, to improve the productivity of their service businesses, managers should *analyze their business position, formulate ambitions, and take action*. To help them do so, we presented a framework with which they can analyze the current status of their service business and that points them toward the specific ambitions they can formulate and the specific actions they can take.

7.2   Outlook for Further Research

We identify two aspects that merit further research. The first aspect relates to the fact that many service businesses report "customer intimacy" as their main strategic focus. Apart from the question whether every business attaches the same meaning to those words, it seems that the desire to individualize is universal. This notion seems to be in the genes of service businesses. Nevertheless our reasoning and analysis shows that service businesses *can and do* follow a variety of approaches to improve productivity. Not every service business has to *individualize*, many – indeed most – of them will perform better when adopting a *standardization* or *flexibility* orientation. There exists therefore a discrepancy between what service businesses communicate and what they actually do. The question is then how this drive to offer individualized services can be reconciled with the necessity to achieve the cost advantages of standardization or flexibility.

A second aspect for further research is the relation between individual service businesses and the wider service system, i.e., the value creating ecology, in which they act. It is unknown whether businesses within the same ecology should use the same perspective on productivity improvement or not. Based on our reasoning above, namely that it is important to coordinate activities within a single perspective, arguments could be given for coordinating all the businesses in a service ecology into a single perspective. However, when reasoning from theories of adaptivity and resilience, it makes sense to accept or create a certain variety of perspectives within a service ecology. If this is the case, what should this mix of different perspectives in the ecology look like and how can it be brought about? And when productivity is a good compass to measure the innovativeness of service businesses, can we develop an analogous instrument for measuring the innovativeness of service ecologies?

References

Araujo, L., and Spring, M. (2006). Services, products and the institutional structure of production. *Industrial Marketing Management*, 35, 797–805.

Bangma, K., Gibcus, P., Kuijpers, J., and De Wit, G. (2004). *Arbeidsproductiviteit in de Nederlandse dienstensector: een literatuurstudie en enkele eigen empirische bevindingen.* Research Report H200405. Zoetermeer: EIM.

Baumol, W.J. (1967). Macroeconomics of unbalanced growth: the anatomy of urban crises. *American Economic Review*, 57(3), 415–426.

Boone, T., Ganeshan, R., and Hicks, R.L. (2008). Learning and knowledge depreciation in professional services. *Management Science*, 54(7), 1231–1236.

Brynjolfsson, E., and Hitt, L.M. (2003), Computing productivity: firm-level evidence. *The Review of Economics and Statistics*, 85(4), 793–808.

Chesbrough, H., and Spohrer, J. (2006). A research manifesto for service science. *Communications of the ACM*, 49(7), 35–40.

De Jong, J.P.J., and Vermeulen, P.A.M. (2003). Organizing successful new service development: a literature review. *Management Decision*, 41(9), 844–858.

Demirkan, H., Kauffman, R.J., Vayghan, J.A., Fill, H.-G., Karagiannis, D., and Maglio, P.P. (2008). Service-oriented technology and management: perspectives on research and practice for the coming decade. *Electronic Commerce Research and Applications*, 7, 356–376.

Diewert, E. (2000). *The challenge of Total Factor Productivity measurement.* Working Paper, University of British Columbia.

Dorgan, S.J., Dowdy, J.J., and Rippin, T.M. (2006). The link between management and productivity. *McKinsey Quarterly.com*, February 2006.

Dosi, G. (1982). Technological paradigms and technological trajectories: a suggested interpretation of the determinants and directions of technical change. *Research Policy*, 11, 147–162.

Drucker, P.F. (1994). The theory of the business. *Harvard Business Review*, September–October, 95–104.

Drucker, P.F. (1999). Knowledge-worker productivity: the biggest challenge. *California Management Review*, 41(2), 79–94.

Hamel, G., and Prahalad, C.K. (1993). Strategy as stretch and leverage. *Harvard Business Review*, March–April, 75–86.

Heskett, J.L., Jones, T.O., Loveman, G.W., Sasser, Jr., W.E., and Schlesinger, L.A. (1994). Putting the service-profit chain to work. *Harvard Business Review*, March–April, 164–174.

Johnson, B.C., Manyika, J.M., and Yee, L.A. (2005). The next revolution in interactions. *McKinsey Quarterly*, 4, 21–33.

Karni, R., and Kaner, M. (2007). An engineering tool for the conceptual design of service systems. In: D. Spath and K.-P. Fähnrich (Eds.) *Advances in services innovations.* Berlin: Springer.

Maglio, P.P., Srinivasan, S., Kreulen, J.T., and Spohrer, J. (2006). Service systems, service scientists, SSME, and innovation. *Communications of the ACM*, 49(7), 81–85.

Nelson, R.R., and Winter, S.G. (1982). *An evolutionary theory of economic change.* Cambridge: The Belknap Press of Harvard University Press.

Penrose, E. (1959). *The theory of the growth of the firm.* New York: Wiley.

Porter, M.E. (1985). *Competitive advantage: creating and sustaining superior performance.* New York: Free Press.

Prahalad, C.K., and Hamel, G. (1990). The core competence of the corporation. *Harvard Business Review*, May–June, 79–91.

Solow, R.M. (1957). Technical change and the aggregate production function. *The Review of Economics and Statistics*, 39, 312–320.

Spohrer, J., Maglio, P.P., Bailey, J., and Gruhl, D. (2007). Steps toward a science of service systems. *IEEE Computer Society*, 40(January), 71–77.

Tien, J.M., Berg, D. (2003). A case for service systems engineering. *Journal of Systems Science and Systems Engineering*, 12(1), 13–38.

Triplett, J.E., and Bosworth, B.P. (2003). Productivity measurement issues in services industries: "Baumol's disease" has been cured. *FRBNY Economic Policy Review*, September, 23–33.

Van Ark, B., and De Jong, G. (2004). *Productiviteit in dienstverlening. Deel 1: Wat het is en waarom het moet.* Study for Stichting Management Studies (Foundation of Management Studies, affiliated with the Confederation of Netherlands Industry and Employers, VNO-NCW). The Hague: Royal Van Gorcum.

Van Asseldonk, A.G.M. (1998). *Mass-individualisation: business strategies applying networked order to create economic value in heterogeneous and unpredictable markets.* Veldhoven: TVA management bv.

Wolff, E.N. (1999). The productivity paradox: evidence from indirect indicators of service sector productivity growth. *The Canadian Journal of Economics*, 32(2), Special issue on service sector productivity and the productivity paradox, 281–308.

Zegveld, M.A. (2000). *Competing with dual innovation strategies: a framework to analyse the balance between operational value creation and the development of resources.* Den Haag: Werk-Veld.

Zegveld, M.A. (2004). The productivity and governance of company-specific knowledge. *International Journal of Learning and Intellectual Capital*, 1(3), 317–333.

Zegveld, M.A., and Den Hartigh, E. (2007). *De winst van productiviteit: sturen op resultaat in dienstverlening.* Study for Stichting Management Studies (Foundation of Management Studies, affiliated with the Confederation of Netherlands Industry and Employers, VNO-NCW). The Hague: Royal Van Gorcum.

Value Co-creation from the Consumer Perspective

Steve Baron and Gary Warnaby

University of Liverpool Management School, Chatham Street, Liverpool L69 7ZH, UK

Abstract The paper provides the basis for a classification of organizational operant resources as seen from a customer perspective. It facilitates, particularly, research and further understanding of Foundational Premise 9 (FP9) of the service-dominant logic of marketing (i.e. all social and economic actors are resource integrators), and suggests areas for more focused research on other foundational premises relating to value co-creation. It is based on research undertaken for, and with, the British Library, and offers an alternative research approach to the more conventional customer satisfaction survey in order to ascertain value from a consumer perspective.

Keywords Consumer experience, operant resources, service science, service systems, value co-creation

1 Introduction

Chesbrough and Spohrer (2006) have posed the question "How do people and organizations negotiate the creation of intangible assets that produce value for both?"

Through a case study of a specific organization – the British Library (BL), the national library of the UK – this paper addresses the co-creation of value and the notion of 'value in use', that are central to the service-dominant logic of marketing, by focusing on understanding value co-creation from the *consumer* perspective. More specifically, it aims to further understand how consumers integrate their resources by engaging in experiences, and how consumers may perceive organizational operant resources. Working on the premise that individual consumers, as well as organizations, are service systems, the paper offers frameworks that:

- Provide insights into the roles of the service science elements of people, technology, shared information and consumer input in value-creation networks

- Offer a new lens through which to improve customer-perceived service quality
- Integrate consumers into the process of service creation and delivery

Sections 3 and 4 of this chapter discuss the role of operant resources in the service-dominant logic of marketing. Section 5 outlines the specific context of the research (i.e. the British Library), before discussing the nature of the operant and operand resources of both the Library's users and the organization itself (Sects. 6 and 7), and their interaction (Sect. 8). Sections 9 and 10 discuss the managerial implications, before concluding with suggestions for further research (Sect. 11).

2   Operant Resources and the Service-Dominant Logic

Foundational Premise (FP4) of the service-dominant logic of marketing states that operant resources are the fundamental source of competitive advantage (Vargo and Lusch 2008). However, currently, there is a lack of empirical work that takes a *consumer* perspective on operant resources, or on how consumers use and integrate their own operant resources. By gaining empirical, case-study-based insights, it is hoped that FP4 can move beyond conceptualization to enabling frameworks. As the co-creation of value will involve the interplay of operant resources of both consumers and organizations, a brief summary of each is given.

3   Consumer Operant Resources

Arnould et al. (2006) provide a very helpful categorization of consumers' operant resources. They are:

- Physical resources (physical and mental endowment, energy, emotion, strength)
- Social resources (family relationships, consumer communities, commercial relationships)
- Cultural resources (specialized knowledge/skills, history, imagination)

Often supported by ICT-mediated communication, consumers find ways to integrate their own operant resources and, through C2C interactions, integrate their operant resources with other consumers, often to great effect. However, there is, as yet, little practical evidence of the employment of consumer operant resources within the existing canon of research.

4   Organizational Operant Resources

In general, an organization's operant resources are said to be made up of its controls, routines, cultures and competencies, as well as the skills and knowledge of its employees, its technology and information-gathering capabilities and its relationships with competitors, suppliers and customers (Madhavaram and Hunt 2008).

Of course, an organization's view of its operant resources may not tally with the views of its customers – certainly in terms of which resources are of value to the customer beneficiaries. So a consumer perspective on organizational operant resources can provide valuable insights, which, in turn, can serve to improve organizational effectiveness.

5   Case Study: The British Library

When British Library (BL) users became aware in January 2007, through a national newspaper report (Woolf 2007), that UK Government spending cuts could potentially result in the library opening hours being slashed by a third, and charges being made for researchers to use the reading rooms, over 800 detailed consumer messages of support for the BL, solicited by the organization, appeared on the BL website. Members of Parliament were bombarded with protests, and, as a result questions were tabled in parliament. Typical of the supporting emails is the one below from a US academic:

> I am a graduate student in English Literature. I have been a British Library patron for several years now as I do my research in late-medieval travel accounts. I am writing in support of the funding issue brought to my attention by my colleague. I strongly urge the Treasury to continue your funding. There are resources available at the British Library that are available nowhere else. I myself have used the library's manuscript collection on numerous occasions, and the resources I use are one-of-a-kind materials that cannot be accessed in any other form. In addition to my research, I have also used the BL as a learning tool for my students. I have twice taught for my university's London Study Centre, covering courses such as Shakespeare and British Literature. While teaching these classes I brought my students to the Ritblatt Treasures Room to see the Magna Carta, Shakespeare folios, the Luttrell Psalter, and other important manuscripts and first editions. This was a valuable resource to use, and I would hope those resources remain free and open to the public.

Although the word 'resource' is used many times about the BL itself, the excerpt demonstrates explicitly, and indicates implicitly, the operant resources (physical, social, cultural) at the disposal of this BL consumer. The physical and mental endowment is demonstrated by the repeated travel to the UK, the organization of student visits to the BL, and the academic qualifications obtained. Social resources are implied by the student network and personal network which included the colleague who alerted her to the potential cuts. Cultural resources include a history of living and working in the USA, and the imagination to incorporate field work into the study centre's curriculum.

This was just one of 800 entries to the BL website. Undertaking a detailed analysis of these messages, it was possible, in almost all cases, to identify examples of consumers' use and integration of their own operant resources. Equally, many messages of support identified the BL's organizational operant resources that contributed to consumer value-in-use. Short excerpts are given below to provide illustrations.

Truly the British Library is one of the treasures of the world... (1)
The British Library is an incredibly precious resource...and needs all the support it can get (2)
...the atmosphere in the reading rooms is very conducive to productive work and it's an exceptionally lovely building to work in (3)
The Library constitutes a major part of our national heritage (4)
The BL staff...provide the most concise and thorough guidance on locating difficult-to-find materials (5)
I was made incredibly welcome, given lots of help by the excellent reading room staff... (6)
...none comes close to the quality of the BL's online services (7)
The staff are pleased and enthusiastic that you want to come in, and want to help you in any way they can (8)
I use the BL café as a social place to meet people and network. (9)

A thorough analysis of the BL user voice on the organization's operant resources resulted in the following categorizations:

- Representational (further sub-divided into Reputation, Goodwill, Comfort/Congeniality) – as illustrated by quotes 1–3 above.
- Cultural (further sub-divided into Ethos, Knowledge, Capabilities) – as illustrated by quotes 4–7 above.
- Social (further sub-divided into Staff Friendliness/Helpfulness, Social Atmosphere) – as illustrated by quotes 8–9 above.

6   Operant and Operand Resources of Customers and Organizations

A full analysis of consumer and organizational resources will include operand resources of each (as in Table 1). However the focus of this paper is the potential value co-creation that results from the interplay between the customer and organizational operant resources (i.e. columns headed 'Customer Operant Resources' and 'Customer-Articulated Organizational Operant Resources' in Table 1). Such a focus explicitly recognises FP 4 of the service-dominant logic of marketing, and that operant resources act on operand resources to produce effects, but clearly does not acknowledge completely the complexity of the service systems involved.

The categorizations in the column headed 'Customer Operant Resources' are those advocated by Arnould et al. (2006). Those in the column headed 'Customer-Articulated

Table 1. Operant and operand resources of customers and organizations

Customer operand resources	Customer operant resources	Customer-articulated organizational operant resources	Customer-articulated organizational operand resources
Economic	Physical	Representational	Geographical location/place
	Sensorimotor	Reputation	
	Endowment	Goodwill	
	Energy, emotions, strength	Comfort/congeniality	
Material objects	Cultural	Cultural	Building/space
	Specialized knowledge and skills	Ethos	
	Life expectancies and history	Knowledge	
	Imagination	Knowledge management	
		Know-how	
		Capabilities	
		Service quality	
		Technology	
Physical Spaces	Social	Social	Products (library collections)
	Family relationships	Staff friendliness/ helpfulness	
	Brand communities	Social atmosphere (C2C networking)	
	Consumer tribes		
	Commercial relationships		

Organizational Operant Resources' resulted from the analysis of the BL user support messages. Initially, it was anticipated that the labels 'physical', 'cultural' and 'social' may also apply to organizational operant resources. However, the process of deriving a prototype classification system of customer-perceived organizational operant resources raised an issue related to the primary classification 'physical' that was used for customer operant resources. As with all organizations that have customers on-site, the physical space, or servicescape, is a key *operand* resource over which the organization has allocative capabilities to influence customers' perceptions of physical-space-related organizational operant resources, especially those social resources that support the customer community. Whereas, in the resource-based theory of the customer (Arnould et al. 2006), 'physical' resources (strength and emotion) are classified as operant resources, the label 'physical' was found to be somewhat confusing as a label of organizations' operant resources. So the label 'Representational' has been introduced to encapsulate the strength of feelings that the BL's image evokes. Hence, physical space has been classified as an operand resource, and perceptions of community (operant resource) that follow from organizational decisions on design of physical space have been assigned to the category 'social atmosphere (C2C networking)'.

A tenet of this book is that service, defined as the application of competence and knowledge to create benefit (or value) for another, derives from interactions of service systems. As stated before, an individual customer, as well as an organization, is a service system. Therefore, the middle two columns of Table 1 throw some light on the potential interactions of the customer service system with the organizational service system through possessed and perceived (from the customer perspective) operant resources.

Each organization has multiple customers, and therefore multiple service system interactions. Equally, customers create experiences through interacting with many other service systems, including other customers. Before pulling these ideas together, it is useful to highlight recent work on consumer experience and C2C interactions.

7   Consumer Experiences

Caru and Cova (2007) argue that there are two distinct ways for consumers to become immersed in an experience: passively, or actively. The passive way refers to consumer immersion in a firm-manipulated experience, such as in a leisure-related elaborate servicescape (for example, Disney parks). The active way is where consumers are able to immerse themselves in an experience, so that immersion can be "…thought of as a whole set of operations that consumers carry out to produce the experience by manipulating to their own advantage whatever is being done to manipulate them" (Caru and Cova 2007, p. 37). The goal in analyzing the BL user-support messages was to undertake research which results in a greater understanding of active consumer immersion in experiences, to complement the existing research by academics and practitioners on organizational consumer experience management. It ensures that the consumer's perspective is maintained throughout (Merholz 2007).

8   Consumer-to-Consumer Interactions

Any attempt to understand co-creation of value and consumer experiences inevitably involves a consideration of C2C interactions. They are the manifestations of the application of consumer social resources: family relationships and consumer communities. It is only by taking a consumer perspective on co-creation of value that due consideration is given to C2C interactions. While C2C interactions have always taken place at on-site service settings, it is probably the on-line C2C interactions, as exemplified by the British Library example, which have re-emphasized their importance today's service environment. Communication from one academic to another (as contained in the US academic's support message to the BL) is but one of many on-line C2C communications that result in exponential increases in the scope and extent of consumer campaigning, with organizations (such as BL) having to re-orientate their thinking just to handle the volume of consumer support.

The BL case has focused on consumers articulating their support for an organization. Of course, the problems are far greater when the consumer campaign is *against* an organization. Consumers also actively seek advice from other consumers, using the latest technology, on what hotel to stay in, which books to buy, what music to download, what pub to frequent prior to a sporting event, etc. How many of us have decided against booking in a hotel on the basis of previous guest comments in 'Trip Advisor'? How many hotel managers really know how to manage their service offer in the light of increased consumer information, both positive and negative, via C2C interactions?

9   Insights from the Case Study

In the spirit of offering guidance on how to invest in improving organizational service systems, and encouraging better management practice, Figs. 1 and 2 below present a way of conceptualizing consumer experiences with an organization, and with other consumers.

Suppose an organization has n customers. The co-creation of value through operant resource interactions, between customer i ($i = 1, 2, ..., n$) and the organization, can be represented by Fig. 1, which takes the middle two columns of Table 1, and highlights the operant resource linkages.

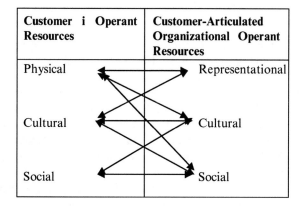

Fig. 1. Co-creation of value: organization and customer *i*

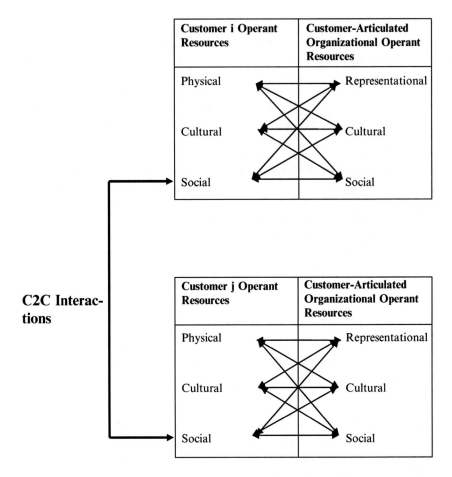

Fig. 2. Co-creation of value: organization and multiple customers

Moreover, Customer i (i = 1, 2, ..., *n*) may have C2C social interactions with other customers of the organization, i.e. Customer j (i ≠ j, j = 1, 2, ..., n) as represented in Fig. 2.

The network in Fig. 2 is incomplete, in that it only includes the one organization, and not the many and varied interactions that consumers will have with other organizations and experience enablers, which may in turn support the focal organization. So it does not capture the total consumer experience. Nevertheless, it does provide a framework for a more detailed understanding of value co-creation possibilities with consumers.

Figures 1 and 2 provide a focus for guiding further empirical research aimed at finessing FP9 of the service-dominant logic (i.e. all social and economic actors are resource integrators). Figure 1 forms the basis for a better understanding of "the interplay of the consumers and firms operant and operand resources" (Arnould et al. 2006, p. 98). Taken together, the greater specificity of the operant resources of both the organization and the customer can stimulate research into the specific nature of value co-creation (FP6 of the service-dominant logic).

10 Some Managerial Implications

The case study offers directions on how organizations can gain insights into the roles of people, technology, shared information and consumer input in value-creation networks. The case-study analysis alerted us to implications for marketing research and how data are collected. As noted above, all the data were solicited by the BL, being responses to a *single* question on the organization's website (viz. "If you want to support us, please let us know why the British Library is important to you"). The analysis was extremely time-consuming, and the authors became involved precisely because the organization did not have time to carry out the analysis in a systematic way. Such analysis requires a dedicated resource, as it is a resource-intensive process. It was, however, recognized as extremely valuable by the BL managers when the results were presented to them. Maybe, organizations can re-direct resources normally employed in designing and analyzing customer satisfaction surveys, addressing numerous company-designed questions, into quali-tative analyses of customer-generated data? Building on active customer participa-tion, in this case through analyzing heart-felt customer voice, provides subtle clues not only to the operant resources that customers bring to value co-creation pro-cesses, but also to their higher-level values which underpin their relationships with the organization.

Generally, studies that aim to improve customer-perceived service quality have tended to be based on survey-based marketing research methods, using, for example, instruments such as SERVQUAL (Parasuraman et al. 1988). However well-designed such surveys are, they do not necessarily capture key elements and networks that contribute to customer experiences. Most surveys of this kind, for example, focus on service encounters with an organization, and pay little attention to C2C interactions and social networks, or indeed the creativity of customers in employing their operant resources. Eliciting customer-articulated organizational operant resources, as for example in the third column of Table 1, offers a new direction for research that acknowledges both organizations and customers as service systems.

By focusing on the interplay between customer operant resources and customer-articulated organizational operant resources, it is possible to identify potential for integrating consumers into the process of service creation and delivery. By way of illustration, a positive feedback loop that is taking place in the BL's 'Business and Intellectual Property Centre' (BIPC) is presented in Fig. 3. The BIPC is used by entrepreneurs and small business managers to facilitate the launch and expansion of new businesses, thereby facilitating their ongoing, sustainable success.

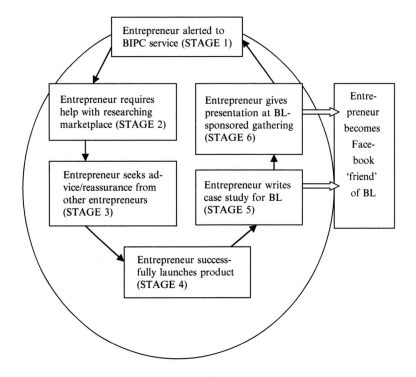

Fig. 3. Example of virtuous circle brought about by interplay of organizational and customer operant resources

At stage 1, an aspiring entrepreneur is alerted to the BL's BIPC service as a result of the organization's representational resources (by means of advertising campaigns, website, and other marketing communications activities). At stage 2, the organization recognizes the entrepreneur's lack of expertise in effective information searching (deficiency of customer cultural resource) and offers specialized help (organizational cultural resource). At stage 3, the organization recognises the entrepreneur's need to talk to other similar people (lack of customer social resource), and facilitates business/social events for entrepreneurs both online and face-to-face on BL premises (organizational social resource). Up to this stage, the entrepreneur is mainly expending physical resources, whilst building up cultural and social resources. At and after stage 4, the entrepreneur has developed customer cultural resources that can be channelled into action at stage 5 – the writing up of a case study of the BL's part in a success story, published on the BL's website and in its annual report. (The BL explicitly solicits such case studies for marketing communication purposes, targeted at all user groups). This adds to the organization's representational resources. At stage 6, the successful entrepreneur then becomes a lead figure/role model in subsequent business/social events for entrepreneurs, adding to customer social resources. Finally, back to stage 1, other potential entrepreneurs are alerted to the BL's BIPC service, and the virtuous circle is completed and ready for further cycles. During this process, the BL have used their cultural and social resources to set up a Facebook page in recognition of the C2C interactions that contribute to the entrepreneurial experience, but which may not directly involve the BL.

As seen above, the framework presented in Fig. 2 provides a very helpful way of managing the manner in which customers can be integrated, in a mutually beneficial way, to service creation and delivery.

More generally, customers of organizations may use and integrate their operant resources in tandem with an organization's customer-perceived operant resources, in a positive or negative way, often in situations when the organization is threatened, either through environmental changes (e.g. governmental funding reviews, as in the BL case), or through its own service failures being made transparent and well-known via C2C networks. Such triggers seem to unearth latent consumer values that translate into operant-resource-fuelled consumer action.

What can organisations do in response?

The approach adopted in this chapter emphasizes the need for organizations to understand the operant resources possessed by their customers and how they use, integrate and articulate them. It is unlikely that such understanding can be obtained via conventional customer surveys, and innovative research methods will be required to study consumers in action, and consumer practices. A focus on understanding what consumers think about the organization's operant resources can foster more effective marketing communication – a communication emphasis on organizational value propositions that have proven resonance with consumers.

11   Conclusion

The focus of this chapter is on value co-creation from a consumer perspective. The BL case study illustrates that if an organization is important to consumers, they will voice their viewpoints if sufficiently motivated to do so. Through analyzing the content of the consumer voice, it is possible to uncover how consumers use and integrate their resources, and how they perceive the organization's operant resources. By categorizing the two sets of operant resources, it is possible to delve into the value co-creation dynamics brought about by the interplay of the operant resources of two social systems – the consumer and the organization – and to create positive feedback loops that enhance the operant resources in each social system. The ideas put forward in this chapter are intended to provide basic frameworks that can be refined and tested through further case-study research with different organizations.

There are limitations to the classification of organizational operant resources. First, the elements in Figs. 1 and 2 need to be refined to embrace organizations that do not have onsite customers, for example E-Businesses, or Food-Processing firms.

Second, this is a first attempt at classification and needs further testing to ensure that the categories are completely exhaustive. Indeed, while carrying out this analysis, the authors identified scope for ambiguity among/within some categories. Nevertheless, we believe it is a step that needs to be taken in order to encourage focussed empirical research on value co-creation within the context of the service-dominant logic of marketing.

References

Arnould, E. J., Price, L. L. and Malshe, A. (2006). Toward a cultural resource-based theory of the customer. In R. F. Lusch and S. L. Vargo (Eds.), *The Service-Dominant Logic of Marketing: Dialog, Debate and Directions* (pp. 320–333) Armonk: ME Sharpe.

Caru, A. and Cova, B. (2007). Consuming experiences: an introduction. In A. Caru and B. Cova (Eds.), *Consuming Experience* (pp. 3–16). Abingdon: Routledge.

Chesbrough, H. and Spohrer, J. (2006). A research manifesto for services science. *Communications of the ACM*, July, 35–40.

Madhavaram, S. and Hunt, S. D. (2008). The service-dominant logic and a hierarchy of operant resources: Developing masterful operant resources and implications for marketing strategy. *Journal of the Academy of Marketing Science*, 36, 67–82.

Merholz, P. (2007). Experience *is* the product. *Business Week*, June 22.

Parasuraman, A., Zeithaml, V. A. and Berry, L. L. (1988). SERVQUAL: a multiple-item scale for measuring consumer perceptions of service quality. *Journal of Retailing*, 64 (1), 12–37.

Vargo, S. L. and Lusch, R. F. (2008). Service-dominant logic: continuing the evolution. *Journal of the Academy of Marketing Science*, 36, 1–10.

Woolf, M. (2007). British Library to start charging. *The Independent*, 28 January, http://www.news,independent.co.uk/uk/this_britain/article2192972.ece. Accessed 21 June 2007

Metrics That Matter: Measuring and Improving the Value of Service

Thomas J. Buckholtz

Goldman School of Public Policy, University of California, Berkeley

157 Westridge Drive, Portola Valley, 94028, CA, USA

Abstract This chapter features two metrics for the value of service and provides how-to advice for using them to attribute value, improve service, create service-innovation roadmaps, select metrics, and promote service science. The chapter also presents perspective and advice regarding service offerings and measurement and provides examples of using the two metrics.

Keywords Metrics, value, innovation, roadmap, functionality, proficiency, service science, service systems

1 Introduction and Usage

How can an entity... Request needed service? ... Provide service someone wants? ... Ascribe value to service? ... Foster optimal-value service?

A service recipient, provider, innovator, consultant, researcher, or a service-as-a-science catalyst needs to answer those questions – regarding its clients, itself, and its providers. This chapter features perspective and how-to advice for all service-ecosystem participants. Section 2 discusses a framework for shaping services and using metrics. Sections 3 and 4 provide two measuring scales for determining value associated with almost any service activity. Section 5 gives examples of shaping services and guidance for using the scales and framework. Section 5.2 provides an example, which catalysts can consider emulating, of building a grassroots movement. Section 6 notes benefits people can derive by applying the scales. Section 7 extends Sects. 2, 3, 4, and 6 by providing more advice for using metrics.

Additionally, for researchers, Sect. 2 provides a framework for cataloguing and analyzing metrics and their uses; Sects. 3 and 4 connect the scales to theoretical bases and to other techniques that can be considered applications of those bases; Sect. 5 provides instances supporting the validity and utility of the scales and framework; Sect. 6 points to opportunities to use the scales in researching service innovation and science; and Sect. 7 suggests bases for selecting research metrics.

H. Demirkan et al. (eds.), *Service Systems Implementation*, Service Science:
Research and Innovations in the Service Economy, DOI 10.1007/978-1-4419-7904-9_13,
© Springer Science+Business Media, LLC 2011

2   Service and Service Measurements

This section provides perspective about service and measurements.

Service denotes both (a) the impact of some *activity* on a *client* entity or result and (b) the activity generating such impact. *Impact* denotes effects that would not have happened without the activity. *Entity* can be a person, organization, nation, society, system, animal, etc., or combination thereof.

Society provides various definitions of service (Vargo and Lurch 2004; Spohrer et al. 2007) and *results* that entities need, want, achieve, or happen to experience. Frameworks for envisioning or measuring results include Maslow's hierarchy of needs (Maslow 1943); customer-satisfaction measuring systems; applications of *Six Sigma* and predecessors thereof; aspects of financial accounting, including *shareholders' equity*; aspects of investment, including *rate of return*; applications of *critical success factors* (Rockart 1986; Ronald 1961); and categories of purposes for coalitions and relationships (Buckholtz 2007).

Service measurements help answer prospective or retrospective questions (Table 1). Prospective estimates support choosing the extents to which to pursue courses of action. Retrospective statements contrast service-based results with estimated results based on assuming the service did not occur.

3   A Measuring Scale for the Functional Value of Service

This section discusses a measuring scale (Table 2) useful for addressing the functionality question (Table 1), "How and how much do activities contribute to results and to each other?" Service activities supporting specific results can be classified via this functional-category hierarchy.

Table 1. Questions addressed by measurements

Service impact

　Who is a client?

　How much do client entities and results differ, because the service occurs, from what they would be without the service occurring?

Service generation

　What activities occur?

　For various activities, …

　　Who is a client?

　　Who is a *provider*?

　　How and how much do activities contribute to results and to each other? (*service functionality*)

　　How and how well do activities proceed? (*service proficiency*)

Table 2. Service-functionality scale

Realizing – using or measuring results of service

Accomplishing – receiving or performing service

Planning – selecting service scenarios

Understanding – building knowledge of opportunities for service

Marshaling – gathering resources that perform the above activities or that are used in the course of those activities

This scale may be considered as a *banding* of a value-stratified continuum of service activities (Buckholtz 2007). Other scales that also can be considered as bandings of all or parts of that continuum include the Awareness/Attention, Interest, Decision, Action progression (Ace 2001) by which salespeople can gauge customer activity; the ISPAR model (Spohrer et al. 2008a) for value co-creation; and the Direct Outcomes tool known as Achieve Progress (Buckholtz 2007).

To the extent a client successfully delegates work associated with a band, the client may not need to be concerned with work – in subsequent bands – supporting that activity. Thus, a client may ascribe more value to service in a band than to service in lower bands. Exceptions can arise, for example, to the extent (a) work in a lower band – for example, providing computer systems (Marshaling) – needs to support work that is not being delegated; or (b) the client desires to control or provide services in lower bands.

This sense of value dovetails with *principles of lean consumption* (Womack and Jones 2005). Providing high-band service can obviate a client's dealing with low-band work, thereby solving the client's problem more completely than otherwise might be the case and reducing the number of decisions the client makes.

Ascribing value to higher-band work should not be interpreted as devaluing (a) work in lower bands (for example, a failure in any band can be significant.) or (b) the reusing of work from lower bands.

Clients, providers, and other entities can consider the extent to which (a) a vision for how to achieve success in a band points to needs for innovation or action in subsequent bands (Plan downward); (b) difficulties in planning related to a band point to potential problems or risks in planning for subsequent bands; (c) success in a band creates potential for innovation or success in preceding bands (Plan, work, or create value upward. For example, hiring an employee (Marshaling) may create opportunities based on knowledge the person brings (Understanding)); (d) difficulties in carrying out work in a band point to potential problems or risks regarding work in preceding bands; and (e) an activity – in any band – can itself be studied by reusing the hierarchy (*nesting, recursion*, or *fractal properties*).

The following are approximate relationships between ten foundational concepts (Spohrer et al. 2008b) of service science and the functionality scale: (1) Resources – Marshaling; (2) Entities – Marshaling; (3) Access Rights – Marshaling; (4) Value-Cocreation Interactions – All (perhaps especially Accomplishing); (5) Governance Interactions – All; (6) Outcomes – All (perhaps especially Accomplishing and

Table 3. A functionality scale for knowledge-based services

Realizing

Accomplishing

Planning
  Gaining buy-in for service decisions
  Making decisions
  Comparing scenarios
  Analyzing individual scenarios

Understanding
  Qualifying opportunities for service or for service improvement
  Stating opportunities (metrics include statements' extrinsic properties, such as *usefulness* for comparing specific scenarios)

Marshaling
  Focusing attention toward specific data
  Qualifying data (metrics include data's extrinsic properties, such as *relevance*, and intrinsic properties, such as *consistency* [Buckholtz 1995])
  Presenting data
  Synthesizing trends or other data from previously existing data
  Capturing data

Realizing); (7) Stakeholders – Marshaling; (8) Measures – Realizing; (9) Networks – Marshaling; and (10) Ecology – All.

Bands can be subdivided. For example, in the Marshaling category, an information-technology system can have an associated *technology stack* running from user-application software to basic electronic-elements. For knowledge-based services, a sub-banding (Table 3) for some bands (Table 2) illustrates practical needs of enterprises and other entities.

4   A Measuring Scale for the Proficiency Value of Service

This section discusses a measuring scale (Table 4) useful for addressing the proficiency question (Table 1), "How and how well do activities proceed?" When exploring "how well" for an activity, people should consider context in which the activity takes place.

This scale applies to essentially all activities and can be considered to be a sharpening of focus and reduction in scope of other scales, such as capability maturity models and the Direct Outcomes Achieve Style tool (Buckholtz 2007).

For a task, entities may ascribe more value to behavior associated with a category closer to Obviated than to behavior associated with a category farther from Obviated. Such value may emphasize, for example, *efficiency* or *likelihood for successful quality control*. Exceptions arise, for example, to the extent (a) work associated with an upper category (for example, Obviated or Routine) compromises

Table 4. Service-proficiency scale

Obviated – entities do not perform the activity, because performing it is not needed
Routine – entities follow established processes
Experimental – entities try various processes
Ad hoc – entities try to perform the activity without using processes
Pending – entities do not perform the activity, even though outcomes the activity can produce are needed

capability, creativity, or flexibility or (b) it is more appropriate to plan (Pending) than to do (other categories).

This sense of value is harmonious with *principles of lean consumption* (Womack and Jones 2005). Clients want to avoid work (Obviated) or, if they must do work, clients often would like to use Routine means.

5   Interpreting Examples of Service Breakthroughs

This section interprets examples of service breakthroughs (in quality, productivity, innovation, and compliance), each in terms of at least one of the functionality scale (Table 2) and the proficiency scale (Table 4). Some interpretation also emphasizes service-impact and service-generation questions (Table 1).

5.1   The Essence of Knowledge Services and the Information Age

This example uses functionality bands (Tables 2 and 3) to analyze the redrafting of a mission statement. Also, people can consider the extents to which such analysis provides key concepts regarding the essence of the Information Age and the evolutions of (a) knowledge services (or Information-Age services) and (b) services catalyzed by staff-function-led communities, including ones led by chief information officers (CIOs).

In 1980, the Paperwork Reduction Act established *information resources management (IRM)* as a field of practice within the United States federal government. IRM combines knowledge usage and services, records management, computing, and telecommunications. The terminology for CIO was *Designated Senior Official for Information Resources Management.*

In 1989, the United States General Services Administration's (GSA) Information Resources Management Service (IRMS) fulfilled roles including (a) co-CIO for the federal Executive Branch (Work included co-leading the practice of IRM, reviewing the performance of some CIO-led organizations (triennial reviews), and overseeing much Executive Branch IRM procurement. The other co-leader was a group in the

Office of Management and Budget), (b) supplier to federal entities (in all three Branches) of $1 billion per year of telecommunications and professional services, (c) CIO for GSA, and (d) supplier of information to the public.

In late 1989, GSA was doing strategic planning. IRMS needed a mission statement. The following are candidate themes, each with an image the theme might convey (to the perhaps 4,000,000 federal employees IRMS served) and with an assessment of value based on Table 2: (a) *Information proficiency* – using information to make and implement decisions (Planning and Accomplishing); (b) *Information-rich environment* – useful information (Understanding); and (c) *Quality products and services* – computers, telephones, and networks (Marshaling). Previously, IRMS had developed an *information-rich environment* theme, which I (newly serving as the commissioner leading IRMS) found momentarily compelling and then, thinking of *information overload*, not optimal. I devised and IRMS adopted the following mission statement (Buckholtz 1995): *To help clients achieve information proficiency. Information proficiency is the effective use of information to achieve a person's job or an organization's mission.* Associated with this statement were two operational themes: (a) *proficiency with information to make decisions and thereby set goals* and (b) *proficiency through information to communicate and implement decisions and thereby achieve results specified by goals.*

By emphasizing clients' Planning and Accomplishing activities, IRMS provided clients a vision of support for clients' doing their work well and provided a gamut of providers (CIOs, members of CIO-led communities, and IRM vendors) guidance regarding clients' needs and wants (Buckholtz 1996). Subsequent endeavors included (a) a nationwide movement to improve governmental service to the public (Sect. 5.2) and *reinventing government* (Accomplishing) and (b) endeavors (such as *C4I for the Warrior*) to fuse information and intelligence across systems, among governmental organizations, and between governmental and other entities (Marshaling and Understanding).

5.2   *Improving Governmental Service to the American Public*

This example (a) features the evolution of a service – the systematic fostering of improving governmental service to the American public – from Pending and Ad Hoc (Table 4) to at least Experimental, (b) involves efforts in which coalitions progressed from gathering (Marshaling (Table 2)) to other activities (including Accomplishing and Realizing) that benefitted many entities, and (c) points to advantages of focusing on broad concepts of coalitions and impacted entities (Sect. 2).

During the 1980s, thousands of federal, state, and local government agencies served the public. In 1989, Francis A. McDonough, a GSA IRMS deputy commissioner, proposed that – starting with the community of federal CIOs – the nation could build coalitions to make *service to citizens* (or *governmental service to the public*) a topic and to catalyze widespread innovation and improvement (McDonough and Buckholtz 1992). By early 1993, the nation was benefiting from projects, research, and a grassroots coalition – of academic, news-media, private-sector, and local-, state-, and federal-government employees and organizations – that pursued vital opportunities. Later in 1993, the federal government labeled some initiatives *reinventing government*. Subsequent *e-government* (at all levels of government) and *simplified permitting* (for building permits) illustrate outgrowths from this endeavor.

5.3   *Facilitating Compliance by Considering Regulation to be a Service*

This example features a regulator's improving service to regulated entities (Table 1, with the regulated entities considered as clients), thus offering clients opportunities to do compliance work via higher-proficiency behavior (Table 4).

Before and during the early 1990s, IRMS's co-CIO-for-the-Executive-Branch function (Sect. 5.1) propagated the Federal Information Resources Management Regulation (FIRMR), which pertained to much Executive Branch IRM activity. When I served as IRMS commissioner, I spoke with people about three IRMS roles – service, *regulation*, and *catalytic leadership* (activities (such as starting the service to citizens movement [Sect. 5.2]) independent of traditional regulatory and service roles). I encouraged IRMS's regulatory functions to treat regulation as a service that helps clients benefit from and comply with laws, regulations, and good practices. IRMS shrank the FIRMR from 120,000 words to 40,000 words and enhanced IRMS's advisory bulletins. In its role of overseeing procurements (then $20 billion per year, or 3% of the world information-technology marketplace), IRMS reassessed how it estimated procurement risk, rebalanced its oversight to focus on high-risk procurements, and streamlined its consultative work – all to better meet national and client needs. Thus, for example, some client-done compliance work for low-risk procurements became Obviated (Table 4).

5.4   *Who Are the Clients of Procurements?*

This example features the evolution of an aspect of procurement-service practice – the *Government-Wide Acquisition Contract* – from Pending to Routine (Table 4) and illustrates the value of focusing on the questions "Who is a client?" and "Who is a provider?" (Table 1).

In 1990, a typical large United States federal government IRM acquisition effort featured one agency (hypothetically, the Department of Justice) conducting a procurement (for personal computing) allowing only that agency to make purchases, up to a limit ($0.5 billion). During 1991 or 1992, I proposed gaining more value from such endeavors. For a Government-Wide Acquisition Contract (GWAC), an agency might conduct a similar procurement with a higher limit ($550 million) and a provision that only entities other than that agency could use the additional amount ($50 million) of *procurement authority*. Vendors got more potential business more easily. Agencies had more choices regarding what to buy and how much to pay. In effect, contracts competed with each other. The government acquired more-appropriate technology and services, at better prices. By early 1993, agencies were pursuing 24 GWAC procurements. A January 2006 article noted a then-current $290 billion in GWAC activity – procurements that were being planned, were out for bid, or had been awarded and were still in use (Gerin 2006). Between 1990 and 2006, use of the GWAC concept transited from Pending to Routine.

5.5   Pioneering the Enterprise Software License

This example features obviation (Table 4), via the *enterprise software license* (or *corporate license*), of software suppliers' service activities.

Traditionally, software was sold by the copy. Starting in 1983, Pacific Gas and Electric Company negotiated fixed-price licenses allowing personal-computer software use – for PG&E work – on any computer (Schindler 1984). A vendor supplied a few sets of software and manuals at the beginning of a contract and whenever, during the next 7 years, the vendor produced a new version. The licenses obviated suppliers' work and costs that might have scaled with the number of software users (for example, training and help-desk support), number of computers (software copies), or aspects of customer corporate culture (marketing, sales, and processing orders) and operations (billing). While potentially challenging revenue-based salesperson-compensation practices, the licenses supported interests of suppliers (achieving and maintaining profitability) and PG&E (improving capabilities and containing costs). PG&E tabulated – for each of 12 enterprise licenses – savings of at least 90% compared to per-copy list price (based on estimates of numbers of computers on which software ran, but not including savings from not paying for copies of software upgrades) (Buckholtz 1986). Vendors added corporate licensing to their marketing, sales, and services activities.

5.6   Preserving Public Tidelands

This example features evolution of a service – defending the natural ecology of specific coastline – from Ad hoc to Routine (Table 4) and then, with the addition of a new Accomplishing goal (Table 2), to Obviated.

During the 1950s, people proposed uses – such as boat harbors, parking lots, and a city maintenance facility – for the 7 km (4.5 miles) of Pacific Ocean coastline and 280 ha (700 acres) of parkland within the City of Palos Verdes Estates, California, USA. A coalition of citizens persuaded the city council to vote down each proposed development. The coalition's proficiency at countering proposals grew from Ad hoc to Routine. But, the agenda was being set by pro-development entities and the coalition's Accomplishing activities were defensive and tactical. In approximately 1957, I proposed that the coalition's Accomplishing goals feature creating a wildlife preserve. With this Understanding insight, the coalition broadened its view of its opportunity. The coalition's reactive and proactive work (including helping coalition allies become planning-commission members and city-council members) constituted Accomplishing work toward durable strategic impact. During the 1960s, the State of California granted title for the tidelands to the City and the City established the Palos Verdes Estates Shoreline Preserve. Defense of the natural resources became Obviated.

6   Applying the Functionality and Proficiency Scales

People can apply the functionality scale (Table 2) and proficiency scale (Table 4) usefully throughout service ecosystems and activities.

People can create candidate innovation opportunities by envisioning (a) new or enhanced service offerings throughout the functionality scale and (b) how extant activities can be performed differently – by changing behavior within activities' current proficiency categories or by changing behavior to other categories. Using the scales thus can make ideation and innovation more Routine and Experimental and less Ad Hoc and Pending (Table 4).

People can create roadmaps for marketplaces, service offerings, and products. For example, during the first decade of the twenty-first century, much search-engine service featured presenting-data activities (Table 3). Opportunities suggested by the functionality scale include developing qualifying-data services. Opportunities suggested by the proficiency scale include helping clients achieve higher-proficiency behavior in the clients' qualifying-data activities. Similarly, and as suggested by Sects. 5.1 and 5.2, people can use the scales develop *service innovation roadmaps* (University of Cambridge 2008).

People can use the scales to (a) improve links in a *service-value chain* (Heskett et al. 1994); (b) generate value-proposition concepts, including in categories such as *all benefits*, *favorable points of difference*, and *resonating focus* (Anderson et al. 2006); (c) optimize value and sequences of steps for working with customers – for example, throughout a *service production process* (Mills and Moberg 1982); (d) develop hierarchies regarding the provision of service (One such hierarchy pertains to *building blocks* for a *service-oriented enterprise* [Demirkan and Goul 2006].); (e) develop and use plans and theories regarding service, including in areas such as *service innovation*, *service systems*, *service science*, and *stakeholder priorities* (Spohrer et al. 2007; University of Cambridge 2008); (f) guide – anticipate, plan, and measure the value of – initiatives to enhance the service-science movement, perhaps including via parallels to the service-to-the-citizen movement (Sect. 5.2); and (g) similarly guide service-science research activities.

When developing roles for team members, people can consider the extents to which individuals have (or can gain) skills and like to do work associated with various functionality bands; proficiency categories; and pairings, each of one or more functionality bands with one or more proficiency categories.

7   Selecting Metrics

When selecting metrics for service scenarios, people can decide (based, for example, on the significance of choosing prospectively among scenarios or understanding retrospectively differences between scenarios) the extent to which to make measurements. Then, people can choose metrics, based in part on advice in Table 5.

8   Conclusion, Recap, and Acknowledgements

Throughout their work, people can consider opportunities to provide service that is situated – from clients' perspectives and regarding clients' needs – optimally on the functionality scale (Table 2) and that helps clients behave at optimal proficiency (Table 4).

Throughout service-systems ecosystems, people can improve the value created by their and other people's endeavors by using service-shaping and metrics-selection

Table 5. Advice regarding choosing metrics

Consider diversity, regarding choices as to what to measure, in categories such as the following

Outcomes; inputs

Needs or wants of clients; needs or wants of providers

Work improvement or reduction; work transfer

Qualitative effects; quantitative effects

Consider *to what extent?* metrics before adopting *which one?* metrics

Consider using a functionality scale (for example, Table 2 or 3) to envision activities for which measurement might prove useful

Consider using the proficiency scale (Table 4) to envision the success of applying a specific metric to a specific circumstance

Consider that ostensibly quantitative metrics can have qualitative bases (for example, customer-satisfaction scores may be averages of numbers representing ranges of or points on qualitative scales. And, financial-benefit numbers depend on judgment calls, such as regarding the likelihood of and timing for receiving payments)

Consider that using qualitative measures and quantitative non-financial measures can support the following activities

Determining the extent to use financial measurements

Determining financial measuring techniques to use

---

frameworks, two scales (and related tools and theory) for measuring value, advice, and examples – all discussed in this chapter.

I would like to acknowledge that Jim Spohrer, Haluk Demirkan, and each anonymous reviewer provided valued suggestions regarding this chapter.

References

Ace, C. (2001). *Successful Marketing Communications: A Practical Guide to Planning and Implementation*. Butterworth-Heinemann, Woburn, p. 7 ff.

Anderson, J. C., Narus, J. A. and Van Rossum, W. (2006). Customer Value Propositions in Business Markets, *Harvard Business Review*, March 2006.

Buckholtz, T. J. (1986). Site Licensing Lets Users Spend Less Money to Get More Software, *InformationWEEK*, June 2, 1986.

Buckholtz, T. J. (1995). *Information Proficiency: Your Key to the Information Age*. Wiley (originally, Van Nostrand Reinhold), New York.

Buckholtz, T. J. (1996). Evaluating the CIO. *Computerworld Leadership Series*, Volume II, Issue 2. Computerworld, Framingham, Massachusetts, March 18, 1996.

Buckholtz, T. J. (2007). *Innovate Incisively: Gain Impact. Save Time.* http://stores.lulu.com/ThomasJBuckholtz

Demirkan, H. and Goul, M. (2006). AMCIS 2006 Panel Summary: Towards the Service Oriented Enterprise Vision: Bridging Industry and Academics, *Communications of the Association for Information Systems*, Vol. 18, 2006.

Gerin, R. (2006). New dawn for GWACs. *Washington Technology*, Volume 21, Number 02. January 2006. http://www.washingtontechnology.com/print/21_02/27841-1.html

Heskett, J. L., Jones, T. O., Loveman, G. W., Sasser, Jr., W. E. and Schlesinger, L. A. (1994). Putting the Service-Profit Chain to Work, *Harvard Business Review*, March–April 1994.

Maslow, A. H. (1943). A Theory of Human Motivation. *Psychological Review*, 50, 370–396

McDonough, F. A. and Buckholtz, T. J. (1992). Providing Better Service to Citizens with Information Technology. *Journal of Systems Management* 43(4), 32–40

Mills, P. K. and Moberg, D. J. (1982). Perspectives on the Technology of Service Operations, *The Academy of Management Review*, 7(3), 467–478.

Rockart, J. F. (1986). A Primer on Critical Success Factors. C. V. Bullen (editor). *The Rise of Managerial Computing: The Best of the Center for Information Systems Research*. Dow Jones-Irwin, Homewood, IL

Ronald, D. D. (1961). Management Information Crisis. *Harvard Business Review*, September–October 1961.

Schindler, Jr., P. (1984). Buying Rights to Copy Disk. *Information Systems News*. October 1, 1984.

Spohrer, J., Maglio, P. P., Bailey, J. and Gruhl, D. (2007). Steps Toward a Science of Service Systems, *Computer*, 40(1), 71–77.

Spohrer, J., Vargo, S. L., Caswell, N. and Maglio, P. P. (2008a). The Service System is the Basic Abstraction of Service Science, *Proceedings of the 41st Annual* Hawaii International Conference on System Sciences, IEEE Computer Society, Washington, DC, p. 5.

Spohrer, J., Anderson, L., Pass, N. and Ager, T. (2008b). Service science and service-dominant logic, *Proceedings of Otago Forum 2: From Propositions to Practice,* School of Business, Dunedin, New Zealand, December 8–12, pp. 6–9.

University of Cambridge Institute for Manufacturing and International Business Machines Corporation (2008), *Succeeding Through Service Innovation*, 2008.

Vargo, S. L. and Lurch, R. F. (2004). Evolving to a New Dominant Logic for Marketing, *Journal of Marketing*, 68, 1–17

Womack, J. P. and Jones, D. T. (2005). *Lean Solutions: How Companies and Customers Can Create Value and Wealth Together*. Free Press, New York, p. 15.

Succeeding Through Service Innovation: Consumer Directed Care in the Aged Care Sector

Linda Wilkins

Honorary Fellow, Australian Catholic University, Melbourne, Victoria, Australia

Carmel Laragy

Social Work Lecturer, School of Global Studies Social Science and Planning,

College of Design and Social Context, RMIT University, Melbourne, Victoria, Australia

Hossein S. Zadeh

Senior Lecturer, School of Business, and Logistics, Information Technology, College

of Business, RMIT University, Melbourne, Victoria, Australia

Abstract The growing challenge and diversity of ageing populations is a key global issue for struggling health systems. Consumer Directed Care (CDC), an innovative service delivery system, opens up possibilities for re-defining consumer expectations, prompting change in how health service providers operate. As a service delivery model, CDC offers improved responsiveness to individual requirements; and increased transparency in the use of allocated funding. Where implemented, CDC has established new relationships and interactions between key stakeholders, co-creating value for older citizens. This chapter reviews some drivers for the development of service innovation, surveys various in-country approaches, highlights current trends in CDC delivery and describes an EU policy impact assessment instrument to aid funding bodies. The chapter concludes by speculating on organizational outcomes from CDC and the likelihood that the introduction of this innovative service delivery model will require closer collaborative relationships between service providers and information technology specialists.

Keywords Consumer directed care, ICT and aged care, healthcare services, service innovation, service systems, case study

H. Demirkan et al. (eds.), *Service Systems Implementation*, Service Science: Research and Innovations in the Service Economy, DOI 10.1007/978-1-4419-7904-9_14, © Springer Science+Business Media, LLC 2011

1   Introduction

Service systems have been described as "dynamic configurations of resources (people, technologies, organisations and shared information) that can create and deliver value to customers, providers and other stakeholders" (IfM and IBM 2008: p. 18). In both the public and private sectors, transactional models are evolving where the consumer pays for selective use of services, pooling and sharing them with a resultant intensification of the use of products and reduction of their consumption. As service delivery agencies transition to new ways of operating, service providers need to accommodate a variety of approaches that enable them to determine the optimal organizational or network configuration to maintain their service offerings as well as optimal payment mechanisms in exchange for providing the service (Lusch et al. 2006). The service sector in developed countries such as the United States and Australia currently accounts for some 80% of all economic activity (DFAT 2008; Spohrer et al. 2007). The service economy encompasses not only private enterprise but also the diverse services provided by government, such as education, health and welfare. The development of service systems, in close association with the growth of the service economy, has largely displaced the traditional product-driven, one-model-fits-all approach.

In such a rapidly evolving field it is hardly surprising that a normative, well-accepted view of service systems and what they comprise is yet to be developed. Some define the service sector primarily by contrasting it with manufacturing (Tien and Berg 2003; Quinn and Paquette 1990; Quinn et al. 1987); others have argued that services should not be seen as a distinct set of activities (Ramirez 1999) and that even to seek such a dichotomy is misguided (Araujo and Spring 2006). An integrated theory of service systems that spans multiple disciplines does not yet exist whilst those models that do exist are recognized as being of limited value (IfM and IBM 2008). Service systems studies suffer from a pronounced imbalance in service research between academic output and practical interest. Significant gaps also remain in general understanding of the nature and behaviour of service systems. There are no instruments or key performance indicators to measure progress in service science innovation and no guidance or any kind of roadmap available to organisations on what investments to make to see predictable performance improvements. Investment in service research and development mirrors the same lag and imbalance. Whilst in many developed countries the service sector's contribution to the economy amounts to some two thirds of total GDP and jobs, investment in service related studies represents only one third of total R&D spending (IfM and IBM 2008).

Despite these frustrating barriers, there are also significant drivers for investment in service innovation. Government agencies and NFPs need improved service systems to enable them to respond more effectively to calls for improved quality, productivity and innovation. Recognition is growing that service science has the potential to benefit society by drawing on the integrated talents of a diverse community and enable adaptive innovators to identify the seeds around which innovation can take root and grow.

Table 1. Global Demographics (Tien and Berg 2003: p. 16)

Continents	Percentage of population aged 60 or older		Working age persons per aged 60 or older person	
	2002	2050	2002	2050
Europe	20.0	37.0	3.9	1.8
North America	15.7	27.1	5.0	2.8
Asia	8.6	22.9	11.1	3.9
Latin America	7.9	22.1	11.0	3.8
Africa	5.0	10.0	16.8	8.9

The growth of ageing populations has been flagged by WHO as one of three global challenges likely to overwhelm struggling health systems (The World Health Organisation Report 2008). The issue is particularly urgent in developed countries (see Table 1) and hence provides a strong impetus for service innovation.

The implications of an ageing population bring to the fore questions such as how to optimize service systems to interact and co-create value in this sector. There is little doubt that service innovations will be needed to underpin the substantial reorientation required to deal with the challenging social issues associated with delivery of aged care.

2   Consumer Directed Care

We believe that funding should be more directly linked to people rather than places
(A Healthier Future for all Australians (NHHRC) Interim Report 2008: p. 162)

Consumer directed care (CDC) is a term used to refer to an approach to obtaining care for frail elderly and people with disabilities, under which the person needing care has direct control over the resources provided for their care, and these can be used flexibly to meet their individual needs (Laragy and Naughtin 2009). This can take several forms; it can range from simply providing the person requiring care with a sum of money which they can spend as they wish, to providing them with a budget and some management support, but with few restrictions on how the budget may be spent, or to providing them with a budget which can only be spent on identified services delivered by approved providers. Services and equipment can be purchased from traditional service agencies and funds can be used for options outside the formal service system. Consumer directed care provides greater control and choice to the consumer and reduces reliance on case management services. It is increasingly being used in aged care internationally to promote independence and achieve cost efficiencies.

Since the 1960s, CDC projects in the US and Canada have supported people with disabilities to live in the community (Hutchison et al. 2006). CDC projects expanded into Europe and into aged care during the 1990s (Ungerson and Yeandle 2007). Projects usually commenced with a pilot that was evaluated and later expanded to become a viable service option along with traditional agency-based services (Barnes 2004; Hutchison et al. 2006). Projects often encountered implementation challenges when adapting to the needs of their consumer group as well as to specific national and service system requirements. Change has been incremental and has required policy leadership from government and involvement from service providers and advocacy organizations to be effective.

Clearly there is pressing need for change and additional options in aged care services. Demographic changes in developed societies will increase the number of older citizens needing care in coming decades and consequently increase pressure on providers to make optimum use of available resources. These social shifts and sustainability issues are challenges that require new policy frameworks. Furthermore, there are strong demands from consumers and their advocates to have more choice and control than is currently available. CDC provides an additional option when addressing these issues.

3   Discussion

> The rigidity of how the aged care system operates is very different to our expectations about choice in other aspects of our lives. As the baby boomers age, it is likely that people will expect more choice, not less, in how they are able to receive aged care services when they need them. (A Healthier Future for all Australians (NHHRC) Interim Report 2008: p. 166)

Evaluations of CDC projects consistently report high consumer satisfaction and improved outcomes. Governments internationally are expanding this approach because it has resulted in greater independence and social participation for consumers, and because of its potential to deliver cost efficiencies. When consumers take a greater role in managing their allocated funds there are potential savings because of the reduced use of case management. Furthermore, when consumers have greater bargaining power they can achieve cost efficiencies by meeting their needs in more flexible and creative ways outside of the formal service sector. 'Thinking outside the square' and developing innovative ways to meet needs often lead to improved outcomes for the person concerned, their family and carers, and support workers.

A number of studies have sought to identify features of CDC projects contributing to successful outcomes (see Leadbeater et al. 2008; Individual Budgets Evaluation Network 2008; Mahoney et al. 2007; Office for Disability Issues 2008; Reynolds 2007; Robert Wood Johnson Foundation 2006; Social Care Institute for Excellence 2007; Ungerson and Yeandle 2007). These studies found that successful CDC projects featured professional staff displaying positive attitudes and being well informed; ready access to information and support services for consumers; manageable financial accountability requirements; readily available account-keeping services; protective mechanisms in place for the vulnerable; and appropriate training and working conditions for support workers.

Some of the more commonly raised objections to implementing CDC delivery are:

- The possibility of older people, carers and support workers being at increased risk without ongoing supervision from case managers
- Concerns about less accountability for public funds
- Development of support plans being more difficult and protracted

Laragy and Naughtin (2009) have identified a range of strategies that can be developed to address these concerns including an agreed plan for each consumer that details activities; regular reviews; the availability of support and financial accounting services as well as, where required, a nominated person responsible for a consumer with cognitive impairment.

4   CDC Outcomes

Outcomes resulting from the introduction of CDC in the aged care sector are of considerable interest to government and other agencies charged with a duty of care for this sector of the population. Three positive outcomes frequently associated with CDC implementations in the literature are: improved responsiveness to individual requirements; greater cost efficiencies and increased transparency regarding use of allocated funding for consumers and government alike. The following section of this paper provides an analysis of each of these outcomes followed by a proposal for a policy assessment framework.

4.1   *Improved Responsiveness to Individual Requirements*

A recent meta-analysis of CDC evaluations conducted by the UK's Social Care Institute for Excellence concluded that consumers were generally more satisfied with a CDC approach than with traditional support services because their individual needs and preferences were better met (2007). Control of the allocated funds gave consumers more bargaining power with service providers, case managers and other professionals who become more responsive to their needs (Nicholls 2007).

Consumers reported that professionals 'become more like advisers, counsellors and brokers, guiding people to make better choices for themselves' (Leadbeater et al. 2008: p. 11; Commission for Social Care Inspection, England 2006a). Simple changes such as a support worker being available to assist consumers into bed at a preferred time or to undertake tasks as agreed, greatly enhanced their quality of life (Nicholls 2007; Österle and Hammer 2007). CDC offered new options to people of all ages, including those who were older. The desire to maintain autonomy is articulated by many respondents as indicated by an example quoted in a submission to the Commission for Social Care Inspection (England): 'Age, in itself, is not a disability but it brings disabilities and we have to adjust . . . We still want to be masters of our own destiny.' (2006a: p. 1). The literature offers numerous submissions from respondents referring to the opportunities CDC creates for increased social inclusion and social participation (O'Donovan and Doyle 2006; Poll et al. 2006). CDC is often used to complement other available resources such as payment for transport to take part in activities that would have been inaccessible to consumers otherwise (Commission for Social Care Inspection (England) 2006b: p. 7).

The fact that consumers could select their support workers has been perceived as a major advantage of CDC (Carmichael and Brown 2002; Gauthier 2006). Choice of support staff is strongly preferred to assistance from agency staff on rotating shifts. 'Direct Payments give me control. I now have a say in what I eat and drink, what I do and when I do it. I can choose carers that can help me to live my life. I can have continuity instead of a different carer every day' (Commission for Social Care Inspection (England) 2006b: p. 4).

CDC appears particularly well suited to specific populations as it offers the opportunity for culturally and linguistically diverse populations to organize supports in culturally appropriate ways (Joseph Rowntree Foundation 2008; Nicholls 2007). Reports from Britain and the US indicate that consumer directed care is more responsive to cultural differences than the 'one size fits all' approach offered through many traditional service agencies.

4.2   Greater Cost Efficiencies

The importance of payment mechanisms in exchange for service provision has already been referred to in this chapter. Improved cost efficiencies clearly represent a key variable when providers are determining the optimal organizational or network configuration to select (Lusch et al. 2006). Whilst current academic evidence on efficiencies and costs of CDC is inconclusive, there are indications of government agencies expanding CDC projects due to anticipated cost savings (Leadbeater et al. 2008; Office for Disability Issues 2007; Wisconsin Department of Health and Human Services 2008a). Based on their own analysis of costs and efficiencies, these government agencies have expanded consumer directed care projects in disability services without waiting for independent data analysis.

Significant cost savings have been reported in two recent studies from the US and the UK. Head and Conroy (2005) published results from a US study that randomly allocated service users to either CDC or to a control group receiving services from a traditional agency. Although accurate comparisons were not possible (many people assigned to the agency were left on waiting lists or received few services), after allowing for these differences, savings of 8% were still reported. Savings of 10% were reported in the UK in Control project (Leadbeater et al. 2008). Both studies acknowledged difficulties in validating findings as individual staff allocations could be increased or decreased when people moved to CDC. A meta-analysis of research findings conducted by the English Social Care Institute for Excellence (2007) concluded that current academic evidence on efficiencies and costs of consumer directed care is inconclusive and more work needs to be undertaken.

From a government perspective, CDC may provide a means of supporting increasing numbers of people on lower per capita costs while maintaining quality. In the US, availability of CDC has resulted in consumers being able to live at home longer where they usually chose less formal and less expensive supports to meet their needs.

Programs that reduce or defer the need for institutional care provide huge cost savings to communities. One US government program that invested $1.4 billion annually to support people continuing to live at home, succeeded in leveraging an additional $4 billion from other public, community and private sources for over eight million elderly individuals (Administration on Ageing 2006).

In Australia, older people will double in number as a proportion of the population in the next 40 years (Fig. 1). At present more than half a million older Australians receive Home and Community Care services, predominantly (95%) from private NFP or government providers (Department of Health and Ageing 2008). A large proportion of the funds allocated for support are used by service agencies for case management and administrative overheads (Summers 2007). Case management and administrative overheads appear to be areas for potential savings. For example, the costs of case management can be significantly reduced in situations where consumers or their representatives have the capacity and willingness to use their time to organize services, equipment and other related requirements. Support is growing for a more flexible range of care subsidies that would give older Australians receiving community care packages the option to

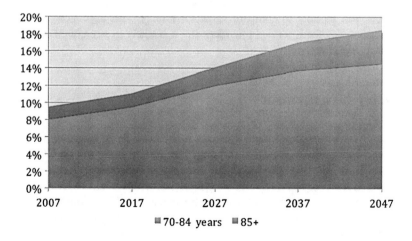

Fig. 1. Population Projections for Australia 2007–2047
(Australian Bureau of Statistics 2008)

determine how the resources allocated for their care and support are used (NHCC 2008: p. 178).

Consumers who self-manage have access to more of their allocated funds, even when they utilize some funds for information, brokerage and accounting services. New services established to offer these services to self-managing consumers in Australia and overseas charge fees of less than 10% of the allocated funds. CDC achieves cost efficiencies through the development of a more informed consumer perspective enabling individuals to seek best value for their available funds in the aged care market place.

From a user perspective, CDC offers access to more funds and greater bargaining power. Consumers can seek opportunities to meet their needs in flexible and creative ways with potential cost savings because they are not restricted to purchasing services from the formal aged care sector. Effective use of consumer purchasing power is an important element of improved financial outcomes from the CDC approach.

4.3   Increased Transparency

An advantage of CDC is that it offers more transparency for consumers and governments regarding the use of allocated funding. Informed consumers are increasingly questioning the use of government funds that are allocated to them through service providers. Some consumers, for example, are questioning why they receive less than half of the value of their total package in the costs of the services provided. Service providers have historically pooled available funds and allocated them across all clients based on the agency's perceptions of need. CDC will require agencies to be directly accountable to consumers for the use of their funds and consumers will be able to compare value for money. This approach will require more transparency from service providers and it is likely to strengthen consumers' purchasing capacities.

5   Policy Measurement

A major issue for government agencies is the capacity to measure policy outcomes and hence access recurrent funding. The current literature on CDC implementation has not yet produced an acceptable analytical framework and evaluation system – one that recognizes people as beings who can learn and adapt over time and offers governance mechanisms that allow IS to respond proactively to strategy changes and predictable technological advances (IfM and IBM 2008: p. 18). Millard's adaptation (2008) of the European Commission (2006) policy impact assessment approach (see Fig. 2) offers a conceptual background and reference system to aid understanding of the holistic context of particular CDC implementations.

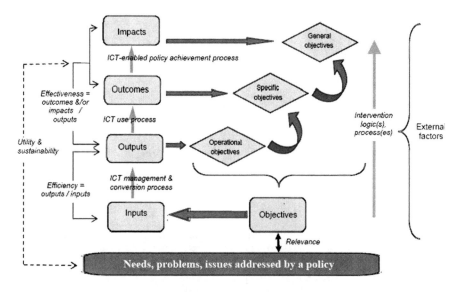

Fig. 2. Generic Policy Impact Analysis and Measurement
Reference System (Millard 2008)

The proposed framework sets out:

- How the objectives of a given policy need to be derived from identified needs or problems and evaluated for relevance
- How the objectives need to be implemented in terms of the inputs needed to produce a set of outputs
- How the efficiency of the policy can be assessed by relating the outputs produced to the inputs employed

The framework also indicates that outputs should themselves lead to outcomes and in turn, to impacts, and these should then be evaluated against the outputs to determine the policy's effectiveness. The whole sequence of inputs to impacts, matched to objectives is linked by one or more processes, which provide the rationale for their specification and inter-relationships. The overall utility and sustainability of the policy's impacts can subsequently be related back to the needs originally identified (Millard 2008).

6   An Overview of CDC Service Provision in Five Countries

Models for CDC service provision have developed differently across different countries. Table 2 sets out aspects of the comparative state of CDC delivery in the United States, England, Sweden, Austria and Australia. Within the US there are

Table 2. CDC in-country provision for aged care

Country	Primary responsibility	Legislation and policy responsibility	Dominant funding source	Public resource allocation	In-country consistency	Dominant service model	CDC trend	Employment flexibility
USA	I	State	Private	Low	Low	Market	Growth in some areas	Variable
England	S	N	Mixed	Med	Med	Mixed	Strong consistent growth	Variable
Sweden	S	N	Public	High	Med	Mixed	Growth in some areas	Flexible
Austria	F	N	Mixed	Low	Low	Mixed	Widely available	Very flexible
Australia	S	N	Mixed	Med	High	Mixed	Interest	Low

N national, *S* society, *F* family, *I* individual

wide variations in funding and service models with most areas permitting employment from family and informal networks.

England provides a public resource allocation that is higher than that of the USA but lower than that of Sweden. Although there are variations in regional implementation, England actively promotes CDC and supports innovative trials nationally. There is a strong move towards different forms of CDC (such as individualized budgets) with some districts allowing and encouraging employment from family and informal networks.

Sweden provides tendered competition in some municipalities with traditional municipal monopolies in 50% of areas. Employment from family and informal networks is permitted.

In Austria, CDC has been widely available for over 15 years and has increased sharply in recent years. Austria introduced major policy reforms in both the aged and disability sectors in 1993 and consumer-directed care became available to everyone needing ongoing support. In 2004, over 300,000 people – around 4% of the population – used CDC. Employment from family and informal networks is encouraged. The Austrian long term care allowance scheme is among the most unregulated in Europe (Österle and Hammer 2007). Consistency of care offerings varies considerably across the nine provinces. Co-payments for services such as home help and nursing have become more widespread since the introduction of a long-term care allowance scheme. Approximately 90% of consumers self-direct their care while living in the community. CDC is available to all adults regardless of their type of incapacity. Recipients of the allowance, 45% of whom are aged over 80 years, are cared for at home with daughters and daughters-in-law as the main caregivers. In Australia, the agency holds funds and employs workers. The for-profit sector is increasing but NFPs are still significant providers. There is some reluctance to allow employment of family members and recruitment of family members has not been actively encouraged. In cases where a consumer holds the funds, there may be a requirement to engage support workers only from approved service providers and not from the open labour market.

In each country, certain critical design considerations have emerged that affect outcomes from the introduction of CDC such as: balancing freedom for the person needing care with protections against the misuse of the funds; and taking into account the administrative responsibilities that CDC can place on the individual self-managing their own care (NHHRC 2008: p. 168).

7 Conclusion and Future Work

Changes in online delivery models have accelerated the shift in people's sense of ownership and methods of acquiring services. Providers need to create new frameworks capable of connecting the various players under a shared umbrella. Innovative service delivery models such as CDC will require closer collaborative relationships between service providers and information technology specialists. IT support can link all stakeholders in a central node capable of coordinating inter-faces, flow of information and expertise and multi-faceted market demands, whilst providing a high degree of self-service and mass customisation. Such an approach would benefit agencies allowing new strategies and consequent alliances to emerge. Policy makers and providers in the NFP sector are well positioned to challenge existing approaches in the aged care sector. As sustainability becomes an increas-ingly urgent global concern, there are opportunities to expand the definition of stakeholder value to include and expand new measures such as CDC. Hence the introduction and/or expansion of CDC represents a significant step in changing the orientation of existing service systems from a provider-centric to a consumer-centric one.

Government agencies can demonstrate the value of service science by creating methods, data sets and tools to inform and challenge current support. Funding to develop relevant measurements and reliable data on knowledge intensive service activities across sectors – including nationally directed data collection about employment opportunities, skills, career paths and IT-enabled activities – is required to underpin leading practice for service innovation. Value creating service innovations such as CDC require systematic support if they are to be utilized effec-tively to develop service innovation roadmaps. Government agencies should encourage public hearings, workshops and briefings with other stakeholders to review such service innovations.

The benefits of 'learn as you go' approaches have been related to positive out-comes for services users of consumer-directed support by studies from Canada, the USA and Australia (Lord and Hutchison 2003). Providers of innovative services will however need to learn from local and overseas experience when considering appropriate mechanisms to protect vulnerable individuals, whether these are clients or support workers. In the case of clients, they will need to maintain a balance between implementing detailed planning and risk management tools to promote choice and independence. Providers will also need to consider how to maximize safeguards and maintain informality and flexibility for support workers without jeopardizing working conditions. Future work must attend to provision of a well-accepted policy framework and more conclusive evidence on efficiencies and costs of CDC delivery.

References

Administration on Ageing (2006). "Choices for Independence: Modernizing the Older Americans Act, Department of Health and Ageing", Washington, DC.

Araujo, L. and Spring, M. (2006) Services products and the institutional structure of production, Industrial Marketing Management, Vol 35, pp 797–805.

Australian Bureau of Statistics (2008) http://www.abs.gov.au/ (retrieved 10th December 2010).

Barnes, C. (Nov 2004). Independent Living, Politics and Implications, Paper presented at the "Conference on Independent Living", Copthorne Tara Hotel, London.

Carmichael, A. and Brown, L. (2002). The Future Challenge for Direct Payments, Disability and Society, Vol 17, No 7, pp 797–808.

Commission for Social Care Inspection. (2006a). "Making Choices: Taking Risks", Commission for Social Care Inspection, Newcastle, England.

Commission for Social Care Inspection. (2006b). "Real Voices, Real Choices: The Qualities People Expect from Care Services", Commission for Social Care Inspection, Newcastle, England.

Department of Foreign Affairs and Trade, Australia (2008). "About Australia service sector world class tertiary industries", http://www.dfat.gov.au/facts/service_sector.pdf, retrieved Nov 7, 2008.

Department of Health and Ageing (2008). Report on the Operation of the Aged Care Act 1997 1 July 2007 to 30 June 2008 Commonwealth of Australia, Canberra.

European Commission Impact Assessment (2006) http://ec.europa.eu/governance/impact/commission_guidelines/commission_guidelines_en.htm (retrieved 10th Dec 2010).

Gauthier, P. (2006). "Employers Review of the CSIL Program", Paraplegic Association, British Columbia, Vancouver, Canada.

Head, M. and Conroy, J. W. (2005). Outcomes of Self-Determination in Michigan, In R. Stancliffe and C. Larkin (Eds.), "Costs and Outcomes of Community Services for People with Intellectual Disabilities", pp. 219–240, Paul H. Brookes Publishing Co, Baltimore.

Hutchison, P., Lord, J., and Salisbury, B. (2006). North American Approaches to Individualised Planning and Direct Funding, In J. Leece and J. Bornat (Eds.), "Developments in Direct Payments", pp. 49–62, The Policy Press, University of Bristol, Bristol.

IfM and IBM. (2008). "Succeeding through Service Innovation: A Service Perspective for Education, Research, Business and Government", University of Cambridge Institute for Manufacturing, ISBN: 978-1-902546-65-0, Cambridge, United Kingdom, http://www.ifm.eng.cam.ac.uk/ssme/.

Individual Budgets Evaluation Network. (2008). "Evaluation of the Individual Budgets Pilot Programme: Final Report, Social Policy Research Unit", University of York, York.

Joseph Rowntree Foundation. (2008). "Person-Centred Support, What Service Users and Practitioners Say", Joseph Rowntree Foundation, York.

Laragy, C., and Naughtin, G. (2009). "Increasing Consumer Choice in the Aged Care Services: A Position Paper/Carmel Laragy and Gerry Naughtin", Social Policy and Ageing Program Research and Policy Centre, Brotherhood of St Laurence, Melbourne.

Leadbeater, C., Bartlett, J., and Gallagher, N. (2008). "Making It Personal", DEMOS, London.

Lord, J. and Hutchison, P. (2003). Individualised Support and Funding: Building Blocks for Capacity Building, Disability and Society, Vol 18, No 1, pp 71–86.

Lusch, R.F., Vargo, S.L, and Malter, A J (2006). Marketing as Service-Exchange: Taking a Leadership Role in Global Marketing Management, Organizational Dynamics, Vol 35, No 3, pp 264–278.

Mahoney, K., Wieler Fishman, N., Doty, P., and Squillace, M. (2007). The Future of Cash and Counseling: The Framers' View. Health Services Research, Vol 42, No 1, pp 550–566.

Millard, J. (2008). eGovernment Measurement for Policy Makers, European Journal of ePractice, http://www.epracticejournal.eul, No 4, August 2008. ISSN: 1988-625X, retrieved Feb 18, 2008.

NHHRC (National Health and Hospitals Reform Commission) (2008). A Healthier Future for All Australians Interim Report, Commonwealth of Australia pub 2009.

Nicholls, A. (2007). "Older peoples' services and individual budgets: good practice: examples and ideas", Commissioned by Judith Whittam, Individual Budget Pilot Advisor, for Care Services Improvement Partnership, http://www.integratedcarenetwork.gov.uk/index.cfm?pid=462&catalogueContentID=1978, Leeds, retrieved Feb 2009.

O'Donovan, M.A., Doyle, A. (2006). "Measuring Activity and Participation of People with Disabilities – an Overview", Health Research Board, MAP Bulletin, November 2006, Dublin, Ireland.

Office for Disability Issues. (2007). "The Costs and Benefits of Independent Living", Office for Disability Issues, England.

Office for Disability Issues. (2008). "Independent Living: A Cross-Government Strategy About Independent Living for Disabled People", Office for Disability Issues, England.

Österle, A. and Hammer, E. (2007). Cash Allowances and the Formalization of Care Arrangements: The Austrian Experience. In C. Ungerson (Ed.), "Cash for Care in Developed Welfare States", pp. 13–31, Palgrave Macmillan, Basingstoke, Hampshire.

Poll, C., Duffy, S., Hatton, C., Sanderson, H., and Routledge, M. (2006). "A Report on in Control's First Phase 2003–2005", In Control Publications, London.

Quinn, J.B. and Paquette, P.C. (1990), "Technology in Services: Creating Organizational Revolutions", Sloan Management Review, Vol 31 No 2, pp 67–78.

Quinn, J. B., Baruch, J. J., and Paquette, P. C., (1987). "Technology in Services", Scientific American, Vol 257, No 6, pp 50–58.

Ramirez, R. (1999) Value Co-Production: Intellectual Origins and Implications for Practice and Research, Strategic Management Journal, Vol 20, pp 49–65.

Reynolds, I. (2007). "Systems of Support and Brokerage: Report on Interim Research Evaluation for West Sussex In Control Brokerage Pilot", Respite independence and supporting employment for carers in West Sussex (RISE), West Sussex.

Robert Wood Johnson Foundation. (2006). "Choosing Independence: An Overview of the Cash and Counseling Model of Self-Directed Personal Assistance Services", Robert Johnson Wood Foundation, Princeton.

Social Care Institute for Excellence. (2007). "Choice, control and individual budgets: emerging themes", London, England. http://www.scie.org.uk/publications/briefings/files/scare20.pdf, retrieved Feb 2009.

Spohrer, J., Maglio, P. P., Bailey, J. and Gruhl, D. (2007). "Steps Toward a Science of Service Systems", IEEE Xplore, retrieved Oct 29, 2008.

Summers, M. (2007). "Great Expectations: A Policy Case Study of Four Case Management Programs in One Organisation", The University of Melbourne, Melbourne, Australia.

The World Health Organisation (2008). "The World Health Report", http://www.who.int/whr/2008/en/index.html, retrieved Feb 17, 2009.

Tien, J. M. and Berg, D. (March 2003) A Case for Service Systems Engineering, Journal of Systems Science and Systems Engineering, Vol 12, No1, pp 13–38.

Ungerson, C. and Yeandle, S. (2007). Conclusion: Dilemmas, Contradictions and Change. In C. Ungerson and S. Yeandle (Eds.), "Cash for Care in Developed Welfare States", pp. 187–207, Palgrave Macmillan, Hampshire, England.

Wisconsin Department of Health and Human Services. (2008a). "Statewide expansion of managed long-term care", Wisconsin, USA, http://dhfs.wisconsin.gov/ManagedLTC/, retrieved April 2008.

Measurement in Service Businesses: Challenges and Future Directions

Rajesh Kumar Tyagi

Department of Logistics and Operations Management, HEC Montreal, Montreal, Canada

Abstract This chapter presents challenges faced by service businesses while implementing a measurement system. A review of existing frameworks is presented and a new framework, the Service Scorecard, is introduced. The Service Scorecard is an adaptation of the Six Sigma Business Scorecard for the service sector. The framework has also been influenced by existing frameworks such as the Malcom Baldrige award criteria, the Balanced Scorecard, the European Quality award and the Service Profit Chain model. The seven elements of the Service Scorecard are Growth, Leadership, Acceleration, Collaboration, Innovation, Execution, and Retention. The examples of measurement systems are presented with concrete real-world case examples. Final thoughts and the challenges faced are also presented.

Keywords Service scorecard, measurement in services, balanced service scorecard, tableau de bord, measurement, service innovation, service chain design, employee engagement, measurement of performance, service productivity

1 Introduction

The importance of measurement models and key performance indicators has been identified as one of the important areas of future research in service science literature (Rust and Miu 2006; Maglio and Spohrer 2008). In the product world, a firm faces variability only in the production process. In service businesses, customers introduce additional variability as customers are often an integral part of the production process. Additionally, service businesses do not have inventory levels, the number of turns, or significant assets, to measure utilization. The most critical elements – employee engagement and customer experience – are difficult to measure. Some service companies attempt to remedy these challenges by measuring productivity in terms of revenue per employee, but doing so can have its drawbacks and considers only part of the measurement issue. Recent publications (Brignall and Ballantine 1996; Heiskala 2005; Klassen et al. 1998; Lees 2004; Marr and Schiuma 2003; Tangen 2003, 2005) have provided new insights in the domain of measurement in service systems. General references such as Spitzer (2007), Wilcox and Bourne (2003) and Bourne (2008) on these topics also provide additional understanding of this topic. In this chapter, a clear distinction is made between service processes, a providers' perspective, a service experience, and an end users' perspective. The service experience incorporates the dynamic actions of the processes, often referred to as provisioning.

Crédit Lyonnais reportedly implemented (Pezet and Sponem 2006) some form of French tableau de bord as far back as in 1890! Recent examples of popular measurement systems are, Balanced Scorecard (Kaplan and Norton 1997) and Performance Prism (Adams and Neely 2000). A few popular auditing frameworks are the Malcom Baldrige Award (Flynn and Saladin 2001; Curkovic et al. 2000; Wilson and Collier 2000), and European Quality Model (Wongrassamee et al. 2003). The most popular model, Kaplan and Norton's Balanced Scorecard, was designed to improve the bottom line performance of companies by focusing on non-financial measures of the vision, strategy, objectives, targets, and actions. Experience shows that most Balanced Scorecard measurements (Kaplan and Norton 1997) follow the 'SMART' (specific, measurable, action, realistic, and target) principle. However, the service business consists of difficult-to-measure, difficult-to-quantify, knowledge-driven, subjective and intangible measurements. The service sector operations are bound to have more subjective performance measurements. Hence, there is a need for a performance measurement system designed specifically for a service-dominant context, and that includes explicit measures to implement the scorecard. The newly developed framework should also incorporate the foundational concepts of service science.

Only a select few models that were designed specifically for the service businesses can be identified: the service profit chain model, a scorecard in financial services provided by Christopher Ryder Jones (2004) and the service model presented by Fitzgerald et al. The service profit chain model is a strategic tool and includes a service profit chain management audit. Heskett et al. (1997) present a service profit chain model, which has been applied in a retail setting (Silvestro and Cross 2000). Fitzgerald et al. (1991) conducted the most comprehensive study in this area. The model proposed by them for service firms included measures related to *results* (financial measures, competitiveness) and measures that related to *cause* (quality, resource utilization, innovation). The concept of causality is included in this model and the business unit is considered as the main unit for performance management.

The aim of this chapter is to discuss challenges in service businesses while implementing a measurement system. This chapter seeks to address the following questions: What are the challenges in the measurement of service systems that are relevant for the service-dominant context? Could a framework that is relevant for the Service Science context be developed? What will this framework look like and how can it be implemented in different contexts? What are the challenges and future directions? The following sections of this chapter describe the measurement of each of the elements of the scorecard, the rationale for each element and present a few case studies.

2 Methodology

This chapter presents a conceptual framework, developed and presented by Tyagi and Gupta (2008). The work presented in this chapter is in continuation of the research presented in Tyagi and Sawhney (2010) and Wayne et al. (2008). The research followed a case research methodology proposed by Dul and Hak (2008). First, a comprehensive literature review was conducted and relevant literature was critically evaluated. Key literature articles were in the areas of performance measurement in service businesses, application of the balanced scorecard in the service sector and application of Six Sigma in the service sector. The literature review led to a tentative framework of the Service Scorecard. To refine and validate the tentative theoretical framework, semi-structured interviews of executives at service firms were conducted. The information is complemented with in-depth case studies. Details of a few case studies are presented in this chapter. Since information on strategy for performance measurement is confidential for an enterprise, the names of some of these enterprises cannot be revealed publicly. The Service Scorecard is an adaptation of the Six Sigma Business Scorecard (Gupta 2007) for the service sector. The framework has also been influenced by existing frameworks such as the Malcom Baldrige award criteria (Wilson and Collier 2000), the Balanced Scorecard (Kaplan and Norton 1997), the European Quality award (Wongrassamee et al. 2003) and the Service profit chain model (Heskett et al. 1997).

3 Architecture of the Service Scorecard

The Service Scorecard framework consists of seven elements (i.e. GLACIER model) that represent certain intangible attributes of a service business. As shown in Fig. 1, the seven elements of the Service Scorecard are Growth, Leadership, Acceleration, Collaboration, Innovation, Execution, and Retention. Each element of the Service Scorecard represents a significant aspect of business and has interdependency with the other elements. The rationale for the measurement of each element will be discussed in the next section.

The Scorecard architecture includes processes and methods at an operational level (execution), strategic decisions at a corporate level (leadership) and at tactical level (engagement and innovation). The architecture of the scorecard incorporates the foundational concepts of service science: the stakeholders in the service chain (customers, employees, community, managers and service chain partners), outcomes (win-win, value co-creation with partners), measures (productivity, innovation, quality, improvement or acceleration), resources (people, organizations, information and technology), interactions and entities (service systems). This specific architecture is the foundation of the scorecard. The following sections of this chapter describe the measurements of each the elements of the scorecard, the rationale for each element and present a few case studies.

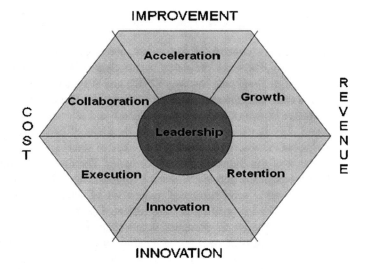

Fig. 1. Service scorecard architecture (Adapted from Tyagi and Gupta 2008)

3.1   Leadership

Leadership is considered to impact corporate performance (Northhouse 1997; Ogbonna and Harris 2000; Phillips and Schmidt 2004) and hence should be the central part of any measurement framework. However, the complexity and lack of understanding of the leadership concepts make it difficult to prove the causal link between leadership and corporate performance using rigorous statistical techniques. Current understanding of leadership states that leaders diagnose and understand the "situation" and take appropriate actions by adopting certain types of measures. The Leadership Scorecard by Jack Phillips and Lynn Schmidt (2004) provides a scorecard methodology for leadership. The following seven types of information could be reported showing the results of effective leadership development: indicators presenting the volume and reach of the program (number and variety of programs, percent of employee participation, hours of training per employee, investment in a leadership program, length of time a leadership position is open), satisfaction with the development program, learning from the program, application of the skills and competencies in real job situations, business impacts of applying newly gained skills and knowledge, return on investment and intangible benefits.

In the Service Scorecard, the leadership element is critical to set the bar, demand performance, and align the organization to achieve business objectives. There can be so many important measures that could be established to measure leadership. However, too many measurements for CEOs could lead to 'runaway' CEOs, because they do have to deal with subtle aspects of the business. In Service

Scorecard, selecting the two or three best measures for the leadership turned out to be about bringing out the best in people. One measure is to inspire employees to do their best for producing outstanding results and that creates significant value for the organization. Employees or teams love to be recognized with the CEO Award for Exceptional Value. A trivial-looking aspect of the CEO Award is its publicity. The second leadership measure represents the CEO's commitment to create value for stakeholders. (This requires CEOs to continually monitor financial performance of the corporation not to satisfy the street what the fundamentals of the business by ensuring return on equity). The third leadership measure denotes corporate social responsibility of the firm. A service firm should identify key investment in the area of corporate social responsibility, provide indices where the firm might be listed, any awards won by the firm and or provide indication of the impact of these efforts. The concept of including social and environmental impact, in addition to financial impact, is called triple bottom line concept.

3.2   Acceleration

Acceleration, defined as rate of improvement, promotes involvement of the customer for ensuring growth and exceptional customer service. Benefits of accelerating improvement are multi-fold. Due to the aggressive improvement goals, teamwork is required. It creates interdependence among departments and sensitizes them of each other's goals. Each department understands that acceleration in improvement is a corporate goal for everyone, so cooperation is critical and benefits are mutual. Initiatives using Six Sigma or Lean are implemented to reduce waste and streamlining service business processes. Most importantly, once committed to accelerate improvement at an aggressive rate, the leadership and managers must both get passionately involved; otherwise failure is eminent. Without the leadership involvement, a corporation cannot accelerate improvement.

Innovation is an outgrowth of acceleration in business performance. Normally, improvement and innovation are considered to contradict each other. Incremental improvement is about consistency, while innovation is about disruption and variation. When the improvement becomes dramatic, it requires innovation, as the new process must become consistent at the different level. Improvement can reduce consistency, while innovation can raise the bar. The typical goal for improvement must exceed the comfort level, forcing the new solution to be significantly different from others.

The typical measure of acceleration is the rate of improvement that is needed for each department. Besides being a new measure, another challenge is that this rate of improvement measure causes discomfort for managers, as it requires them to set an aggressive rate of improvement. Based on the market position, and internal opportunities for improvement, a typical rate for improvement may range from 15% to 30% in service processes. The improvement measures reduction in waste of both time and material. For example, if a service business process is yielding 80%, the rate of improvement goal could be set between 30% and 70% of the 20% waste. Similarly, if a sales process is producing a certain level of sales or margins towards the established profitable targets, the improvement goal could be a 15–30% reduction in slack of the targets. The plan for accelerating improvement must be developed with extensive cross-functional participation.

3.3   Collaboration

In the Service Scorecard, the focus is on the reliability of the partner and the trust between partners. Measures for collaboration will depend upon the long-term goals of the partnership (Segil 2004). If the strategic goal is to reduce cost and improve productivity, the metrics will focus on the process side. If the strategic goal is to improve market position, the measures will focus on the related metrics. Longer-term partnerships will focus on trust development, communication and learning aspects. Common metrics used to measure the partnership in a product-centric environment are cost, speed of delivery and conformance or quality. A broader index called "the Collaboration Index" has been suggested to measure the strength of a partnership (Simatupang and Sridharan 2005). The index consists of three different elements: information sharing and knowledge management, decision-making alignment and incentive alignment. Information sharing represents the degree of collaboration. The extent of collaboration could also include measuring the extent of mutual cooperation, which leads to improved quality and mutual assistance in problem solving, which then leads to improved quality. Ideally, the *overall health, reach,* and *relevance* of the collaboration should be measured.

One obvious measurement of partnership relationship is partner satisfaction. Another measure of the partnership relationship is trust between partners. The trust between partners is an important indicator of the strength of the partnership. Trust affects the performance outcome of a relationship. Performance outcomes could be in the form of time to completion, the financial outcome or satisfaction. However, no common understanding of the way trust should be measured exists.

How (sourcing or service chain) partner selection affects firm performance is an important research topic. A Harvard Business School study by MacBeth and Ferguson (1994) suggested that a key driver to the decline of US manufacturing firms' competitiveness in the global marketplace is underinvestment in intangibles such as supplier/partner relationships. Customers do not see any difference between the partner firm and the firm itself. A strategic partnership and collaboration could lead to faster new services introductions, added flexibility and strengthened financial stability. A service firm will often depend upon its partner to provide a certain level of service quality.

3.4   Service Innovation (Employee Engagement)

At a typical service firm, the cost of human capital is usually more than 50% of revenue, and can be even higher for a professional service firm. The major organizational asset includes employee skill, knowledge and competency. These assets that drive innovation and growth can also move to another firm and are not easy to retain. In spite of the importance of this element, very few firms report measurements of the human asset in corporate financial reports. Some firms report measures such as revenue per employee. However, this measure is a simplistic and lagging measure. Some firms might consider not disclosing publicly these measures in order to have a competitive advantage.

Employees at service firms deal directly with the customers and need to be engaged positively. Customers usually have longer contacts with employees at service firms. Therefore, employee engagement is even more important in the service offerings context, as it influences customer retention and innovation. Employee engagement drives human capital when employees are considered as assets (Davis 1996). Measurement methodologies fall into two broad categories: the Human Economic Value Added (HEVA) approach and the Return on Investment (ROI) approach. Human Economic Value Added, HEVA, is defined as net operating profit after tax minus the cost of capital.

The Return-on-Investment (ROI) methodology forces managers to justify various employee engagement decisions. Organizations using the ROI methodology move from providing human resource programs based on activity to focusing on bottom-line results (Fitz-enz 2000). In a specific situation, it becomes a reasonable task to assign monetary values to these measures. The benefits are then compared to the monetary value of a particular program to develop the ROI. Firms use return on investment methodology to keep track of investments in training, development and other workforce initiatives.

Employee ideas, employee involvement/engagement and *employee satisfaction* are possible measures of the employee innovation/engagement. Employee ideas measure provides leading indication about the pipeline of innovation at a particular service firm. Number of ideas implemented is another measure that could be considered. Employee satisfaction is another leading indicator. Lower satisfaction will likely lead to higher employee turnover.

A study by Mark Huselid (Becker and Huselid 2001), "High Performance Work Practices," shows a relationship between work practices and company performance. Firms utilizing so-called "high performance work practices" tend to have lower employee turnover and higher overall productivity. This study's authors concluded that when a one-third improvement in high performance work practices occurs (over the average firm in a particular sector); the shareholder value of the firm would increase by about 10–15%. A recent article on Human Sigma in the Harvard Business Review (Fleming et al. 2005) claims to measure the effectiveness of the employee-customer encounter. The study occurred at service firms and shows the importance of engaged employees and engaged customers. Service firms with engaged employees and (emotionally) engaged customers tend to be 3.4 times more effective compared with the baseline group.

3.5   Execution

Operational execution enhances process performance in terms of value and responsiveness. Operational excellence also provides a standard methodology and a common corporate wide language. The importance of Execution has been identified by Larry Bossidy and Ram Charan in their book *Execution: The Discipline of Getting Things Done*. The Execution element incorporates two dimensions – executing the operations strategy or what is required, and improving the responsiveness of execution. The use of various operational improvement methodologies is relatively new in the service sector. The reasons for the lack of use of these methodologies could be attributed to the mindset of managers and a mentality that service processes and systems are intangible (thus no standard methodology should be applied). Some service firms have applied execution methodologies and reaped the benefits; some have adopted methodologies such as Six Sigma (Patton 2005), ISO 9000 or the process audit. An international standard such as ISO 9000 emphasizes internal quality and focuses on process management.

Successful service firms have reduced service system complexity by breaking down the experience into discreet steps and by providing the required customer intimacy. For example, Hard Rock Café has very clear metrics from the beginning of the experience of seating at the table to providing dessert and the bill. The key is to understand the customer's needs, provide solutions to the needs, and measure performance by applying process-based thinking.

A service firm should provide *responsiveness*. The degree of responsiveness refers to meeting the customer demands in terms of variety of offerings, on demand availability (24 × 7 availability, online availability), degree of customization, and a prompt service recovery. Consider a service delivery system facing demand-uncertainty from the customer side. An emergency room at a hospital is a prime example of such a system. The emergency room faces an uncertain demand in terms of how many patients will show up, when they will show up and what type of response that might require.

Typical hospital executives want to have high patient satisfaction; shorter patient stays at the facility, higher throughput of patients, and higher revenue/profits. A recent report discusses the installation of self-service do-it kiosks at the Emergency Room at Parkland Memorial Hospital, Dallas, TX. The ER facility, handling about 300 patients a day, has reduced its wait time after installing the system (Stangle 2007). Patients take about 8 min to enter the information. Serious patients still go through the line faster. Once the information is entered, the information pops up at the nurse's touch screen. Patients with chest pains, stroke symptoms or other serious and worrisome complaints get priority. The system is an example of using industrialized customer intimacy. The Emergency Room represents a service system with very high variability. ER providers have to embrace this variability or complexity and try to institute processes that can streamline the healthcare process and still can maintain the responsiveness.

A new methodology, Six Sigma for Services, used Innovation as a step in the DMAIE methodology, replacing "I" for the Improvement step (Goel et al. 2005). The inherent weakness of productivity improvement is balanced by making service innovation part of the methodology.

3.6   Retention

The purpose of customer metrics is to focus on firm profitability and growth. A firm incurs customer-related costs to acquire and retain a particular customer. These costs include acquisition cost, operating cost, and customer retention costs. On the revenue side, a firm gets base revenue, future revenue and some price premium from early adopters. A higher loyalty and retention will lead to reduced acquisition costs and perhaps higher revenue, if a firm is able to cross-sell other offerings to its existing customers. The net effect is higher profit. Retention shows that customers have repurchased from the same firm, but does not give any indication about the true satisfaction of customers. Loyalty could be "bought" by providing some incentives such as coupons, promotions and/or some special deals for existing customers.

Customer satisfaction is the most common measure used at a firm level and at the national level. Frederick Reichheld proposed a metric called the "Net Promoters Index" and suggested that this is the *only* index a firm requires to grow. The hypothesis behind using one number is that "The only path to profitable growth may lie in a company's ability to get loyal customers to become, in effect, its marketing department." The basic idea is that a firm should grow the size of promoters and reduce the size of detractors. A typical net promoter's score is between 10% and 20% for most firms. The index is simple, easy to measure and has gained some traction among practitioners. Firms that have used this index are General Electric, The Wall Street Journal, Intuit and Symantec. Firms have started using the Net Promoters Score as one important score to tie compensation and other rewards throughout the organization. A recent academic study by Keiningham et al. (2007) compared the Net Promoters Index to other benchmarks such as ACSI. The study refutes two assertions, namely that the net promoter's index is superior to other indices, and that ACSI and growth are unrelated.

3.7   Growth

A service firm could grow by acquiring new customers, entering into new markets using existing offerings, creating and delivering new offerings, and selling more offerings to existing customers. However, the most important and sustainable way to grow a service business is by creating and delivering new offerings. The nature of innovation in service businesses is multidisciplinary. Differences between innovations in these two contexts are still debated. Service firms typically do not have a department called Research and Development and seldom apply for a patent for intellectual property. Innovation in the service sector is driven by employee engagement, customer engagement, business practices and human resource management practices of a firm. The intangibility, simultaneous production, and consumption aspects of service offerings create an added challenge in terms of defining the value of innovation and its impact on customer behavior. Since customers experience the offering and do not look at it as a collection of processes, a firm needs to study the experience aspect upfront.

Growth through service innovation could be considered a process. The metrics could be considered at three different levels: input metrics such as number of ideas per employees (discussed in the employee innovation section), employee engagement; process velocity metrics tracking the employee responsiveness to ideas; and output metrics such as revenue/profit growth from new offerings. For example, when an employee has an idea, how long does it take to get heard, and how long does it take to get implemented? A company that is very responsive will likely have more employees that want to participate. By using % revenue from new offerings in combination with other metrics, companies and managers can stay informed about how their employees are doing generating ideas. Typical metrics could include one or the combination of the following: revenue (profit) from existing customers with existing products, revenue (profit) from existing customers with new products, revenue (profit) from new customers with existing products, revenue (profit) from new customers with new products, or number of new customers added.

4 Examples of Measurement Systems

In this section, a few select cases of service firms that have implemented elements of the Service Scorecard. The implementation of measures and measurement systems will vary based on the sub-sector. For example, the healthcare sector has its own additional challenges related to regulations and privacy issues, while professional service firms need to focus much more on human capital and knowledge management issues. The size of the firm also plays a role during the design and implementation stages. A small firm in the early stages will likely use only a few select elements of the Service Scorecard. Table 1 summarizes various measurements representing different elements of the GLACIER architecture. This chapter presents examples of service firms in IT services, elderly care, call center and online marketing services. The large technology service provider measurement system is summarized in Table 2. Some of the measurements represent a good cross-section of the business, including resources, capital, ethics, improvement, rework, collaboration, diversity, revenue, cost, margin, and client. Overall, there are

Table 1. Example of process measurements (Adapted from Tyagi and Gupta 2008)

Element	Process measurements
Growth	Revenue from new customers with (existing) new products
	Revenue from new customers with existing products
	Number of new customers added
Leadership	Percent of employees recognized by CEO
	Profit margin from existing (new) products, Net income or EBITDA
	Corporate social responsibility measures: Investment $, projects
Acceleration	Number of major improvement projects completed
	Reduction in recurring problems or customer complaints
Collaboration	Partnership performance index
	Cost per transaction, system utilization
Innovation	Number of new ideas submitted (implemented) per employee
	Value of new business generated/cost saving by the new ideas
	Employee satisfaction index, Annual employee turnover
Execution	Process sigma level, On-time service delivery
Retention	Growth in business with existing customers
	Number of new customers with referrals from existing customers

Table 2. Measurement system of a large service provider

Framework	Performance measures
Leadership	Contribution to the foundation
	% Improvement margin, revenue
	Accounts receivable
	Return on capital employed
Retention	% Revenue increase from large accounts
	Annual client satisfaction index, client references
	% of revenue from services introduced in last 2 years
Execution	Rework cost as % of total effort
	% Utilization
Employee engagement	% of recruits receiving top grade in tests
	% of annualized attrition

six elements, 32 objectives, and 39 measures. Firms' 5-year CAGR averages about 40% for revenue and profit.

Good Shepherd Services (GSS), based in Seymour, WI, provides faith based care to the elderly. The facility attracts residents from Illinois, Indiana, Michigan and Wisconsin. To implement the values of the organization, the facility had to become a high performer. To sustain the success of GSS in fulfilling its fundamental objectives of care, share, respect, and support, its leadership developed short-term and long-term objectives and corresponding measures without using a predefined scorecard framework. The organization's focus is to improve performance by using best practices, raising funds, and controlling expenses. This case study provided an opportunity to examine and refine the Service Scorecard framework.

The third case is an outsourced call center. An outsourced call center is a typical example of a cost-driven partnership agreement. Performance measures include the revenue/cost/total cost per call, the customer retention rate, and the percent of downtime, the percent of overflow calls, and the accuracy of calls or errors. Total cost per call is usually calculated by taking the total cost for a particular period and dividing by the total number of calls received. A partner can enhance revenue by suggesting add-on services and by understanding customer needs.

Call centers often get calls from customers to cancel or to terminate customer services. Depending upon the skills and competence of the staff, the call center should be able to persuade some of these customers to continue with the service contract. A high quality supplier will not only help enhance the revenue per call but will also help improve the customer retention rate. The accuracy of orders and calls could be measured by callbacks or by measuring the accuracy of the order taken.

Q Interactive, an online marketing service firm employs about 200 employees with revenue of about $150 million and CAGR of 35% in 2007. The Q Interactive firmly believes in its Rewards and Recognition program that serves to highlight the excellence existing in all areas and job functions across the company. The recognition program consists of three awards: On-the-spot recognition, monthly or quarterly recognition and annual corporate recognition. In most of these awards, the CEO is involved in presenting the award in person, or recognizing the individual through a card, or even participating in selecting the award winners. The annual awards may appear to be formal CEO awards, but the other awards also include the CEO's participation.

5 Final Thoughts and Challenges

The Service Scorecard is presented in this chapter and practiced by service firms as indicated in this chapter. The distinguishing feature of the Service Scorecard is the utilization of operational measures to proactively monitor financials, while facilitating growth through employee involvement, innovation and superior leadership. A rigorous validation of the framework of the Service Scorecard is underway. A rigorous statistical analysis of the Service Scorecard will provide higher confidence to the Service Scorecard users and justifies their commitment to its methodology.

There are service businesses that have implemented aspects of the Service Scorecard well and realized the benefits associated. Opportunities for growth and productivity improvement are addressed using Six Sigma and Lean principles, and growth is achieved through service innovation. The service innovation begins with employee engagement and could happen at various levels: process, delivery system or the solution provisioning. Based on the literature review and field experience, specific challenges associated with service firms' performance measurement are:

- *Employee engagement part needs to be prominently included*: Employee engagement drives financial performance and the innovation potential of a service firm. Employee engagement is critical in the service dominant context (Becker and Huselid 2001).
- *Service Innovation dimension needs to be included*: Our understanding of innovation and the innovation process in service sector is derived from a manufacturing setting (Fitzsimmons and Fitzsimmons 2000). Performance measurement system needs to capture the inherent differences (Gallouj and Weinstein 1997; Luteberget 2005).
- *Measurement and measures*: The challenges related to the elements of the Service Scorecard are in the measurement of *customer experience*, *trust* among value chain partners and *leadership*. Measures are being developed to measure the customer experience and to measure an effective leadership. The challenge for the measurement of leadership is that there are can be so many important measures that could be established. Selecting the best measurement for the leadership must define roles clearly for the CEO.
- *Concept of value co-creation*: Service businesses face additional variability due to customer presence in the system. A service firm needs to not only manage the added variability but also needs to manage the value co-creation process. Due to customer involvement in the service provisioning, four types of additional variability are introduced: arrival/request, capability of the customer, effort exerted by the employees and subjective preference of the customer (Frei 2006).

References

Adams, C. and Neely, A. (2000). The performance prism to boost M&A success. *Measuring Business Excellence*, 3, 19–23.

Becker, B. E. and Huselid, M. A. (2001). *The HR scorecard: Linking people, strategy, and performance*. Boston, MA: Harvard Business School Press.

Bourne, M. (2008). Performance measurement: Learning from the past and projecting the future. *Measuring Business Excellence*, 12 (4), 67–72.

Brignall, S. and Ballantine, J. (1996). Performance measurement in service businesses revisited. *International Journal of Service Industry Management*, 1, 6–31.

Curkovic, S., S. Melnyk, R. Calantone, and R. Handfield. (2000).Validating the Malcolm Baldrige National Quality Award Framework through structural equation modeling. *International Journal of Production Research*, 38, 765–791.

Davis, T. R. (1996). Developing an employee balanced scorecard: Linking frontline performance to corporate objectives. *Management Decision*, 4, 14–18.

Dul, J., and Hak, T. (2008). *Case study methodology in business research*. Amsterdam: Elsevier Butterworth-Heinemann.

Fitz-enz, J. (2000). *The ROI of human capital – measuring the economic value of employee performance*. New York: AMACOM – American Management Association.

Fitzgerald, L., Johnston, R., Brignall, S., Silvestro, R. and Vosss, C. (1991). *Performance measurement in service businesses*. London: CIMA.

Fitzsimmons, J. A. and Fitzsimmons, M. J. (Eds.). (2000). *New service development – creating memorable experiences*. Thousand Oaks, CA: Sage.

Fleming, J. H., Coffman, C. and Harter, James K. (2005). Manage your human sigma. *Harvard Business Review -On Point* 7, 107–114.

Flynn, B. B. and Saladin, B. (2001). Further evidence on the validity of the theoretical models underlying the baldrige criteria. *Journal of Operations Management, 6*, 617–652.

Frei, X. (2006). Breaking the trade-off between efficiency and service. *Harvard Business Review*. Nov, 93–101.

Gallouj, F., and Weinstein, O. (1997). Innovation in services. *Research Policy*, 26, 537–556.

Goel, P. S., Gupta, P. Jain, R. and Tyagi, R. K. (2005). *Six sigma for transactions and service*. New York: McGraw-Hill.

Gupta, P. (2007). *Six sigma business scorecard: Creating a comprehensive corporate measurement system*. New York: McGraw-Hill.

Heiskala, M. (2005). *A conceptual model for modeling configurable services from a customer perspective*. Master Thesis, Helsinki University of Technology, Helsinki.

Heskett, J. L., Sasser, E. W. and Schlesinger, L. A. (1997). *The service profit chain – How leading companies link profit & growth to loyalty, satisfaction, & value*. New York: The Free Press.

Jones, C. R. (2004). A 'scorecard' for service excellence. *Measuring Business Excellence*, 8, 45–54.

Kaplan, R. S., and Norton, D. P. (1997). *The balanced scorecard: Translating strategy into action*. Boston, MA: Harvard Business School Press.

Keiningham, T. L., Cooil, B., Andreassen, T. W. and Aksoy, L. (2007). A longitudinal examination of net promoter and firm revenue growth. *Journal of Marketing*, 71 (July), 39–51.

Klassen, K. J., Russell, R. M. and Chrisman, J. J. (1998). Efficiency and productivity measures for high contact services. *The Service Industries Journal*, 18, 1–18.

Lees, G. (2004). Improving strategic oversight: The CIMA strategic scorecard. *Measuring Business Excellence*, 8, 5–12.

Luteberget, A. (2005). Customer involvement in new service development: How does customer involvement enhance new service success? Master Thesis Paper, Agder University College Faculty of Engineering and Science, Norway.

MacBeth, D. K. and Ferguson, N. (1994). *Partnership sourcing: An integrated supply chain management approach*. London, Pitman.

Maglio, P. P. and Spohrer, J. (2008). Fundamentals of service science. *Journal of the Academy of Marketing Science*, 36, 18–20.

Marr, B. and Schiuma, G. (2003). Business performance management – Past, present & future. *Management Decision, 41*, 680–687.

Northhouse, P. G. (1997). Leadership – Theory & practice. Thousand Oaks: Sage.

Ogbonna, E., and Harris, L. C. (2000). Leadership style, organizational culture and performance: Empirical evidence from UK companies. *International Journal of Human Resource Management, 11*, 766–788.

Patton, F. (2005). Does six sigma work in service industries? *Quality Progress*, 38, 55–60.

Pezet, A. and Sponem, S. (2006). *Did the French tableau de bord appear in banks? The case of the Credit Lyonnais 1870-1890*. Working Paper MPPEP project 2006–2009.

Phillips, J. J. and Schmidt, L. (2004). *The leadership scorecard*. Oxford/England: Elsevier Butterworth-Heinemann.

Rust, R. T. and C. Miu. (2006). What academic research tells us about service. *Communications of the ACM*, 49 (7), 49–54.

Segil, L. (2004). *Measuring the value of partnering – How to use metrics to plan, develop, and implement successful alliances.* New York: AMACOM – American Management Association.

Silvestro, R. and Cross, S. (2000). Applying the service profit chain in a retail environment challenging the 'satisfaction mirror'. *International Journal of Service Industry Management*, 11, 244–268.

Simatupang, T. M. and R. Sridharan. (2005). The collaboration index: a measure for supply chain collaboration. *International Journal of Physical Distribution & Logistics Management*, 35(1), 44–62.

Spitzer, D. R. (2007). *Transforming performance measurement – Rethinking the way we measure & drive organizational success.* New York: AMACOM – American Management Association.

Stangle, J. (2007). ER patients check-in at computer kiosks, *USA Today*, Online version, 9/13/2007.

Tangen, S. (2003). An overview of frequently used performance measures. *Work Study*, 52, 347–354.

Tangen, S. (2005). Analyzing the requirements of performance measurement systems. *Measuring business excellence,* 9(4), 46–54.

Tyagi, R. K. and Gupta, P. (2008). *A complete and balanced service scorecard: Creating value through sustained performance improvement.* Prentice Hall, NJ, Financial Times Press.

Tyagi, R. K. and Sawhney, M. (2010). High performance product management: The impact of structure, process, competencies, and role definition. *Journal of Product Innovation Management,* 27, 81–94.

Wayne, J., Tyagi, R.K., Reinhardt, G. Rooney, D., Makoul, G., Chopra, S. and DaRosa, D. (2008). Simple standardized patient hand-off system that increases accuracy and completeness. *Journal of Surgical Education*, 65(1), 476–485.

Wilcox, M. and Bourne, M. (2003). Predicting performance. *Management Decision*, 41, 806–816.

Wilson, D. D., and Collier, D. A. (2000). An empirical investigation of the Malcolm Baldrige National Quality Award Causal Model. Decision Sciences, 31, 361–383.

Wongrassamee, S., Gardiner, P. D. and Simmons, J. E. L. (2003). Performance measurement tools: The balanced scorecard and the EFQM excellence model. *Measuring Business Excellence*, 7, 14–29.

An Integrated View of Service Innovation in Service Networks

Renu Agarwal

University of Technology, Sydney, Australia

Willem Selen

United Arab Emirates University, UAE

Abstract This chapter provides an insight into how service innovation may be enabled in service systems. In particular, we look at the ability of the organizational networks to collaboratively generate the capacity to adapt to changing circumstances rather than as individual firms on their own, using the RARE (*R*esources, *A*ctivities and *R*outines configured and reconfigured through *E*ntrepreneurial actions) strategic framework. This leads into unraveling the complexity of strategic decision making in service networks through co-evolutionary adaptation, or the learning of organizations over time and the resulting virtuous process of experience, learning, and dynamic capabilities enabling them to respond to and launch a variety of competitive actions. Finally, we report on how service networks can address the duality of dynamic control capacity and responsiveness, known as the Paradox of Flexibility, through linking strategic and operational capabilities, as well as customer-supplier duality capabilities, in real time. This in the end results in innovation in services or our notion of "elevated" service offerings.

Keywords Service systems, service network, elevated service offering, dynamic capabilities, service innovation, co-evolutionary adaptation, paradox of flexibility

1 Introduction

"Service systems are all around us. We live in a world where it is a daily experience to interact with various service systems such as banking, communications, transport and health care. This is driven by global sourcing of organizational capabilities. It is also enabled by an increasing use of technologies to ensure the fulfilment of service level agreements between organizations" (University of Cambridge Report

H. Demirkan et al. (eds.), *Service Systems Implementation*, Service Science: Research and Innovations in the Service Economy, DOI 10.1007/978-1-4419-7904-9_16, © Springer Science+Business Media, LLC 2011

2008, p. 6). *Service systems* are dynamic configurations of *people, technologies, organizations* and *shared information* that create and deliver value to customers, providers and other *stakeholders* (University of Cambridge Report 2008, p. 1). Service systems are complex adaptive systems that typically interact with other service systems via value propositions, which may form stable relationships in extended value chains or service networks (University of Cambridge Report 2008, p. 18).

A particular service system, referred to as service value networks or SVN, was recently described as: "*a network of value chains, which vibrates its essence from the combined core competencies of the stakeholders in the chain, mobilizes the creation and reinvention of value of its assets, requires strategic focus and revives roles and responsibilities amongst different stakeholders. Through the use of relationship, technology, knowledge and process realignment and management, a SVN connects to the customer via the channel of choice, heightens the transformation of the nature, content, context and scope of the service offerings, opens up new market opportunities, keeps the social infrastructure intact and secures competitive advantage*"(Agarwal and Selen 2005). Conceptually, a service value network is all about building and fostering dynamic capabilities to yield a service innovation or "elevated service offering", one that can only result because of collaborative efforts of the service network partners, as illustrated in Fig. 1.

As such, a SVN displays both horizontal (across network partners and possible competitors) and vertical (suppliers, producers, and marketing intermediaries) structures. The motivation for networking includes gaining flexibility to cope with the rapidly changing and intensely competitive marketplace; developing skills and leveraging resources needed to identify and move innovations quickly to commercial success, and achieving operating efficiencies essential to offer value to customers, stockholders, and other stakeholders (Cravens et al. 1994). In the context of the larger framework of service systems, we can consider service value networks as *service networks* and will refer to them as such for the remainder of the chapter and for consistency.

This chapter provides an insight into how service innovation may be achieved in service networks. First, we look at the ability of the network to collaboratively generate the capacity to adapt to changing circumstances rather than as individual firms on their own, using the RARE (*R*esources, *A*ctivities and *R*outines configured and reconfigured through *E*ntrepreneurial actions) strategic framework. This leads into unraveling the complexity of strategic decision making in service networks through co-evolutionary adaptation, or the learning of organizations over time

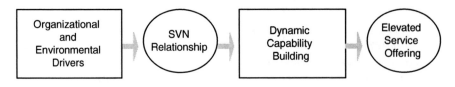

Fig. 1. The conceptual Service Value Networks (SVN)

through exploring and exploitation, and the resulting virtuous process of experience, learning, and building of dynamic capabilities enabling them to respond to and launch a variety of competitive actions. Next, we unravel this co-evolutionary adaptation into five strategic logics and present an integrated framework of service innovation in a service network. We then report on how such networks can address the duality of dynamic control capacity and responsiveness, known as the Paradox of Flexibility, through linking strategic and operational capabilities, as well as customer-supplier duality capabilities, in real time. A health care service network is subsequently presented, in which some of the concepts of the chapter are illustrated, followed by conclusions.

2   The RARE Framework for Strategy Development in Service Networks

Mathews (2006) recently described the salient concept of a "disequilibrium" in strategy development between on the one hand *strategising*, or organizations manoeuvring for position, and ability to differentiate and seek competitive advantage over competitors, and *economising*, defined as a behaviour meeting the optimality and efficiency criteria (all resources being put to their best possible use), on the other. Mathews (2006) put this disequilibrium concept in his RARE framework, which is about "*R*esources, *A*ctivities and *R*outines configured and reconfigured through *E*ntrepreneurial actions". According to Mathews, "*Resources [are] best thought of as the means through which the firm is able to conduct its activities*"; "*Activities may be considered as discrete economic processes; when linked together, they form a value chain*"; and *R*outines are associated "*with the strategic goal of building competencies through learning by doing*". We also notice that value chains nowadays are transformed into value networks: "*value chains are rapidly evolving into value networks, with multiple entry and exit points, creating enormous complexity for all the players involved*" (Li and Whalley 2002), hence the formation of service networks.

For service networks, the economic significance lies in the ability of the network to collaboratively generate the capacity to adapt to changing circumstances rather than as individual firms on their own. As such, strategising in a service network is done collaboratively through the reconfiguration of its activities, its resource base, and the routines that link resources with activities. Accordingly, the concept of disequilibrium is very important, whereby issues such as strategising are required in the formation of networks, and being innovative is required to provide solutions and new service offerings.

Executing the RARE framework at the operational level in a service context, we suggest that during service encounters, customer-facing employees are faced by unpredicted situations and variations in customer demands. These varied customer inputs define a state of disequilibrium during customer engagement, interaction and delivery. Yet, such unpredicted situations and unexpected variations in customer demands can turn into learning opportunities for the customers, for the employees who work for the service provider, and for the service organization itself at both an operational and strategic level. As such, employees within their operational guidelines and boundaries set by the leaders of the service network have to act, engage, and work with the customer in satisfying their needs, optimally and efficiently, resulting in learning across both sides. In an urge to satisfy customers and to provide a memorable experience, employees often have to spontaneously develop new routines, and maintaining this balancing act between adhering to existing, as well as developing new, routines is a challenging task. Activities and routines that are generally planned, and by their nature of being planned, no longer remain in a state of disequilibrium (Mathews 2006).

Service innovation can be related to changes in various dimensions, such as innovation in the service concept, the client interface, the delivery system, and technological options (Cook et al. 1999; Gadrey et al. 1995a; Chase et al. 1998). In this chapter we define service innovation as an "elevated service offering (ESO)", or a service innovation that may display multiple dimensions as described earlier, but that can only eventuate as a result of a collaborative arrangement, one that could not otherwise be delivered on individual organizational merits (Agarwal and Selen 2009). While we realize that a better service offering is possible through improved capacity management, improved customer interaction, improved training, and many more reasons leading to service innovations that can be implemented using an organization's existing resources and capabilities, our perspective in this chapter is particularly on innovation that can be implemented through partnering in service networks – arrangements that may create new competencies, capabilities, and resources that result in ESO. Thus, organizations in an urge to deliver elevated service offerings will require strategic and operational changes such that they can operate seamlessly both inter- and intra- organizationally.

Innovation is critical as an organizational strategy. To ensure continued economic prosperity, and to gain competitive advantage, organizations are more so collaborating with other firms in an urge to innovate. Here, the key focus lies in the strategic formulations and operational implementations of the service network. The ability of senior managers to seize opportunities through the orchestration and integration of both new and existing resources and the ability to simultaneously explore and exploit to overcome the inertia and path dependencies are both central to dynamic capabilities and the firm's ability to adapt over time. This entails co-ordination, integration, alignment, focus, and ability to embrace the strategic capabilities and execute operational tasks. Not only that, dynamic capabilities are seen as an essential ingredient which build on the notion of core competencies culminating into higher-order capabilities made up of routines or processes (Winter 2003; Zott 2003) or routines to learn new routines (Eisenhardt and Martin 2000) that are fundamentally rooted in relationship building, learning, and knowledge management. As such dynamic capabilities are defined as *"the organizational and strategic routines by which firms achieve new resource configurations as markets emerge, collide, split, evolve and die"* (Eisenhardt and Martin 2000). According to Helfat and Peteraf (2003),

"Dynamic capabilities do not directly affect output for the firm in which they reside, but indirectly contribute to the output of the firm through an impact on operational capabilities". In service networks, dynamic capabilities processes develop enhanced strategic and operational capabilities that are unique and inimitable and are a result of new configuration of resources, operational activities and routines resulting from associated interactive processes. Teece et al. (1997) define dynamic capabilities as *"the firm's ability to integrate, build, and reconfigure internal and external competencies to address rapidly changing environments"*. As such these organizational capabilities dynamically evolve and renew over time – and this encapsulates the very notion of co-evolutionary adaptation, or the learning of organizations over time and the resulting virtuous process of experience, learning, and dynamic capabilities enabling them to respond to and launch a variety of competitive actions.

In a service network context, dynamic capability skill-sets provide customer-facing employees with an ability to become innovative, agile, efficient, and effective. Referring back to the RARE strategic framework, in addition, customer learning and agility, developed by the customer as a result of customer engagement, may also play a significant role in achieving a stable and equilibrium state during the service encounter.

Technology is also a prime driver of growth and innovation, and plays a significant role in strategy development through information and communication technology (ICT) competence and ICT deployment. ICT acts as an enabler for the co-ordination, integration and management of organizational processes and activities, enhances relationship ties, provides superior value, increases customer retention, and increases organizational learning (Froehle and Roth 2004, 2007; Harris and Goode 2004; Parasuraman and Grewal 2000; Amit and Zott 2001; Day and Schoemaker 2000; Walters and Lancaster 2000).

Gattorna (2003) has been advocating the importance of strategic alignment within organizations through subcultures and leadership styles. In our context of service networks, it is the co-ordination, integration and alignment amongst internal and external factors, which makes strategic decision making and its execution even more complex, hence making the process difficult to manage and execute effectively and efficiently. Referring to the RARE framework, we will now attempt to unravel this complexity by dissecting the logic of co-evolutionary adaptation into five logical perspectives across achieving effective outcomes (strategizing) and efficiency (economizing), as follows:

- Logic of *Positioning (strategizing)*
- Logic of *Leveraging (strategizing and economizing)*
- Logic of *Opportunity and Innovation (strategizing)*
- Logic of *Experiential Learning*
- Logic of *Customer Engagement (economizing)*

These logical perspectives are elaborated on next, culminating into an overarching nomological framework of the process of service innovation through elevated service offerings in a service network.

3   Co-evolutionary Adaptation in Service Networks

3.1   The Logic of Positioning

According to Porter (1980, 1996, 2001), positioning establishes an organizations unique value of products and services associated with the activities it executes in order to obtain economic rents or profits. Several researchers have emphasized that value is a key element for ensuring company success. Customer value expectations, together with the key success factors of resources, cost structures and technology (Walters and Lancaster 2000), combine to create value propositions, which positions the service network in the market in terms of what they can offer and to whom they market and deliver. These decisions and directions are embedded in the competitive priorities of the alliance. As such, after the definition of competitive priorities, value positioning is key in managing the customer, industry, and the organizational perspectives of a market-driven strategy (Hill 2005), something that requires constant and consistent management attention with ongoing renewals.

3.2   Logic of Leveraging

The service network attempts to consolidate and assimilate any type of collaborative firm resources into a complex set of evolutionary and adaptive resources to gain competitive advantage. According to Barney (1991b) organizational performance is built through the deployment and use of idiosyncratic, valuable and inimitable resources; as well as capabilities that might be heterogeneously distributed across the organization. As such, organizations need to build dynamic and inimitable activity business systems in response to market pressures.

According to Galbreath (2005) resources can be classified as tangible resources (those that include financial assets and physical assets) and intangible resources, identified as strategic assets (what the firm has), which include:

- Intellectual property assets (Hall 1992)
- Organizational assets (Barney 1991a; Fernandez et al. 2000)
- Reputational assets (Roberts and Dowling 2002); or skills (what the firm does), which include capabilities (Hall 1992; Amit and Schoemaker 1993; Day 1994)

According to Makadok (2001), organizations leverage two types of resources: resource-picking and capability-building. Sambamurthy et al. (2003) argue the need for capability-building leverage resources over resource-picking for the sake of supernormal performance. Resource-picking is advantageous in situations when organizations apply superior information or knowledge in procuring resources that are cheaper than their own operations when deployed in conjunction with other resources (Barney 1986). Although it is questioned whether resource-picking is a source of competitive advantage (Sambamurthy et al. 2003) on its own, especially when others also have access to similar market factors, we believe that the challenge of inimitability and uniqueness lies in new resource configurations, methods deployed, and uses extracted (Eisenhardt and Martin 2000). This is accomplished through "capability-building leverage", defined as the firm's ability to integrate, build, and reconfigure internal and external resources in creating higher order capabilities that are embedded in their social, structural, and cultural context (Grant 1995; Teece et al. 1997).

Recent empirical studies on dynamic capabilities confirm that competitive advantage does come from new configurations of resources and operational capabilities and not from dynamic capabilities per se. In fact, knowledge-enabled dynamic capabilities impact and result in new operational capabilities, which are an output of dynamic capabilities, and hence are a source of competitive advantage (Cepeda and Vera 2007; Kale and Singh 2007; Agarwal and Selen 2009). Thus, leveraging processes are fundamental to strategic and economic actions taken by organizations, which include establishment and ongoing maintenance of strategic relationships with partners – suppliers, customers and other stakeholders. This provides the ability to build, change or mobilize resources and assets through the establishment of networks where organizations team in a plug and play mode, on a need-to-need basis and explore and exploit solutions and opportunities collaboratively.

3.3   Logic of Opportunity and Innovation

According to the strategy literature (Eisenhardt and Martin 2000; Helfat 1999; Lavie 2006; Teece et al. 1997), dynamic capabilities explain long term competitive advantage through the ability of a firm to reconfigure assets and existing capabilities, whilst based on organizational design literature (March 1991; Duncan 1976; Tushman and O'Reilly 1997), ambidexterity provides firms an ability to simultaneously explore and exploit, thus allowing firms to adapt over time. O'Reilly and Tushman (2007) suggest ambidexterity acts in itself as a dynamic capability. It is in this context, that service networks need to be capable of not only inventing, but stretching themselves beyond the norm when searching for elevated service offerings. The network's ability to continuously come up with creative ideas, explore and exploit every opportunity, and actually execute them with agility into deliverable outcomes, provides it with an extra compounded capability required for excelling – an inimitable valuable resource, which is its "innovative capability". Based on the logic of opportunity, whereby organizations are on a constant lookout for persistent innovations and creative ideas (D'Aveni 1994; Young et al. 1996), the superior firm is shaped through relentless innovation and competitive actions.

According to Sambamurthy et al. (2003), competitive advantage built through positioning or leverage can be damaged or wiped out completely due to rivalry, new entrants actions and insights about competitors actions, and resource building or leveraging. Cultural, socioeconomic, or technological changes that threaten the environment can further effect competitive advantage, and hence cause obstacles to current developments. In light of these arguments, *"continuous innovations and creativity in products, services, or channels and vigilance to emerging opportunities or countervailing threats are vital for superior performance"* (Sambamurthy et al. 2003). In the service context, non-technological innovations such as marketing, managerial, or organizational business models are also relevant.

Service networks need not only recognize the pursuit of incremental and radical innovations within their service delivery methods and service operations, but in fact should also be on the lookout for add-on services that embellish the service experience for the customer (Johne and Storey 1998; Gadrey et al. 1995b; Oke 2007). In services, service interaction with a customer is an integral part of any business offering, and it is therefore important that every touch point with its customer is exploited and turned into opportunities, making the customers experience attractive and memorable.

Recent work by Oke (2007) has emphasized the need for innovation management practices to carry out an innovation. In this context, the Pentathlon framework (Goffin and Pfeiffer 1999; Oke and Goffin 2001) provides a platform to achieve successful innovation management, comprised of innovation strategy, creativity and ideas management, selection and portfolio management, implementation management, and human resource management. This innovation management framework can assist in encouraging creativity and innovation within organizations (Oke 2007) at both the strategic and operational elements of innovation, and hence also applies to service networks.

3.4   Logic of Experiential Learning

According to D'Aveni (1994), competitive advantage has three dimensions – it is short lived due to the quest for disrupting rival actions, it must be continuously growing, and the greater the number of competitive actions, the greater the opportunity to seize opportunities, and hence achieve competitive advantage. In this context, the logic of opportunity draws attention to co-evolution as a strategic process, which continuously enhances organizational capabilities and skills. Such co-evolution is deemed essential at both the strategic and operational level. In this context knowledge, whether individual, organizational or developed as a result of an integrated value system, is ever increasing, requiring the right environment for it to explore, exploit, flourish and expand. On one hand firms are inert and change occurs through an evolutionary process, as such, knowledge ought to be co-evolutionary in service networks, because individuals and organizations learn over time, and that knowledge is also adaptive, which refers to the virtuous process of feedback and experiential learning. Hence, the logic of experiential learning through competitive actions enhances the dynamic capabilities and provides a mechanism for recursive learning (Sambamurthy et al. 2003). This entails learning-by-doing by inertial organizations as environments shift, especially when functioning under dynamic relationships with partners (ibid).

3.5   Logic of Customer Engagement

Organizations nowadays are customer-centric, and this is even more prominent in service organizations. When customer contact is passive or nonexistent, service processes may be designed with manufacturing-like principles in mind which take advantage of standardisation and automation to enhance the efficiency and effectiveness of operations (Chase 1978). On the other hand, when customer contact is high and active, service processes bring about unavoidable inefficiencies, and human relation skills become a dominant factor in designing the process (Chase 1978). In this regard, processes handling web-site interactions also constitute front-offices (Safizadeh et al. 2003). Therefore, it can be argued that back-office efficiencies lead to cost-based competitive advantages, whilst front-office based efficiencies lead to differentiation advantages. It is assumed in the service network framework that customer contact is ever-present, either on the periphery or as a core aspect of the service offering.

Bitner and Brown (2008) present five ways organizations compete through services, and identify the customer's viewpoint as the most impacting factor. Furthermore, they state that value creation and delivery to the end-customer must be a point of attention throughout the innovation process. Extant literature justifies that organizations who give importance to customer focus in their product development processes are the most successful (Henard and Szymanski 2001; Edwardsson et al. 2006). More importantly, it is the role of the customer as a co-creator, and that too for service innovation of any type, which is crucial for customer engagement (Bitner and Brown 2008; Walters and Rainbird 2006). In services, the success of the service interaction is based on the process-embedded knowledge in systems where the customer is the provider of the input (Roth and Menor 2003).

Customer experiences can be positive or negative, and to a greater or lesser extent memorable (Carbone and Haeckel 1994). However, customers play a greater co-producing role in the delivery of experiences (Grove et al. 2000). Fitzsimmons and Fitzsimmons (2004) suggest that services are *"in the process of witnessing a transformation from the traditional concept of a service transaction to one of an experience"*.

Stuart and Tax (2004) point out that exceptional service firms enhance their customers experience (and hence loyalty) by designing their service system in a way that encourages greater active customer participation, and/or makes the environment more conducive to customer absorption. Recently, an empirical study on experiential services shed light on the customer journey concept wherein the customer has a central role in service innovation and its design; which was not technology driven (Voss and Zomerdijk 2007). In light of the definition by Pullman and Gross (2004) service experience design is defined as *"an approach to create emotional connection with guests or customers through careful planning of tangible and intangible events"*.

Service organizations have started to view the systematic designing and managing of customer experiences as a powerful way of improving service levels and differentiating from competitors (Pine and Gilmore 1998). In light of these developments, today's service organizations are spending more time and effort on this important aspect of service design and service delivery. Through the use of knowledge-based ICT systems or tools, customers participate and provide their inputs through blogs and discussion forums. This customers' knowledge allows for interactive design of services in real-time. Co-opting of customer involvement in the value creation process is thus becoming a necessity (Vargo and Lusch 2004). According to Voss and Zomerdijk (2007), *"providing compelling customer experiences is also seen as an important factor influencing customer loyalty, for customers are more likely to make repeat purchases and give positive word of mouth when they had a good experience."*

As such, participation and engagement of the customer during the customer encounter is a key element of the service network approach to elevated service offering (ESO) delivery. Not only that, it is anticipated that the ESO's will have a measurable impact on performance – financial for profit organizations; improved client/customer satisfaction through new service offerings or new ways of delivery methods; and possibly productivity in terms of reduced service delivery times.

In summary, the role of strategy in shaping superior performance is influenced by five distinct logics of operations which underpin the *logic of service operations outcomes* – the logic of positioning; the logic of leverage, the logic of opportunity and innovation; the logic of experiential learning; and the logic of customer engagement. All these logics form elements of strategizing and relate to strategic effectiveness – i.e. doing the *right things!* On the other hand, the service network execution and implementation is all about efficiency, which is an operational issue – i.e. *doing the right things right* (Porter 1996). It is to be noted that efficiency is not just about cost reductions, but all about doing tasks and activities governed by strategic decisions in an optimal manner.

We now turn to a more detailed discussion of the control capacity of the service network and the service network's controllability or responsiveness, and the inherent paradoxes and alignment issues involved.

4   Control Capacity and Responsiveness in Service Networks

According to Volberda (1996), *"A firm is said to be 'under control' when for each competitive change there is corresponding managerial capability and firm response"*. In the case of service networks, changes can arise from competition, collaboration, or environmental uncertainty; with an additional change in the parameter of services – i.e. multiple variations in customer inputs.

Flexibility can be seen as a managerial task addressing the question *"Can managers respond at the right time in the right way?"*, fundamentally questioning the managerial capability of an organization that endow the firm with flexibility. Flexibility can also be looked at as an organizational design task addressing *"Can the organizations react at the right time in the right way?"* resulting in the creation of a right environment to foster flexibility. This creates a duality of control capacity and controllability, referred to as the Paradox of Flexibility (Volberda's 1996).

Realising the inherent paradoxical nature of organizational flexibility, added with the hyper-competitive turbulent environments, with change being frequent and speedy in the service sector, there are increasing chances for organizations to drift away from their norm.

Referring to the earlier RARE framework, it becomes clear that a service network organizational structure operates under the principles of the Paradox of Flexibility. The *dynamic control capacity of the service network management* and the *controllability or responsiveness of the service network* is seen as the dual of each other, and they need to be aligned across the two tasks. Further, these strategic and operational decisions are centered on the network resources, activities and routines which, when activated through entrepreneurial action, underpin the RARE framework. In here, *strategizing* enables the discovery of strategic options through entrepreneurial actions which is possible through the notion of *"extraordinary discovery"* (Yu 2001), which refers to radical implications and events, and re-interpreting those incoming events into new ideas (Klein 1999). We postulate that the service network resumes its "under control" state when the managerial capability of the service network provides a corresponding organizational response, presumably for each competitive or customer preference change as shown in Fig. 2.

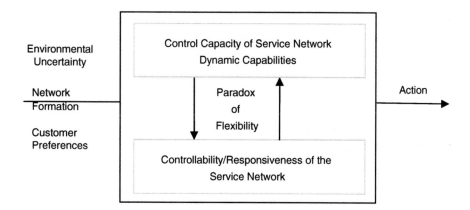

Fig. 2. Paradox of flexibility – control capacity and controllability/responsiveness in service networks (Adapted from Volberda 1996)

For the service network to be able to sense and respond to business opportunities, and remain innovative and competitive, the higher order activities and routines for decision making, both intra- and inter-organizational, are paramount. These newly developed skills and capabilities are critical for enabling change in strategies, setting competitive priorities, and selecting new collaborative partners. Accordingly, we also believe that agility requires high responsiveness in terms of being able to handle changes with speed, manage variety and variations as differentiated in the context of services by Schmenner (2004)); whilst innovative capacity requires creativity in ideas and solutions; and entrepreneurial alertness requires the ability to foresee, visualise and exploit options (Joiner and Josephs 2006). Added to these is the partnership with customers which is pivotal to the value creation of the service network, and is central to the customer engagement capability and other capability building competencies and skill-sets. As such, each of these new dynamic capabilities will enhance the decision making process – i.e. the ability to take the right decisions at the right time will become the service network's control capacity. It is believed that the ability to initiate the suite of managerial capabilities will depend on the design adequacy of organizational conditions, such as the technology and the connectivity across the service network(s), its structure, and culture (Zelenovic 1982). These determine the service network's organizational controllability or responsiveness. Combining the managerial and organizational design tasks often requires a process of alignment – an ability to develop dynamic capabilities that enhances flexibility and an adequate organizational design to utilize those capabilities. If no balance exists, this would result in failure. Assuming that the service network has an adequate organizational design, its controllability of the network in terms of coherent responsiveness and effectiveness in regard to each competitive or customer preference change, will be affected.

The same theoretical explanation as applied for *strategising* can now be applied to the concept of *economising*. In order to manage the service network managerial and design tasks in real-time in an agile manner, and to provide innovative/ customized service offerings and service delivery solutions in the most effective and efficient manner, a set of higher-order specific skill-sets is essential for both the operational framework and the operational work-force.

Next, we discuss organizational alignment through linking strategic and operational capabilities.

5   Organizational Alignment: Linking Strategic and Operational Capabilities

Establishing a service network requires three key elements – namely resources, activities, and routines; whereby routines are built by management which connect the organizational resources with their current activities through entrepreneurial endeavours (Mathews 2006). The co-ordination of these three important elements spans across inter- and intra-organizations resources and capabilities; activities and decision making; and finally routines, processes and interfaces.

In the context of service networks, factors that are central to providing an enduring source of competitive advantage include the relationships between strategy formulation (decisions that are related to service design choices, target markets, selection of partners), strategy execution and the operational framework (related to delivery practices, operational processes spanning across partner organizations), and competitive capabilities required to manage the customer encounter interface. Service networks are very much dependent upon the role of management in building, leveraging and adapting higher-order competencies in order to address the needs of rapidly changing environments at both the strategic and operational level. As is well-known, core competencies are embedded in organizational processes or routines around co-ordination, integration, learning and transformation functions, and are an outcome of operational realisation of strategic decisions. Yet, by padding capabilities with other abilities centred on the needs of the customer may arm organizations with inimitable capabilities at an operational level, bounded within a service network.

Flexibility in responsiveness involves the management and development of new capabilities for unwarranted situations, enabled through variety and agility. Variety can be connoted in terms of quantity (the number) of capabilities or the quality of capabilities (e.g. entrepreneurial endeavour, ability to innovate ideas). Agility relates to the ability to combine and recombine resources and processes in different ways with speed, often resulting in the creation of new routines. On the other hand, the ability to initiate the repertoire of dynamic capabilities depends on several factors – organizational (e.g. competitive priorities, structure and culture of the service network) and environmental factors (e.g. environmental uncertainty).

Summing up, these conditions dictate the service network's controllability of responsiveness, and its alignment to strategic activities. Next we discuss the linking of customer-supplier duality capabilities in real-time.

6   Linking Customer-Supplier Duality Capabilities

In the context of services, the stochastic nature of customer-supplied inputs (Sampson 2001) with random arrivals, inconsistent specification, and varying input quality, not only adds to the vulnerability of the dimension of uncertainty (Sampson and Froehle 2006), but it subjects the operations management with challenges that are never ending. In order to deal with this on a day-to-day basis, the operations management and customer-facing employees require additional and different skills and capabilities to deal with such situations. According to Yu (2001), an opportunity exists only if it is perceived and will not be discovered if the alertness system is switched off. Yu (2001) defines "*ordinary discovery*" (Yu 2001) events, one which depict a '*backward*' interpretation for individuals who are entrepreneurs who endeavour to exploit opportunities by doing some things better, and exploiting things that were so far unnoticed. This indeed concurs with deBano's backward interpretation that *"something that is there and working it over"* (de Bano 1977) largely promotes *"change within an existing situation"* (Cheah 1992). As such, pre-defined boundaries under which the front-of-house staff can operate will only equips employees with an ability to handle situations that are either existing, or predictable, or both. The ability to operationally sense and foresee variations in customer needs and the possibility to fulfil customer needs are restricted by the agility to act based on the knowledge of the service network boundaries, and progressive development of dynamic capabilities. This is because they occur as customer-encounter interactions happen, and are skills that are likely to assist employees when dealing and interacting with customer needs in real-time – thus together constituting the responsiveness of the service network through its front-of-house employees. As such, it is important that the front-of-house employees are entrepreneurial, agile and innovative, whilst being empowered and equipped with processes that will allow them to take decisions with speed and novelty, and arm them with the ability to keep control of the situation – the control capacity of the service network.

The control capacity and controllability or responsiveness issues of a service network are summarized in Fig. 3 below.

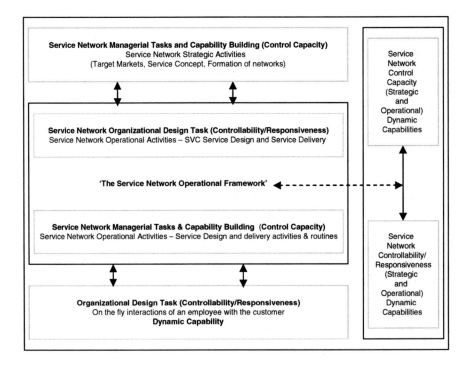

Fig. 3. The control capacity and controllability/responsiveness
of a service network

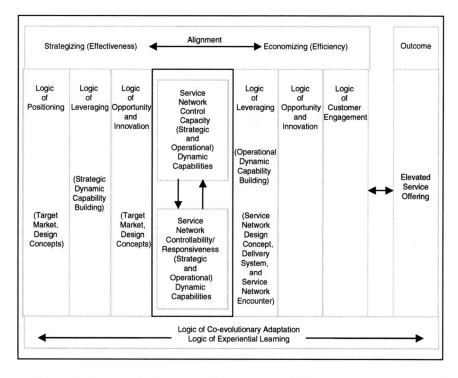

Fig. 4. An integrated view of service innovation (ESO) in service networks

Overall, we summarize the relationships between the different logics, the control capacity of the Service Network, and its controllability/responsiveness to respond to change and uncertainties, in Fig. 4. In accordance with the logic of co-evolutionary adaptation, organizations learn over time; and through a virtuous process of experience, learning, and dynamic capabilities, are able to respond to and launch a variety of competitive actions.

In the next section, we illustrate a service network in health care with the concepts and frameworks we have introduced.

7   An Industry Example of a Service Network: Virtual Critical Care Unit

The Sydney West Area Health Services, CSIRO and CenTIE in Australia, collaboratively developed an advanced Virtual Critical Care Unit (ViCCU). ViCCU is a tele-health system that supports critical care services between a referral/tertiary hospital and a rural hospital by transmitting very high quality, real-time multimedia information, including images, audio and real-time video, over an IP based network

(Li et al. 2006). This is a classic example of a true collaborative outcome resulting from the reconfiguration and mobilization of resources, tasks and activities who strategically decided to partner in coming up with an elevated service offering (*Logic of Positioning, Logic of Leverage, and Logic of Opportunity and Innovation; Strategizing*). This innovation in health services not only uses technology as a prime enabler, but also involves the co-operation of customers – human beings e.g. doctors, nurses and patients, using the technology in complex emergency clinical environments. Time-criticality in an emergency situation often deters people from trialing new ways of clinical practice with no room for human error. Under this situation, the patient is deterred the most, however the customers understanding of the emergency support system and the value-added service he is getting from the new medical system, adds to the customers experience; only possible due to customer engagement and participation resulting from collaboration (*Logic of Customer Engagement – Economizing*). From the medical teams perspective as well, their communication and interaction with the customer, their participation and engagement, and the patient's endurance and understanding, helps them give the patient the best possible treatment.

The radical approach of treating emergency patients located remotely; especially in areas where the reach of appropriate emergency services was difficult to deliver in time, was a far-reaching discovery. Through the use of relationship management (patient, nurses, doctors, telecommunications company, CSIRO), knowledge management (the use of tacit and explicit knowledge of partners in coming up with the practical solution of this need), technology management (appropriate use of technology – IP based network with excellent video quality), and process management (design of new routines and tasks, and the integration with old practices, through ICT systems and processes integration), individual patient needs in delivering hospital care, synonymous to the notion of "*extraordinary discover*" (Yu 2001), was implemented. On the other hand, once the organizational framework for this radical discovery was in operation, the notion of "*ordinary discovery*" events came into play. The real-time input from all stakeholders, in particular the patient's engagement and input was found to be different in each event providing different inputs – the patient's body, his condition and his symptoms (*Logic of Customer Engagement – Economizing*). Not only that, employees being entrepreneurial in their tasks could explore opportunities by doing some tasks and activities better, and exploiting things that were so far unnoticed (*Logic of Opportunity and Innovation – Economizing*). The co-operation of the patient in these critical stages even became very important in providing the best care and customized medical solution at speed, by the doctors and nurses on duty (*Logic of Customer Engagement – Economizing*). Through this ongoing iterative process of continuous engagement and learning, each time the service delivered was different, unique and satisfying for the patient, especially when the patients' life was ultimately saved (*Logic of Experiential Learning*).

The role of the cultural values of the remote and local hospitals (collaboration, freedom of speech, and being entrepreneurial), the collaborative governance and management of the team spanning across local and remote hospitals, their synchronized co-ordination and integration abilities with aligned goals and objectives, significantly influence each stakeholder's role-play during the delivery of the elevated service offering (during both the stages i.e. the strategic execution of the radical tele-health infrastructure project and its day-to-day operations). This tele-health elevated service offering may produce or exhibit a new customer encounter interface, new delivery method, new service offering, increase in on-time delivery, a reduction in customer waiting time, increased customization, retention, satisfaction and, above all, a memorable experience for the customer. It is a real-time collaborative effort that demonstrates the dynamic capability building processes in an adaptive manner at both strategic and operational levels (embedded under the phenomena and concepts of *Control Capacity and Controllability/ Responsiveness in Service Networks, Organizational Alignment – Linking of Strategic and Operational Capabilities, and linking of Customer-Supplier Duality Capabilities*). The collaborative, innovative, agile and entrepreneurial action processes in real-time from all stakeholders perspectives (Li et al. 2006) was indeed paramount in coming up with this new service offering.

Thus, fostering dynamic capabilities is paramount in contemporary service organizations as it is an approach to building higher-order competencies and skills to address rapidly changing environments. This is consistent with the recent views regarding the notion of higher-order dynamic capabilities through learning and alliance formation (Zollow and Winter 2002; Cepeda and Vera 2007; Harreld et al. 2007; Agarwal and Selen 2009), wherein dynamic capabilities enable an organization to modify, extend and improve its strategic and operational capabilities to manage any given task (Kale and Singh 2007). Consequently, innovations are increasingly brought to the market by networks of firms, selected for their unique capabilities, and operated in a coordinated manner through concerted efforts. Not only that, these dynamic capabilities can be fostered and inculcated within service networks resulting in elevated service offerings (Agarwal and Selen 2009).

8   Conclusions

We have provided an integrated view of managing innovation in service networks, built on the Paradox of Flexibility concepts, the RARE framework, and various strategic organizational logics. Our conceptual chapter provides a deeper integrated understanding of the phenomena related to interacting service systems, a better understanding of the interplay of people, organizational practices, and business models in collaborating service organizations in an urge to deliver elevated service offerings. We also provided further insight into the different dynamic capabilities at play within a service network, and their ongoing and adaptive evolutionary process. In today's service and knowledge-based economy, managers of service organizations need to understand the dynamics of capability building and their importance in fostering new capabilities and its impact on service innovation.

References

Agarwal, R. and Selen, W. (2009) Dynamic capability building in service value networks for achieving service innovation. *Decision Sciences*, August 2009, 40, 3, 431–475.

Agarwal, R. and Selen, W. (2005) Services Value Network Consortia: recent literature and operational definition. *ANZAM Symposium* (Australia and New-Zealand Academy of Operations Management), June 13–14, 2005, Capricorn Coast, Queensland, Australia.

Amit, R. and Schoemaker, P. J. (1993) Strategic assets and organizational rent. *Strategic Management Journal*, 14, 33–46.

Amit, R. and Zott, C. (2001) Value Creation in e-businesses. *Strategic Management Journal*, 22, 493–521.

Barney, J. (1991a) The resource-based model of the firm: origins, implications and prospect. *Journal of Management*, 17.

Barney, J. B. (1986) Strategic factor markets, expectations, luck and business strategy. *Management Science*, 32, 1231–1241.

Barney, J. B. (1991b) Firms resources and sustained competitive advantage. *Journal of Management*, 17, 99–120.

Bitner, M. J. and Brown, S. W. (2008) The service imperative. *Business Horizons*, 50th Anniversary Issue.

Carbone, L. P. and Haeckel, S. H. (1994) Engineering customer experiences. *Marketing Management*, 3, 8–19.

Cepeda, G. and Vera, D. (2007) Dynamic capabilities and operational capabilities: a knowledge management perspective. *Journal of Business Research*, 60, 426–437.

Chase, R. B. (1978) Where does the customer fit in a service operation. *Harvard Business Review*, 56, 137–142.

Chase, R. B., Aquilano, N. J., and Jacobs, F. (1998) Service innovation in Hong Kong: attitudes and practice. *Operations Management for Competitive Advantage*. McGraw-Hill, Boston, MA.

Cheah, H. B. (1992) Revolution and evolution in the entrepreneurial process. *World Conference on Entrepreneurship*. Singapore.

Cook, D. P., Goh, C. H., and Chung, C. H. (1999) Service typologies: a state-of-the-art survey. *Production and Operations Management*, 3(1), 35–44.

Cravens, D. W., Piercy, N. F., and Shipp, S. H. (1994) New organization forms for competing in highly dynamic environments: the network paradigm. *Proceedings of the Second Research Conference on Relationship Marketing*, Atlanta, GA.

D'aveni, R. A. (1994) *Hypercompetition: Managing the dynamics of strategic maneuvering*. The Free Press, New York.

Day, G. S. (1994) The capabilities of market-driven organisations. *Journal of Marketing*, 58, 37–52.

Day, G. S. and Schoemaker, P. J. H. (2000) *Managing emerging technologies*. Wiley, New York.

De Bano, E. (1977) *Lateral Thinking*. Middlesex, Penguin.

Duncan, R. B. (1976) The ambidextrous organization: Designing dual structures for innovation. In R. H. Kilmann, L. R. Pondy and D. Slevin (eds.). *The management of organization design: Strategies and implementation*. North Holland, New York: 167–188.

Edwardsson, B., Gustafsson, A., Kristensson, P., Magnusson, P. and Matthing, J. (2006) *Involving customers in new service development*. Imperial College Press, London, UK.

Eisenhardt, K. and Martin, J. (2000) Dynamic capabilities – What are they? *Strategic Management Journal*, 21, 1105–1121.

Froehle, C. M. and Roth, A. V. (2004) New measurement scales for evaluating perceptions of the technology-mediated customer service experience. *Journal of Operations Management*, 22, 1–21.

Froehle, C. M. and Roth, A. V. (2007) A resource-process framework of new service development. *Production and Operations Management Society,* 16, 169–188.

Fernandez, E., Montes, J. M. and Vazquez, C. J. (2000) Typology and strategic analysis of intangible resources: a resource-based approach. *Technovation,* 20, 81–92.

Fitzsimmons, J. and Fitzsimmons, M. (2004) *Service Management: Operations, Strategy and Information technology,* 4th ed. McGraw-Hill, London.

Gadrey, J., Gallouj, F. and Weinstein, O. (1995a) Innovation in services. *Research Policy,* 26, 537–556.

Gadrey, J., Gallouj, F. and Weinstein, O. (1995b) New modes of innovation: How services benefit industry. *International Journal of Service Industry Management,* 6(3), 4–16.

Galbreath, J. (2005) Which resources matter the most to firm success? An exploratory study of resource-based theory. *Technovation,* 25, 979–987.

Gattorna, J. (Ed.) (2003) *Introduction and frameworks.* Gower Publishing Company, Hants, England.

Goffin, K. and Pfeiffer, R. (1999) *Innovation Management in UK and German Manufacturing Companies.* Anglo-German Foundation, London.

Grant, R. M. (1995) *Contemporary Strategy Analysis.* Blackwell,Oxford.

Grove, S. J., Fisk, R. P. and John, J. (2000) Services as theatre. In Iacobucci, D., Swartz, T.A. (Ed.) *Handbook of Services Marketing and Management.* Thousand Oaks, CA, Sage Publications.

Hall, R. (1992) The strategic analysis of intangible resources. *Strategic Management Journal,* 13, 135–144.

Harreld, J. B., O'Reilly, C. A. I. and Tushman, M. L. (2007) Dynamic capabilities at IBM: Driving strategy into action. *California Management Review,* 49, 1–23.

Harris, L. C. and Goode, M. M. H. (2004) The four levels of loyalty and the pivotal role of trust: A study of online dynamics. *Journal of Retailing,* 80, 139–158.

Helfat, C.E. (1999) Know-how and asset complemantarity and dynamic capability accumulation: The case of RandD. *Strategic Management Journal,* 18, 339–360.

Helfat, C. E. and Peteraf, M. A. (2003) The dynamic resource-based view: Capability lifecycles. *Strategic Management Journal,* 24, 997–1010.

Henard, D. H. and Szymanski, D. M. (2001) Why some products are more successful than others. *Journal of Marketing Research,* 38, 362–275.

Hill, T. (2005) *Operations Management.* Palgrave Macmillan, Hampshire, New York.

Johne, A. and Storey, C. (1998) New service development: A review of the literature and Annotated Bibliography. *European Journal of Marketing,* 32, 184–252.

Joiner, B. and Josephs, S. (2006) *Leadership agility.* Jossey-Bass, San Francisco, CA.

Kale, P. and Singh, H. (2007) Building firm capabilities through learning: the role of the alliance learning process in alliance capability and firm-level alliance success. *Strategic Management Journal,* 28, 981–1000.

Klein, D. B. (1999) Discovery and the deepself. *The Review of Austrian Economics,* 11, 47–76.

Lavie, D. (2006) Capability reconfiguration: An analysis of incumbent responses to technological change. *Academy of Management Review,* 49, 553-570.

Li, F. and Whalley, J. (2002) Deconstruction of the telecommunications industry: from value chains to value networks. *Telecommunications Policy,* 26, 451–472.

Li, J., Wilson, L. S., Qiao, R.-Y., Percival, T., Krumm-Heller, A., Stapleton, S. and Cregan, P. (2006) Development of Broadband Telehealth System for critical care – process and lessons learnt. *Journal of Telemedicine and e-Health Oct 2006,* 12(5), 552–560.

Makadok, R. (2001) Toward a synthesis of the resource-based and dynamic-capability views of rent creation. *Strategic Management Journal,* 22, 387–402.

March, J. G. (1991) Exploration and exploitation in organizational learning. *Organization Science,* 2, 71–87.

Mathews, J. A. (2006) *Strategizing, disequilibrium and profit.* Stanford University Press, Stanford, CA.

Oke, A. (2007) Innovation types and innovation management practices in service companies. *International Journal of Production and Operations Management*, 27, 564–587.

Oke, A. and Goffin, K. (2001) Innovation management in the service sector. *Management Focus*, 16, 8–10.

O'Reilly, C. A. and Tushman, M. L. (2008) Ambidextrity as a dynamic capability: Resolving the innovator's dilemma. *Research in Organizational Behaviour*, 28, 185–206.

Parasuraman, A. and Grewal, D. (2000) The impact of technology on the quality-value-loyalty chain: A research agenda. *Journal of the Academy of Marketing Science*, 28, 167–174.

Pine, J. B. and Gilmore, J. H. (1998) Welcome to the experience economy. *Harvard Business Review*, 76, 97–105.

Porter, M. E. (1980) Competitive strategy: techniques for analysing industries and competitors. The Free Press, New York.

Porter, M. E. (1996) What is strategy. *Harvard Business Review*, 74, 61–78.

Porter, M. E. (2001) Strategy and the Internet. *Harvard Business Review*, March 2001, 62–78.

Pullman, M. E. and Gross, M. A. (2004) Ability of experience design elements to elicit emotions and loyalty behaviors. *Decision Sciences*, 35, 551–578.

Roberts, P. W. and Dowling, G. R. (2002) Corporate reputation and sustained superior financial performance. *Strategic Management Journal*, 23, 1077–1093.

Roth, A. V. and Menor, L. J. (2003) Insights into service operations management: A research agenda. *Production and Operations Management*, 12, 145–164.

Safizadeh, M. H., Field, J. M. and Ritzman, L. P. (2003) An empirical analysis of financial services processes with a front-office or back-office orientation. *Journal of Operations Management*, 21, 557–576.

Sambamurthy, V., Bharadwaj, A. and Grover, V. (2003) Shaping agility through digital options: Reconceptualizing the role of information technology in contemporary firms. *MIS Quarterly*, 27, 237–263.

Sampson, S. E. (2001) *Understanding business services*. Wiley, New York.

Sampson, S. E. and Froehle, C. M. (2006) Foundations and Implications of a Proposed Unified Services Theory. *Production Operations Management Journal*, 15.

Schmenner, R. W. (2004) Service businesses and productivity. *Decision Sciences*, 35, 333–347.

Stuart, I. F. and Tax, S. (2004) Toward an integrative approach to designing service experiences lessons learned from the theatre. *Journal of Operations Management*, 22, 609-627.

Teece, D. J., Pisano, G. and Shuen, A. (1997) Dynamic capabilities and strategic management. *Strategic Management Journal*, 18, 509–533.

Tushman, M. L. and O'Reilly, C. A. (1997) *Winning through innovation: A practical guide to leading organizational change and renewal*. Harvard University Press, Boston, MA.

University of Cambridge, and IBM. (2008) Succeeding through service innovation (a service perspective for education, research, business and government), *University of Cambridge Institute for Manufacturing (IfM) and IBM*.

Vargo, S. L. and Lusch, R. F. (2004) Evolving to a new dominant logic for marketing. *Journal of Marketing*, 68, 1–17.

Volberda, H. W. (1996) Toward the flexible form: How to remain vital in hypercompetitive environments. *Organization Science*, 7, 359–374.

Voss, C. and Zomerdijk, L. (2007) Innovation in Experential Services: An Empirical View. In UK Department of Trade and Industry (DTI) Economic Papers (Ed.) *Innovation in services*. London, UK: DTI, 97–134.

Walters, D. and Lancaster, G. (2000) Implementing value strategy through the value chain. *Management Decision*, 38, 160–178.

Walters, D. and Rainbird, M. (2006) *Strategic operations management – A value chain approach*. Palgrave Macmillan, London.

Winter, S. G. (2003) Understanding dynamic capabilities. *Strategic Management Journal* 24, 991–995.

Young, G., Smith, K. G. and Grimm, C. M. (1996) Austrian and industrial organization perspectives on firm-level competitive activity and performance. *Organization Science,* 7, 243–254.

Yu, T. F.-L. (2001) Entrepreneurial alertness and discovery. *The Review of Austrian Economics,* 14, 47–63.

Zelenovic, D. M. (1982) Flexibility – A condition for effective production systems. *International Journal of Production Research,* 20(3), 319–337.

Zollow, M. and Winter, S. G. (2002) Deliberate learning and the evolution of dynamic capabilities. *Organization Science,* 13, 339–351.

Zott, C. (2003) Dynamic capabilities and the emergence of intra-industry differential firm performance: Insights from a simulation study. *Strategic Management Journal,* 24, 97–125.

A Service Systems Perspective of E-Government Development

Chee Wei Phang

Department of Information Management and Information Systems, School of Management, Fudan University, 670 Guoshun Road, #707, Shanghai 200120, China

Atreyi Kankanhalli

Department of Information Systems, School of Computing, National University of Singapore, Computing 1, 13 Computing Drive, Singapore 117417, Singapore

Abstract There have been increasing efforts by governments worldwide to innovate public service delivery, one of the means being through e-government. However, the mixed success of e-government initiatives highlights the need to better understand citizens' requirements and engage them in the development of e-government service offerings. In response to this need, we propose a service systems perspective to analyze a participatory e-government service system based on the key resources of people, organizations, shared information, and technologies. By doing so, this study bridges the gap in existing research that has separately examined the different resources without considering their inter-relationships in a systematic manner. For practitioners, the resulting framework provides a tool to understand how the key resources as well as stakeholders of the e-government service system inter-relate, which allows more comprehensive strategies to be formulated for improving e-government service offerings.

Keywords Service science, service systems, e-government development, e-participation

1 Introduction

Governments around the world are seeking to innovate their service provisioning via electronic means as part of an overall movement towards e-government. E-government refers to the use of information and communication technologies (ICT) to transform how the public sector performs its roles in serving its constituents

H. Demirkan et al. (eds.), *Service Systems Implementation*, Service Science:
Research and Innovations in the Service Economy, DOI 10.1007/978-1-4419-7904-9_17,
© Springer Science+Business Media, LLC 2011

(Heeks 1999; Phang et al. 2008). It is expected that e-government will bring about improved communication with constituents, enhance democratic processes and reduce social exclusion, which can result in higher public satisfaction (Olphert and Damodaran 2007). As a result, there has been a steady growth of investment in e-government efforts. For example, the spending in this area by the U.S. government is estimated to reach US$62.4 billion in 2009 compared to US$55 billion in 2004; while the spending in the Asia-Pacific region is expected to reach US$31.7 billion by 2010, from US$22.7 billion in 2006.[1] Yet despite the rising investments, citizens may not always be able to realize the benefits and numerous cases have been reported of the slow take up of e-government service offerings (Accenture 2006; Olphert and Damodaran 2007).

To increase e-government service acceptance by citizens, it has been suggested that the development of e-government should not focus solely on providing the technical infrastructures, but also consider the social aspects related to the role of potential users in the development process (Olphert and Damodaran 2007). Specifically, it is imperative to engage citizens to understand their actual needs for e-government service development. Extending this argument, this article proposes a service systems perspective of e-government development that systematically considers the dynamic configuration of resources that include not only technology, but also people, organization, and shared information, in order to co-create value (Chesbrough and Spohrer 2006; IfM and IBM 2008; Maglio and Spohrer 2008). Employing a service systems perspective to analyze e-government service offerings resonates with prior work that identifies e-service, or how service provisioning is handled over the Internet, as a promising research area for service science (Chase and Apte 2007). It also responds to the call for demonstrating the value of service science to government agencies, so as to make government service systems more citizen-responsive (IfM and IBM 2008). Further, while previous research has noted the importance of considering people e.g., citizens and public administrators (Anthopoulos et al. 2007), and technology e.g., online bulletin boards and chat tools (Phang and Kankanhalli 2008), in improving e-government service offerings, there remains a lack of a systematic endeavor to consider the different resource elements of a service system (Chesbrough and Spohrer 2006; IfM and IBM 2008; Maglio and Spohrer 2008) in a holistic manner. This article seeks to address this gap so as to provide guidance on how the acceptance of e-government service offerings can be enhanced.

Of central interest in this article is the improvement of e-government service offerings through a participatory approach that can be informed via a service systems perspective. It is worth noting that in recent years, there has been an increasing trend of implementing initiatives to engage citizens in government decision-making (Macintosh and Whyte 2008). Instances of these initiatives, known as e-participation (Phang and Kankanhalli 2008), include Estonia's Osalusveeb (www.osale.ee),

---

[1] http://www.ctg.albany.edu/publications/reports/advancing_roi?chapter=4

Israel's SHIL (shil.info), Singapore's REACH (www.reach.gov.sg), UK's Camden Consults (www.camden.gov.uk), and US' Paradise Utah (paradise.utah.gov/). The participation of citizens in government decision-making is expected to lead to the formulation of policies that are more comprehensive and better grounded in citizens' needs (Irvin and Stansbury 2004). Through participating in these initiatives, citizens may also feel a greater sense of ownership towards the resulting e-government service offerings and policies (Olphert and Damodaran 2007). Yet despite their potential benefits, citizens' response towards such initiatives has often been disappointing (Wojcik 2007). Further, while such initiatives have been employed to engage citizens in public policy decisions such as in city planning (Gronlund 2002), their utilization to inform how e-government service offerings can be better designed remains lacking (Olphert and Damodaran 2007). We will therefore focus on participatory initiatives where e-participation is applied to engage citizens for the development of e-government service offerings. We then relate this to the key concepts of a service system to shed light on how such initiatives can be improved. Specifically, we aim to address the question "What can be done to improve participatory e-government service development by considering such initiatives as a service system?"

In Sect. 2 that follows, we discuss each of the key resource dimensions of a service system (people, organizations, shared information, technologies), and based upon which analyze how a participatory e-government service development can be improved. The inter-relationships among the key service system resources are then summarized in Fig. 1 at the end of the section. Section 3 concludes by discussing the implications of this study for both researchers and practitioners, and the future research directions.

2   Participatory E-government Development as a Service System

A science of service systems could inform theory and practice around service innovation (Spohrer et al. 2007), which aligns with the objective of e-government service providers to innovate the delivery of public service offerings. Service systems are dynamic configurations of people, organizations, technologies, and shared information that create and deliver value to their stakeholders including service providers and clients (IfM and IBM 2008). Essential to a service system is that both the service providers and clients work together to create dynamic value through the resources constituting the system (Demirkan et al. 2008; Spohrer et al. 2007). Below we will employ the service systems perspective as a guiding framework to analyze a participatory e-government service system along the key resource dimensions of people, organizations, shared information, and technologies, which enables us to systematically derive possible enhancements for e-government service offerings.

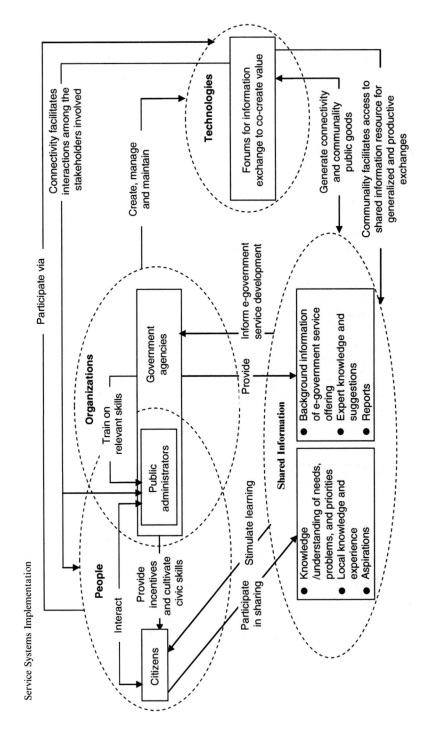

Fig. 1. Participatory e-government service development as a service system

2.1   People

People can be seen as resources that can be accessed in creating value propositions, which are packages of benefits and solutions offered and delivered by the service system (IfM and IBM 2008). They are the stakeholders in a service system and typically take on the roles of service providers and customers. Following this conceptualization, the key people who are involved in a participatory approach for e-government service development include the public administrators responsible for running the initiative and the citizens who participate to provide their feedback. They may also include citizens who are indirectly involved in the service system i.e., those who do not participate but benefit from the resulting e-government service offerings.

With regard to the people resource, two current issues that are faced in participatory e-government service development are the lack of participation and the deficiency in skills or capabilities of the people involved in the initiatives (Olphert and Damodaran 2007). To address these issues, below we propose (1) the specific incentives that government organizations may provide to citizens to motivate their participation; and (2) the specific skills or capabilities that are needed for both citizens and public administrators to make such initiatives effective.

The problem of how citizen participation may be promoted has a long tradition of research in the political science and public administration literatures (e.g., Barber 1984; Glass 1979). Research on this topic has given rise to a number of theories to explain factors leading to citizen participation, which can be broadly classified as socio-economic theories and rational choice theories. Early *socio-economic theories* (e.g., Verba and Nie 1972) attempted to explain citizen participation based on individuals' socio-economic characteristics such as age, education, and financial status. However, subsequent research recognized the limitations of socio-economic characteristics in explaining participation, since individuals with higher socio-economic status were not necessarily found to be more active participants in democratic processes (e.g., Piven and Cloward 1989). Attempts to refine this set of theories led to the identification of different classes of antecedents of participation including participation resources, motivations, and mobilization (Verba et al. 1995).

Participation resources include time, money, and civic skills i.e., the organizational and communication abilities that can facilitate an individual's participation. These resources show the link between an individual's socio-economic characteristics and his participation. For instance, high-income individuals are likely to have more monetary resources, which should better enable them to participate in political activities such as campaigning and party donation. *Motivations* that are identified as salient to participation include individual and group incentives as well as a sense of political efficacy (Verba et al. 1995). Individual incentives refer to the ability to influence specific outcomes that an individual favors, whereas group incentives include an individual's identification with a group such as a political party.

Political efficacy refers to individual's belief that "political change is possible, and that the individual citizen can play a part in bringing about this change" (Campbell et al. 1954, p. 187). Apart from resources and motivations, individuals also need *mobilization*, which typically comes in the form of requests to participate from surrounding people e.g., to sign a petition.

The other class of theories i.e., *rational choice theories*, see citizen participation as a rational activity in which the aim is to maximize benefits while minimizing costs (e.g., Green and Shapiro 1994; Olson 1965). These theories assume that individuals are by nature economically rational actors, who base their decision to participate on cost-benefit calculation (Pattie et al. 2002). However, this set of theories has been criticized for its inability to explain certain participation behaviors, most notably election voting. Based on rational choice theories, a rational actor will likely not participate in voting given the costs incurred e.g., in terms of time and effort of traveling, and the uncertain benefit of influencing the election outcome (being one of many voters). Subsequent research has tried to refine this perspective by proposing a more comprehensive set of participation incentives beyond the rational economic ones, including *collective incentives, selective process incentives, selective outcome incentives, group incentives, expressive incentives,* and *social norms-derived incentives* (Seyd and Whiteley 2002). A summary of these incentive definitions is provided in Table 1. It is to be noted that both the group incentives and expressive incentives are related to an individual's attachment to a group e.g., a political party. Therefore, the two incentives may be less applicable to

Table 1. Definitions of different participation incentives
(From Seyd and Whiteley 2002)

Incentives	Definition
Collective incentives	Benefits that are available for all citizens to enjoy regardless of whether one participates
Selective process incentives	Gratification that is experienced during the participation process, related to the enjoyment of interacting with others
Selective outcome incentives	Privatized outcomes accruing from participation that are related to self-interest e.g., furthering one's political career
Group incentives	Individuals' perception about the efficacy of the group e.g., a political party, to bring about desired social change
Expressive incentives	Incentives to participate that are grounded in a sense of affection and loyalty towards a group e.g., a political party
Social norms-derived incentives	Motivation to conform to the influence of social referents to participate, similar to the notion of mobilization (both capture the influence of other people on an individual's willingness to participate)

general participation contexts where citizens are not necessarily members of a political organization, unless the initiative is designed such that representatives from different political organizations are invited to debate on an issue. It can be seen that citizens need different kinds of incentives/motivations as shown in Table 1, and resources including time, money, and civic skills to participate. These incentives and resources can be provided or cultivated by the government organization concerned, as discussed in the next section.

Recent studies of e-government implementation have also revealed the need for public administrators, especially those appointed to key roles such as formally designated "e-champions", to possess the skills of initiating, facilitating, and managing participation (Phippen and Lacohee 2006). These public administrators also need to possess communication techniques and skills in interacting with citizens to ensure the effectiveness of the participatory e-government service development initiatives (Olphert and Damodaran 2007). Thus, the public administrators should be trained by the government organization concerned to develop the relevant skills, as discussed below.

2.2   Organizations

From a service systems perspective, an organization is an accessible non-physical resource that has the ability to establish formal and informal relationships with other stakeholders (IfM and IBM 2008). In the context of our study, organization refers to the government agency that is responsible for the participatory e-government service development initiative. The government agency concerned is the service provider that needs to ensure successful value creation through the initiative. To achieve this, several interventions can be implemented by the government agency.

First, the government agency may provide various incentives (see Table 1) to citizens to encourage their participation. For instance, the agency can highlight *collective incentives* to participants by publishing how prior inputs of citizens had led to improved e-government service designs that benefited the whole community. The process of participation may also be made more enjoyable (i.e., *selective process incentives*) by facilitating interaction among the participants. Additionally, opportunities to further their political career (a kind of *selective outcome incentives*) can be highlighted to participants, such as the possibility to join a citizen panel formed by the agency. *Mobilization* efforts can be carried out from time to time to effectuate *social norms-derived incentives* e.g., to urge citizens through mass media, including those who haven't participated, to be involved in the initiative.

Second, while government organizations may not be able to provide the time and monetary resources for citizens to participate, civic skills of citizens (the organizational and communication abilities that can facilitate participation) may be cultivated through a long-term effort of government agencies. Civic skills include an individual's abilities to speak and write well, organize their ideas or views, and feel comfortable to engage in discourses (Verba et al. 1995). Such skills can be developed through citizens' involvement in three key social institutions i.e., the workplace, civic organizations (e.g., rotary clubs, unions, volunteer associations), and religious institutions. These institutions provide opportunities for citizens to hone their civic skills e.g., through engaging in discussions, planning for functions, and giving presentations (Verba et al. 1995). A citizen who has developed civic skills will likely find it less daunting to participate in government decision making initiatives. Government organizations may provide resources to encourage the formation of civic organizations e.g., study circles (Rubenson 2000), and other avenues for citizens to develop their civic skills needed for participation.

Third, there is also the need to train public administrators who are tasked to run the initiative. The skills that need to be inculcated include those of initiating, facilitating, and managing participation, as well as communication techniques and abilities in interacting with citizens (Phippen and Lacohee 2006). These may be enhanced through the sharing of best practice knowledge and experiences among the government agencies and public administrators. External consultants and experts in communication and discussion facilitation can also be engaged by the government organization for this purpose.

Last, the government agency needs to provide the information required for citizens to participate as well as to create, maintain, and manage an effective technological platform for citizen participation in e-government service development. We will discuss these issues in the following sections on *shared information* and *technologies* of the service system.

2.3   Shared Information

Shared information constitutes the conceptual resource that can be accessed by all stakeholders in a service system to create value (IfM and IBM 2008). In the case of a participatory e-government service development initiative, shared information is contributed by both the government agency concerned and the citizens who participate in the initiative. The government agency needs to provide information such as the background of the e-government service to be developed, expert knowledge about the possible alternatives for the development, and reports on the estimated costs and expected benefits, to facilitate citizen participation. Citizens will contribute their opinions regarding the e-government service development, express their needs, preferences, and aspirations, and offer possible solutions which may be substantiated with relevant local knowledge and experience (Olphert and Damodaran 2007). With ongoing dialogue among the government agencies and citizens, the shared information base will continue to grow and facilitate joint value creation among the stakeholders.

Through access to the shared information, the stakeholders involved will be able to combine relevant knowledge into useful ideas and solutions that can inform the development of e-government service offerings. The process of exchanging information with public administrators and fellow citizens also allows individual citizens to learn about government decision-making practices and exposes them to the diverse views and knowledge of others. The latter may promote mutual learning among the stakeholders of the service system concerned. Consequently, citizens may come to appreciate the intricacies of government decision-making and the rationales of views held by others. This can lead to a greater sense of ownership towards the resulting e-government service offering by having contributed to their development process (Irvin and Stansbury 2004). The use of the shared information by the service system stakeholders to co-create value can be facilitated with appropriate technologies as discussed below.

2.4   Technologies

A variety of technologies have been employed to support citizen participation in government decision-making e.g., online bulletin boards, e-mail, chat tools, and online surveys (Phang and Kankanhalli 2008). Our discussion thus far suggests two requirements of technologies that are particularly relevant for a participatory e-government service development initiative i.e., the technologies should facilitate (1) *interaction among the stakeholders*; and (2) *access to various shared information* to aid value co-creation in the service system. These are consistent with prior research that has identified several differences between technologies supporting a service system and those supporting a product manufacturing system (Mills and Moberg 1982). Specifically, technologies supporting a service system need to handle the close interaction between the service providers and the customers, provide high capacity for information processing, and facilitate customers' involvement in creating what they need by allowing easy access to the relevant information.

Technologies that support the creation of an online forum for interpersonal communication may be particularly appropriate to fulfill the above requirements of a service system. Based on the public goods theory (Samuelson 1954), such interactive communication technologies are able to provide two types of public goods that can facilitate individuals' collective action in joint value creation, namely connectivity and communality (Fulk et al. 1996). *Connectivity* is the ability afforded by technologies that allows individuals who share common goals or interests to easily communicate with each other (Fulk et al. 1996; Kumar and Benbasat 2002). *Communality* refers to technology capabilities that provide a commonly accessible pool of information for generalized and productive exchanges (Fulk et al. 1996; Monge et al. 1998). *Generalized exchanges* refer to patterns of social exchange where an individual contributes to and receives resources from different people. In *productive exchanges*, information is assembled to create something new, such as the formulation of better solutions resulting from combining the ideas contributed by different stakeholders. Both connectivity and communality demonstrate the characteristics of public goods (Fulk et al. 1996) i.e., they can be consumed by all people (*non-excludable*) and one person's consumption does not reduce the amount available to anyone else (*jointness of supply*) (Marwell and Oliver 1993).

Connectivity and communality afforded by online forum technologies can facilitate the co-creation of value among the relevant stakeholders i.e., government organizations (*service provider*) and citizens (*customers*), in several ways. First, connectivity may facilitate the *close interaction* among the stakeholders that is required for a service system (Maglio and Spohrer 2008) by making it easy for them to communicate with others who share common goals or interests. For instance, individuals who are interested to explore a certain measure of improving e-government service may want to discuss this with others who are also interested in the measure. An online forum makes it easy for them to do so by searching through the contributions of others in the forum. Through clicking a "reply" button, they may then engage in discourses with the people found to have the same interest. They can deliberate about the service improvement measure e.g., by collectively scrutinizing its pros and cons, and deepening understanding of how the measure can be refined. The interactions facilitated by the connectivity capability may then lead to a more comprehensive measure for improving e-government service offerings, which will be of value to both the government agency and citizens.

Second, communality may fulfill the *information needs* of the service system stakeholders in joint value creation (Mills and Moberg 1982). An online forum can serve as a repository of civic knowledge (Kumar and Vragov 2005) by accumulating the information contributions of all stakeholders in a common place over time. Such an information resource can be made easily accessible to all stakeholders by processing and organizing the information in a structured format, such that responses are attached to their target message in a chronological order in the forum. This will allow the flow of information between the different stakeholders to be easily observed. With easy access to a common pool of information, the service system stakeholders can more readily engage in generalized and productive exchanges to create value (Monge et al. 1998). For example, they may *combine* relevant contributions by different stakeholders to come up with a more comprehensive measure to improve the design of an e-government service offering.

It is worth noting that the public goods of connectivity and communality in an online forum demonstrate the characteristic of simultaneity of production and consumption in a service system (Maglio and Spohrer 2008). As more individuals interact with each other in the forum, a higher level of connectivity can be generated since the larger number of the stakeholders involved and associated information in the forum will make it more likely that there are people who share similar interests or goals. Also with more individuals contributing information resources to the forum, a higher level of communality can be generated since more shared information is now accessible from a common repository for information exchange purposes.[2] At the same time, the higher levels of connectivity and communality can

---

[2] There is the possibility of congestion and overload effects if the information contributions exceed a certain threshold beyond which finding information and connecting with like-minded people becomes arduous.

facilitate stakeholders' involvement in collective value creation activities e.g., in interacting and exchanging ideas for improving e-government service development. However, stakeholders must continue to interact and contribute in order for the connectivity and communality public goods to be sustained (Monge et al. 1998).

Our preceding discussion is summarized in Fig. 1, which depicts the inter-relationships among the key service system resources and stakeholders for a participatory e-government service development initiative.

3   Conclusion

In this article we have demonstrated the use of a service systems perspective to analyze participatory e-government service development initiatives. Specifically, through analyzing these initiatives as a service system based on the key resources of people, organizations, shared information, and technologies, we systematically derive possible areas of improvement for e-government service development. Starting from the *people* resource, we draw attention to the need to provide the relevant incentives and cultivate civic skills of citizens to encourage their participation. For the public administrators concerned, they must possess the skills of initiating, facilitating, and managing participation, and communication abilities to interact with citizens. We then move on to *organizations* to suggest what the concerned government agency can do to facilitate both the citizens and public administrators to engage in the initiative. For the *shared information* resource, we highlight the kinds of information that need to be provided by the different stakeholders involved in the value creation activities. Finally, we contend that the *technologies* to support a participatory e-government service development initiative should provide both connectivity and communality public goods to facilitate stakeholders' co-creation of value.

This article contributes theoretically by extending the application of concepts from service science, specifically service systems and the related configuration of resources, to the e-government and e-participation context. The resulting framework serves to provide a holistic view of the inter-relationships among the key resources as well as stakeholders of a participatory e-government service system (as depicted in Fig. 1). The importance of these resources has been separately identified in previous research (e.g., Anthopoulos et al. 2007; Olphert and Damodaran 2007; Phang and Kankanhalli 2008).

For government practitioners engaging in developing e-government service offerings through a participatory approach, the study offers a comprehensive framework that helps visualize the important areas for which attention is required and identify inadequacies and opportunities for service improvement or innovation. It helps to formulate systematic interventions to manage such initiatives by considering the inter-relationships among the pertinent resources and stakeholders together as a service system.

Future research may build on this study to extend the stakeholders of an e-government service system from public organizations and citizens to also include private organizations. This is in response to the emergence of the public-private-partnership (PPP) model in implementing e-government service (Langford and Harrison 2001). In the PPP model, the private sector is engaged in the design, financing, construction, ownership, and/or operation of a public service (Akintoye and Li 2003). The rationale is that such an arrangement would allow both the public and private sectors to pool together their resources and competences in providing better service; and share the costs and rewards from the cooperation (Snabe 2005). However, a PPP-based service system is likely to entail a web of more complex inter-relationships among the different stakeholders. To better understand such complex inter-relationships, researchers may consider adopting the notion of a service ecology. A service ecology is a system of actors that together create a sustainable service, and often involves several organizations that exchange value in a mutually beneficial way (Bonnie and O'Day 1999; Morelli 2002). Key to a successful service ecology is the synergy created among the cooperating organizations in applying their specialization and realizing value towards the collective provision of a total service offering.

Overall, the application of a service systems perspective to e-government service development reinforces the paradigm of viewing citizens as customers. As O'Donnell et al. (2007) noted, "This is the era where government is 'modernized' and the citizenry is 'consumerized' (p. 1). The paper contributes towards the advancement of this paradigm.

References

Accenture (2006). Leadership in customer service: Building the trust. http://www.accenture.com/xdoc/en/industries/government/acn_2006_govt_report_FINAL2.pdf. Accessed 15 May 2008.

Akintoye, A., and Li, B. (2003). *Public private partnership: Managing risks and opportunities, an overview of public private partnership.* Oxford: Blackwell Science.

Anthopoulos, L. G., Siozos, P., and Tsoukalas, I. A. (2007). Applying participatory design and collaboration in digital public services for discovering and re-designing e-government services. *Government Information Quarterly,* 24(2), 353–376.

Barber, B. (1984). *Strong democracy: Participatory politics for a new age.* Berkeley, CA: University of California Press.

Bonnie A. N., and O'Day, V. L. (1999). *Information ecologies: Using technology with heart.* Cambridge, MA: MIT Press.

Campbell, A., Gurin, G., and Milner, W. (1954). *The voter decides.* Evanston, IL: Row Peterson & Co.

Chase, R. B., and Apte, U. M. (2007). A history of research in service operations: What's the big idea? *Journal of Operations Management,* 25, 375–386.

Chesbrough, H., and Spohrer, J. (2006). A research manifesto for services science. *Communications of the ACM,* 49(7), 35–40.

Demirkan, H., Kauffman, R. J., Vayghan, J. A., Fill, H.-G., Karagiannis, D., and Maglio, P. P. (2008). Service-oriented technology and management: Perspectives on research and practice for the coming decade. *Electronic Commerce Research and Application,* 7, 356–376.

Fulk, J., Flanagin, A. J., Kalman, M. E., Monge, P. R., and Ryan, T. (1996). Connective and communal public goods in interactive communication systems. *Communication Theory*, 6(1), 60–87.

Glass, J. J. (1979). Citizen participation in planning: The relationship between objectives and techniques. *American Planning Association Journal*, 45(1), 180–189.

Green, D., and Shapiro, I. (1994). *Pathologies of rational choice theory*. New Haven, CT: Yale University Press.

Gronlund, A. (2002). Emerging infrastructures for e-democracy: In search of strong inscriptions. *e-Service Journal*, 2(1), 62–89.

Heeks, R. (1999). *Reinventing government in the information age: IT enabled public sector reform*. London: Routledge.

IfM and IBM. (2008). Succeeding through service innovation: A service perspective for education, research, business and government. Cambridge: University of Cambridge Institute for Manufacturing.

Irvin, R. A., and Stansbury, J. (2004). Citizen participation in decision making: Is it worth the effort? *Public Administration Review*, 64(1), 55–65.

Kumar, N., and Benbasat, I. (2002). Para-social presence and communication capabilities of a web site. *e-Service Journal*, 1(3), 5–25.

Kumar, N., and Vragov, R. (2005). The citizen participation continuum: Where does the US stand? In *Proceedings of the Eleventh Americas Conference on Information* Systems, Milwaukee, WI: Omnipress, pp. 1984–1990.

Langford, J., and Harrison, Y. (2001). Partnering for e-government: Challenges for public administrators. *Canadian Public Administration,* 44(4), 393–416.

Macintosh, A., and Whyte, A. (2008). Towards an evaluation framework for eParticipation. *Transforming Government: People, Process and Policy*, 2(1). 16–30.

Maglio, P. P., and Spohrer, J. (2008). Fundamentals of service science. *Journal of the Academy of Marketing Science,* 36(1), 18–20.

Marwell, G., and Oliver, P. (1993). *The critical mass in collective action: A micro-social theory*. Cambridge: Cambridge University Press.

Mills, P. K., and Moberg, D. J. (1982). Perspectives on the technology of service operations. *Academy of Management Review*, 7(3), 467–478.

Monge, P., Fulk, J., Kalman, M., Flanagin, A., Parnassa, C., and Rumsey, S. (1998). Production of collective action in alliance-based interorganizational communication and information systems. *Organization Science*, 9(3), 411–433.

Morelli, N. (2002). Designing product/service systems: A methodological exploration. *Design Issues*, 18(3), 3–17.

O'Donnell, D., McCusker, P., Fagan, C. H., Newman, D. R., Stephens, S., and Murray, M. (2007). Navigating between utopia and dystopia in the public sphere through eParticipation: Where is the value? Presented at the *International Critical Management Studies Conference*, Manchester.

Olphert, W., and Damodaran, L. (2007). Citizen participation and engagement in the design of e-Government services: The missing link in effective ICT design and delivery. *Journal of the Associations for Information Systems*, 8(9), 491–507.

Olson, M. (1965). *The logic of collective action: Public goods and the theory of groups*. Cambridge, MA: Harvard University Press.

Pattie, C., Syed, P., and Whiteley, P. (2002). Citizenship and civic engagement: Attitudes and behavior. Presented at the *Political Studies Association Annual Conference*, University of Aberdeen, UK, 5–7 April.

Phang, C. W., and Kankanhalli, A. (2008). A framework of ICT exploitation for e-participation initiatives. *Communications of the ACM*, 51(12), 128–132.

Phang C. W., Kankanhalli, A., and Ang, C. Z. (2008). Investigating organizational learning in eGovernment projects: A multi-theoretic approach. *Journal of Strategic Information Systems*, 17(2), 99–123.

Phippen A., and Lacohée H. (2006). E-government – issues in citizen engagement. *BT Technology Journal*, 24(2), 205–208.

Piven, F. F., and Cloward, R. A. (1989). *Why Americans don't vote*. New York: Pantheon.

Rubenson, D. (2000). Participation and politics: Social capital, civic voluntarism, and institutional context. Presented at the *Political Studies Association-UK 50th Annual Conference*, London, UK, 10–13 April.

Samuelson, P. A. (1954). The pure theory of public expenditure. *Review of Economics and Statistics*, 36, 387–389.

Seyd, P., and Whiteley, P. (2002). *New labor's grass roots: The transformation of the labor party membership*. London: Palgrave Macmillan.

Snabe, J. H. (2005). Public private partnerships. *The Bimonthly Magazine on E-Governance*, pp. 6–8.

Spohrer, J., Maglio, P. P., Bailey, J., and Gruhl, D. (2007). Steps towards a science of service systems. *IEEE Computer*, 40(1), 70–77.

Verba, S., and Nie, N. (1972). *Participation in America: Political democracy and social equality*. New York: Harper & Row.

Verba, S., Schlozman, K., and Brady, H. (1995). *Voice and equality: Civic voluntarism in American politics*. Cambridge, MA: Harvard University Press.

Wojcik, S. (2007). How does eDeliberation work? A study of French local electronic forums. In A. Avdic, K. Hedström, J. Rose, and A. Gronlund (Eds.), *Understanding eParticipation: Contemporary PhD eParticipation research in Europe* (pp. 153–165). Örebro: Örebro University Library.

Predictive Systems for Customer Interactions

Ravi Vijayaraghavan, Sam Albert, and Vinod Kumar Singh

24/7 Customer Innovation Labs

Pallipuram V. Kannan

24/7 Customer Inc

Abstract With the coming of age of web as a mainstream customer service channel, B2C companies have invested substantial resources in enhancing their web presence. Today customers can interact with a company, not only through the traditional phone channel but also through chat, email, SMS or web self-service. Each of these channels is best suited for some services and ill-matched for others. Customer service organizations today struggle with the challenge of delivering seamlessly integrated services through these different channels. This paper will evaluate some of the key challenges in multi-channel customer service. It will address the challenge of creating the right channel mix i.e. providing the right choice of channels for a given customer/behavior/issue profile. It will also provide strategies for optimizing the performance of a given channel in creating the right customer experience.

Keywords Service systems, predictive systems, customer interactions, call center, contact center, self-service, text mining, channel optimization, customer experience, customer satisfaction, sentiment analysis, online customer service, customer care

1   Introduction

Several rapid changes in the global business environment have made traditional approaches to customer service non-competitive and obsolete. Major changes have occurred in the "Front Stage" (customer-provider interactions) and "back-stage" (operational performance) (IfM and IBM 2008). These changes are being driven by the presence of increased customer touch points, increased number of customer contact channels, explosion of tools to capture the "voice of the customer" and a step increase in the ability to leverage global resources for service delivery. The rapidity of these changes has not allowed service systems to adapt and optimize to

H. Demirkan et al. (eds.), *Service Systems Implementation*, Service Science:
Research and Innovations in the Service Economy, DOI 10.1007/978-1-4419-7904-9_18,
© Springer Science+Business Media, LLC 2011

the new reality. The changes in these systems have been organic, slow (relative to environmental changes), market-driven and evolutionary, creating sub-optimal solutions. The objective of this work is to provide a frame-work for optimizing a particular service system – B2C customer service organizations (such as call/contact centers) and their interactions with customers. Past work in this area has focused on a single contact channel such as a call center (Maglio et al. 2006; Cheng et al. 2006) or self-service (Meuter et al. 2000; Lee and Lin 2005; Salomann et al. 2005; Piccoli et al. 2004) and on operational improvements (Maglio et al. 2006; Cheng et al. 2006; Piccoli et al. 2004) of the channel rather than establishing a strategic framework to optimize the multi-channel service provider-customer interaction. This work proposes a methodology for integrated deployment of various customer contact channels to maximize customer experience/satisfaction while driving up operational performance. The end-goal is to develop a data-driven framework and a set of tools for businesses to continuously optimize the interaction across multiple channels between the two key stakeholders, the customer and the service provider (referred to as the "provider" in this chapter).

Each service interaction between a provider and the customers is an opportunity for the provider to satisfy, surprise, delight and disappoint its customers. The traditional view of service encounters always being "low-tech high-touch" is no longer true (IfM and IBM 2008; Meuter et al. 2000).With the coming of age of web as a mainstream sales and support channel, providers have invested substantial resources in enhancing their web presence for customer service. Today service encounters occur across various virtual "Low/high touch" and traditional "high-touch" channels. Customers can interact with the provider, not only face-to-face and through the traditional phone channel but also through chat, email, SMS or web self-service. With the convergence of phones and computing devices, each of these channels is becoming ubiquitous since they are accessible through computers, mobile phones and PDAs. In addition to individual preferences, each of these channels is best suited for some service offerings and ill-matched for others. For example, email may be the right channel for confirmation of a web purchase and for tracking shipping information. However, a phone call may be appropriate to discuss issues with a wireless provider's rate plan. While web chat may be the preferred channel to shop for a camera where different models can be visually compared and specific questions about each of the models can interactively be answered live.

A key dimension to this problem is the lifecycle of the customer (Fig. 1). Throughout the customers' lifecycle there are often several interactions between the customer and the provider, some initiated by the customer while others by the provider. The interactions occur across different channels based on the customer and provider needs. Another evolving dimension of this problem is the growth of social media. Blogs/micro-blogs, community forums and other social networking sites are fast replacing traditional customer service in certain domains. Customers are using these channels to discuss product issues, find problem resolution and express their delight/frustrations over products, service offerings and brands. Providers have traditionally understood the importance of social networks in improving customer service (Cross et al. 2005) and as a logical next step are starting to leverage social

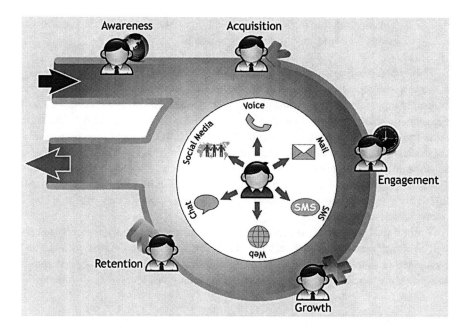

Fig. 1. Interactions across customer lifecycle

media to improve customer experience through mining knowledge from them and proactively engaging customers based on this knowledge (Bernoff and Li 2008).

Given that the same customer may interact with the provider through different channels, Soussa and Voss (2006) present a framework for measuring quality of channel integration. In this framework, the two dimensions used to measure integration quality are *channel-service configuration* (availability of multiple channels, their quality and transparency to the customers) and *integrated interactions* (consistency of interactions across channels). This chapter provides a practical approach for optimizing customer interaction and customer experience based on this philosophy.

Customer service providers today clearly see a need for their offerings to be through multiple channels. However, they struggle with key challenges in delivering these offerings through different channels while maintaining high integration quality and customer experience. Some of the challenges include

1. Creating the right channel mix – Providing the right choice of channels for a given customer/behavior/issue profile. Key aspects of this problem include:
   - Understanding the right channel for the right issue based on historical customer experience and resolution success.
   - Managing the channel choice available to the customer based on the expected value of the customer and the channel cost implications.

2. Optimizing the performance of each of these channels for customer experience and revenue/profit generation.

This chapter will address both these challenges. The problems will be addressed through a solution called *ServiceCube*. The specific example being discussed in this chapter is that of deflection of customer service phone calls to other channels such as chat, email, SMS or self-service. The interactions that are targeted for deflection are those that have low or negative value to the provider and the customer. Fortunately, the patterns of these calls are often predictable. The core of the *ServiceCube* solution is a Text mining engine and a problem prediction engine. The solution exposes opportunities for providers to proactively communicate with the customer through the appropriate channel to avoid an expensive phone call that provides a poor customer experience.

To limit the scope of this study, only four key customer-provider contact channels will be considered – web self-service, email, chat and phone (including SMS and automated channels such as Interactive Voice Response). Impact of customer interactions through peer-to-peer social networking channels will also be discussed.

2   ServiceCube: A Solution for "Right-Channeling" Customer Interactions

Figure 2 illustrates an aggregate view of customer contacts and channel mix in the United States of America across major industry verticals (previsor 2008). Based on this view 89% of all contacts are served by the phone channel either through a

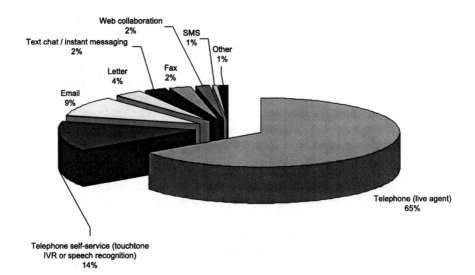

Fig. 2. Channel mix of customer interaction

live agent (65%) or through automated solutions (14%) such as Interactive Voice Response (IVR) and/or speech recognition. This data only considers "customer-provider" interactions and excludes web based self-service and peer-to-peer interactions through social media/community forums/blogs whose growing impact in providing resolutions to customer service issues has not been satisfactorily estimated till date.

The mix shown in Fig. 2 is sub-optimal from both cost and customer experience perspective. Rather, this is the dynamic evolution to a "current state" i.e. call centers existed well before internet and web-based customer support. The adoption and dominance of phones and call centers for customer service represents the burden of a legacy channel mix. In reality, Voice calls are among the most expensive interactions for a provider. Often they provide poor customer experience since they end up as a medium for escalating customer issues rather than for proactive communication due to their high costs.

Theoretically, the "right-channel mix" is one that maximizes long-term profitability (Rust et al. 2000). Practically, it is a complex optimization problem where there is a need to make the right trade-offs based on issue type, issue frequency, channel costs, customer experience and customer life time value where necessary. Figure 3 provides a schematic representation adapted from the "Return on Service Quality" approach (Rust et al. 1995). The schematic points out opportunities for both improving and measuring each step in the process, resulting in greater profitability.

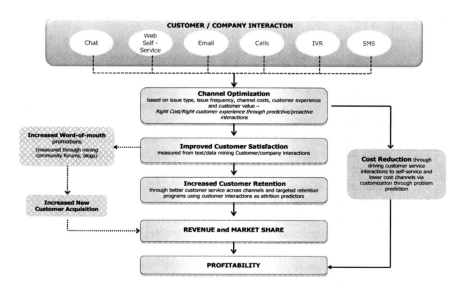

Fig. 3. Model to estimate ROI for optimizing customer-provider interactions

Practical challenges in being able to optimize the channel mix include:

1. A poor understanding of customer contact distribution across various channels. Specifically, limited understanding of the issue distribution for which customers contact a provider. Root causes of this include the dynamic nature of customer issues combined with relatively static processes/tools to capture data, human error and lack of integration of multiple interaction channels.
2. Lack of a *customer friendly* strategy to drive adoption to other channels that reduce cost or improve customer experience. For example, a customized web-based self-service solution that solves customer issues, is able to drive down service costs while driving up customer experience. On the other hand, hiding the customer service phone number in the provider's web page may drive down costs but at the same time also reduce the quality of customer experience and potential future revenues.

Both these challenges can be addressed through focused efforts in mining and understanding the vast volumes of customer interaction data that exist in voice recordings, chat transcripts, emails, web analytics reports, blogs and community forums. The customer interaction data contains a wealth of information that is being dynamically updated. Issues customers face, their resolution success and the customer experience during the interaction are all embedded in this data.

One of the core assumptions of the following approach is that the initial opportunity that provides the greatest potential for channel optimization is the deflection of customer service calls to chat, email and web self-service. The case for this approach is obvious since:

- Voice/Phone is the costliest (http://solutions.liveperson.com/sb/channel_comparison.asp) "highest touch" channel for customer service.
- Voice has the highest share of contacts due to historical reasons. It is the most mature channel both from the perspective of service delivery and customer adoption.
- Online channels such as chat, email and self-service have huge potential for expansion since adoption of web as a customer support channel is growing (Piccoli et al. 2004). These channels also have substantial opportunity to improve in quality of customer service (Lennon and Harris 2002) as they mature.
- The approach itself is not to force customers to other channels but to provide them better choices by improving their experience in other channels. It is a partly emergent rather than a completely prescriptive approach for channel optimization. A prescriptive methodology would take a top-down view of channel optimization. However, this strategy assumes that as we keep improving the customer experience in each of these channels and provide the right channel choices for the right customers, the customers themselves

will determine the optimal channel mix that will over a period of time move significant share of customer contacts from voice to other online channels.

Critical process steps in being able to move contact volumes from calls to other channels with a net positive impact on customer experience include:

1. Analyzing contact drivers – Categorizing the distribution of key issues that drive customers to contact the provider.
2. Predicting issues – Developing models to predict issues that specific customers are likely to contact about.
3. Driving adoption of online customer service – Increasing usage of web self-service, email and chat for customer service through increasing awareness and improved service experience.
4. Developing strategies for proactive communication – Addressing customer issues proactively through other channels.
5. Continuous optimization of channel mix.

3   Analyzing Contact Drivers

The first step in identifying key contact drivers is to categorize the distribution of issues that drive customers to call the provider. A challenge is that customer contact data is often captured poorly in the CRM systems and has to be mined from either actual customer conversations or from detailed verbatim notes captured by the call center representatives based on the customer conversation. This is accomplished through text mining based Query/Issue Categorization (Albert and Vijayaraghavan 2011) where a customer queries/issues are assigned to one or more pre-defined categories. A typical query/issue categorization model contains a custom taxonomy/dictionary of relevant categories. The taxonomy construction typically uses a combination of human resources with some domain expertise and automated approaches to be able to create a lexicon with domain-specific terminology terms and a mapping between the subjects and terms (Chuang and Chien 2003). This taxonomy provides a hierarchical categorization of business queries/issues. The categorization models are repeatedly re-created and evolved over time depending on the dynamism of the business system. The end goal is to be able to view customer issues across multiple dimensions including product, lifecycle, process, customer type and channel. Figure 4 provides an example of such a view for customer service over chat channel. The data obtained from mining chat transcripts is a typical example of distribution of customer queries for an online retailer during the immediate post-purchase phase of the customer lifecycle. The categorization shown here provides the aggregate distribution of customer queries. Each of these categories can be mined further for greater granularity of issue types.

The Query categorization models provide a historical context for the key issues driving contact. To add to this, mining community forums and other social networking

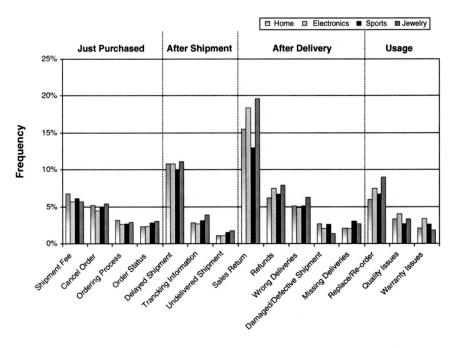

Fig. 4. An example view of query categories for a typical online retailer

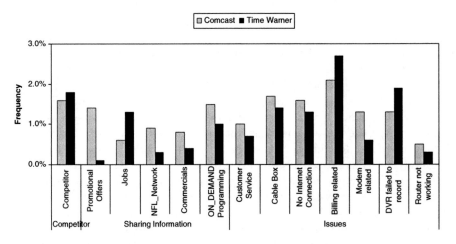

Fig. 5. Example query categorization based on tweets

sources can provide a complementary view and are valuable particularly in providing indicators for future contact drivers. Often, early adopters are more active in social networks and mining these forums serve as valuable early warning systems. Social network forums also provide a unique view for conducting competitor analysis in the service domain. Figure 5 shows a sample query categorization for Comcast and Time Warner, both competitors in providing telephone and cable service offerings. The textual data for query categorization has been obtained from Tweets (http://twitter.com) about the providers. The results of such query categorizations is used to forecast call types, better train call center agents and devise proactive communication strategies over email, chat, web, twitter and other online channels.

4   Predicting Issues

Once the overall distribution of customer queries and issues are mapped out, the next logical step is to build a predictive model that can be deployed in various customer contact channels. The steps in accomplishing this include data fusion of the structured CRM data with the text mining results of query categorization. Once this integrated data structure is created, a problem predictor is built. The goal of the problem predictor is to calculate the probability that a certain query will be asked by a customer with a given set of demographic, behavioral, temporal, engagement and contact attributes. Figure 6 illustrates the architecture of the problem predictor. Naïve Bayes algorithm (Witten and Frank 2005) has been used in this model.

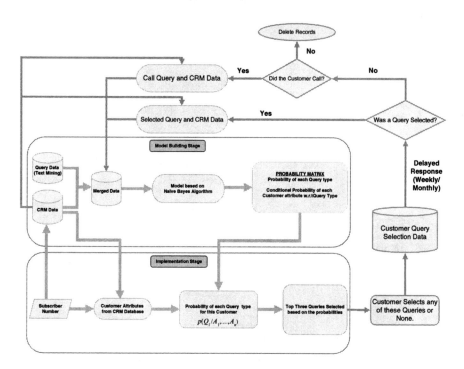

Fig. 6. Architecture of the problem predictor

$$p(Q_i / A_1, A_2 \ldots A_n) = p(Q_i) \cdot p(A_1 / Q_i) \cdot p(A_2 / Q_i) \ldots p(A_j / Q_i) \ldots p(A_n / Q_i)$$

where Q_i is a query type i and A_j is a customer attribute j.

Naïve Bayes was chosen for its simplicity in implementation for supervised learning. Obviously, the generic architecture can support other algorithms as well. Furthermore, for these types of classification problems where the focus is more on classification and rank-ordering than on actual predicted probability, Naïve Bayes is competitive in performance in spite of its unrealistic independence assumption (Domingos and Pazzani 1997). The universe of queries is then rank-ordered based on decreasing probabilities. The top few (typically 3–5) are displayed to the customer. Figure 7 shows a lift chart for a problem predictor created to predict problem types for a credit card customer.

Practically, the predictor can be deployed in any of the customer channels as an automated solution or to support and improve the quality of human interaction. As a self-service solution it can be deployed either as an auto-response to emails, a customized support page once a customer logs in, a predictive IVR tree for customers who call into the call center or a pre-chat bot that provides answers to the questions that particular customer is likely to ask. Figure 8 illustrates a typical implementation for web self-service. In this illustration, if a customer logs into a billing page of their phone or cable provider, a pane is populated with answers/hyperlinks to the issues the customer is most likely to have.

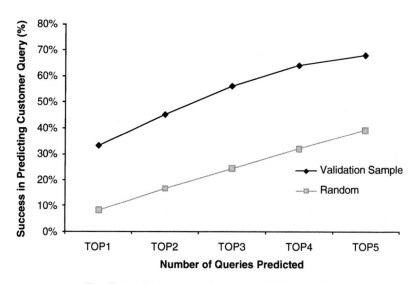

Fig. 7. Prediction results on a validation sample

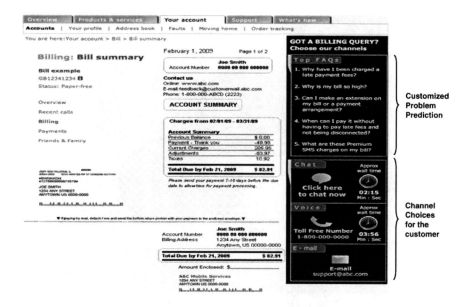

Fig. 8. Illustration of a problem predictor implementation for web self-service

5   Driving Adoption of Online Customer Service

Two factors that can drive down customer service calls are increased awareness of online channels for customer service and increased customer adoption and loyalty to these channels:

1. Increased awareness to drive up usage of online customer service can be accomplished through proactive communications on paper bills, email and IVR promoting online customer service options. Incentives to use the web (i.e. no fee to pay over the web) can often drive up adoption. These campaigns are targeted using the problem predictor. However, the investments to drive traffic online to support pages are of little use if the quality of service experience does not keep them online and they return to the phone for resolution.

2. Improved customer loyalty towards online channels is a direct function of their service experience. A significant volume of customers initiate a voice call after attempting to resolve their issues over the support web page. An opportunity exists to solve the customer's problems online to avoid an expensive call. The issue predictor can provide targeted resolution to visitors, particularly when they are authenticated (Fig. 8), driving up customer experience. In addition, easy availability of multiple

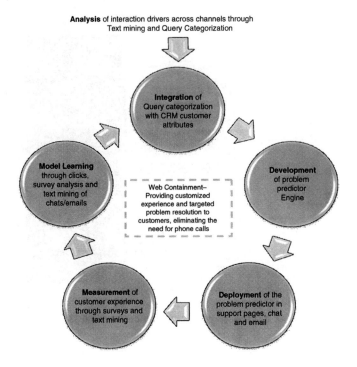

Fig. 9. Web containment – resolving issues online

channels online (such as chat and email) can improve customers' online experience since customers have the ability to chose the channel and level of interaction depending on complexity and type of issue.

A robust web containment strategy should continuously adapt to the evolving visitor behavior. The problem predictor can help accomplish this (Fig. 9).

6   Developing Strategies for Proactive Communication

Another important component of a robust customer service strategy is addressing customer issues proactively through lower cost channels that are non-intrusive and convenient. For example, a customer service call to a prepaid card provider to enquire about account balance could often be avoided if the provider sent a simple email or SMS or Tweet with the same information. This looks like an obvious strategy. However the key to implementing this strategy cost effectively is answering the question "who will call, when and for what?" The problem predictor can be used

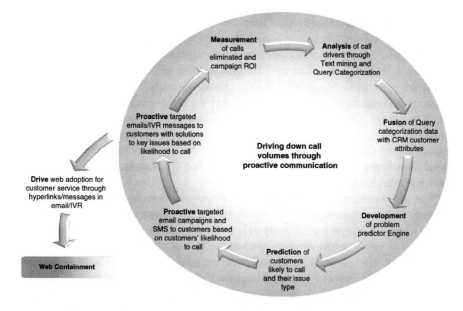

Fig. 10. Use of proactive communication strategies to reduce call volumes

to answer this question which in turn triggers proactive communication that is targeted and is through the right channel (Fig. 10).

Social media is evolving as an increasingly powerful source of information to drive proactive communication strategies. For example, mining micro-blogs such as twitter and community forums provides an opportunity for the provider to understand the current issues customers are facing and provides a platform to address these issues proactively.

7   Continuous Evaluation of Channel Mix

As a more balanced channel mix evolves it is critical to continuously measure customer experience in each of these channels as a function of process, product/ service, customer profile and seasonality. The goal is to ensure that any channel deflection/migration is not at the cost of customer experience, particularly for the high value customers.

In addition to the traditional survey mechanism the customer experience is measured using a text-mining based approach. A hybrid method of keyword spotting and lexicon affinity (Liu et al. 2003) is used. This makes use of ConceptNet (Liu and Singh 2004), and WordNet (Fellbaum 1998), to extend the scope and context of the emotion that is being expressed.

Customer sentiment extraction used for business intelligence is from various sources and channels including blogs, micro-blogs, email, voice, chat and online communities. Substantial work on opinion mining from online communities, blogs and review sites exists in literature (Taboada and Grieve 2004; Pang and Lee 2008). However measurement approaches vary across channels. For example, blogs are broadcasts that contain texts which are proactive and more verbal, and the emotions are typically at a constant level through the document. In contrast, in interactive conversations such as voice and chat, the tone is reactive in nature and the emotions expressed are dynamic and fluctuate based on response received. While document level classification might be suitable for blogs and community forums, it may not be for interactive conversations.

The methodology of mining the text to detect emotions in interactive conversations considers various dimensions which dynamically impact customers' sentiment. Since a primary reason for the analysis is to improve customer service agent performance, it is important to measure the change in customers' emotions through the conversation. The customer sentiment model includes analyses on phases of the conversation, establishment of a baseline emotion at the start of the conversation, position of the emotional content in the conversation, weighted evaluation of emotions and extreme emotions of customers, time variables of the interaction, emoticons, special characters and emphasizers (the last three in the case of chat/email) . These scores are computed separately and then used to arrive at a final score referred to as the Net Experience Score (NES) (Albert and Vijayaraghavan 2011). The structure of the NES model is illustrated in Fig. 11. The scores in various layers are finally aggregated into a Net Experience Score which varies between −1 and +1 (Fig. 12). The broad

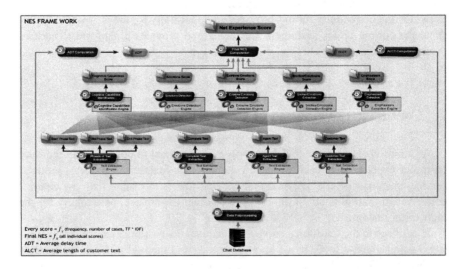

Fig. 11. A framework for measuring Net Experience Score (NES) (Albert and Vijayaraghavan 2011)

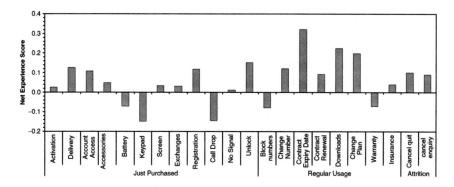

Fig. 12. Net Experience scores for different issue categories for a typical wireless carrier across online customer service and social media channels

approach is to measure a normalized difference between positive and negative tones. Factors such as agent response time and length of the conversation are also used for the normalization:

$$Net\ Experience\ Score\ (NES) = \frac{(S_+ - S_-)}{(S_+ + S_-)}$$

where S could represent any attribute that measures emotion.

Key benefits of this methodology of scoring customer conversations and using NES to measure customer experience over conventional customer satisfaction (CSAT) surveys are the following:

1. Customer satisfaction surveys often have response rate bias(Peterson and Wilson 1992; Lebow 1982) and data collection bias (LeVois et al. 1981). With the NES methodology all conversations can be scored removing response rate bias. Similarly, since the data is collected from actual "in the moment" conversations between provider and customer, the data collection bias is also eliminated.

2. Customer satisfaction surveys measure an aggregated view based on a small sample of customer who respond and are often not appropriate for measuring sentiments of micro-segments of customers based on multiple (i.e. process/product/demographic) dimensions. The NES methodology can provide measures of customer experience at a higher dimensionality and granularity. In addition, measures across different channels can be compared for calibration and consistency.

3. Reasons 1 and 2 make it challenging to use surveys as predictors for future customer behavior at an individual or micro-segment level. Though numerous models have been developed for understanding antecedents and consequences of customer satisfaction survey scores

(Szymanski and Henard 2001; Cronin et al. 2000; Reichheld 2006) these are at an aggregate level. They help in driving strategic direction for organizations. However, the NES methodology provides a targeted approach to predicting and managing consequences of customer satisfaction measures such as positive/negative word-of-mouth, repurchase and attrition. The methodology can also be used to drive focused actions on improving product, process or customer service agent performance.

So far, we have looked at the application of text mining to measure customer experience. This assumes that text transcripts of customer interactions are readily available. An additional complexity exists in mining sentiment from voice. The text is not readily available and transcription technologies are error prone, particularly since the system in this scenario cannot be trained to a voice. A hybrid approach is used to measure customer experience. Non-linguistic features such as loudness, pitch, speaking rate are measured and their trends over the course of the conversation are used as one source of input. Transcripts based text mining is used as another source of input to derive an NES.

The dynamic nature of customer interactions creates a need for continuous channel optimization since customer needs, provider offerings and channel availability are all evolving. Two key dimensions need to be continuously evaluated for each of the customer channels. Customer issues and the customer experience in resolving those issues. As this matrix evolves over time, each channel is evaluated for cost and customer experience (which implicitly incorporates both resolution success and channel friendliness).

Future research will focus on improving methods for normalizing measurements of factors such as customer sentiments across channels. This is required since customers use each of these channels differently. For example, a chat may be used more as a mechanism to resolve a specific issue while Twitter may be used predominantly for expressing joy or frustration with a provider. The mix of positive and negative sentiments in each would be different. A robust measurement should normalize for these differences.

8   Conclusion

This work provides a new framework for managing customer-provider service interactions across the life-cycle of the customer. The framework promises potential gains relative to the current state of customer service, in each of the three dimensions, Efficiency, Effectiveness and Sustainability (Sphorer et al. 2006). However, the focus of the framework is more on effectiveness and sustainability and less on efficiency gains.

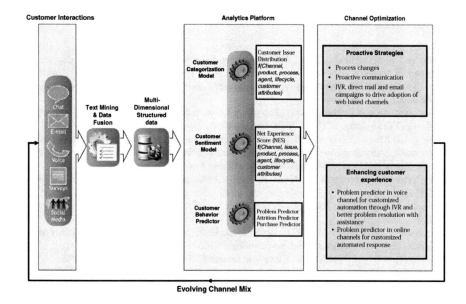

Fig. 13. A framework for optimization of customer service channel mix

Customer-provider interactions are evolving from their traditional focus on operational optimization and efficiency of various channel "Silos" i.e. call/contact centers. Today customers' view of the provider is shaped by their multi-channel interactions with the provider. This has created substantial value for optimization of the entire framework of customer-provider interactions across channels. A critical aspect of channel optimization is a robust framework for deriving intelligence out of customer interactions (Fig. 13). Key components of this framework include, the ability to integrate/"fuse" structured and unstructured data from different customer interaction channels and the competency to build predictive systems that enable a proactive interface with the customers. In addition, given the dynamic complexity of this system, it is important to be able to measure the impact of changes created by these proactive strategies on customer experience so that the system learns and evolves over time as customers and their engagement mode with the provider changes. Future work should measure the dynamic adaptability of the approach as customers' channel preferences evolve, new channels get introduced and other channels become obsolete. In addition, for practitioners, this work provides tools and strategies for managing customer contact in a manner that improves customer experience and their life-time value to the provider while driving down costs.

Acknowledgments The authors would like to thank members of the Innovation Labs team at 24/7 Customer for various insightful discussions.

References

Albert and Vijayaraghavan (2011). Net Experience Score – a measure of customer experience, *paper in progress*.

Bernoff and Li (2008). Harnessing the power of the Oh-So-Social Web, *MIT Sloan Management Review*.

Cheng, Boyette and Krishna (2006). Towards a low-cost high-quality service call architecture, *Services Computing, SCC '06. IEEE International Conference*, Chicago, IL, pp 261–264.

Chuang and Chien (2003). Enriching web taxonomies through subject categorization of query terms from search engine logs, *Decision Support Systems*, 35(1), 113–127.

Cronin, Brady and Hult (2000). Assessing the effects of quality, value, and customer satisfaction on consumer behavioral intentions in service environments, *Journal of Retailing*, 76(2), 193–218.

Cross, Liedtka and Weiss (2005). A practical guide to social networks, *Harvard Business Review*, 83(3), 124–132.

Domingos, P., and Pazzani, M. (1997). Beyond independence: Conditions for the optimality of the simple Bayesian classifier. *Machine Learning* 29:103–130.

Fellbaum (1998) (Ed) *WordNet: An Electronic Lexical Database*, MIT Press, Cambridge, MA.

IfM and IBM (2008). *Succeeding through service innovation: A service perspective for education, research, business and government*. Cambridge: University of Cambridge, Institute for Manufacturing. ISBN: 978-1-902546-65-0.

Lebow, J. L. (1982). Consumer satisfaction with mental health treatment. *Psychological Bulletin* 91, 244–259.

Lee and Lin (2005). Customer perceptions of e-service quality in online shopping, *International Journal of Retail & Distribution Management*, 33(2), 161–176.

Lennon and Harris (2002). Customer service on the Web: A cross-industry investigation, *Journal of Targeting, Measurement and Analysis for Marketing*, 10(4), 325–338.

LeVois, M., Nguyen, T. D. and Attkisson, C. (1981). Artifact in client satisfaction assessment: Experience in community mental health settings. *Evaluation and Program Planning* 4 (April): 139–I50.

Liu and Singh (2004). ConceptNet – a practical commonsense reasoning tool-kit, *BT Technology Journal*, 22(4).

Liu, Lieberman, and Selker (2003). A model of textual affect sensing using real-world knowledge. *In Proceedings of IUI'03*, Miami, FL, pp 125–132.

Maglio, Srinivasan, Kreulen, and Sphorer (2006). Service Systems, Service Scientists, SSME, and Innovation, *Communications of the ACM*, 49(7).

Meuter, Ostrom, Roundtree, and Bitner (2000). Self-service technologies: Understanding customer satisfaction with technology-based service encounters, *Journal of Marketing*, 64, 50–64.

Pang and Lee (2008). Opinion mining and sentiment analysis, *Foundations and Trends in Information Retrieval*, 2(1–2), 1–135.

Peterson and Wilson (1992). Measuring customer satisfaction: Fact and artifact, *Journal of the Academy of Marketing Science*, 20(1), 61–71.

Piccoli, Brohman, Watson and Parasuraman (2004). Net-based customer service systems: Evolution and revolution in web site functionalities, *Decision Sciences*, 35(3), 423–455.

Previsor (2008). The US Contact Center Operational Review (2008). Whitepaper, 2nd Edition.

Reichheld (2006). *The ultimate question – Driving good profits and true growth*, Harvard Business School Press, Boston, MA.

Rust, Zahorik and Keiningham (1995). Return on quality (ROQ): Making service quality financially accountable, *Journal of Marketing*, 59, 58–70.

Rust, R., Zeithaml, V. and Lemon, K. (2000). *Driving customer equity: How customer lifetime value is reshaping corporate strategy*. Free Press, New York.

Salomann, Kolbe, and Brenner (2005). Self-Services in customer relationships: Balancing high-tech and high-touch today and tomorrow, *e-Service Journal* 4(2), 65–84.

Sousa and Voss (May 2006). Service quality in multichannel services employing virtual channels, *Journal of Services Research*, 8(4), 356–371.

Sphorer, Maglio, Bailey and Gruhl (2006). Steps toward a science of service systems, *Communications of the ACM*, 49(7).

Szymanski and Henard (2001). Customer satisfaction: A meta-analysis of the empirical evidence, *Journal of the Academy of Marketing Science*, 29(1).

Taboada and Grieve (2004). *In Proc. of AAAI Spring Symposium on Exploring Attitude and Affect in Text,* Stanford, CA, pp. 158–161.

Witten and Frank (2005), Data mining – Practical machine learning tools and techniques, 2nd Edition. Elsevier, Amsterdam.

CPSIA information can be obtained at www.ICGtesting.com

228827LV00001B/87/P